Contested Culture

CULTURAL STUDIES OF

THE UNITED STATES

ALAN TRACHTENBERG, EDITOR

CONTESTED Culture

THE IMAGE, THE VOICE, AND THE LAW

JANE M. GAINES

THE UNIVERSITY OF NORTH CAROLINA PRESS   CHAPEL HILL & LONDON

© 1991 The University of
North Carolina Press
All rights reserved

Library of Congress Cataloging-in-
Publication Data
Gaines, Jane, 1943–
    Contested culture : the image, the
voice, and the law / by Jane M. Gaines.
        p.   cm.—(Cultural studies of the
United States)
    Includes bibliographical references
and index.
    ISBN 0-8078-1977-8 (cloth : alk.
paper).—ISBN 0-8078-4326-1 (pbk. :
alk. paper)
    1. Performing arts—Law and
legislation—United States—Cases.
2. Entertainers—Legal status, laws,
etc.—United States—Cases.
3. Intellectual property—United
States—Cases.   4. United States—
Popular culture.   5. Socialism and
culture.   I. Title.   II. Series.
KF4290.A7G35   1991
344.73′097—dc20
[347.30497]   91-10770
                    CIP

Manufactured in the United States of
America

95 94 93 92 91   5 4 3 2 1

Chapter 3 appeared in somewhat different
form as "Dead Ringer: Jacqueline Onassis
and the Look-Alike" in South Atlantic
Quarterly 88, no. 2 (Spring 1989): 461–
86, © by Duke University Press. Chapter 7
appeared in somewhat different form as
"Superman and the Protective Strength of
the Trademark" in Logics of Television, edited
by Patricia Mellencamp, © 1990 by the
Indiana University Press.

FOR RICHARD DYER

Contents

Foreword

Contested Culture is the sort of book that makes a fundamental difference. A work of extraordinary synthesis of methods, theories, and materials, it changes the way we will hereafter understand the actual work performed by contemporary entertainment images such as photographs, films, sound recordings, advertisements, and commercials. One way to state the difference is negatively: Jane Gaines treats entertainment images not as self-contained structures of experience but as, in the first instance, a kind of property, artifacts produced and controlled within systems of ownership that define their character as cultural experience. But this recognition, already familiar to many readers, only launches the most significant lesson she has to teach. In a series of brilliant readings of case law in the field of entertainment, Gaines directs our attention to *contest,* to struggles in the form of juridical litigation between and among interested parties over rights to contested image-properties, rights of control, and rights of profit-taking. The cases themselves and their personae, ranging from historical celebrities like Jackie Onassis and Bela Lugosi to fabricated celebrities like Superman and Dracula, perform a drama in their own right, a courtroom meta-entertainment in which the otherwise invisible character of images as contested property becomes vividly plain in Gaines's astonishing readings.

Reading *Contested Culture* one encounters fascinating surprises one after another, all accumulating into a comprehensive analysis that strips commercial entertainment images of any remaining innocence. The images of popular cinema and television, the book argues, bear the impressible imprint of capitalist property relations, which is to say of unstinted competitive antagonism among interested parties, including performers, studios or production companies, agencies, distributors, publishers, and not least, lawyers and law firms. But, as descriptively rich and engaging as they are in their own right, the narrative accounts of specific cases in each chapter do not exhaust the significance of the book. The real challenge and the fullest value to cultural studies lies in the historical argument. The argument is not just that laws governing intellectual property, definitions of the subject, privacy, publicity, and trademarks are as important as cameras and sound booms in how entertainment artifacts get made. It is not simply that law matters, but that law changes in the face of new challenges, that the forms of legal and cultural contest are themselves shaped and reshaped by contention. The book holds to a resolutely historical method in the sense that each instance, each case, is treated in its particularity and in its appropriate context.

Each case becomes a cultural text in its own right, a text in which issues of law and culture appear locked in conflict but in which resolutions negotiate new conditions and produce new forms. The book translates the language of case law into the drama of cultural contestation, not only between producers and owners (the simplest, and as Gaines shows persuasively, a simplistic version of the issue) but between and among entities that are themselves legal fictions arising from litiginous improvisation. The development traced in the book culminates in the final chapter, where the author reveals how copyright law has undergone transformation into trademark law as a means of protecting corporate ownership of that strangely elusive kind of property designated by inscriptions, verbal and graphic, such as "Superman."

Not least among the intellectual exercises and pleasures of *Contested Culture* is the work of synthesis performed by the book. In a real sense the book emerges at the intersection of several separate disciplines, critical methods, and theories, the most prominent of which are film history, film theory, critical legal studies, popular culture studies, feminism, and most important, Marxist cultural theory, especially as it has been refined and practiced by British cultural studies. By exemplifying a fertile crossing over from one genre of criticism to another, which results in something new and original, the book implicitly confronts the danger of balkanization in the general field of cultural studies. Readers will recognize many of the concerns of particular fields and approaches in cultural studies, including questions of the subject, of realism, of the star system, of serialization, and the general question of cultural commodity-production. The result is a remarkably coherent study, a breakthrough, I think it is no exaggeration to claim, to a new coordinated study of popular cultural forms. Jane Gaines shows that the consideration of legal doctrine and juridical process has an essential place in the interpretation of cultural forms. She shows that law connects image to society, to the material processes that under-gird and pervade culture. And that students of contemporary culture must develop the means, such as the study of relevant legal doctrine, to identify those processes and their institutions, to examine their role in the cultural work of images. *Contested Culture* speaks to many of the new concerns presently reconfiguring the broad terrain of American studies. As a provocation and a challenge, a signal work of interdisciplinary synthesis, the book contributes enormously to the project of remapping the American field of historical cultural studies.

—Alan Trachtenberg

Preface

This book began as an attempt to fathom commodity "tie-ups"—the consumer goods and services that have been linked with the release of motion pictures. In its American manifestation, the phenomenon had its first exuberant phase in the thirties, producing the Shirley Temple doll, as well as promotions for Lux soap, Chesterfield cigarettes, and Dixie cup ice cream. In the late seventies the strategy was revived again on a grand national scale in the STAR WARS and SUPERMAN merchandising campaigns. What first intrigued me about the tie-up phenomenon was its ephemerality. In their transition from the local theater to canonical status as objects of serious scholarship, the films of the early classical period shed their associations with the automobile, the cereal box, and the refrigerator, which had once been part of the context that launched them. The Dixie cup lid imprinted with Jean Harlow's photographic image became in time a valuable collector's item.

What also attracted me to the tie-up was the way it seemed to epitomize Marx's analysis of the commodity form: that which holds the key to capitalist production, the core that appears at first to be "an extremely obvious, trivial thing" but that later turns out to be a "very strange thing," full of "metaphysical subtleties and theological niceties."[1] What I have always liked about the promotional commodity is that it is at once obvious and devious, spontaneous and orchestrated, flat and deep. On the hypothesis that some of the subtleties of this phenomenon had so far eluded us, I began to interview publicists from the thirties, as well as their contemporary equivalents who now work in the advertising and merchandising wings of Columbia Pictures, Warner Communications, and Twentieth-Century Fox Entertainment, which developed out of the old studio publicity departments. Those contacts led me in turn to Gregory Battersby and Charles Grimes's *The Law of Merchandise and Character Licensing*, where I discovered that the merchandising industry—this relatively new, completely parasitical multimillion-dollar business—had its own body of law. I learned that merchandising is based on the structure of the limited term license, which was perfected in the thirties with the Disney characters and with the Buck Rogers and Lone Ranger promotions. Battersby and Grimes, however, led me to something much more important: Melville B. Nimmer's law school textbook, *Cases and Materials on Copyright and Other Aspects of Entertainment Litigation—Including Unfair Competition, Defamation, and Privacy*. As Nimmer, the former Paramount Pictures lawyer, says in the introduction, his book is about entertainment transactions. But it also shows us the film studies canon in inverted form. In entertainment law, *Gaslight* (1942) is important not as a canonical film melodrama but as the object of a radio parody; *The Maltese Falcon* (1941) is the center of a dispute over serial rights; and Warner Brothers' *Dark Passage* (1947), which later became the television series "The Fugitive," figures in the definitive case on the "indivisibility of copyright." Reading Nimmer's *Cases and Materials* is an uncanny experience for the historian of American film. It begins exactly where film historians begin: with photographic technology and popular entertainment forms. The first case reprinted in Nimmer deals with issues surrounding the reproduction of a circus poster, the second with copyright in an 1882 photographic portrait. In a way, my approach in this book has been to write a series of essays that construct Nimmer's entertainment law volume as a companion piece to American film history and to contemporary film and television theory. Each of the six case study chapters grows out of current preoccupations in this field. Chapter 2, on the 1882 Oscar Wilde photograph, examines the subject in photography, the better to elucidate our understanding of the subject in cinema; chapter 3, on Jacqueline Kennedy Onassis and the look-alike phenomenon, revisits the problem of photographic realism and the feminist analysis of the image. Star study informs both the chapter on star contracts and the consideration of the Bela-Lugosi-as-Dracula case; challenges posed by the ontology of sound inform chapter 4, where I discuss the Nancy Sinatra sound-alike case, and chapter 7 covers the many media lives of Superman. There I ask if the ascendancy of the trademark over the copyright in intellectual property doctrine is related to the evolution of the television series form out of the motion picture as an entertainment medium.

While this book directly engages issues in film studies, it also has an American studies subtext. Because it returns so repeatedly to the divergence of U.S. intellectual property doctrine from French and British law, this study also raises some hope of new answers to the recurring question "What is American?" If we want to look to U.S. variations in Anglo-American law for some understanding of the particularity of American-ness, we must be prepared to examine large shifts *and* structural changes. Legal historians have often commented on the broadest differences be-tween U.S. and British law: the particularly American emphasis, for instance, on judge-made common law. But British and American legal doctrine have historically shared the same structure, so local develop-ments that show up in American law and not in British are all the more pronounced. Such is the case with the peculiarly American privacy right (and its reverse side, the publicity right) and with the American transfor-mation of Anglo-American trademark doctrine, which allows the mer-chant to take his hard-earned marketplace goodwill, turn it inside out, and transfer it to another merchant. While this legal phenomenon is probably an important companion formation to the development of consumer culture since the turn of the century, we cannot know that without looking at other aspects of American society. And it is here that the American studies interdisciplinary approach enables us to put legal doc-trine back into the context of U.S. history, literature, and mass culture from which it has been divorced by the very methodology of legal studies. From this vantage, the project of considering legal doctrine as cultural text is not just one of adding missing links to the study of American society; it is rather one of rereading written law by supplementing it.

James T. Farrell once described the American entertainment industry as the "grandiose Luna Park of capitalism."[2] But while film studies has taken it for granted that its critical antagonist is American capitalism, other branches of American studies have historically described U.S. society in other terms, even when those critiques are generated from a Leftist perspective. Michael Denning's important recent overview of Marxism and American studies makes it clear that U.S. film history, theory, and criticism stand out from the rest of American studies in their reliance on Marxist theory.[3] One way of explaining this difference is to start with the object of study itself. Film studies, unlike American studies in general, begins with the forms of mass communications technologies themselves and the marked features of the American culture industry. But in addition, film theory itself is bound in a particular contestatory way to American culture, since its French, British, and German sources were derived largely as a critical response to American mass culture. With the exception of the valorizing *Cahiers du Cinéma* auteur theory, the sources of contemporary film theory—the later French ideological critique of the apparatus, the pessimistic Frankfurt School critique, and the British *Screen* tradition—all represent criticism that "cut its teeth" on the product of the American film industry in an effort to counter U.S. cultural hegemony. Thus while the popular culture tradition in this country that grew out of American studies has been concerned with things American, new scholars in the U.S. have been attracted to film theory because of its European Marxist components as much as or more than any interest in analyzing classic American film texts. Meanwhile, British cultural studies has also upstaged the American popular culture movement by offering a more potent methodology for analyzing popular music, racial imagery, and television advertising, often by looking comparatively at American and British cases.

Yet another transatlantic crossing that informs my approach is the appearance of the American critical legal studies (CLS) movement in the late seventies, which has its companion development in British critical legal studies, officially formed in 1984. The differences in the two movements could be charted on the basis of their varying reliance on Western Marxist thought. Whereas British critical legal studies is theoretically compatible with British cultural studies in its reliance on Marxist thought, its American CLS counterpart accommodates more theoretical variation, including positions skeptical of Marxist theory.

I have set out to consider iconic similarity, the author's right in the work, and post mortem rights in the celebrity image (rights after death) as a contribution to an emerging American cultural studies. But ultimately I want to demonstrate the effectivity of the Marxist features of British cultural studies. I could not have excavated the structural premises of American entertainment law without those theoretical tools.

Acknowledgments

This book has benefited from the considered advice of friends and colleagues. Among those I would like to thank are John Belton, Stanley Fish, Simon Frith, John Frow, Peter Gabel, Rod Gibbs, Larry Grossberg, Iris Tillman Hill, Fredric Jameson, David Lange, Vincent Porter, Mark Rose, and Philip Rosen. Graduate students in the Department of English, the Graduate Program in Literature, and the Law School at Duke University, as well as the Department of Communications Studies, University of Iowa, provided invaluable research backup and help with manuscript preparation. For that work I would like to thank Anca Cristofovici, Paul Deutsch, Bob Lane, Jim Lastra, Dana Phillips, Arnold Winter, and Cary Wolfe. The Duke University Research Council provided generous support for the project.

The following is dedicated to Richard Dyer, a scholarly legend in his own time. I'm sure that my colleagues in cinema studies will understand and agree, for I am only one of many others who have drawn political inspiration as well as emotional sustenance from his work.

Contested Culture

CHAPTER ONE

On Likeness

THE LAW

In this book, Melville Nimmer meets Bernard Edelman. It was inevitable that Nimmer, the author of the standard treatise on U.S. copyright law, former lawyer for Paramount Pictures, and, during his life, one of the one hundred most powerful lawyers in the country, would meet the French Marxist legal theorist who specializes in the intellectual property aspects of new communications technologies.[1] Although Edelman is primarily a French legal scholar, he occasionally comments on U.S. legal doctrine, as well as American popular forms. Recently, for instance, he discussed the plagiarism and parody issues arising out of cases that involved Edgar Rice Burroughs's Tarzan and a French pornographic version of Charles Schultz's Snoopy. Given the relevance to intellectual property doctrine of poststructuralist interest in the *work*, in the *subject* who utters the *work*, and in the discourses that utter that *subject*, Edelman is pivotal.[2] For his work stands quite alone in the way it hinges on intellectual property doctrine as well as contemporary theories of meaning. Edelman transplants a poststructuralist style of language "play" into legal theory, and in doing so he produces a kind of hybrid discourse that is anomalous to legal studies in the United States.

Here, for example, is Edelman on legal parody: "Parody is a creation based on a creation: it creates from the already created. Hence its ambiguity. On the one hand, it has to be distinct and distinguishable from the work being parodied, while borrowing its characters. On the other hand, so as not to run foul of the legal obligation of 'respect,' it cannot falsify the work being parodied."[3] This subtle play on the law of parody, familiar to readers accustomed to the poststructuralist production of puns as theory, is somewhat strange in the context of intellectual property law. Within this doctrine, language is like hard coin. Words and precise phrases, 1 transferred intact from judicial opinion to commentary and back to opinion, are themselves the carriers of valuable entitlements. Legal discourse is designed to guard against ambiguity, and even the use of synonyms is avoided because it produces unwanted ambiguity rather than clarity. Meaning is bound again and again to linguistic terms through the ritual of citation.

This is not to say that juridical discourse is without verve, play, or wit. Often established doctrine evolves out of a judge's subtle humor. The wry description of portrait painting delivered by Justice Oliver Wendell Holmes, Jr., in *Bleistein v. Donaldson Lithographic Co.* (1903), for instance, has become part of the foundation of copyright doctrine. Defending the copyrightability of circus posters reproduced by lithography, Holmes addressed the difference between reproducing a copy and producing a painting from the same original: "But even if they had been drawn from life, that fact would not deprive them of protection. The opposite would mean that a portrait by Velasquez or Whistler was common property because others might try their hand on the same face. Others are free to copy the original. They are not free to copy the copy."[4] More often, though, U.S. intellectual property discourse is not turned upside down or inside out. It isn't regularly submitted to a critique of its premises. After all, if it is to do the work of guaranteeing property value, it cannot be found to be (as Edelman finds it) unstable, self-contradicting, or incoherent.[5] It must represent itself as scientific and airtight.

It is perplexing to me that there has been so little response to Edelman's work in either Britain or the U.S. When his *Ownership of the Image* (published in France in 1973) was translated into English in 1979, the British film journal *Screen* published two important reviews.[6] Three years later, John Tagg made productive use of Edelman in an essay on power relations in the photographic image.[7] And in the U.S., *Social Text* published an analysis of Edelman and E. B. Pashukanis, the Soviet legal theorist of the twenties, to whom Edelman is indebted.[8] Aside from this instance, however, the response has been muted at best, and what is surprising is that although *Ownership of the Image* appeared coincident with new critiques of the literary and cinematic subject (especially in the pages of *Screen*), Edelman's quite original application of these theories to legal subjecthood has never been integrated into the *Screen* tradition.

The reason for this neglect could not have been that Edelman's starting point in his study is the still photograph, because it was clear by 1979 that critiques of "representation" pertained to photography as well as film.[9] It may have been, instead, that the English title of Edelman's book suggested a "captains of industry" approach to the organization of mass culture, one that might have led potential readers to think that this was yet another analysis of concentrations of power in the entertainment industry.[10] The question "Who owns the image?" might have implied, in other words, that the book was about property disputes involving publishing companies, motion picture studios, and television broadcasting networks.

Edelman's French title, *Le droit saisi par la photographie*, suggests, however, that the book is about photographic technology's indictment of traditional legal doctrine. And such an inquiry is in the spirit of the work on the politics of meaning in the image, which, like Edelman's book, also has its origins in post-1968 French intellectual thought. Why, then, was Edelman not claimed by a tradition to which he clearly belongs?

Two other possible explanations suggest themselves. First, we might surmise that film theorists and literary critics have usually seen legal doctrine as foreign terrain. And second, these same critics might view the legal subject as essentially irrelevant to the questions of gender, desire, and sexuality that have been central concerns since the late seventies. The second possibility will have to wait for a fuller investigation in another undertaking. But I want to elaborate on the first possibility by asking why, given the existing model of Michel Foucault's work (which draws no hard boundaries between medical, literary, penal, religious, or legal institutions), legal discourse was never pulled into the orbit of the *Screen* tradition—unlike, say, medical discourse, which was readily critiqued and incorporated into feminist film theory.[11] Part of the answer has to do with the configuration of critical fields and their respective methodologies. Within the ten years since the appearance of the English translation of Edelman, the once cinema-centered *Screen* tradition has given way to cultural studies. For a short time in the seventies, British cultural studies and *Screen* theory were considered rival traditions.[12] Today, however, cultural studies is often represented as encompassing all of the theoretical work on contemporary communications technologies, work which has some basis in poststructuralist theories of meaning. Because of this new development, I want to be clear that I am sticking quite closely to the original concerns of British cultural studies. My reference point, then, will be the identifiable body of work generated in the early seventies within and around the Centre for Contemporary Cultural Studies in Birming-

ham, England, and centered on the work of Stuart Hall and others.[13] This
gives me a point of entry into the analysis of legal doctrine, a methodolog-
ical overlap (although not necessarily a perfect correspondence) with
Edelman, and a political vantage point on Nimmer and the entertainment
industry.[14]

Probably the most fundamental principle I take from cultural studies is
Raymond Williams's definition of culture as a "way of life," as the sum of
all aspects of a society.[15] I start, then, from the assumption that although
intellectual property law has its specialized traditions, codes, and practices, it can also be studied as an object of culture. Practical law, however,
is also a discourse of power, one that restrains persons and regulates other
objects of culture. I will want to investigate, therefore, how intellectual
property law impinges upon such forms of culture as names, cartoons,
recorded voices, novels, television dramas, photographic images, and
motion pictures.

I am asking some old questions about the configuration of culture, but
asking them from a new angle. Does intellectual property law proscribe
certain aesthetic forms? Does it ensure the existence of some forms and
not others? Do we therefore want to say that this law has a part in the
social production of meaning? Does the consideration of intellectual
property as another code that determines the availability of popular signs
need to be factored into our theories of meaning? Before I continue this
line of inquiry, let me clarify what I will mean by "intellectual property
doctrine."

Technically, Anglo-American intellectual property doctrine encompasses the unfair competition, copyright, and patent branches of the law.
Here I limit myself to the unfair competition and copyright areas, since I
am looking more at the cultural software than the industrial hardware side
of production, where patent law is pertinent. By "doctrine," I mean the
body or corpus that is composed of the rulings of judge-made or common
law, as well as of legislature-produced or statutory law. But in addition,
"doctrine" encompasses commentary (law review articles, treatises) within which legal theorizing takes place. Although my discussion in some
cases will range over the literature of the commentary, I will start with the
written judicial opinion or decision rather than with any general principles. Each chapter takes one or more written opinions as its organizing
focus.

The Double Movement of Legal Culture

Legal doctrine as a discourse has some structural similarity to popular culture as defined by British cultural studies. Stuart Hall, in "Notes on Deconstructing 'The Popular,'" describes popular culture as neither a fully appropriated territory (a space of containment) nor a space seized by the popular classes (a space of resistance). "The popular" is instead a middle ground between opposing social forces. In his theorization of this ground, Hall might be speaking about the space Anglo-American law occupies in relation to the wider culture. In the transition from agrarian to industrial capitalism, Hall explains, one sees an ongoing struggle over the culture of the poor and the working classes, a contest created because of the need to re-form society to meet the new needs of capital.[16] Attempts to analyze popular culture, he goes on, have tended to view it as a space of either containment or resistance, as either totally conservative or inherently radical. Hall corrects that overstatement by giving us a better definition of popular culture than I have yet to find elsewhere: "Popular culture is neither, in a 'pure' sense, the popular traditions of resistance to these processes; nor is it the forms which are superimposed on and over them. It is the ground on which the transformations are worked. In the study of popular culture, we should always start here: with the double-stake in popular culture, the double movement of containment and resistance, which is always inevitably inside it."[17] Over this "battlefield," the dominant culture will try to "disorganize and reorganize" social meaning as it attempts to settle definitions and fix forms. But the dominant culture always encounters resistance points at which these forms are re-articulated and redefined as acts of "refusal." From this vantage, it would be a mistake to understand popular culture as either entirely saturated and corrupt or entirely authentic because it is somehow people's culture.[18] And so it is with all social forms. Following the Soviet literary theorist V. N. Volosinov, Hall reminds us that all classes use the same language and that "differently oriented accents intersect in every ideological sign."[19]

Hall's theorization owes something to Raymond Williams's notion of popular culture as an "uneasy mixture" of radicalism and adaptation.[20] But in its theorization of the "refusal" of dominant culture, it also shares something with the Frankfort School's lesser-known analysis of not the bleakness but the utopian dimension of mass culture. Although Hall himself is less inclined to think of the double movement of mass culture in terms of the concept of utopia, other culture theorists have found in mass culture a desire for something better, a utopian urge that balances the degradation of consumer culture with a promise of community and plentitude. In Walter Benjamin's dialectic of the commodity, we find an intimation of this revolutionary social transformation, and certainly it is there in Ernst Bloch, who even saw a connection between the goals of revolutionary struggle and the human "liberties" and aspirations found in natural law.[21] But the idea of utopianism in mass culture has had to be reformulated for the contemporary period, the period within which we suspect that consumer culture is exponentially taking away more than it is offering. The classic statement of why we find a utopian dimension at all within contemporary mass culture is Fredric Jameson's theorization of the "fantasy bribe": "[T]he works of mass culture cannot be ideological without at one and the same time being implicitly or explicitly Utopian as well: they cannot manipulate unless they offer some genuine shred of content as a fantasy bribe to the public about to be so manipulated."[22] And here is where I find my analogy between mass culture and legal discourse. For in order for the law to have viability at all, it too needs to hold out that "genuine shred" of something, and it does so in the promise to uphold rights, to secure benefits equally, and to ensure "liberty." But the law holds out this promise, not to manipulate but to respond to its constituency. It cannot rule without seeming to be fair, and without seeming to be fair it cannot secure the consent of those whom it governs. To secure a viable consensus, the law must work for those out of power as well as for those in command of it, and to this end, the law will under some circumstances even undermine the long-term interests of those who are most able to make it work for them.[23] Some of the more dramatic illustrations of this point occur in the literature on Anglo-American slave law.

The approach to the law that finds it open to struggle and movement has been worked out by historians Eugene Genovese and E. P. Thompson. In *Roll, Jordan, Roll*, Genovese discusses the adherence of the Southern states to the legal principle of the slave as property. Pressed to its logical conclusion and held to its word, however, the "slave as property" argument produced not the slaveowners' desired result but quite the opposite. What it produced was not the protection of real estate property but rather the enactment of prohibitions against punishment involving humanity. That is, the "slave as property" principle produced human beings—potential legal subjects—who were capable of acting as well as of being criminally acted upon. The slave laws worked not only to secure the compliance of the ruled but also to reinforce a cosmic view of justice and to represent a code *to* the ruling themselves. That code upheld again and again a set of rights for slaveholders that constituted them as persons able to testify in court, to bear arms, and to protect their property, and it withheld the same rights from their slaves. But because the same law had to be consistent and uniform in principle, it could be used to condemn an abusive master who murdered a slave. Or again, the law might hold to its own principle that a slave could not testify against a white man, but the white law would then have to suffer the consequences of its own racism, as in the case of a Louisiana court that had to acquit a white man who incited a slave rebellion because it could not hear the testimony of slaves.[24] In these ways and in others, the very law that protected the institution of slavery could in the long run sabotage the slaveholders.

In order for the law to work effectively, it cannot seem to be anything other than neutral and fair. And it will be, says E. P. Thompson:

> If the law is evidently partial and injust, then it will mask nothing, legitimize nothing, contribute nothing to any class's hegemony. The essential precondition for the effectiveness of law, in its function as ideology, is that it shall display an independence from gross manipulation and shall seem to be just. It cannot seem to be so without upholding its own logic and criteria of equity: indeed, on occasion, by actually *being just*.[25]

Thompson's analysis of the "rule of law" in eighteenth-century Britain articulates a case for seeing the law from a materialist standpoint as a structure that is able to serve opposition to the interests of capital even though it is bound to those interests. In fact, Thompson goes so far as to say that even though the law *is* mystifying and faithfully works to the advantage of the class that implements it, this same law, untarnished, can be an effective instrument of equalization. At the conclusion to his study of an eighteenth-century penal code designed to punish "blacking" (poaching) in the royal forests, Thompson makes his most controversial statement on the law: "We ought to expose the shams and inequities which may be concealed beneath this law. But the rule of law itself, imposing the effective inhibitions upon power and the defence of the citizen from power's all-intrusive claims, seems to me to be an unqualified human good. To deny or belittle this good is, in this dangerous century when the resources and pretensions of power continue to enlarge, a desperate error of intellectual abstraction."[26]

An "unqualified human good"? We might take issue with Thompson by pointing out that American intellectual property law in this century has produced a merchant's "goodwill" as a property, has extended the copyright monopoly grant in the 1976 reform, and has yielded to market pressure to turn copyright into trademark protection. Could all of these developments be called just, fair, and impartial—particularly when the law has undeniably favored controlling interests in such shifts, often to the detriment of the common good? Still, says legal theorist Mark Tushnet, "[N]othing in the law prevents it from advocating such ideals as equality and community,"[27] and what we find in a closer look at U.S. legal doctrine is that it does, in fact, contain the provisions for social and economic equality. While it might not be fair in practice, it is built upon the premises of equality and the interests of the common good.

By way of example, let us look at the utopian provision and its antithesis in contract law. This double movement or double-stake of the law is often lost sight of in contemporary Marxist analyses as well as in U.S. law review commentary (although for different reasons). A recent political analysis of contract doctrine, for example, holds that the law, in its representation of "free exchange," produces unequal relations as equal. Contract law, in other words, is blind to the power differentials of the parties entering into the agreement. That may be, but contract discourse, in the representation of "freedom of contract" also generates precisely the opposite: a completely utopian idea that has been a rallying point in labor struggles, a concrete focus for protests against oppressive employment conditions. This is not to say that the same concept couldn't then be turned against workers who had entered into unfair contracts; in such cases "freedom of contract" could make it seem that workers had freely entered into and even desired the oppressive labor to which they were contractually bound.[28]

While this reading of the doubleness of contract doctrine relies upon existing analysis, my interpretation of the dichotomous structure of copyright law is somewhat more tentative and is entirely my own. Part of the difficulty in highlighting the duality of copyright law stems from the fact that, in legal studies as well as in the wider culture, copyright is accepted so unconditionally as a provision for the public good. My fundamental premise—that copyright is a monopoly grant—is not even readily available in the legal literature. What has almost totally disappeared from the U.S. law review commentary is the notion of the copyright monopoly as a necessary evil—necessary in order to provide incentive to authors to produce literary works for an ultimate public good, a good that includes furthering the "pleasure" of reading.[29]

In the U.S. Constitution, the purpose of copyright and patent monopoly grants is "[t]o promote the Progress of Science and the useful Arts by securing for limited Times to Authors and Inventors the exclusive Right to their respective Writings and Discoveries."[30]

It is not so much the monopoly grant, however, as it is the way in which copyright law monitors it that makes this law function in two opposite ways. Either it can limit elements of culture (by recognizing the monopoly right) or it can make those elements available for others by *not* affording copyright protection. As we will see in chapter 4, for example, one can claim copyright monopoly protection for a musical composition and the vocal performance of it. But, the singer's "style" of performance is left unprotected by intellectual property law, on the assumption that to allow such a monopoly on performance signs would limit the available pool of expressive gestures. Hence we find in copyright law the self-correcting mechanism of what I call the double movement of circulation and restriction.

Let me be clear that the circulation-restriction dichotomy does not correlate exactly with the double movement of resistance and containment in popular culture. Some forms of popular culture, because of their proximity to the people, can be reappropriated by the people as signs of refusal almost as soon as these forms are produced. But because of the clumsy mediation of institutions, the law is systematically distanced from the people. Still, the law, like popular culture, is a common ground, and it must *seem* responsive to all interests, large or small. Conflicting groups and class interests must use the same law, just as they use the same national language, but in both instances significant differences in application stem from the structures of institutional access and implementation.[31] In other words, it is the schools and the courts that make the language and the law work for some groups and not others. Not surprisingly, then, what has happened historically in unfair competition law is that powerful market interests have learned to use the more generous "availability" and "circulation" provisions in the law, thus taking advantage of their privileged access to legal institutions.

Take the following example: If Superman is now an archetype available to all and is not a trademark, property of DC Comics, that means that ABC is free to use the character type in its series "The Greatest American Hero." But it also means that ABC could then copyright its antihero Ralph Hinkley, thus restricting use of the character. ABC could even register the image of Hinkley with the U.S. trademark office for use on coffee mugs. If Hinkley became a popular figure, in forty years he too might be returned by the courts to circulation in the common culture. In practical terms, what legal "availability" really means is that another corporate entity can set up another monopoly through copyright and trademark registration. And so it is that the dynamic of circulation-restriction starts all over again. In reality, then, intellectual property law makes and unmakes monopolies. In that respect, it is like other U.S. trade regulation, which steps in when monopoly, capital's firstborn monster, threatens capital's favorite child, free enterprise. Unrestrained, trademark or copyright, like any other monopoly, can grow powerful, can cast a pall and deaden.

But the utopian light that shines within the law will become progressively fainter as I move into the following chapters. Property claims will win out over "freedom of speech" claims. And even then, "freedom," when it is invoked, will usually mean unrestricted freedom to compete. Persons are consistently invoked as owners. Most of the cases I will discuss deal with disputes over potentially valuable properties, and very little of the commentary on this law is sympathetic to notions of public culture. Some of my characterization of the law as oppressive is a function of my reliance upon Edelman, whose theorization of the law as a key structure in the production of ideal subjects is bleak indeed. Here, I would have to agree with others who have criticized Edelman's failure to provide relief from an oppressive structure of bourgeois law by looking to provisions within it that allow for resistance and critique. For those provisions do, in fact, exist. The American doctrine of fair use, for instance, does make allowance for the dissemination of ideas in an educational context, no matter how critical or subversive. As Vincent Porter has argued with reference to fair use, it is not necessarily in the ultimate interests of capitalism to allow photocopying for academic purposes, a possibility that does not figure in Edelman's theory.[32]

Judicial Opinion and Commonsense Knowledge

The doubleness of the law, what Alan Hunt and Peter Fitzpatrick call the "deep perplexity" of its positive and negative character,[33] is a result, at least in part, of what Raymond Williams has described as the "asymmetry" of contemporary mass society. The disjunctures between the various aspects of social life are more pronounced than in earlier centuries, when education, the state, law, moral life, and the market were mutually reinforcing, or in Williams's terms, relatively symmetrical.[34] Symptomatic of the structural asymmetry that Williams describes is the way capitalism tends to produce the very seeds of its dissolution. Here is Williams's famous example: "A Marxist book, an anarchist's guide, attacks on the institution of the family, songs celebrating physical violence or showing crime as justifiable and successful, can and do become, whatever their varying cultural sources, profitable commodities in a market within a state and culture which officially (and no doubt, within the terms of its insoluble contradiction, really), disapproves of or opposes all these things."[35] As Terry Lovell describes it, self-expanding capital in its "anarchy" produces its antitheses as it produces a widening range of commodities carrying counter-values that undermine the official values of the culture.[36] And U.S. intellectual property, even though it is driven more often by the logic of capital than by any of its counter-logics, will contribute in its way to the production of commodities willy-nilly, since what it generally does (after the fact of commodity production) is to retrace the conditions for that production. But the mechanism of intellectual property performs its work blindly; as it draws boundaries between what is and is not property, it doesn't ask about the content of what it does or does not recognize as a cultural property. It only sees value and interests. The judges who implement and interpret the law, however, are a different matter.

Having made such a point about the structure of intellectual property, however, I must immediately qualify my assertion. For while this law characterizes itself as a neutral space, safe from politics, above social vicissitudes, a space where reason reigns, it is at the same time *of* the community—and that is especially true of American legal discourse, with its emphasis on the common law and its evolution in custom and use. The U.S. common law system, taken from old British law, has subsequently become more American than British.[37] And it is this judge-made law, as opposed to the statutory law of the legislature, that I pause to look at here.

For what I will return to again and again in the following chapters is the feature of juridical discourse that is most like commonsense knowledge. Yes, judges do apply legal rules and principles, and yes, most of what they write in their opinions pertains to the review of precedent and the clarification of points of law. But that purely legal discourse is often mixed with pithy sayings, homely analogies, personal judgments, and frank characterizations. What I mean by defining this knowledge as "commonsense" is that it is drawn directly out of the reservoir of shared knowledge in the culture, the common pool of norms, beliefs, and values from which we all draw in our attempts to make sense of the world.

The concept of "commonsense knowledge" was first introduced into cultural studies as critics rediscovered the work of Antonio Gramsci, and it became clear that it was a key concept closely linked to Gramsci's notion of hegemony.[38] For Gramsci, commonsense knowledge concretized the contradictory consciousness of the working class, a consciousness whose contradictions could be revealed by that class and only by that class. The commonsense knowledge I am talking about, which appears to be produced by judges (but is produced *for* them as well), is that same sense, which the class out of power borrows. Such a "borrowed" consciousness is not necessarily "theirs," and it doesn't serve their interests in the long run. Although this consciousness doesn't exactly fit their experience, they make do with it anyway. In its contradictoriness, this store of wisdom *does* benefit groups in power, but this consciousness is also the terrain within which the official values of the society clash with the ever-expanding needs of capital. For all of its composite eclecticism and incoherence, commonsense knowledge works over time to the advantage of dominant interests.[39] The significance of studying judicial opinions as cultural texts is that they illustrate two things about commonsense knowledge: One, we see how it "gets the job done" in the culture, so to speak; and two, we see how a sphere of activity other than the law makes its inconsistencies felt in legal doctrine.

Juridical discourse, for instance, will hold forth on the strict legal definition of "original work" as nothing more than a work produced by an originator. But it may then abruptly lapse into value judgments that betray a preference for elite culture's dismissal of anything that is "imitative" of something "genuinely original." Judge Greenfield, for example, in his ruling in *Onassis v. Christian Dior–New York, Inc.*, disparagingly dismissed the claim of the Onassis look-alike because she was only a "coun-terfeit" of the real. Here the judge clearly aired value-laden opinions that were fundamentally at odds with the basic principles of copyright law, principles that have no use for the notions of genuineness and authenticity that are found at large in the wider culture. The official values of the society, in other words, are here at odds with the legal conditions requisite for industrial production. Where the strict legal definition of "original work" facilitates corporate ownership and the transfer of entitlement between owners, humanist standards of excellence are totally irrelevant and can only confuse an already complicated legal issue.

The clash between official values and the imperatives of industrial production is nowhere more dramatic than in the wresting of a right of publicity out of the right of privacy. In the period from 1930 to 1970, and especially in cases involving the commercial appropriation of celebrity images, judges espoused the traditional value that a famous person had freely chosen to live in the public eye and that therefore he or she could not object to the consequent invasion of privacy. In other words, "they asked for it." But at the same time, more and more agreed that since advertisers paid the famous for the use of their images, there might be a property right involved. In one of the pivotal opinions, *O'Brien v. Pabst Sales Co.*, the majority held that since O'Brien had been named outstand-ing football player of the year in 1938, he could not complain when his photograph appeared in a Pabst beer advertisement. But Judge Holmes, dissenting in *O'Brien*, anticipated the development of the law in this area in his reference to advertisers' common practice: "They are undoubtedly in the habit of buying the right to use one's name or picture to create demand and good will for their merchandise. It is the peculiar excellence of the common law that, by general usage, it is shaped and moulded into new and useful forms."[40] It is this "general usage," this "peculiar excel-lence of the common law," that produces juridical discourse as the dra-matic scene in which social beliefs meet in all of their antipathy. Such discourse is crisscrossed by warring premises. Mark Tushnet explains that judicial opinions in particular help us understand the consciousness that is dominant at any given time in history because they undertake the function of institutional justification. That is, in these discourses, the institution that ostensibly serves the community justifies itself to the community that it serves, even as it explains the community to itself. Because these opinions, as he says, "articulate attempts to reconcile decisions with commonly accepted premises, [they] reveal those premises almost directly. And from the premises we can reconstruct the consciousness."[41]

There is finally another way in which we can consider the juridical opinion as a cross section of commonsense knowledge: we can define these texts of culture by their distinctive relationship to material conditions. One way of defining common sense in Gramscian terms is by connecting it directly to lived experience. It is a mixed consciousness, certainly, with its imaginary and mystifying devices, but it will always have a foot (and thus a "grounding") in economic circumstances and social relations. One can say the same of juridical discourse, which addresses conflicts arising directly out of material reality and experience. Judicial opinions, then, pinpoint cultural trouble spots. As Peter Gabel and Jay M. Feinman have observed in their discussion of these opinions: "Most of the time the socioeconomic system operates without any need for law as such because people at every level have been imbued with its inevitability and necessity. When the system breaks down and conflicts arise, a legal case comes into being."[42] The cases I discuss in the following essays grow out of social conflict-irritants, and legal discourse grows around them as it performs its ameliorative and conciliatory functions. One way of reading the face of a culture is to look at the conflict-irritants it produces, which are then taken up as case law. Case law identifies the trouble spots, but it also prioritizes issues by deciding which causes of action it will allow and which points of law it will decide on appeal.

Critical Legal Studies and Cultural Studies

I have thus far argued for seeing judicial opinions as common-sense knowledge, which means that we will understand them as containing conflicting ideas, both in the sense of holding those ideas and in the sense of managing them. This wisdom will even combine such contradictory concepts as privacy and publicity and render them as smoothly evolving doctrine. What I have not yet said is that these opinions work ideologically. Although within cultural studies "commonsense knowledge" is often used interchangeably with "ideology," in other fields "common sense" is often used to mean the opposite of mystification: good, solid, time-tested sense.[43] This knowledge *does*, however, have good sense as its "core," which, as I have said, is also its material grounding.[44] What, then, should our objection be to such common sense? The objection is the same objection we would make to ideology. With its mixed bag of knowledges, its characteristic inconsistencies, ideology cannot deliver analysis, cannot give us any distance on a culture within which its primary function is to keep existing social relations intact. And it is therefore a significant challenge to legal doctrine to charge that it promises science and gives us ideology instead.

As Stuart Hall puts it, following Louis Althusser, ideology moves "constantly within a closed circle, producing not knowledge, but a recognition of things we already knew"; it treats as "already established fact exactly the premises which ought to have been put into question."[45] What Hall writes of ideology is also true of the law, which cannot question its own categories (authorship, private property, right), since it depends upon them for its perpetuation. The law will maintain these categories with a circularity. When it is asked, for instance, "What is an author?" it answers, "An author is an originator." And when asked "What is an originator?" it will say, "An originator is an author."

I find corroboration for this view of juridical discourse as ideology in the critical legal studies movement, which has in recent years mounted a challenge to the U.S. legal community. Critical legal studies dates from a 1977 conference in Madison, Wisconsin, which brought together both radical academics and practicing lawyers. It has its equivalent groups in Germany and France and is especially strong in Britain, where in 1984 the Critical Legal Conference was established.[46] The easiest way of distinguishing American from British critical legal studies is to say that the former encompasses a wider variety of intellectual strains than the latter. As critical legal studies has evolved in Britain, it has clearly been shaped by contemporary developments in Marxist and feminist theory, in postmodernism and deconstruction, and by the renewal of interest in the Frankfurt School critics.[47] In the following, I range among sources in both British and U.S. critical legal theory, since that broad field is resonant with so many themes and preoccupations in cultural studies. But it has also been through the U.S. "CLS" tradition that I have come to understand the particularity of American legal doctrine that is both congruent with French and British law in some aspects and sharply divergent in others.

One of the main challenges for cultural studies has been the clear definition of the object of its critique. Is it mainstream media, the humanist tradition, bourgeois ideology, classical narrative fiction, or aesthetic realism? American critical legal studies, in contrast, has a more clearly delineated antagonist in "liberal legalism," the legal tradition that provides the foundation of American law and its concepts of the public/private distinction and the separation of powers. This is the same tradition that adheres to the Lockean understanding of property, to which I will turn shortly. An important critique of this tradition was launched by the legal "Realism" movement between 1920 and 1939, and it has been part of the project of a new generation of Leftist scholars to carry on where the "Realists" left off.[48] Not insignificantly, then, my own reading of the internal rhetoric of privacy doctrine is also indebted to the work of the Realists.

There are other ways in which the concerns of cultural studies overlap with those of critical legal studies: both see the social world not as given but as "constructed"; both take interest in people's struggles and in challenges to the dominant consciousness; and both insist on the importance of history and economics and of opening up ideological contradictions. For comparative purposes, I want to focus on one area of mutual concern—the very one, as it happens, that addresses the problem of bringing together divergent disciplines while recognizing what Marxist theory calls their "relative autonomy." It is regrettable that a concept that refers to the one theoretical problem that fires the imagination of so many Marxist scholars should be so terminologically awkward. Still, "relative autonomy," Engels's peculiar invention—and an oxymoron, Colin MacCabe points out—has its justifications. The concept may be best understood as a corrective to the tendency to find cause and effect relationships between the economic base and the superstructure (composed of the spheres of culture, education, law, the family, the state).[49] What Étienne Balibar calls the "non-correspondence" of these levels or spheres is a theoretical antidote to an older propensity in Marxist theory: "economism," or the explanation of all cultural phenomena in terms of economic arrangements.[50] To give a bald example, an attempt to explain the content of motion pictures as the direct result of industrial capitalism would be an economistic explanation. Similarly, critical legal studies is a reaction to a comparable mechanical tendency in an older, "instrumentalist" theory of law that read Anglo-American law as simply the implementation of ruling-class interests.[51]

In terms of the following chapters, the theoretical challenge of relative autonomy is how to represent political, social, economic, legal, and cultural forms as connected and yet disconnected. How, for example, do I represent the manifold relationships between musical recording and the following: U.S. political priorities in 1909 and 1976, the structure of the American family, the uses of leisure time, the internal logic of copyright law, the state of recording technology, the growth of monopoly capital, and the cultural construction of hearing? Let me try to make this more manageable. Since I ultimately want to ask questions about the relationship between the concrete forms of sound recording and the way musical recording is constructed through statutory and common law, I am interested in how "extrinsic" changes in the material production of sound are felt "intrinsically" in the internal formal structures of law and culture. I borrow this dichotomy from Fredric Jameson, who refers to the "scandal of the extrinsic," which "comes as a salutary reminder of the ultimately material base of cultural production." But the real scandal, Jameson argues, is not in finding that the mode of production has had its effect on the forms of culture. Rather, it is in the difficulty of accounting for how things change in a society that can produce only discontinuities, and therefore can be understood only as distributing its causes and effects unpredictably, so that we are forced to read the "symptoms" of one cultural phenomenon in another.[52] A very rough but humorous analogy for this beguiling phenomenon is Walter Benjamin's example of the sleeper who suffers from indigestion: "The economic conditions under which society exists come to expression in the superstructure just as with someone sleeping, an over-filled stomach, even if it may causally determine the contents of the dream, finds in those contents not its copied reflection, but its expression."[53]

Can we describe the relation between legal doctrine and mode of production with the metaphor of the sleeper and his dream? According to Marxist thought within critical legal studies, the law is not strictly a superstructural phenomenon, but it is certainly not an economic phenomenon either. Unlike other cultural phenomena such as television serials and narrative fiction, however, the law is often confused with the economic. For instance, a mistake we could easily make would be to represent the law of copyright as the determining base for the superstructural "work of authorship."[54] This mistake is instructive, however, because it calls our attention to something Marx and Engels themselves commented upon: the way the law under capital *represents itself* as determining economic relations.[55] In my later discussion of the way in which the right to privacy becomes a property right, we will see precisely this self-characterization in the increasing bravado with which U.S. law represents itself as creating value. But that is a long way indeed from dispelling our doubts about where the law fits in the social totality. Is there a proper Marxist theory of law? Marx and Engels themselves did not leave a coherent answer to that question.[56] But such a theory has been attempted by others, and I want to turn now to one example of the way in which the theory of commodity production has been ingeniously turned into a theory of law.

The Commodity Exchange School of Law

Soviet legal theorist E. B. Pashukanis, writing in the twenties, gives us the most complete theorization of bourgeois law. His theory sees the entire legal structure as organized around the individual as opposed to the group, around the juridical subject as the holder of property rights.[57] I should emphasize *entire* here, because it is really when one tries to extend Pashukanis's theory to all branches of the law that it breaks down.[58] And it has been argued as well that the law is not sufficiently elastic in the Soviet theorist's work, that Pashukanis does not allow for the possibility that the law could serve oppositional interests (as, for instance, Eugene Genovese and E. P. Thompson have shown it to do). Criticism of Pashukanis often points out that because he had no theory of ideology to speak of, his analysis doesn't yield an understanding of what I have called the double movement of law.[59] However, if we keep the shortcomings of the theory in mind, there is no reason that we can't apply it to those areas of law where it has much to tell us: the laws of trademark and unfair competition, and the law of copyright. As Paul Hirst has suggested, one of the values of Pashukanis's work is the framework he provides for seeing "right" as a historically specific "bourgeois right" rather than as a universal entitlement. Pashukanis, he concludes, provides us with a basis for posing a "challenge to the validity of 'right' as a category in the public sphere."[60] And it is the validity of "right" as a legal category that concerns me in my discussion of the *right* of publicity.

Pashukanis's analysis of legal relations begins with the individual the subject, the "atom of legal theory, its simplest, irreducible element."[61] This subject has two basic "characteristics": He has rights, and he can own property. That seems fairly simple and obvious. But as soon as it is asserted that "right" and "property" are foundational, these givens slip away from us. Because "right" and "property" *are* so fundamental to Anglo-American law as we know it, we cannot achieve any critical distance on these categories simply by identifying them. To see these concepts critically, we need to imagine the antithesis of bourgeois man freely holding a property: in medieval man, for instance, who was fettered by that property.[62] Or again, we have to consider the institution of slavery in order to understand the precondition to the property right as the right to own oneself.

This discussion takes us back momentarily to John Locke, in whose *Two Treatises of Government* we find three basic principles to which I will refer throughout the following chapters. The first and second Lockean principles concerning private property are closely linked. Property is premised upon freedom, the ownership of oneself and one's own labor. Hence, property in things is contingent on property in the self. We should note that Locke's formula allows for a circularity that denies legal personhood and property to slaves. For if you can't own yourself you can't own other property, and if you can't even own property, then how can you possibly be said to own yourself? In Locke's third principle (one of his more colorful theorizations), property is the product of man's labor, which he has "mixed" with nature.[63]

Locke's labor "mixed" with nature to produce property is perfected in Hegel, who finds in the exertion of the will nothing less than the appropriation of all nature. Hegel sets the stage for the rights-holding subject as we know it by conceiving of subject and right as simultaneous. Thus, it is impossible to see how "subject" as category might precede "right." After Hegel, it is impossible to imagine how subject and right could be separated, and it is thus difficult to see that it is the former, *not* the latter, that guarantees the conditions for ownership. Hegel's basic statement on "subject" and "right" should sound terribly familiar to us, but that is the point; we are tracing the construction of the idealist foundations of society as we know it: "A person has as his substantive end the right of putting his will into any and every thing and thereby making it his, because it has no such end in itself and derives its destiny and soul from his will. This is the absolute right of appropriation which man has over all 'things.'"[64] Hegel provides the legal subject with its living and breathing equivalent, the human person. And personhood, in turn, is further embellished and made pertinent to every one of us in the notion of individual personality. For Hegel, "personality" and "right" are reciprocal: "Personality essentially involves the capacity for rights and constitutes the concept and the basis (itself abstract) of the system of abstract and therefore formal right. Hence the imperative of right is: 'Be a person and respect others as persons.' "[65] By tying rights to personality, Hegel can argue that abstract rights emanate from human beings; right becomes synonymous with individual self-expression, with the investment of personality, through will, in material objects. In Hegel, to quote Pashukanis, the right has become an "attribute," even a characteristic, that "belongs to" every person.[66]

Where Pashukanis's theory is most original is in his critique of the Hegelian foundation of contract theory. For those acquainted with Marx's theory of value, the Soviet theorist's "commodity exchange theory of law" will have a certain familiar appeal because it is superimposed over the theory of commodity production.[67] Pashukanis argues that property develops from the need for owners to exchange commodities (whether the labor or the good). Whereas in U.S. intellectual property law we are given the impression that property exists because the law protects it, Pashukanis shows how this principle actually works the other way. It is not that the legal form determines the commodity form; the commodity form determines the legal form: "Property in the legal sense did not arise because it occurred to people to invest one another with this legal capacity, but because they were able to exchange commodities only in the guise of property-owners. The unlimited power of disposal over objects is nothing but the reflection of unlimited commodity circulation."[68] This symmetrical relationship between two property owners exchanging commodities is the basis of the contract in which "the wishes of commodity owners meet each other halfway."[69] The contract is the place where two independent Hegelian "wills" are measured equally. Blind to anything except two freely willed commodity owners entering into exchange, the law of contract treats unequal persons entering into contractual relations as equals, as I noted earlier. The apparent symmetry of contract law in fact fosters inequality.[70]

Where critical legal studies scholars take issue with Pashukanis is in his overlap of the commodity form and the legal form, a conflation that does not help us to see the important differences in the economic and the juridical. Law and mode of production, these scholars remind us, are not synonymous and interchangeable! But if we put aside this important criticism, Pashukanis's critique of contract relations is close, in two key aspects, to the critical legal studies analysis of the contract. First, critical legal studies too argues that the contract masks all manner of inequity, unfairness, and contradictoriness.[71] And second, for Pashukanis as well as for Edelman and critical legal studies, the contract is the place where legal abstraction is translated into our experience of law. As Pashukanis theorizes it: "Outside the contract, the concepts of the subject and of will only exist, in the legal sense, as lifeless abstractions. These concepts first come to life in the contract."[72] But in Edelman it becomes clear that those categories that "come to life" are still not necessarily filled by real historical individuals: "So we shall see these categories *coming alive*. We shall see them signing labour contracts, and justifying convictions for illegal strikes. We shall see them applying the necessary rules of the relations of production."[73] But we must ask, Who is the "them" who signs the contract? Does "them" refer to "categories" or to persons, and how can we tell the difference? The legal contract is one text of culture that situates us in a completely novel relation to one another.[74] So we need to ask, Who is the "subject" who "comes to life" in the legal contract?

The Subject in Law

Edelman, following Pashukanis, starts from the premise that bourgeois law is organized around the "subject in law." This subject who holds rights and can own property by virtue of his ownership of himself, to quote Pashukanis again, "is the simplest and most complete" element of this law.[75] What is the category Edelman is invoking in his use of the concept "subject"? How is it related to the uses of the "subject" in other poststructuralist theories of culture?

It is impossible to overestimate the importance of the category of the "subject" to contemporary theory and criticism in the humanities. But because the philosophical concept of the subject has had so much utility, it may finally have lost its positional value within critical language. The term "subject" is often difficult to distinguish with enough exactitude from other concepts that appear to overlap its boundaries: individual, man, human, ego, person, author. And now, as though the concept weren't philosophically troubled enough, why do I propose the importance of the "legal subject"?

Certainly the subject assumed by law is important for historical and comparative purposes. The link is there to be made between the seventeenth-century evolution of a "subject" as a philosophical term, the classification of personal pronouns ("I," "he," "she") in English grammar, and the Lockean rights-holding individual who could own property.[76] So in terms of our grasp of this historical bourgeois subject, the legal contribution would seem to be crucial because it tells us that property owning, as well as speaking, centers the "I" in relation to the world. Free and equal subjects exchange goods and ideas from the secure vantage point of a legal-grammatical "I."

Contemporary theories of meaning in linguistics and literature have rethought the discourses of the novel as well as literary language itself in terms of the subject. Basically, this is an exercise in asking about the hypothetical point where meanings converge—the "point of unity" where sense is made.[77] Structural linguistics, for instance, is interested in the subject ("point of unity") presumed by the use of "I" or "me." Literary criticism asks questions about the kind of subject-as-reader assumed by point of view, mode of address, and character construction, since such a hypothetical construct is basic to the operation of novelistic form. This subject is said to be "inscribed" and sometimes even "prescribed" by the form, whether it be expository essay, poem, or novel. One of the most productive ways to use this notion is to consider how the author and reader could be said to "inscribe" each other as points of reception or origin. The inscribing certainly has to do with one "writing the other into" the script of discourse, with performative expectations and images of one another. In this sense, the author "imagines" a reader just as a reader envisions an author and reads accordingly.

I should be clear from the start that, as this notion of "subject" has been developed, it deals exclusively with spaces or places for hypothetical readers and authors and has no cognizance of the real historical persons who write and read. Hence the utility of the term "subject-position," which emphasizes the place-holding aspect of the conception and associates it more concretely with literary, linguistic, and even cinematic devices. But even as the question of the subject is made concrete and viable for aesthetics, it is often concurrently said that "texts produce subjects," which opens up larger philosophical questions to which I will shortly turn. Here, I want to broach the possibility of moving from a consideration of the subject as inscribed in literature to the subject as inscribed in legal discourse, and one place to start may be with the position of the author in literature, who, as reevaluated by Foucault, works to validate, to confer value, to situate the reader, and to control or restrict meaning, among other things. Fortunately, Foucault's concept of the "author-function" sufficiently depersonalizes this textual activity so that we can understand its structural operations in literature as a whole.[78] The concept of the author in legal discourse, as I take it up in the following chapter, will have its function as focal point in common with the literary author, although in copyright law the focal point is not the convergence of meaning but the point of entitlement.

Let me digress here with a word about comparisons between law and literature. To date, most of the interesting work has centered on problems in interpretation, the question being what happens to the coherence of the law when poststructuralist modes of analysis are brought to bear on it, a question I raised at the outset of this chapter.[79] This concern always seems to assume that the effectivity of legal discourse is somehow of a different (oftentimes higher) order than that of literary form and language. Behind that concern is the belief that the interpretation of legal discourse has real "consequences." As we know, definitions of criminality, social and economic equity, and even "life and death" are a matter of legal interpretation. With a conviction of this, practicing lawyers and legislators must inevitably come to think of their expertise as smoothing out ambiguity in legal language in order to settle perplexing matters with finality. In answer to this implication that legal discourse has "consequences" while literary discourse does not, Stanley Fish has argued that the difference between the two has to do with "differing spheres of and routes to consequentiality, not the difference between consequentiality and its opposite." But while he argues that the interpretations of literary critics are "far-reaching" because they affect the canon, the curriculum, the classroom, and the cultural fabric of values and myths, I would take a shorter route.[80] Since, as I am arguing in terms of intellectual property, there are structural similarities between legal and literary discourse (both essentially positing the bourgeois subject in their notion of what constitutes an author), comparisons of the two in terms of "effects" are irrelevant. In this branch of Anglo-American law at least, the two discourses inform each other because they share the same cultural root buried deep in the seventeenth century.

But having introduced the problem of the subject, we cannot remain at the level of either interpretation or textual convention, since the concept is caught up in the whole political and philosophical history of the Western world. We must be concerned, in other words, not only with the subject addressed by the text (whether the novel or the text of legal doctrine) but with the greater subject implied in every aspect of the culture. To come to terms with the larger implications of the subject, we need to return not to Pashukanis but to Edelman's other primary source.

One might describe Edelman's theory as the only existing marriage of Pashukanis and French Marxist theorist Louis Althusser. Edelman leads us back not only to Althusser's important "Ideology and Ideological State Apparatuses" (ISAs) essay but also to Althusser's curious suggestion that it is legal ideology as well as bourgeois ideology that gives us the category of the subject as we now understand it. The one passage that contains this allusion to the subject in law, as it happens, also raises the controversial question of the historical specificity of the subject: "By this I mean that, even if it only appears under this name (the subject) with the rise of bourgeois ideology, above all with the rise of legal ideology, the category of the subject (which may function under other names: e.g., as the soul in Plato, as God, etc.) is the constitutive category of all ideology, whatever its determination (regional or class) and whatever its historical date— since ideology has no history."[81] In a footnote Althusser adds that legal ideology "borrowed the legal category of 'subject in law' to make an ideological notion: man is by nature a subject."[82] It is this kind of borrowing (of the bourgeois subject from legal ideology and the legal subject from bourgeois ideology) that necessitates my discussion of both the larger subject and the specificity of the subject in law.

Two important points come to our attention here, both of which are relevant to Edelman's project: the subject in history and the naturalization of subjecthood. I want to first take up the more accessible problem of the subject in history and return to a discussion of how man is "by nature" a subject. First, although Althusser says that ideology has no history, he also says that historically the ideological category of the subject has gone by other names (the Platonic soul, God). (We might add to this list the Roman subject-citizen, the Christian soul, the Cartesian "I," the Kantian transcendental subject, and the Freudian experimental subject.)[83] And, I should stress as well Althusser's distinction (basic to cultural studies) between "Ideology" in general (sometimes capitalized to emphasize that it *is* universally operative in all societies) and historically specific "ideologies." At this time in history, then, the ideological centerpiece in Western culture, the point of coherence at which cultural forms converge and without which they would not mean what they do, is "Man."

Although Althusser doesn't make a connection between the category "Man" and the bourgeois subject to which he refers in the ISAs essay, he is more helpful elsewhere on this as well as on the differences between the theoretical category of the "subject" and the historically specific human beings who might occupy this category:

> "Man" is a myth of bourgeois ideology: Marxism-Leninism cannot *start* from "man." It starts "from the economically given social period"; and, at the end of its analysis, when it "arrives," *it may find real men*. These men are thus the *point of arrival* of an analysis which starts from the social relations of the existing mode of production, from class relations, and from the class struggle. These men are quite different men from the "man" of bourgeois ideology.[84]

This passage is notable as well for its contrast of the humanist approach, which starts with "man," with the materialist analysis, which starts with the mode of production. And poststructuralism has further supplemented Althusser's position by unmasking the humanist myth of individual agency. For the humanist, we act as individual agents by using language as self-expression and by proceeding as though we can determine the outcome of our actions. Poststructuralism, however, would say that our ability to act as agents is due not to any innate capacity for linguistic self-expression and social determination but to the fact that we are constructed as this kind of agent-subject. In place of the human agent, poststructuralism gives us the constructed and positioned subject, the subject who does not choose the linguistic or iconic signs with which to "speak" a language but who is instead "spoken by" that language. "As subjects," says Umberto Eco, "we are what the shape of the world produced by signs makes us become."[85] The impossibility of agency implied in this view finally signals what is sometimes referred to as the "death of the subject," or the end of the reign of humanism's "man."

Insofar as I find the legal subject, the natural rights-bearing person displaced by a corporate trademark or copyright owner, I also find a "death of the subject" in intellectual property law. But within legal doctrine, the demise of the subject-in-law is not represented as a crisis. It is *figured*, though, and no more clearly than in the current movement to introduce a *moral rights* provision into U.S. copyright law.[86] The moral right of the artist, which would extend over the work *after* it is sold, asserts the artist over the owner, and advances the author's right with the aid of humanism's fondest ideals: artistic integrity, creative vision, and personal expression. To give the artist a lifetime moral right over his or her work would mean, among other things, that he or she could prohibit the distortion of intention produced by altering the work. But as admirable as such initiatives may be, they are finally less significant as attempts to secure rights for artists than as symptoms of the displacement of the author.

The point is not to mourn the demise of the legal subject in Anglo-American intellectual property law.[87] Rather, the point is that to return the author to the work through an argument for moral rights is to bring back the same category that facilitated the transfer of rights in the work to a third-party owner in the first place. In this I differ from Edelman, who somewhat romantically sees the photographer (who is denied authorship in the photograph in French history) as the proletarian of creation. In Edelman's theory, the intercession of the legal subject in photographic creation is as it should be. This is not to say that Edelman isn't ironic about the manner in which the legal subject was historically introduced into the photographic act. The photographer, as Edelman wryly observes, was "wrested from the machine" and put back "into the domain of the actuating subject."[88]

Note that Edelman here employs "author," "photographer," "creator," and "subject" almost interchangeably. To do that, I think, can be misleading, and in my own discussion I try to make some important distinctions by using adjectival qualifiers. For instance, to emphasize how the concept of "legal subject" overlaps with the concept of "author" in both nineteenth-century French and U.S. cases, I use the term "author-subject."[89] Only as an author can a legal subject have a right in a work, and only as a legal subject can an author be said to have a "right" to defend or to assign to a third party. My hope here is to be more specific about the category of "subject" in order to spare the reader the often confusing and alienating experience of reading contemporary criticism dealing with poststructuralist theories of the subject. At the same time, however, I want to do justice to the more difficult aspect of Althusser's discussion of the subject, especially since it is crucial to Edelman's conception: the naturalization of subjecthood, the way in which, to use Althusser's phrasing, "for you and me, the category of the subject is a primary 'obviousness.'"[90]

As Althusser points out, ideology works through us, often with our own enthusiastic cooperation. In working through us, it "fits up" ideal subjects for the kind of society that must be produced in order to reproduce the capitalist mode of production. Ideology "recruits," as Althusser puts it, but it doesn't coerce subjects.[91] In a way, it doesn't need to coerce because it is we who self-identify ourselves as these very subjects; we are the ones who see no other way of being because we recognize ourselves in the absolute obviousness of the existence that ideology constructs. What Edelman gains in his reliance upon this notion of the recruited subject is the implication that the structure of capitalist society *requires* the position of the rights-holder, the subject-in-law. The criticism leveled at this theorization of the subject has consistently been that Althusser tended toward an idealism that is incompatible with materialist theory.[92] In Althusser's theory, ideology alone sometimes appears to be responsible for constructing subjects. Some critics have asked how real historical persons might act when circumscribed within subject-positions.[93] Others, among them E. P. Thompson, have been concerned that Althusser's structuralist underpinnings denied a role to human agents in the making of history.[94] For a Marxist theory of ideology, this is a point of some significance, because the crucial feature of Marxist analysis is that economic practices are privileged as determinations over a transcendently floating superstructure. Material conditions are classically privileged over Ideology. This critique of Althusser began to appear in the early eighties and held its own through the decade as Marxist literary criticism and film theory turned to other concerns by examining reception theory or taking up the problem of defining postmodern culture.

As British cultural studies critiqued Althusser, some of the problems that arose in his ISAs essay had to do with his attempt to incorporate some aspects of Jacques Lacan's conception of the subject into his reworking of Marxist theory. The French psychoanalytic theorist's conception of the symbolic order was thus taken over into Althusser's new characterization of ideology.[95] Before going further we need to ask whether the substantial body of thought that develops a poststructuralist psychoanalytic subject has any relevance for a discussion of the legal subject.

In his well-known critique on the ISAs essay, Paul Hirst gives us some help with this. From a position generally supportive of Althusser's project, he recommends other approaches to the problem of the subject that Althusser does not address. First, he suggests that Althusser himself did not fully consider the implications of his use of psychoanalysis, since his subject operates only at the conscious level of the psyche (which in both Freud and Lacan is always split between conscious and unconscious). Considering the divided aspect of the subject would have produced different conclusions, Hirst thinks.[96] Does the same point apply to Edelman, whose subject, like Althusser's, is quite clearly the conscious subject?

Edelman's legal subject (who is produced by structures and fails to recognize his positioning) partakes of something of the psychoanalytic influence in Althusser, but *Ownership of the Image* does not rely on psychoanalytic theory. Although it may be possible to write legal theory from the point of view of psychoanalysis, considering, for instance, the function of gender, language, and personhood, this is not that type of analysis. Instead, once he has situated himself within Althusser's general theory of the subject, Edelman constructs a discussion closer to what Hirst describes as a theory of subjects as "supports for processes," a second example of an approach that, if taken, might have led Althusser in another direction.[97]

I would take Hirst's intervention as an example of the way in which any consideration of the legal subject problematizes poststructuralism's theorization of subjecthood. The law constructs its entities by recognizing their rights, and in this act of recognition the law sees them as unified and coherent. Furthermore, legal discourse confers various statuses on these entities; Hirst's example has to do with possession or responsibility of some kind. And finally, the law posits its subjects as able to take legal action, whether to ask a court for an injunction or to sue another entity for damages. But one of Hirst's most convincing points has to do with the way the law can either refuse subject status to some entities (slaves and subordinate persons) or produce nonhuman entities as unified legal subjects. In this way, corporations, joint stock companies, and even animals (through trusts) can inhabit legal subject-positions.[98] Elsewhere, to emphasize the disjuncture between Althusser's theory and the internal structure of Anglo-American law, Hirst asks, "Can companies be interpellated in circular form?"[99]

The question remains as to what critical legal studies can contribute to the project Edelman has begun. Where British cultural studies has focused primarily on the struggle and contest within ideology over cultural territory, critical legal studies, with its different internal history, has put a premium on the analysis of discourse.[100] And consequently, in this field,

where the material conditions of legal subjects are of paramount importance, the ideological construction of those subjects is now a more central
concern. But still, in American critical legal studies, there has been relatively little interest in the work of either Pashukanis or Edelman. Is it that
the two taken together are seen as representative of the extremes of
Althusserian formalism? It may be that the high Althusserian phase of film
and literary studies (during which time it seemed that entire cultures were
constructed from within the structures of textual discourse) is not foreseeable for legal studies because of a built-in check: Legal studies, by definition, starts with an interest in what people do or do not do with legal texts
in their capacity as taxpayers, employees, or lawsuit claimants. Academic
studies of cultural texts, in contrast, have historically been under no
obligation to consider museumgoers, reading publics, or live concert
audiences. This issue, of "what people do with the law," arises in Nancy
Anderson and David Greenberg's review of *Ownership of the Image*: "Specifically, the acceptance of legal ideology may be uneven, depending upon
the particular case at stake. People do not take law into account in carrying
out their affairs. When they do, however, they do not merely *follow* the
law. They attempt to evade it, they bend it to their purposes and assert
their own interpretations of what it is and should be. So, too, they may
calculate the likelihood of law enforcement in organizing their conduct."[101]

I want to contrast this version of how people live in relation to the law
with Edelman's theorization of the legal subject in ideology. His crucial
point, adapted from Pashukanis, is that the ideological "effect" of bourgeois law is to produce subjects who think of themselves as free-willed.
But for Edelman, as for Pashukanis, free will is an illusion. As Edelman
writes of the false equality of the contract: "[I]n the end, the relation refers
to *free will*, to the illusion that private property rests on the individual
private will. In law, the 'I will' is an 'I can.' The contract is a Hegelian act, a
pure meeting of wills."[102] Anderson and Greenberg might protest that
people enter into contracts knowing full well that they are participating in
a fiction, and that it is that very knowledge that leads them to find ways of
eluding the provisions of unfair contracts. By litigating a dispute in small
claims court or by striking over employment conditions, people often
challenge the fiction of free will and fair bargain.

And yet there is a way in which we *are* imprisoned by legal discourse. As
rights-holders, we are built into an invisible structure that requires our

symbolic agreement *whether or not we act in any empirical way in concert with this structure*. While as critics we may have thought long and hard about our cooperation in the construction of ourselves and others as gendered readers and viewers, we may not have considered how capitalist property relations depend upon our collective "return to it of its power."[103] To illustrate how a notion of the legal subject complements as well as critiques that other subject, the subject of cultural discourse, I want to turn to the place of the subject in cinema, where the concept found one of its most creative applications in the period coincident with the first publication of *Ownership of the Image*.

The Subject in Law/The Subject in Cinema

The relation between Edelman's work and the critique of classical film theory undertaken by the editors of *Cinéthique* and *Cahiers du Cinéma* in the late sixties and early seventies is an intriguing topic for an entirely different book. But for our purposes, what is of particular interest is the way that Edelman, in 1973, criticizes this emerging theory of the ideological function of the motion picture apparatus on the very same basis that he himself has been challenged from within critical legal studies. I refer, of course, to the charge that Althusser's theory of the subject is indifferent to actual class struggle and that it gives the impression that struggle against such thoroughgoing determination of one's subject-position is futile. For Edelman, that is precisely the danger of suggesting that subjects are made by the mechanisms of cinema. The doom sounded by the idea that ideology is implanted in the photographic machine, he concludes, amounts to "ideological fatalism."[104]

In what was perhaps the earliest formulation of this theory of the cinema subject, Marcelin Pleynet challenged the idea of the "non-signifying" neutrality of the mechanical and creative production of cinematic imagery.[105] Pleynet argued that the photographic "instruments" used to produce cinema—the lenses in particular—could *only* represent bourgeois ideology. The bourgeois view of the world, embodied in the technology that produced cinematic perspective, was literally "built into" the camera. Pleynet supported this position by pointing out the uncanny historical coincidence of experiments with the photographic lens and the reign of Renaissance humanism. Arguing against the notion that motion picture technology is a scientific instrument, Pleynet asserted: "It produces a directly inherited code of perspective, built on the model of the scientific perspective of the Quattrocento."[106]

As this critique of the close relationship between the technological history and the ideological effect of motion pictures was expanded (in subsequent issues of *Cinéthique* and *Cahiers du Cinéma*, and later *Screen*), other aspects of the institutional conditions of cinema spectatorship were incorporated into it. In addition to the perspective of the photographic scene, the seat in the darkened theater and the style of continuity editing were now seen as devices that produced ideal subjects. The individual singularity of the subject, for instance, was assumed by the monocular perspective of the camera and the projector, which "forced" the individual audience member to see as the camera saw.[107] Viewers would be returned again and again to the same positions, because making sense of the narrative (the very impression of reality itself) depended upon their assumption of these places. All cinematic meaning, then, was construed by such single "centered" subjects. In a nutshell, as Jean-Louis Baudry puts it in "The Ideological Effects of the Basic Cinematographic Apparatus," the "subject constitutes the meaning . . . continuity supposes the subject and circumscribes his place."[108] But the cinema, it was argued, is also dependent on this subject who, in effect, completes the "circuit of meaning" by occupying the place he is supposed to occupy. The continuance of cinema as we know it is thus underwritten by the conditions upon which it is viewed. The institution of cinema must produce the very viewing subjects that it requires in order for it to continue to produce these subjects.

Edelman's idea of legal subjectivity and the theory of cinema subjectivity that he criticizes nevertheless echo each other with their shared Althusserian heritage, their critiques of the circularity of ideology, and their theorization of the subject-position. In both, an institution sets up structural positions that anticipate hypothetical subjects. Just as the institution of cinema assumes a viewing situation that organizes a particular kind of engagement with the film, so the legal institution assumes a particular participation on the part of its subject. Basic to Edelman, for example, is the idea that bourgeois law "postulates the necessary relation between two subjects."[109] These are the subjects who, following Edelman and Pashukanis, freely enter into contracts as commodity owners. These commodity owners are by contract structured symmetrically in the law.[110]

Considered strictly as discourses, the law and the cinema-viewing situation postulate the same subject. This is a subject who thinks he or she is free to speak, to take out a real estate mortgage, or to sign an employment contract. But this subject is not free. He or she is in an antagonistic relation to other individuals; his or her cultural life is predicated on singularity and self-sufficiency. This sense of singularity is reinforced daily—even when the individual looks at a roadside billboard, a painting in an art museum, or a photograph in a magazine, where again a coherent world is organized around a singular vantage point.

But that is where the similarity stops. Film theory, following Lacan's lead in considering how language constructs whole cultures, has been much more interested in spectators than in creators. And Edelman begins with the creator when he asks about the photographer as legal subject. But his work should call us back to a consideration of the legal position of producers and directors in the context of motion picture production— ultimately collective production. For the cinema culminates his overview of the nineteenth-century creator as subject in French law that starts with the photographer, since in French law the producing company can now stand where the photographer once stood in relation to the photographic work. This means, says Edelman, that *"the true creative subject is capital."* He goes on, "Capital becomes the very person it interpellates. Capital assumes the mask of the subject, it is animated, it speaks and signs contracts."[111]

If there is any validity in focusing on the places carved out in culture for the subject in ideology, it may be in the discovery that different discursive systems, by assuming the same subject, are at times acting in harmony. But the comparison of such systems also opens up the possibility that subject construction is more "hit or miss" than was once thought. To take a solution offered by Paul Smith, one might consider the process of constructing the subject as an overdetermination, that is, the "effect of a continual and continuing series of overlapping subject-positions which may or may not . . . constitute a person's *history*."[112] If we don't consider the interrelation of these positions, we give the impression that the job of enculturating whole societies is performed by one monolithic institution to the exclusion of others. To imply that we are fully constructed as we sign a contract would be as fallacious as to say that we are formed as we look and listen to popular entertainment.

The Actor-Subject and the Star System

Probably the most provocative approach to the study of images has been the work done in cinema studies on the star as a microcosm of capitalism.[113] In this approach, the star is at once ego ideal for the spectator-subject, ideological rectifier of cultural contradictions, industrial product, and economic strategy in the studio's bid for monopoly domination of the market. It would seem from this perspective that the star is there at every level, a phenomenon of both the base and the superstructure. And the star phenomenon is further complicated by the coincidence of at least three entities: roughly, "private" person, character role(s), and public image.[114] Most work in cultural studies follows Richard Dyer's important semiotic analysis of the star image as text, which sees the star/person/work relation as a composite construction, the sum of calculated promotion, public appearances, motion picture roles, and personality.[115] Dyer has always taken care to give the impression that behind the star image there is no real "private" person whom we can ever hope to know. The real person (if there is one) is more functional than real in the way he or she is invoked as an authenticating presence. However, Dyer's interpretation of the subversiveness of such stars as Lana Turner, Judy Garland, Marilyn Monroe, and Paul Robeson suggests that an actor who carries a strong sexual-political charge can and does break through and "trouble" the star construction in real ways.[116] More recently, Barry King has offered a modification of Dyer's star image schema by suggesting that the person and the screen image are merged in the marketable persona. King's theorization of the "personal monopoly" depends upon some notion of a professional who successfully manages his own labor commodity in a market in which there is an oversupply of actors.[117] To secure this monopoly on his or her own carefully developed persona, the actor "types himself in real life according to his image on screen."[118]

In the following chapters I have used King's "persona" almost synonymously with Dyer's "star image," but in doing so I have become aware of the need for a somewhat more comprehensive theorization. Christine Gledhill has recently pointed the way toward this by reconceptualizing the first three entities and adding a fourth. Thus the persona, as in King, is separate from the real person and the character roles, but it draws from both—"authenticity" from the former and "typicality" from the latter.

Her fourth entity, the image, is subsidiary to person and fictional roles, and is in a sense "spun off" from them, circulating in tandem.[119] The advantage to theorizing a public "persona," as King and Gledhill show us, is that such a theory emphasizes that a star persona is as much a constructed "character" as any film role and also that it can contradict as well as reinforce screen roles. Hypothetically, yet another image, such as Gledhill suggests, gives us a constructed entity in a new domain produced by book publishing and merchandising—what the entertainment industry calls the space of the "secondary market."

A fourth schema is offered by John Viera, whose analysis of the Elvis Presley image combines a legal point of view with Dyer's work on the star image. In the case of celebrities such as Elvis, there are two images: the "image bearer" (as in Dyer's concept of the concrete signifier, the body of the actor) and the "media image." While the first is concrete, the second is intangible. Following Dyer's notion of the intertextuality of the star, Viera's "media image" is a composite made up of film roles, concert appearances, advertising and other promotions. Also as in Dyer, this intangible media image is the work of industry personnel and professional promoters.[120] But where Viera's model diverges from existing ones is in his characterization of the media image as "mental" and having existence in the "media consciousness of the masses."[121] This mental image is nonetheless protectable as an "intangible property," he argues, thus fitting the intertextuality of the star to the tangible/intangible dichotomy of copyright law by turning multiplicity (although not indeterminateness) into transcendence.

But there is a significant difference between intellectual property doctrine and the poststructuralism that informs the work on stars. Whereas Viera would need to resolve the dilemma posed by the multiplicity of the star phenomena (in order to decide who owns Elvis Presley's image), poststructuralist theories stress the irresolvability of the contents of stardom. The best statement of this is Stephen Heath's theorization of the "shifting circulation between agent, character, person, and image, none of which terms is able to contain, to *settle* the circulation."[122] Lest we make the mistake of attributing this insight entirely to developments in the wake of poststructuralism, we should recall that Edgar Morin worked out the tension between the real person and the star as early as 1961: "Model and imitator, exterior to the film and at its heart, determining it but determined by it, the star is a syncretic personality in which the real person cannot be distinguished from the person fabricated by the dream factories and the person invented by the spectator."[123]

But there is a political flaw in the poststructuralist challenge to "the real" as a category to which we can appeal. We do not want to lose sight of the reality of material conditions, and in Marxist theory there is nothing more real than the worker's relation to production. I want to concentrate, then, on still another aspect of stardom, which has been left out of earlier paradigms: the actor as labor.

Both Barry King and Danae Clark have recently argued for a labor theory of stardom. Clark's approach to the star contrasts the motion picture film worker with the spectator, and she argues that the emphasis in film theory has come at the expense of the former, the subject "facing" the camera. For Clark, we need to pay more attention to the star as "subject of production," as worker in relation to the labor process, to other workers, and to management.[124] Clark enables us to historicize this relation as it is played out in the battles for unionization, from the Actors' Equity attempts in the twenties through the formation of the Screen Actors Guild in 1933 and its recognition in 1937.[125] And the concept of the "subject of production" gives particular urgency as well to questions about the struggle between studio heads and actors over control of actors' private lives, their off-screen as well as on-screen appearances, and their image properties—their own bodies and voices—in relation to commercial advertising.

Barry King is helpful here as well because he has argued that screen acting needs to be considered in relation to the way technological change has produced de-skilling. We can no longer consider the actor's performance as integral or whole, says King, because the motion picture gives us "short bursts of performance."[126] In the process of editing and sound-mixing, the actor's body is divorced from his or her voice; it is reorganized, gestures are recombined, the order of expression is rearranged; other bodies "stand in" for that of the actor; other voices are heard as his or her voice. Technology, says King, "dislocates" the performance in time and space in such a way that the actor has little control over it; the actor is anything but the sole author of the discourse he or she has produced.[127] In terms of the traditional understanding of the labor of the actor as the artistic deliverance of an integral piece of work, the screen star is relatively limited in his or her contribution.

But there are two other ways in which we can view the "labor" of the actor, one of which is not "labor" in any traditional sense of the term. First, we need to consider the work of interpretation, the transformative action that singers, instrumentalists, and theatrical as well as motion picture actors perform on their material. New technologies that allow us to re-record, slow down, speed up, stop, and digitalize may have contributed to the de-skilling of the performer and even to his unemployment (as in the substitution of the "electrical transcription" or electronic copy of the musician's performance for the paid "live" performance). But these same technologies make the case for seeing or hearing interpretative work and performance labors that were heretofore elusive.

These technologies bear upon our second point as well: the need to consider the body and the voice of the actor as visual and audio imagery. Body and voice (those apparent biological "givens") are not entirely produced by the labor of the actor as performer; they are also mechanically and electronically "captured" (as photograph and sound recording) by the labor of technicians. And under the studio system, the natural signs of the private person were produced as popular audio and visual images by the collective labor of many others as well—agents, publicists, voice coaches, lighting directors, makeup artists, and costume designers, as well as directors. In short, the transformation of the physiognomy and psyche of a human being by the process of industrial production for the purposes of cornering a market has no equivalent at any other moment in history, nor can manufactured stardom be found in any other society before its appearance in the U.S. It is true that a preexisting star system was in place in both American vaudeville and theater from the 1820s on. But studio stardom was different in kind and scope because of the factor of technological mass production.[128]

Recent historical accounts of the star locate the appearance of the phenomenon around 1909 to 1910, when the immediate economic function of the star emerges as a means used by the early studios to bid for control of the motion picture exhibition and distribution market.[129] Stars contributed to the requisite product standardization and differentiation and in this regard they were, to quote Janet Staiger, like "product specification," much like other aspects of standardization: spectacle, continuity, and narrative.[130] Later, the star "specification" became something else. In the period from 1919 to 1935, which was characterized by increasing concentration of capital in the industry and marked by the vertical integration of the major studios, the star, the established director, and the story were the keys not only to cornering distribution markets but also to securing capital from outside investors.[131]

The structure of this book depends upon seeing the history of the star system as a dynamic in which one monopoly strategy employed by the major studios is superseded by another monopoly strategy employed by the star but modeled upon that of the industry itself. But this is also a story of how individuals attempted through contract negotiation to wrest from the studios the control of their lives as well as their image product. For my purposes, then, I need to consider where and how the star actor was first split into its basic duality: the figure on screen and the "private" person. Here, Richard DeCordova's recent refinement of early motion picture star history provides a starting point.

DeCordova makes a distinction between the "picture personality," which appeared around 1909, and the "star" (as we know the phenomenon), which did not emerge until 1914. In his analysis, the strictly professional aspect of the "picture personality" merges with a new dimension—a private life—to produce the "star." It was around 1914 that the star's life became available as a narrative paralleling and (at the time) reinforcing the on-screen image. Stories about an actor's idealized family life, for example, actually bolstered the ideology of blood relation worked out in the domestic melodramas so popular in this period.[132] It would also become clear by the early twenties that the studio definition of the star persona could productively extend to the area of private life in cases where the off-screen image contradicted the on-screen one. In the industry changes following the 1921 Fatty Arbuckle scandal (a woman died in a bathtub during one of his parties), the studios actively sought to control players' off-screen activities, and to be safe, studio publicists constructed wholesome "lives" for actors in the popular press.[133] Publicity departments sought to cover up actors' moral lapses (which could tarnish an image) by creating confusion between off-screen and on-screen lives. Larger-than-life screen drama absorbed petty personal scandal. Thus when Clara Bow was discovered on a gambling binge at a Lake Taho casino, the publicity department wrote the incident into a script and called the rumor a publicity stunt.[134]

The standard accounts link the historical appearance of motion picture stars with the growth of advertising and with studio bids for monopoly control. Here the key concept that recurs in these accounts of stardom is "differentiation."[135] Motion picture companies needed to differentiate their products in order to stabilize demand for them, which in turn stabilized price. But rather than starting from the idea of differentiating films by means of stars, as one might expect, the studios hit upon the concept by trial and error. In Cathy Klaprat's account, the studios' attempts to differentiate their product by attaching their trade names to players (the Biograph Girl, the Vitagraph Girl) were unsuccessful. And focusing on differences between narratives didn't seem to help separate one studio's photoplay from that of another. But the response of viewers to the first fan magazine told the studios that it was players, not stories, that distinguished one film from another for fans. As the story goes, *Moving Story Magazine* (founded in 1911 by J. Stuart Blackton as a publicity tool for the Motion Picture Patents Company) encouraged readers to write in about their viewing. But rather than suggesting new endings and ideas for stories, fans wrote in with questions about the players.[136]

So the means of differentiating the product (the star) became in time an end in itself. With stars as with no other competitive angle, the promotion of the film product threatened to turn into the attraction. After Carl Laemmle's 1910 "IMP Girl" publicity stunt, which successfully produced the fiction of Florence Lawrence as the first "star," it was clear that the names and likenesses of the players could be used to attract attention to the motion picture.[137] And whether in a "mention" in planted "news" stories, spelled in lights above the marquee, or printed on handbills, the names of the players came to carry an allure and a fascination. After 1909, their likenesses could be found on the one-sheet posters, which no longer depicted generic scenes of action but instead were lithographs specially printed for each film.[138] Around 1913 the first pressbooks appeared, with ideas for stirring up local interest such as Charlie Chaplin look-alike contests, theater-front displays, and merchant cooperation.[139] Before 1916, newspapers printed little about either stars or films, and early pressbooks appealed to the ingenuity of theater managers to stimulate "word of mouth."[140] But after motion picture news began to help sell papers, pressbooks started to include camera-ready advertising cuts and rotogravure images, as well as copy for reviews and articles on the feature film for the women's page.[141] After 1919, with the formation of National Screen Services, exhibitors could order the promotional banners, posters, lobby cards, and eight-by-ten-inch glossy photographs in bulk.[142] By the time the wide-circulation magazine firm MacFadden Publications bought

Photoplay in the thirties, star images were a mass publishing phenomenon.[143]

To date, most of the studies of the phenomenon of stardom have been limited to an overview of motion picture history, but new histories of broadcasting suggest that radio and television played more of a role in the promotion of motion pictures than earlier accounts suggested. In the twenties with radio, and again in the fifties with television, the studios used broadcast media to promote new releases to wider audiences.[144] But here again the star attraction threatened to compete with the main attraction—so much so that in the early years of radio studio producers tried to keep their contract talent from appearing on the air during hours that would compete with their own theatrical trade.[145]

I need to be clear that my subject is more the off-screen image than the flickering on-screen one about which so much has been written. I am looking primarily at the use of the name, voice, and likeness in the by-products of motion pictures: public appearances, radio broadcasts, commercial product endorsements, and licensed merchandise. And my distinction between the motion picture image and its by-products is not an artificial or arbitrary one. In fact, entertainment law has historically differentiated between the motion picture as image capital and its promotional tangents. First of all, copyright in all aspects of the motion picture product (image and sound track) is held by the producer. Not even a single frame containing the image of the star actor from this self-contained motion picture "work" can be reproduced commercially without permission from the copyright owner. But the publicity photograph of a player in a motion picture role is of a different order. While it is not part of the copyrighted work, this use of a player's image has historically been understood as "exploitation" for the real product—the motion picture. And generally that interpretation has meant that the studio could use the image in advertising copy without permission from the player.

There is really no aspect of commercial practice in any other American industry quite like motion picture exploitation. Elsewhere I have tried to explain the concept by looking to its origins in the promotional work of such early showmen as P. T. Barnum.[146] Exploitation, as an approach to selling, was perfected in the circus and carried over into exhibition practices in the advent of the nickelodeon and finally in the motion picture theater as we know it. But defining exploitation precisely is made difficult because the industry itself has historically cultivated *both* a narrow and a broad concept. Early exhibitors and motion picture managers made distinctions between advertising, publicity, and exploitation, and beginning in the mid-teens, the larger studios even encouraged specialization in these areas. Later, separate studio departments were organized around these promotional functions. According to the early histories of exploitation, "advertising" was the work of laying out display announcements and writing copy for paid promotion in newspapers and magazines; "publicity" was the work of the press agent, who arranged "free" exposure as opposed to paid advertising; and "exploitation" was the miscellaneous category of promotions.[147]

At the same time, however, publicists were quick to point to specific practices within this seemingly amorphous category. One historian calls the Florence Lawrence stunt (which involved "planting" the rumor that the actress had died in a streetcar accident in the city where her film was due to open) the beginning of exploitation.[148] And others cite attention-attracting gags such as the use of wild animals, church sermons, "souped-up" automobiles, and suicide notes.[149] But later, in the thirties and forties, "exploitation" would be associated more and more with the arrangement of commodity tie-ups (a full-time job for some studio publicists).[150] In a previous study of such early practices, I concluded that exploitation was a kind of promotional "disappearing act" that could expand or contract to fit the occasion and the forms at hand. It is thus a parasitic discourse that turns available materials to its advantage; we know it by its achievements and its motivations, but not by its forms. Moreover, exploitation is more complex than simply the one-directional message of advertising and publicity, because it produces its own inflated reception simultaneously with its transmission. Exploitation, for instance, produces the connection between Rita Hayworth (star of *You Were Never Lovelier*) and Lustre Creme Shampoo as a natural and spontaneous relationship.

While the goals of exploitation—to move the product—may be a constant in American entertainment history, the forms, as we have seen, are too varied to classify easily. Nor has entertainment law made consistent and useful distinctions regarding such uses of celebrity name, voice, and likeness. In legal doctrine, advertising, publicity, and promotion, and sometimes exploitation are used interchangeably, even in contractual language. Finally, does entertainment industry "exploitation" have anything to do with the concept as used in corporate public relations and in business in general where "to exploit" is merely "to utilize" in a commercial context? This corporate use always seems to be innocent of the other sense of exploitation, that is, the reckless extraction of human labor power. Appropriately, Henri Lefebvre has looked at modern publicity as a "language phenomenon" characterized by its "efficiency" as well as its wide influence. In this, he says, "publicity assumes in part the role formerly held by ideologies: to clothe, dissimulate and transform reality, that is to say production relations."[151] Is it thus that the concept encompasses the successful "exploit" and the exhaustion of land and labor power? Here is both crowning achievement and selfish overreaching—a kind of summary of the capitalist mode of engagement with the world.

Photography "Surprises" the Law

THE PORTRAIT OF OSCAR WILDE

Oscar Wilde's *The Picture of Dorian Gray* (1884), often considered a discussion of the differences between painting and literature, is not that at all. It is really a metaphor for photography. But not because the author, as his biographer Richard Ellmann tells us, was prone to "brooding" about self-portraits and images in the period of his life before he wrote the short novel.[1] The novel is a metaphor for photography because, to put it bluntly, I choose to use it that way. My case, then, will rest entirely upon the utility of that metaphor, but also on the fortuity of historical circumstances. For as it happens, the very year the book was published, the photographic portrait of Oscar Wilde became the object of a copyright infringement suit heard before the U.S. Supreme Court.

I am not going to imply, as is often done, that the author of *The Picture of Dorian Gray* had an early insight into the issues that I will raise. If he seems to have had any insight into those theoretical developments, it is merely because as a critic I am in a position to make it appear as though he had anticipated contemporary theories of representation. In reality, of course, he could not have foreseen the following interpretation. From what I have read about him (which is not the same as what I truly know about him) it would seem that my discussion is in the spirit of Oscar Wilde; but the possibility of his approval of my project finally doesn't matter. Another author might have served as well as an example, although if I am successful, my reader will disagree.

There are, as I see it, four ways in which the narrative of *Dorian Gray* works to elucidate problems posed by the invention of photography. Two of these are fairly predictable in their dramatization of the relationship between the painting and its object, suggesting as they do an analogy between photographic and painted portraiture. But the second two issues raised by the metaphor are less obvious routes to my main concern in this chapter: authorial originality as a claim to ownership in a work. How did this claim come to have viability in the face of the other claims historically asserted against it? And, at what expense has authorship as the basis for ownership been maintained, if it has been maintained at all?

Before addressing these questions, I want to show how this narrative is a parable about the perverse relationship between the photograph, the photographed, and the photographer, that love-hate triangle in *Dorian Gray* that ends in the death of all three. In the narrative, the youth Dorian (the subject of the portrait) changes places with the painting, which physically ages while his body remains as youthful as it was when Basil Hallwood painted his likeness. While the living painting has a soul, the static Dorian is soulless. We have in Dorian, then, the much-discussed phenomenon of photographic preservation, the photograph's awe-inspiring capacity to "mummify" the body, as André Bazin puts it, "to snatch it from the flow of time, to stow it away . . . in the hold of life."[2] In the nineteenth century, this preservative capacity of photographic representation was even understood as a triumph of mortal life over the certainty of bodily decay. In *Dorian Gray*, however, we have the fleshly mortification and decay of the *representation* and the preservation, instead, of the body itself. In other words, in this story, the representation and its object, so easily confused in the tradition of aesthetic realism, seem to have changed places. Perhaps they are even the same thing. In *Dorian Gray* we have an illustration of Bazin's "mummy complex," but in reverse. And we find as well its companion formation, what Bazin calls the "resemblance complex."[3] For Hallwood's portrait of Dorian embodies the highest aspirations of representational art: to achieve lifelike resemblance. The novel imagines the logical conclusion of those aspirations when the portrait that resembles its subject actually *becomes* that subject. For Hallwood, the portrait reveals the truth of the soul of its subject (Dorian); it is "the real Dorian."[4] The live model thus becomes the photographic "work" fixed in time while the representational image hanging on the wall becomes the living being.

The exchange of places between the body and its image raises questions of preservation and resemblance. But it is the revelation of the self in the work that opens up the main considerations of this chapter. First, what is the origin of the notion that a person, whether author or subject of the work, is "revealed" in that representation? And second, how is the epistemological claim that a personality is "revealed" in the work then translated into the legal claim of ownership in the work? How do we find the author in the photographic work in order to establish that he, rather than the machine, created the photograph itself? The famous preface to *The Picture of Dorian Gray* states the problem for us in inverted form: "To reveal art and conceal the artist is art's aim" (p. 7).

Dorian Gray reminds us that a work of portraiture can reveal as much or more about the subject of the portrait as it does about the artist-creator. (It is Dorian Gray, not Basil Hallwood, whose soul is illuminated, exposed, and displayed on the canvas.) And yet, the narrative suggests as well that Dorian the monster *is* the expression of Hallwood's personality. If that is the case, both Dorians (the living representation and the lifelike portrait) are Hallwood's original conception, not only given visible form but in fact made flesh. It is the *artist's* soul, expressed through the work, that is laid bare. But is this expression of the artist's soul displayed in the living portrait, or in the soulless, photographic Dorian who eventually murders the artist and stabs the living portrait? Since the portrait and its subject are now one and the same, the soulless Dorian dies and the image is restored to lifelikeness-locked-in-time. In *Dorian Gray*, then, we find a metaphor for the shifting relationship between the photographed, the photographer, and the photograph, a relationship that illustrates the problem of the attribution of creativity. The "soul," or "personality," which inheres in its creation, rather than residing in any one of the three positions, is passed among them, referred to three possible points of origin.

From a contemporary point of view, we may be quite comfortable with this circularity, which constantly shifts the point of origin (as well as the blame) of meaning from one term to another. The circuit is shorted, however, when the question of ownership is introduced. When Lord Henry Wotten asks Hallwood if he will sell the image of Dorian to him, the portraitist explains that it is not his to sell; it is Dorian's property (pp. 35–36). Since no monetary exchange has taken place between the artist and the subject of the portrait, the issue of ownership seems to be decided on the basis of the congruence between Dorian and his image. Or, the physical likeness itself stakes out a property claim by means of its self-evidence. Shouldn't the subject portrayed have property in the one thing he indisputably owns, that is, property in himself? At the same time, it can be argued that the artist Hallwood himself is the source of the work, the originator of the conception. For aesthetic theory, the question of ownership dramatized in *Dorian Gray* is an interesting ambiguity. But for legal doctrine it is an ambiguity that must be resolved; intellectual property law must know whether or not there is personality in the work. And yet, as we will see, the property right question historically took the answer it wanted from aesthetic debates, while at the same time it went its own way, under pressure from social, economic, and technological factors.

To explain how it was that aesthetic theory and Anglo-American intellectual property doctrine, once entwined, came to part company (while still seeming to be allied), I need to consider the other possibilities that might have provided a basis for ownership in the image. As I see it, there were other contenders for the coveted position of the origin of the photographic work. These other claimants were nature (the source of light), convention (other works), the photographic apparatus, and the subject photographed. The invention of photography, as Bernard Edelman has shown, took French law by surprise, and during the ensuing period of disequilibrium, French courts debated the ways of establishing ownership in the image. How was it, then, that the other contenders were dismissed one by one in favor of the photographer-artist?

The Law "Seized" by Photography

In his introduction to the English edition of Edelman's book *Le droit saisi par le photographie*, Paul Hirst says that the original title contains a pun, suggesting that the law was "seized" and "caught by" new technologies: photography and cinema.[5] In legal terms, *saisi* also refers to an attachment of goods or a seizure of money owed to a creditor.[6] But although this sense of the tables turned on the law has its appeal, there are even more provocative ways of looking at the title, given that the verb *saisir* also means "to perceive," so that we get the impression that the law is seen or grasped through photography.[7] But finally, if we consider the figurative meaning of *saisir*, it has to do with shocking or startling. As Edelman himself frames this, "The eruption of modern techniques of the (re)production of the real—photographic apparatuses, cameras—surprises the law in the quietude of its categories."[8] *Le droit saisi* suggests the lethargy, unpreparedness, and unresponsiveness of the French legal system, but it also carries some sense of the way this technological innovation jolted a social institution, catching it off guard. The new technologies did not produce a communications "revolution" in any sense, but they did pose problems that required institutional adjustments without which defects in the ideological mortar would begin to show.[9]

The law does not easily accommodate such challenges; there is no better illustration of this than the attempt of nineteenth-century French law to decide whether or not the photograph was the artistic creation of the photographer. As Edelman describes it, when French law was first asked whether the photographer could be afforded the same protection for his work as a painter was for his, the courts balked. As Edelman puts it, "The law is first surprised by the question and its first answer is in 'resistance.'" For French law, the crucial question was whether or not the mechanical product could be said to have anything of "Man" in it at all. An authored work (it was argued) is imbued with something of the human soul, but a machine-produced work is completely "soulless."[10]

No sooner had the French courts issued this dictum than they began to reverse it. This bald-faced contravention is dramatized in the statements by French minister Alphonse Lamartine in the 1840s: "It is because of the servility of photography that I am fundamentally contemptuous of this chance invention which will never be an art but which plagiarises nature by means of optics. Is the reflection of a glass on paper an art? No, it is a sunbeam caught in the instant by a *manoeuvre*. But where is the conception of man? Where is the choice? In the crystal, perhaps. But one thing for sure, it is not in Man."[11] But this same minister who saw photographic reproduction as "plagiarising nature" would later declare photography to be "better than art; it is a solar phenomenon in which the artist collaborates with the sun."[12] What had happened? As it became clearer between the middle and the end of the nineteenth century that many thousands of French people made a living by means of photographic technologies and that France exported photographic images, protection of the product against infringement came to seem essential. As Edelman explains, "The soulless photographer will be set up as an artist and the film-maker as a creator, *since the relations of production will demand it.*"[13]

Crucial to Edelman's theory is the idea that in order for the law to protect the photographic work, the photographer (the creative subject who had disappeared into the machine), had to be reintroduced into the equation; a soul had to be found in the mechanical act, the "soulless labor" of operating a camera. The subject (and here all of the grand potential of humanism's "Man" is unfolded) "invests" the photograph with something of himself, with the combination of humanness and particularity that we have come to call the "original conception." In this original conception, the creative subject and his work, intertwined as they are, become "indivisible."[14] Noting the way in which the landscape scene before the camera becomes an original work of art, Edelman asserts, "In order to 'intellectually' appropriate what belongs to everyone, I must not reproduce it, for then I shall do no more than expose what belongs to everyone, but I must produce it."[15] Here we have made a quantum leap in the same click of the shutter. As Edelman's critique testifies, what was simply a machine act of retrieval and duplication (Lamartine's "plagiarism") of the real world before the camera suddenly becomes an original production of that real world. As the creative subject is brought to bear on the object before the lens, a a wholly new thing is produced from the merger of creative subject and object. And this new thing is the artistic or intellectual property.

And yet, as Edelman argues, in order for the legal subject to claim protection for this new property he had produced, the face and body of the work had to evidence a mark that, although invisible, could be recognized in law. And so it was that around 1862, the French courts translated the expression of the creative soul into the more serviceable concept of the "imprint of personality," a legal means by which the work could be seen as something indelibly etched with this sign of its author.[16] But shouldn't we be suspicious of the declaration that something is there in the photographic product that was not there before? How is it that the photographer could be suddenly transformed from a mindless mechanic into an artist and a creator, even a genius? And how can we account for the fact that the same "rote movement"—the click of the shutter—is now elevated to the status of the stroke of the pen or the brush? We may be credulous, but the French courts, apparently, were not. So Edelman's account reminds us, new technologies may "surprise" old categories, but only to be reformed according to existing conceptions of the world. Science and engineering may produce technologies that outstrip human capabilities, but these strange inventions are soon reconceived—domesticated and humanized—as they are put to use.

This theme has been developed in contemporary film theory's critique of the way in which technological developments have been historically claimed for an idealism that seems incompatible with purely mechanical functions. First advanced by French film theorists in the early seventies, and coincident with increasing interest in the work of Louis Althusser, this critique began with a description of how the camera itself was historically built to reproduce an aesthetic perspective based on the single eye of humanism's man. Much of this critique derived from an emerging French poststructuralism, which argued that the humanist project had been reinforced by linking it with technological advances. For these critics, the early film theorist André Bazin was said to have claimed each new technological change in cinema as confirmation of an idealist metaphysic—as evidence of a divine plan in the "natural" world that could finally be replicated in every detail by science.[17]

For contemporary film theory, however, technological change is no longer viewed as the forward movement of bourgeois progress, but rather as a series of junctures at which new technologies suggest ways to construct the world anew. These technologies are not employed to transformative ends but are instead harnessed to existing conceptions. Consider how the contemporary French critique might reread the late-nineteenth-century prehistory of cinema and the inventions of Eadweard Muybridge and Etienne Jules Marey. After the camera's original challenge to the visible world as "seen" by the "human eye" (that supremely ideological organ), the motion picture camera ceased to be an instrument for the analysis of movement (through its elongation or abbreviation). Although it held the potential for teaching us to see the natural world a different way, it became instead an instrument for representing the time and space continuum as it was believed to be. Rather than challenging "the real" as it was already understood, the camera ended up confirming that real.[18]

Edelman has looked at another such juncture: the period in European history that was faced with the question of whether photography was the creation of an artist or the product of a machine. French legal discourse was thrown into a state of confusion by the introduction of a technical novelty with unforeseen capabilities—a machine that turned out copies of the natural world without the aid of the "human hand" or, for that matter, the human eye. Just as the eye would have to reassess its version of the visible, so the subject in law would have to reassess its part in the creation of mechanically produced culture. What relevance does Edelman's analysis of this momentary crisis in French legal history have for political analyses of U.S. entertainment law? To answer this question, we need to investigate the sources of Anglo-American copyright law.

U.S. Copyright Law and the Photograph

The 1709 Statute of Anne is often cited as the origin of the authorial right to the work in Anglo-American law, but in fact this right was an outgrowth of a completely different set of interests and national concerns, ones that were far removed from any concern about fairness to authors. The British statute aimed in part to dissolve the monopoly power of the Stationers Company (a kind of publishers guild holding publication rights exclusively), which effectively worked as state censorship.[19] What will be important to us here is the way in which the category of "author"—which in the 1709 statute allowed the London publishers or booksellers to justify their publication rights—is turned to the advantage of writers after the expiration of the twenty-one-year copyright extensions given to Stationers in the original statute. Not until the "Battle of the Booksellers," the controversy surrounding *Donaldson v. Becket* (1774), did the issues begin to undergo the realignment that somewhat resembles the now familiar Anglo-American authorial copyright.

In the U.S., the original 1790 copyright act passed by the First Congress gave protection to charts and maps and then books. In 1802 the act was amended to include the engraving or etching and what the amendment called "prints," and an 1831 amendment mentioned "copyright" for the first time in reference to musical compositions in their engraved or printed form.[20] In 1865 photographs and photographic negatives were officially added to the list of copyrightable forms—a change that some legal sources have attributed to the Civil War popularity of Mathew Brady's photographic works. Five years later, drawings, paintings, chromolithographs, statues, and fine art models or designs were added. After 1870 we find a long hiatus: Between the significant 1909 Copyright Act revisions, which reorganized protection into eleven categories, and the complete revision in 1976, the U.S. Copyright Act was amended only twice. First, in 1912, it was expanded to cover moving pictures; and then, almost sixty years later, in direct response to an outbreak of sound tape piracy in the early seventies, "sound recording" was added as a copyright-able work.[21]

U.S. intellectual property doctrine has written its own history within Supreme Court decisions, and it has historically characterized itself as re-sponsive to technological change, particularly when that change translates into economic imperatives. Chief Justice Burger's statement for the major-ity in *Goldstein v. California* (1973), the preeminent position on state protection of "sound recording," summarized this self-characterization:

> The history of federal copyright statutes indicates that the con-gressional determination to consider specific classes of writings is dependent not only on the character of the writing, but also on the commercial importance of the product to the national economy. As our technology has expanded the means available for creative activity and has provided economical means for reproducing manifestations of such activity, new areas of federal protection have been initiated.[22]

This statement stands in conspicuous contrast to the arguments first advanced in French law on behalf of protecting a new technology. As we know from Edelman's critique, French law focused on the artist and not the industry, even if it worked to the eventual benefit of that industry. But the U.S. House Report on the proposed 1912 amendment that added motion picture photoplays to the copyrightable category was quite spe-cific about the economic stakes in the extension of protection: "The money invested therein is so great and the property rights so valuable that the committee is of the opinion that the copyright laws ought to be amended as to give to them distinct and definite recognition and protec-tion."[23] It may at first seem that the French example, so thoroughly critiqued by Edelman, could have no relevance for the treatment of mechanical and electronic technologies in U.S. copyright law. After all, as Paul Hirst reminds us in his commentary on Edelman, French copyright law is historically based on the author's right (*le droit d'auteur*), whereas the parallel Anglo-American law is based upon the right to copy.[24] And it could be argued as well that Anglo-American law, unlike its French counterpart, was not "surprised in the quietude of its categories" by the new photographic technologies, because Britain had already assimilated photography into its copyright law in 1862, three years before the U.S. followed suit.[25]

We should note, however, that in the histories of both French and American intellectual property, the case of photography reveals the absolute importance of authorship as prerequisite to ownership. In French law, Edelman reminds us, the photographer had to "invest" the real with his personality; similarly, in American copyright law the human author had to put "something" of himself into the real in order to turn it into property.[26] In both cases, the investment of personality is the crucial authorial deposit that turns preexisting material and immaterial property into intellectual property. But once the author-subject, as I will call him, originates the work, his contribution is negated and his position evacuated. If the intervention of the author-subject is easier to see in French law, the evacuation of the author-subject is more pronounced in U.S. doctrine. While in nineteenth-century French law we find the legal subject first intervening in photographic production, in U.S. copyright law we see the legal author-subject gradually removed from the work.

My argument depends upon a reading of the U.S. Supreme Court decision in *Burrow-Giles Lithographic Co. v. Sarony* (1884), a case that has particular historical significance because of its challenge to the constitutionality of the 1865 Copyright Act amendment, which covered photography. Moreover, *Burrow-Giles* remains a definitive statement on "originality" in manually as well as mechanically produced work. In this case, we find the pattern of origination and evacuation that I mentioned above played out in detail: "originality" is elaborated as a defense of Sarony's photographic artistry at the same time that it is reduced to nothing more than a point of origin.

Others may argue that *Burrow-Giles* is a moot case as far as contemporary copyright practice is concerned. It was made redundant by *Bleistein v. Donaldson Lithographic Co.* (1903), a case that involved the copyrightability of circus posters produced by chromolithography and that declared reproductions of this kind to be protectable regardless of the degree of artistry expended in their production. The implication, of course, is that if all photographs and lithographs are copyrightable whether they are artistic works or not, then the more elaborate defense of Napoleon Sarony's artistry would seem to be superfluous to copyright law. A current edition of a basic text on intellectual property, for instance, tells us that *Bleistein* is more relevant to questions regarding the photograph than *Burrow-Giles* is:

At least since *Burrow-Giles Lithographic Co. v. Sarony* . . . photographs of real-life situations have been copyrightable. The justification for protection was that the photographer had invested his pictures with serious artistic consideration and creative effort. But after *Bleistein*, it is apparent that such a claim is unnecessary and that photographs are copyrightable not because of any artistic creative effort but simply because they are the work of "one man alone."[27]

And yet the definition in *Burrow-Giles* of an author as an "originator," or "he to whom anything owes its origin," remains a valid characterization of what constitutes authorship in U.S. copyright law. Perhaps the most dramatic illustration of the definition of originality set forth in *Burrow-Giles* is its application in *Time Incorporated v. Bernard Geis Associates* (1968), to which I will return in more detail.[28] Here the question of who owned the Super 8 mm footage of the Kennedy assassination rested not only upon seeing the hand of *one* amateur filmmaker pushing the button (after *Bleistein*'s "one man alone") but upon the filmmaker's conferral of "originality" on the mechanical work by virtue of his intervention in the creative act as a legal subject. Commenting upon these conditions of "originality" in *Time Inc. v. Geis*, the authors of the intellectual property text to which I have been referring observe, "The combination of happenstance and fate that led to these films amplify [*sic*] the fact that originality is minimal indeed."[29] The requirement that there be maximum originality in the photographic work is also the minimum requirement—that there be no originality at all.

Let me start with the maximum of originality. Of the hundreds of celebrity photographs reproduced illegally in the 1880s (that is, reprinted in disregard of the photographer's copyright), only one provides us with a full statement on authorship in mechanical works in American copyright law. The test case arose when New York photographer Napoleon Sarony filed suit for copyright infringement against Burrow-Giles Lithographic Company, charging it with producing 85,000 unauthorized copies of "Oscar Wilde, No. 18," one of the twenty images the photographer took at a sitting in January 1882 (fig. 1). In April 1883, the Circuit Court of New York, Southern District, decided the case in Sarony's favor.[30]

There is no doubt that the protection of industrially produced culture in the U.S. has its origins in the Turkish carpet that was arranged at the feet of Oscar Wilde. And these origins can be traced as well to his curious

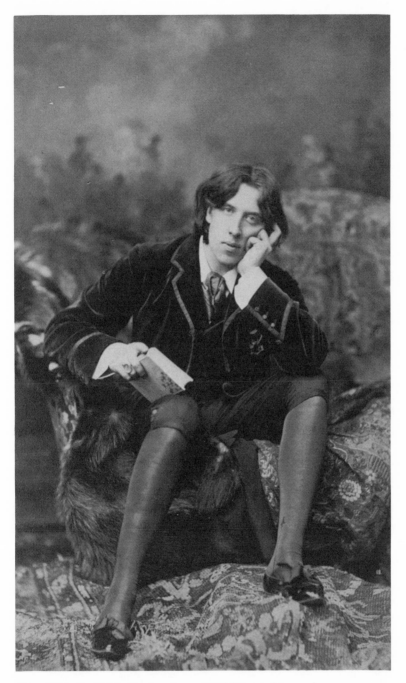

"Oscar Wilde, No. 18," by Napoleon Sarony (1882) (Library of Congress)

lapdog pose, to the assumption of his own signature gesture (the fingers to the face), and to the way he holds the small book poised on his knee. Finally, they are in the whimsical arrangement of Wilde's legs thrust forward to display the silk stockings and shiny patent leather shoes tied with fancy bows. And they are in the shallow depth-of-field of the photograph, which produces a hazy, ethereal soft-focus space above his head. Here, the work and the author's description of his own process of conception fit hand in glove. And the U.S. Supreme Court, in accepting Sarony's description of authorial creation as a valid argument, reauthorized it as law. The court agreed with Sarony that the photograph of Oscar Wilde was

> [a] useful, new, harmonious, characteristic, and graceful picture, and that the plaintiff made the same . . . entirely from his own original mental conception, to which he gave visible form by posing the said Oscar Wilde in front of the camera, selecting and arranging the costume, draperies, and other various accessories in said photograph, arranging and disposing the light and shade, suggesting and evoking the desired expression, and from such disposition, arrangement, or representation, made entirely by plaintiff, he produced the picture in suit.[31]

The elaborated position on originality within this Supreme Court decision also trades upon connotations of aesthetic density because it analogizes "photography" with authors' "writings": "By writings in that clause is meant the literary productions of those authors, and congress very properly has declared these to include all forms of writings, printing, engravings, etc., by which the ideas in the mind of the author are given visible expression."[32] In extending the category of "writings" to lithography and printmaking, the court offered the photographic print legal protection.[33] But there is another legal analogy at work here, namely the French comparison of the photographer and the painter, both of whom may be creative subjects "arranging," "disposing," "suggesting," and "evoking representation." The American theorization of original artistry in the photograph, then, is the product of the convergence of at least three analogies: the written composition, the painted canvas, and the printed lithograph.

Against Sarony's argument in support of photography as an original work of authorship, Burrow-Giles Lithographic Company took the position that the photograph was *not* copyrightable because it was a purely mechanical operation. In a sense, this important challenge to the constitutionality of the 1865 amendment (which recognized the photograph as a "work of authorship") was a recapitulation of the French debates, but with this difference: The "merely mechanical" argument was deployed in the U.S. to dislodge the *already*-positioned subject, rather than to squeeze him out from the start. The lithographic company's argument, as restated by Justice Miller, echoed the early French debates:

> But it is said that an engraving, a painting, a print, does embody the intellectual conception of its author, in which there is novelty, invention, originality . . . while a photograph is the mere mechanical reproduction of the physical features or outlines of some object, animate or inanimate, and involves no originality of thought or any novelty in the operation connected with its visible reproduction in the shape of a picture.[34]

Was this argument, which effectively denied legal protection to the photograph, convincing in a suit for infringement, a suit heard, moreover, during a period that was a heyday for photographic piracy? How could the "merely mechanical" argument stand in light of the emergence of so many self-styled photographic artists in both both France and the U.S., of which Napoleon Sarony was only one of the more prominent examples?

Apparently it couldn't, because the Supreme Court did, in fact, produce a judgment in Sarony's favor. *Burrow-Giles*, however, has been considered somewhat problematic by legal commentators. Even though the court found sufficient evidence of Sarony's authorship to uphold the protection of photographs in which some degree of personality was invested, it did not take a position in regard to the production of what it termed "ordinary" photographs. The court declined to decide on this issue, and Justice Miller's statement discouraged any attempt to look to this decision for such authority. As for the legal status of the photograph produced by "merely mechanical" means, he said: "It is simply the manual operation, by the use of these instruments and preparations, of transferring to the plate the visible representation of some existing object, the accuracy of the representation being its highest merit. This may be true in regard to the ordinary production of a photograph, and that in such case a copyright is no protection. On the question as thus stated we decide nothing."[35] *Burrow-Giles* would in time be interpreted as a case that produced an equivocal statement on the copyrightability of the photograph. It could not provide a clear standard for all photographs—that was not produced until the Copyright Act of 1909. As Judge Learned Hand later put it, the significance of the 1909 clarification was that it allowed protection of photographs "without regard to the degree of 'personality' which enters into them."[36]

Burrow-Giles, as evidenced in its description of Sarony's work process, obviously contains the provision for the protection of works in which authorial "personality" is abundantly displayed. But it also provides for works invested with a zero "degree of personality," since it defines the author as nothing more than the point of origin of the work—as "he to whom anything owes its origin; originator; maker; one who completes a work of science or literature." Later opinions, in fact, have tended to rely on *Burrow-Giles* not for its articulation of authorial "personality" but for its statement of the minimum requirement of originality in other "works of authorship," photographs notwithstanding.[37] What I am suggesting, in other words, is that the very theorization of the legal author-subject in the case of the photograph (the legal prototype for the mechanically produced work) is at the same time an important step in the gradual displacement of the author-subject from his secure position before the work. To put it another way, in U.S. intellectual property law, the intervention of the subject in the photographic work also marked the point of exclusion of the subject.

To provide a picture of what is at stake, it may be useful here to review the sweep of developments from 1709 to 1968, to which I have referred in this section. In the concluding chapters of Lyman Ray Patterson's *Copyright in Historical Perspective*—one of the few historical treatments of Anglo-American copyright law—these developments are read in relation to contemporary concerns about the dangers of the monopoly vested in copyright. In Patterson's view, British and American courts during this period misunderstood the monopoly problem; in an attempt to curtail monopolies on the right to copy (in the interests of the public good), the courts limited the author's right. But, in fact, they should have limited the *publisher's* right, since in current practice publishers, not authors, are owners of copyrights. As Patterson explains it, the courts saw two interests, "author" and "public," when they should have considered a third: "publisher."[38] The contemporary situation that Patterson describes has come almost full circle, back to similar conditions in the eighteenth century when the publisher-monopolists invoked the author's-right pro-vision of the Statute of Anne in an attempt to regain their hold on the rights they no longer held in perpetuity.[39] These rights, the publishers discovered, could be held with more security if they were attached to the "natural right" of the author who had sold the work to them. Patterson characterizes the eighteenth-century publishers' strategy as remarkable for its "transparency."[40] But what of the contemporary situation, in which the publisher-owner acquires the author's lifetime monopoly in the work in order to extend and fortify a right that might have otherwise been limited? What of the example of *Time Inc. v. Geis*, in which the publisher is able to claim a monopoly on the Super 8 mm footage of the Kennedy assassina-tion by means of the authorial right of Abraham Zapruder? Patterson's history reveals a pattern of monopoly effected by using the author as a kind of pawn. But it also shows us a reversal of the outcome of the eighteenth-century battles. For copyright, as he points out, "instead of being a limited right in connection with a work for an unlimited period of time, . . . became an unlimited right for a limited period of time."[41] Patterson may be correct that the House of Lords as well as the book-sellers used authors' rights (absent any authors themselves) to different ends, the former to dissolve and the latter to reconstitute monopoly rights. But Patterson takes this historical background in a predictable direction that negates the logic of his own research. He employs the historical findings that authors' rights were an invention on behalf of an argument for a proper authorial right in Anglo-American copyright law.[42] In this he anticipates the current movement on behalf of a restitu-tion of the author-subject in American law on the model of the French *droit moral* ("moral right").[43] I am willing to follow Patterson only until he uncovers the historically opportunistic uses of author's right. But what Patterson cannot answer is how the authorial creator can be used to construct a legal subjecthood with an attendant "natural right" to an end that does not benefit Patterson's own third interest, the "public."

Patterson's focus on the author's right obscures the historical construc-tion of the legal subject who can have property in his person, a formation that predates and makes possible the construction of the author as owner of his writings. In *Burrow-Giles*, the case under discussion, the author's right obscures the contradictory evidence offered by the technology itself, the evidence that photography *is* mechanical. Authorship in the photograph is a requisite fiction. But then so is authorship in the literary work.

Origin and Originality: "One Man's Alone"

It is true that in intellectual property "originality" has a prag-
matic charge. The concept is used to prevent competing claims to ownership in a work. Nevertheless, within the common law, conflicting claims
have arisen because of the admitted ambiguity of "originality," and it is
this ambiguity that I now want to investigate.[44] Although copyright law
does maintain the distinction between the original and its copy, familiar
from the criticism of fine art, legal doctrine recognizes many more total
works as "original" and views many more kinds of products as "works of
authorship." This is so, in part, because while aesthetic theory disparages
copying, copyright law encourages copying at the same time that it
polices it. It may appear, then, that we are not talking about the same
concept, but what I want to show is that these two concepts of originality
grow out of the same philosophical root: property in the person. The
ambiguity of "originality" complained of by judges and legal commentators can be explained by the divergent histories of legal theory and aesthetic theory in the last two centuries. While the two "originalities" are
still connected at the root, the apparent similarity that this produces in the
two discourses has an ideological function: to mask the threat that each
conception of originality poses to the opposite discourse.

The pressing question for us, of course, is why originality, which in
1884 was required in abundance (as the description above of Sarony's
method attests), has become reduced more and more to the blunt fact of
origin. To answer this question, I need to tell a somewhat longer story
of how "originality"—over "individuality," "uniqueness," "novelty," or
"creativity"—came to be the crucial determining concept in intellectual
property, so that—and again I cite the contemporary word on intellectual
property—"originality does not imply novelty; it only implies that the
copyright claimant did not copy from someone else."[45] A kind of doubleness, in other words, evolved in the legal concept of originality: On the
one hand, the law retained the connotations of artistic creativity and the
ideal of the singular work; on the other hand, "creativity" came to refer
simply to the work's point of origination, not to the unique, soul-invested
nature of the work itself. Before we consider the precarious legal status of
artistic "creativity" in the contemporary period, however, we need to
examine how and under what circumstances the notion became crucial to
assessments of how the work of culture is produced. What we will find is

that the concept of authorial "creativity" has a long and varied history of appropriations and that its use as a means of legally securing property is only one of its more recent manifestations. From this perspective, the appearance of the "creative" subject in relation to the photographic act should have surprised no one, since this subject has appeared historically at so many other times in the service of so many different interests.

Long before the creative subject was ushered into the process of producing the photograph, this subject was inserted into the process of producing objects that had previously been the product of one or more artisans. It is true that the phenomenon of the singular artist who is fully responsible for the work as a whole is first visible in Renaissance Italy at the end of the fifteenth century. But the notion of "creation" in relation to art does not fully emerge until the eighteenth century—and then with a vengeance, as a calculated strategy in opposition to industrial production. Raymond Williams reminds us that the idea of the "creative" artist emerged as the once divine capacity of creation became attributable to humans. And in the current century, Williams continues, "creativity" has become synonymous with innovative, original, and novel, but at the expense of undergoing some devaluation.[46] It is impossible to disregard the striking historical parallel between this linguistic devaluation and the delimitation of the legal concept of "originality."

The impossibility of ever reconciling the two poles of the original/copy dichotomy has become clear for aesthetic theory only in its recent postmodern frame of thought.[47] Historically, the showdown between the original and the copy has been staved off, first and most successfully by the Romantic movement, which attempted to ameliorate the deleterious effects of the industrial revolution. The Romantic view of art as transcendent and of the artist as a superior being evolved as a means of rescuing the artist's work from the market and from the hostile public for whom mass production might make the work available as it had never been before, but at the price of turning it into an industrial product. The Romantics countered the commodification of the work by elevating the artist, but, ironically, the artwork came to be seen as the product of creative genius in proportion to the loss of status of artists in general.[48] The strategy of the Romantics was to project the "humanness" of the creative subject (which they perceived to be under attack) onto the works themselves. As Williams describes it, this amounted to "an emphasis on the embodiment in art of certain human values, capacities, energies, which the development of society towards an industrial civilization was felt to be threatening or even destroying."[49] In short, cultural products were endowed with the same rare and unique qualities that their singular human creators were said to possess. And as the Romantic poets elevated themselves above other humans, they confirmed not only their own originality but also that of their creations, the better to separate those works from mass-produced products.[50]

As we retrace this process, it is useful to recall that the Romantics' insertion of the subject into the work was an artificial one in its time. If poets were only servants of the divine who held a mirror up to nature, then the personal touch of the poet as individual creator could only be intrusive. The pre-Romantic concept of artistic work, as M. H. Abrams reminds us, allowed no space for individual vision, and it therefore left "limited theoretical room for the intrusion of personal traits into [the writer's] product."[51] For Abrams, the Romantic premium on the personality of the writer was a "strange innovation" when it appeared in the nineteenth century.[52]

To see authorship in the work of art as "strange" is difficult today. The notion has become so thoroughly naturalized over the ensuing century as to engender a reverent metaphysics of the existence of the author in his product that would blind the appreciators to the evidence of anything else in the work, especially to the evidence that there is nothing actually *in* the work at all. As an antidote to a persistent but now exhausted Romanticism, we need to remind ourselves of an earlier era when a literary or fine-art work was seen not as the product of a producer at all, but rather as transpersonal and in flux.[53] From a pre- and post-Romantic vantage, we can see that the analogy between the human author and the work is really a kind of anthropomorphism, one that begins to reveal the motives behind the Romantics' historical opportunism. For as they resisted commodification by projecting the personal traits of the author onto the work, the Romantics effected a reification of their own—one through which "the difficulty of the market was not solved," as Williams puts it, "but cushioned, by an idealization."[54] The Romantics' idealization may have temporarily postponed the market restructuring of the work-author relation, but it did so only by legitimizing the same forces that the poets had opposed. It was only a matter of time before the author-subject came to encourage and facilitate mechanical copying.

The Author as Owner

I have already identified the early-eighteenth-century moment in Anglo-American copyright law when the author was introduced into the literary work as the basis of the right to copy. Technically, the author owned the copyright in the work, but because the bookseller/publisher functioned as proprietor, this fact of ownership remained submerged for three-quarters of the century. I now want to show how these two ends (authorship and ownership) came to be tied together, producing the preconditions for the new compatibility between the author and the market. Authorship and mass production, two strands originally separate, became bound together *after* the late-eighteenth-century "Battle of the Booksellers." It is here, at the outset of the industrial revolution, that I want to resume my historical overview.

In his recent essay on the history of the author as proprietor and the birth of the literary "work," Mark Rose provides a valuable critique of the arguments surrounding the 1774 hearings on literary property in the House of Lords as they took shape in the case of *Donaldson v. Becket*.[55] Rose reads these debates as a confluence of developments that made possible legal ownership and literary authorship as we know them today. At this early stage, often lost in later accounts, aesthetic and legal issues were so thoroughly intertwined as to seem indistinguishable: The aesthetic was marshaled in the service of the legal, and the legal applied in reverse to the aesthetic. Both issues were clearly wedded and, it would seem in retrospect, were by chance decided at once. The House of Lords ruled against the booksellers, who ironically were supporting the author's right to the fruits of his labor, the better to reinforce their own monopoly position at the time. In these debates, Rose argues, the author as proprietor became available to link up with the Romantics' theorization of the originality of the author's work, which was just emerging as a new idea at this time. One of the strains that Rose hears in these arguments around literary authorship is, as we might expect, the Lockean articulation of property as derived from the person, a concept that merges in these debates with the idea that the author's personality, his distinctive identity, is imprinted upon his work or expressed through his writing. Coming out of this meeting we have the now familiar combination: authorial property right, originality in the work, and right to copy or reproduce.[56]

This meeting might be mistaken for an inevitability until we look closely at the first attempts to forge the connections among author's right, originality, and copyright that we now take so much for granted. Here, Rose shows us how this combination was produced by means of an almost imperceptible shift in rhetoric. In his 1774 pamphlet, *Argument in Defence of Literary Property*, Francis Hargrave starts with the problem of how one written composition is to be distinguished from another. In this context he reflects upon two related issues: first, the relationship between the author and the composition; and second, the determination of originality. About the authorial stamp on the composition, Hargrave says:

> The subject of the property is a *written composition*; and that one written composition may be distinguished from another, is a truth too evident to be much argued upon. Every man has a mode of combining and expressing his ideas peculiar to himself. The same doctrines, the same opinions, never come from two persons, or even from the same person at different times, cloathed wholly in the same language. A strong resemblance of stile, of sentiment, of plan and disposition, will be frequently found; but there is such an infinite variety in the modes of thinking and writing, as well as in the extent and connection of ideas, as in the use and arrangement of words, that a literary work *really* original, like the human face, will always have some singularities, some lines, some features, to characterize it, and to fix and establish its identity.[57]

What is remarkable about this passage, says Rose, is the way it subtly moves from describing the composition to describing the author—from the property to the proprietor.[58] This shift from property to proprietor is most evident in the analogy between the literary work and the human face. Which is to say that a conflation of the work, the face, and the personality has produced what has been the ruling paradigm in arts criticism *and* Anglo-American intellectual property law for more than two centuries! We begin to see the shared root structure of the two discourses, but also the ascendance of the author over the *work*, which, in the end, is the category that loses out.

Rose finds an additional rhetorical sleight of hand in Hargrave's defense of property in literature. For it is not clear whether in 1774 "originality" refers only to the composition that is not someone else's (not a copy) *or* to the new Romantic sense of something wholly innovative and unique.[59] On the eve of the union between the *author as individual* and the Romantic notion of the *authored work as individuated and unique*, the two concepts still seem oddly paired. Hargrave's conflation of the individual author with the individual work produces the corollary that every literary composition is different because every author is. If we supplement this with the Lockean philosophy that man is the origin of property, then we have the basis for the Anglo-American copyright doctrine definition of authorship set forth in *Burrow-Giles*: All works originating from an individual are individual works of authorship.

In Hargrave's crude early statement, we see the construction of a tautology that has operated historically at the very heart of intellectual property law: All works of authorship are original.[60] Why? Because they originate with authors. As Barthes describes the function of tautology, it is always a temporary "aphasia," which, like the "faint at the right moment," rescues us from having to make the explanation that is not forthcoming.[61] The interchangeable reference to authorship and origin, then, operates in intellectual property law like an automatic lapse, a memory blackout. The law has, in fact, forgotten, and must continue to forget, that before the writer had rights in his literary production, literary property and writer were separate and unbridgeable categories. The long-forgotten alternative, however, may be found in the position against which Hargrave was arguing, in the proposition that the work is "a set of ideas which have no bounds or marks whatever."[62]

In this forgotten proposition, we find the corollary to poststructuralist theories that would come into vogue two hundred years later, theories that would take issue with the Romantic theorization of some works as more original than others. This, then, is where intellectual property doctrine and traditional literary theory each represent a potential undoing of the other. But the threat that literary authorship poses to copyright is only hypothetical. The return of the real author to the work does not mean the imposition of a test of freshness and complexity impossible for courts to administer.[63] Copyright doctrine poses a greater danger to traditional literary theory, since it negates the contradictory philosophical foundations of traditional literary theory. That is, if the individual author produces property in the work in the Lockean sense, then every act of production is an act of origination, *every* work is an original work, regardless of whether it is aesthetically unoriginal, banal, or, in some cases, imitative. Every individual person is also a potential "author" whose "writings" will be as "original" as those of a renowned or acclaimed literary figure.

As Paul Hirst remarks on the consequences of this structure in Anglo-American copyright law:

> Companies coexist within the same framework of rights with individual subjects, football fixtures are defined in the same terms and enjoy the same rights as *Finnegan's Wake*. The law singularly fails to depend on the (supposed) attributes of individual subjects for the foundations of its provisions and persists in treating of legal subjects with indifference to any formal doctrine of subject. Football clubs and heroes of modernism are considered on the same terrain.[64]

Copyright's minimal point of origin requirement, which considers light fixtures and belt buckles as "works of authorship," performs a critique of traditional theory's notion of authorial originality.[65] Copyright law is a great cultural leveler.

As this example indicates, the coexistence of the two overlapping concepts of "originality" is denied in legal discourse. And in traditional aesthetic theory the parallel contradiction—what Rosalind Krauss calls art criticism's "originality/repetition dichotomy"—is similarly accommodated by a kind of "repression."[66] But there is a difference. In high culture aesthetic discourse, the disruptive potential of copying is repressed. But in intellectual property discourse, the Romantic mythos of uniqueness is not repressed but rather persists, cropping up right where it is abolished. Here, then, is what I would say in answer to Hirst's lament about the equal treatment that copyright offers football clubs and heroes of modernism: We should not be surprised that Anglo-American intellectual property law is formally unaccommodating to the human subject bearing natural rights, because copyright doctrine is nothing more or less than a right to prohibit copying by others. Actual authors, in other words, are irrelevant to the operation of a copyright system.

But while maintaining this centuries-old right-to-copy structure, intellectual property, certainly after 1774, began to accommodate the coexistence of the old prohibition against copying and the newer Romantic conception of the authorial property. And this uneasy coexistence produced, in turn, what might be called the positive and negative sides of "originality." On the negative side, there is the definition of originality that is nothing more than *not* having copied. The point of origin, not to mention uniqueness, is not even relevant here. On the positive side is Justice Holmes's 1903 dictum in *Bleistein v. Donaldson*, the expectation that the work will contain some "irreducible" aspect of the author's personality. This positive definition of originality contains none other than the rationale for authorial ownership in the work based upon the analogy between the individuated human being and his writings. Only in Holmes's opinion it is the analogy between the person and his handwriting style that is advanced as an argument for property in the work: "The copy is the personal reaction of the individual upon nature. Personality always contains something unique. It expresses its singularity even in hand-writing, and a very modest grade of art has in it something irreducible, which is one man's alone."[67] This famous dictum is a curious restatement of the 1774 formulation that the author's right is based on his singularity, his separateness from other humans, and it is remarkable in two ways. First, in his phrase "one man's alone," Holmes gives us personality as a formula rather than as depth and complexity of character, and it is this formula that makes possible the apparently contradictory legal argument that a copy is an original work of authorship. Second, Justice Holmes's opinion, appropriately enough, is as mystifying as the Romantic concept of creativity itself; "something" in the work doesn't tell us *what* is to be found, and since the superfluity of creative artistry is stated in the negative ("irreducible"), we are given nothing specific to look for in the authorial product.[68] This irreducible something is the undissolved golden nugget of genius, and it is all that is left in intellectual property doctrine of Sarony's artistry.[69] If the concept of "originality" is ambiguous in intellectual property law, it is because, although the Romantic notion of authorial creation did provide part of the foundation of Anglo-American copyright law, some of its structures have dissolved. Other parts of the Romantics' unfinished project, however, remain undigested in the common law, producing the lumpy ambiguity of the doctrine of originality.

Where Is the Personality in the Work?

With this background on the interrelationship of the two conceptions of originality in mind, I want to return to the problem that the photographic apparatus posed for French law. We have seen that in Anglo-American law, the literary author claimed proprietorship in the

work by means of an analogy between the writer and the written composition. Almost a century later, in French law, the mechanical mediation in
the photographic act put that kind of analogy between author and work in
jeopardy. Let us return to Edelman's analysis of how the French courts
put the subject into the photographic work in order to make him author
of it. The French courts, Edelman says, used the mediation of *technique* to
"invest" the subject in the real; photography was thus "wrested" from the
machine by the concept of the "imprint of personality."[70] What Edelman
means may be better understood if we consider what follows from the
position that the subject does not intervene. If the personality is not in
evidence in the photograph, the subject "disappears" into the machine, or
"disintegrates" into the mechanical.[71] The threat of the machine, in other
words, is the threat of the loss of the legal subject, who is not just relegated
to the status of the mechanic but who is also totally missing in the creative
act. (And is thus unable to provide the basis for protection.) The concept
of "imprint of personality" restores the subject to the photographic work,
but it does not tell us how it is that the soul found its way from the author
through the apparatus and into the photograph. A somewhat closer
consideration of the nineteenth-century French discourse around the
protectability of the photograph reveals that to some degree the creative
process had to be rethought in order to accommodate the photographer
as author. And it is in this reformulation—in which all phases of photographic production are subsumed under the rubric of "conception"—
that "nature" and "the machine," those other contenders for authorial
contribution, are written out of the process.

In conjunction with the record of Sarony's circuit-court-level trial hearing against Burrow-Giles Lithographic Company in 1883 (the year before the U.S. Supreme Court heard *Burrow-Giles*), the *Federal Reporter*
published a summary of legal documents pertinent to the lower court
decision. Among these documents is an English translation of the chapter
on photography from Pouillet's *Propriété Littéraire et Artistique*, which,
the *Federal Reporter* explains, is reprinted in this context because the issues
relevant to copyright in the photograph had been so widely discussed in
France.[72] Pouillet analyzes the positions relevant to the artistic status of
photography that were advanced within French legal theory after around
1860. Since, under the French law of 1793, a photograph had to be
established as an artistic work in order for it to claim protection along

with the painting, the metaphor of painting shapes this discourse. And we hear it faintly echoed in Napoleon Sarony's claim.

In the position for the protection of authorial rights in the photograph, Pouillet's own position, we find that the analogy between the author and the work becomes so submerged that it is, in fact, assumed. It enables the "no two men" formulation (later Holmes's "one man's alone"), which makes it unnecessary to find individuality or personality *in* the work, simply because individuality in the work is guaranteed by the notion of the individual as subject: "We have said many times already that the author's right was derived from the creation which gives to the work its character of individuality. Is this individuality lacking here? Is it not certain that two photographers, reproducing each for himself, the same scene or the same model, will obtain two pictures capable of being distinguished?"[73] But the problem with extending the "no two men" test (which worked for ownership in the written composition) to the production of the photograph is that two different men may very well produce *identical* photographs using the same apparatus identically positioned. What is more, many different individuals can produce the same photographs from the same negative. In order to make the photographer an author, then, the redefinition of the artistic process had to emphasize the prephotographic (and invisible) stage of photographic production. Photographic artistry, then, had to be rethought as something having less and less to do with the mechanical device, that black hole of authorship where all men are undifferentiated mechanics. As the analogy between the photograph and the painting began to break down between 1793 and 1883, the mechanical part of photography had to be circumvented. And once that happened, all aspects of photographic production merged: thinking, making, and end product became one. "Is it not the conception, however expressed, which constitutes the artistic work?" asks Pouillet.[74]

This merger of the material and the immaterial in the notion of "conception" is part of an important ideological rescue mission in the evolution of intellectual property doctrine. For in this doctrine, the immaterial will have to be recognized as the material. As Edelman discusses this operation, it is performed by a juridical fiction, a form of what Marx and Engels identify as the illusion that the law and not the relations of production is the basis of real property.[75] According to Edelman, here is what happens:

Through its own functioning this fiction permits the transition from the invisible—"intelligence," "creation," "genius,"—to the visible—real estate, the "tangible," the "true," the transition from the immaterial to the material. The functioning of the fiction denounces its role. It is a matter of giving to the *invisible*—the thought of man—*the character of the visible*—private property. People knew already, without knowing it, even though it was impossible for them not to know, that the invisible was what is the visible, since it presents itself in the visible. Such, then, is the effectivity of the fiction.[76]

To put it another way, the notion of artistic conception rewrites the process of origination to make the artistic act interchangeable with the only means through which we can know it: the thing produced. Physical acts and mental acts intermingle and become indistinguishable, and labor of mind and labor of hand become equally material. This is what we find in the court's judgment in *Burrow-Giles*, in which Sarony is said to have "given visible form" to "his own original mental conception" by "posing" Oscar Wilde. But well before the U.S. Supreme Court case, Pouillet describes picture-taking as a process in which mental and physical activity are undifferentiated: "The photographer conceives his work; he arranges the accessories and play of light; he arranges the distance of his instrument according as he wants, in the reproduction, either distinctness or size; thus, also, he obtains this or that effect of perspective. After that, what matters the rapidity, the perfection, the fidelity of the instrument with which he executes what he has *conceived, arranged, created*?"[77] (emphasis mine) In support of his position, Pouillet quotes a complementary argument advanced by the legal figure Imperial Advocate Bachelier, which stresses that the means of obtaining the picture do not matter. (After all, Advocate Bachelier argues, even when the mechanical diagraph or pantograph devices were used to aid illustration, the resulting drawing was a protectable work of art.) Shades of Hegel (in which the human will produces property), all that is required is an "exercise of the will," as seen in that smallest of gestures. And this small gesture of will (which went so far to advance the cause of ownership of the image) is none other than "choice." So that in the photographer's "choice" of subject or time of day to shoot, in Sarony's "selecting," "arranging," "disposing," and "evoking," we have the human investment of labor in the thing, the private property-producing gesture.[78]

The arguments both for and *against* authorship in the photograph depend upon the hand-mind duality. But while the former dissolves the role of the hand into that of the head, the latter separates the two in time. The argument against authorship in the photograph stood its ground against the dissolution of manual and mental labor by dividing the photographic act into two steps. Pouillet cites Thomas, Imperial Advocate at the time, as the primary exponent of the position against authorship in the photograph. Although Thomas did not deny that the photographer conceptualized, he argued that this mental labor took place *before* the actual production of the photograph: "The law of 1793 does not protect the labor of thought previous to execution; not that kind of invention which is the work in the mind alone, but it protects the mental labor in its material product."[79] It is in the transmission of this mental labor that Thomas finds the difference between photography and the traditional fine arts, in which "it is always the intelligence of man expressing what his intelligence has conceived, guiding his brush or his graver, and contending with them against material difficulties."[80]

But how, again, is the author's "personality" suddenly found in the work? Thomas's answer is that if the painter's intellect "directed his hand," then that individual irreducible "something" may be seen as organically flowing through the body and directing the conformation of the material object or the vehicles of expression to the shape of his conception. But the personality cannot flow from the subject through the photographic apparatus. The apparatus must be circumvented. If it is not, the authorial credit is voided. Since personality cannot mix and mingle or flow through the machine in any way, it must make its mark without touching. Although the "imprint of personality" is never actually found in the work, it is everywhere else—in choice, technique, artistic practice, and, as we will see, in the life and personal style of the artist-subject.

For Thomas, after the apparatus is set up the photographer "remains a complete stranger" to the process, because, says Thomas, "light does its work; a splendid but independent agent has accomplished all."[81] And in support of this position the acting Imperial Advocate summarizes the decision of an 1864 tribunal, which found that "although the talent of the operator may contribute much to the success of the portraits or views which are desired, it is none the less certain that these products or views are mechanically made, by the action of light upon certain chemicals, and, in this operation, genius can have no effect on the result obtained."[82] As this decision suggests, the reticence of the French courts to understand the photographer as authoring the image may in part be explained by the competing claim for the authorship of nature, enhanced by European discourses on photography that stressed the agency of light. The version of photography as light-drawing, as the creation of nature, after all, reigned for at least twenty-five years after Louis-Jacques-Mandé Daguerre's 1839 discovery. Daguerre's perfected photographic process, as Beaumont Newhall describes it, answered the yearning for a pure image of the world produced by the "pencil of nature," an image that would be superior to the "intrusion of the pencil of man."[83] Typical of the period is one reviewer's comment on William Henry Fox Talbot's *The Pencil of Nature* (1844), which praised the way the photographic plates reproduced in the book seemed "an effect of sunshine, and the microscopic execution sets at nought the work of human hands."[84] Or again, Joseph-Nicéphore Niépce, who later collaborated with Daguerre, named his earliest successful experiment heliography (sun-writing). As the title of his instructional manual attests, the human author-subject was written out of the earliest descriptions of the technology: *On Heliography; or, A Means of Automatically Fixing, by the Action of Light, the Image Formed in the Camera Obscura.*[85]

These two features of photography—the work of natural light and the automatic functioning of the device—were to be reiterated often in the French legal discourse as they were in the formative stages of the technology. This version of how photography worked was reinforced in the published statements of the inventors. By Daguerre's account, the two most remarkable features of his invention were that "anyone can take the most detailed views in a few minutes" and that the daguerreotype was "a chemical and physical process which gives Nature the ability to reproduce herself."[86] But if the image were produced sheerly by the magnanimity of nature, then no requisite exclusivity could be asserted and no fortunes could be made. During the short period in French history when the unique and delicate image on tin was thought to be indifferent to the camera operator and a humanly uncontaminated product of the sun, Daguerre sold his invention to the government.[87] The means for reproducing the works of nature would belong to the French people.

Sarony's Artistry

If the photographer wanted to claim authorship in the work, he could not allow either that "anyone can take the most detailed views in a few minutes" or that the image was nature's miraculous self-reproduction. Both the claim of the machine and the claim of nature were easily dismissed. So for the latter, by the time the apparatus made "anyone and everyone" into photographers, the issue of authorship in the photo had been settled. Between photography's formative years and January 1882, when the Wilde photograph was taken, the emergence of the photographic portraitist altered the popular conception of photographic technique, so much so that by the time Sarony argued for his authorial right, he had a ready-made rationale based on an extremely lucrative trade already flourishing in Paris, London, and New York. In addition, the visual conventions and the institutional practices of portrait photography were thoroughly indebted to traditions of full-length portrait painting—a connection reinforced by the elaborate parlorlike decor of the studios, the ritual of the sitting, and the eccentric theatrics of the photographer. These conventions and practices camouflaged the instantaneity, the effortlessness, of photographic production, but, most of all, they denied photography's multiplicity and reproducibility. As we will see, the history of photography in the nineteenth century reveals an inverse relationship between the mechanical and chemical improvements that increased the speed and ease of image reproduction and the claims made in the name of uniqueness.

The discourse on portrait photography that Sarony inherited originally centered mainly on the pose and the iconography, although sometimes the photographer is credited with using mirrors to manipulate the existing light, which, before the introduction of electric lights, flowed in from the studio skylight.[88] Borrowing the terminology of fine art criticism that photographic portraiture inherited from painting, Justice Miller agreed that Sarony was responsible for "arranging and disposing the light and shade." But curiously absent from Sarony's argument and from the discourse on photography is the labor that actually most resembled that of the painter: retouching, retracing, coloring, and, as advocated by the Pictorialists, printing and rephotographing. Equally strange is the absence of reference to chemical processes, especially given the importance in this period of the advances of the collodian process over the older wet-plate process, and since the new process was having its impact upon photographer and patron alike. But the chemical processes remain the most mysterious aspects of photography in both U.S. and French legal doctrine, in part because they seemed to remain independent of the human hand, a part of nature that could not be absorbed into the process of "conception."

"Conception" was taken out of the recesses of the head and made concretely visible in the personal style and the studio manner of the photographer, who modeled himself after the artist-genius. In fact, Sarony's version of how his personal conception found form in the image resembles nothing so much as the familiar accounts of how the old masters worked with their assistants, whose work was subsumed by the great artist's conception because they "knew" what he wanted. As Sarony described how he relayed ideas to his camera operator: "If I make a position, and his camera is right, my longtime assistant here, Richardson, is able to catch my ideas as deftly and quickly as necessary."[89] If the requisite authorial "personality" could not be detected in the work itself, it could nevertheless be inferred through artistic choice and practical technique.

But especially in cases like Sarony's, the inference of personality in the work was made on and through the body of the artist himself. Napoleon Sarony, whose physical stature was similar to that of his famous namesake, cultivated a volatile temperament and a flamboyant personal style that was epitomized in the red fez he always wore and in the bold red embossed signature on his work. And Sarony's mystique was only enhanced by reports about the posing session. Crucial to the mystique of the photographer as author was the artist-patron relationship, which made up in intensity for what it lacked, compared with the painted portrait, in duration. The pioneer in this tradition of photographic portraiture was Gaspard-Felix Tournachon ("Nadar"). Nadar admitted that the techniques of photography could be easily learned, but he ascribed the superiority of his method to his artistic sensibility, which could be seen in his lighting effects but especially in his capacity for empathy. This empathetic sensibility, the "moral grasp of the subject," enabled him to draw out a likeness much as a theatrical director commanded a performance.[90] Thirteen years after Nadar opened his studio in Paris, Sarony situated his own to take advantage of the Broadway trade, and in that location he perfected the theatrics of photography and established the popularity of the theatrical photograph in the U.S.[91]

It is important to distinguish between the high art aspirations and the ethereal quality of the French portrait school (Nadar, Etienne Carjat, Pierre Petit, Anthony Samuel Adam-Solomon), on the one hand, and on the other, the theatrical photography of Sarony's Broadway studio period. Between Nadar's start and Sarony's heyday, the popular potential of portrait photography was fully realized in Adolphe-Eugène Disdéri's *carte de visite*, which had a short-lived success in France in the years 1854–60.[92] Sarony's Wilde image, however, was taken as a *cabinet* photograph and was much larger (51/2" by 4") than the tiny *carte de visite* that it superseded in popularity.[93] "Oscar Wilde, No. 18" is on the verge of presenting the more psychological effect made possible by placing the photographic subject closer to the camera. The cabinet card aesthetic, with its foregrounding of facial expression, was clearly distinguishable from the aesthetic of the *carte de visite*, whose subject was crowded into the frame stuffed with material possessions.[94] What is significant about the Sarony photographs in particular is that they represent a combination of the aesthetics of the portrait tradition and the wild popularity of the mass-produced *carte de visite*—a merger that encouraged and thrived upon the emergence of the star system in the American theater.[95] In fact, what Sarony largely did was to photograph actors in their roles: Joseph Jefferson in *Rip Van Winkle*, Lillian Russell in *Tzigane*, James O'Neill in *The Count of Monte Cristo*, and Lily Langtry in *As You Like It*.

So it seems that at least two "personalities" mingled their artistry in the photographic work. But how, then, can copyright law deal with two conceptions, two labors of mind and body in the work, when this doctrine is based on a vision of the work as "one man's alone"? Why did the photographer, rather than the celebrity subject, emerge as the creator of the image? There are two broad facets of this question of two artists vying for authorship of the same image: one having to do with authorial power, the other with conventions of representation on the popular stage as they intersect with photographic portraiture. These issues are summarized in an anecdote about Sarony's posing session with the popular melodrama star Adah Isaacs Menken, who came to his studio in Birmingham, England, in 1865. Menken's reputation had been made in her role in the melodrama *Mazeppa*, largely because of the scandalous nature of the scene in which, costumed in pink tights and brief tunic, she rode across the stage tied to the bare back of a horse. Since 1859 she had been promoting herself with *cartes de visite*, which were distributed in conjunction with her performances, but she told Sarony that she had never been satisfied with the photographs taken of her in the role of Mazeppa. As Sarony recalled it, he challenged her by suggesting that she pose herself in eight images, after which he would pose her in a different eight. Much to Sarony's satisfaction, the actress was disappointed in the eight poses she had arranged herself, but she liked his arrangements, which portrayed her in stages of recline, languishing on a fur mat.[96]

Posing, as Sarony's claim implies, involves placing the subject's body in front of the camera in particular positions, eliciting facial expressions, and directing bodily attitudes. In this relatively abbreviated period before shorter exposure times encouraged the myth of spontaneity and chance in photography, the photographer's work consisted, in no small part, of fixing poses that subjects might have to hold for fifteen to sixty seconds. And in this regard, the eye rest and the posing machine (*appui-tête*) are emblematic of the way the subject was made malleable.[97] Having one's picture taken meant being told what to think to encourage an expression and where to look while one was held in the invisible grip of the prosthetic device that shaped the body.[98] In the descriptions of the work of portraiture during the period, it is difficult to tell where the body of the subject as material for arrangement leaves off and where the "costume, draperies, and other various accessories" begin—all of which, in Sarony's argument, are employed to the ends of "evoking representation." But Sarony's artistic practice might better be described as "provoking" a representation in his patrons, since he often threw tantrums and left the room during the photographing session if a subject refused to cooperate with his vision. In Sarony, we see the unsettling implications of the concept of artistic evocation, a concept that suggests there can be no representation unless it is summoned from the subject who, held in the posing machine, yields up an image that is extracted as though it were a confession.

The power relations at work in the posing session suggest a structure of gender relations as well. Certainly the concept of the author as father of the work, which evolved in the Romantic notion of literary genius, could only complement the powers of the new proprietal author emerging at the end of the eighteenth century. Feminist criticism has historically theorized the writer or fine artist as fathering the work by means of the phallic pen or brush and chisel.[99] In contemporary feminist theories of photographic representation, however, the camera is not strictly analogous to the writing or drawing "instrument"; it is instead a dimension of the (male) photographer's instrumental "look," which merges with the camera's view. This controlling and constituting "look," originally theorized as a gendered trajectory, requires a female body as its object.[100] Applying this theory to the power relations involved in photographic sitting, Craig Owens suggests that the photographer's command of the body before the camera produces a power differential: "If, posing for a photograph, I freeze, it is not in order to assist the photographer, it is in some sense to resist him, to protect myself from his immobilizing gaze."[101] But despite the volume of work based on the paradigm of the look in film theory, later applied to still photography, painting, dance, and even literature, little has been done to explain not the controlling eye but the controlling hand. By "controlling hand" I mean the authorial positioning work, the staging and blocking of the theatrical and the motion picture director, and the compositional arrangement of the photographic and fine art portraitist.[102] The gender analysis suggests that there is a relay from eye to hand and from there to the controlling rights in the work.

In the mid- to late nineteenth century, we still find each man entitled to claim the inert matter over which he has exerted his will, in this case the body of the subject before the camera. And in 1882—seventeen years after Congress had recognized copyright in the photograph on the analogy with lithography—we see a strong case emerging for understanding the photographer as more than a servant of his technology.[103] But at least one case was made against the authorial right of the photographer on behalf of the authorial contribution of the subject in the photograph. In this particular case, Benjamin Falk, a New York photographer and Sarony's chief competition, filed suit against Donaldson Lithographic Company for producing a lithograph of the actress Julia Marlowe. Falk argued that the mass-produced lithograph infringed upon his rights to the photograph that he had taken in 1887 of Marlowe in the role of Parthenia in *Ingomar, the Barbarian*. Although the judge decided in favor of Falk, citing *Burrow-Giles* as precedent, Donaldson's case, which rested on the defense that the photograph was unprotectable because the photographer was a mechanic, contested the artistry of the photographer by proposing a competing artistry—that of the actress. Rephrasing the argument as it was put to him, the trial judge summarized: "An examination of the photograph shows that it is the work of an artist. The question is whether the artist was Miss Marlowe, or the complainant. How far the artistic contributions are to be attributed to the talent of Miss Marlowe, it is impossible to say."[104] In weighing the contribution of each artist, the judge read the image itself in an attempt to determine the creative share contributed by each. In answer to the "test" of originality put forward in *Burrow-Giles*, Donaldson argued that it was "absurd to suppose that the complainant (Falk) could have suggested to a trained actress like Miss Marlowe either costume, facial expression, or pose." And they went on to offer the testimony of a gas man working at the Bijou Theatre who had seen the actress on stage in the *same* pose. Further, they argued that the Greek dress was the conventional costume for playing such a part. And finally, the actress's hair was styled in the mode of the day (and therefore could not be seen as the creation of the "photographist").[105]

In support of his decision that Julia Marlowe's pose was the "work" of Falk, the judge argued that the side view represented in the image could only be a pose produced by someone other than Marlowe, who could not have judged on her own how to turn her body or raise her hands "so that the lights and shadows might best reveal the beauties of face and figure." Finally, the judge discovered, in a comparison between two photographs of Marlowe in similar poses, that Falk's interpretation could be detected: "[I]n the one, a pretty woman is standing for her picture; in the other, she has lost her personality in the character she has assumed, as interpreted in the pose chosen by the complainant."[106] The question here is "whose interpretative artistry" is at work? If the photographer emerges here as author with such ease, it may be because of the irony that the personhood of the photographic subject is made invisible by the artistry of the actor who convincingly portrays a character.[107] Later in history, this artistry would have to be reasserted, as I will discuss in later chapters.

This uneven relationship between photographer and photographed in the theatrical portrait business before the turn of the century is paralleled by the economic relations that obtained between them. Lithographers and photographers who claimed authorship in their work on the basis of originality and singularity were nevertheless artist and industrial mass producer in one. They sold theatrical photographs wholesale to salesmen who turned around and sold them in theaters and hotels or by mail order.[108] But, most important, photographers such as Falk and Sarony could make fortunes in this business because they retained the copyright in the theatrical portrait long after actors had contractually signed away any rights they might want to claim. Some actors received royalties later, but the most popular personalities (whose images were called "sure cards" in the trade) often had to be paid royalties in advance. A few of the spectacularly famous commanded large payments for sitting, and in effect challenged, in economic terms, the singular authority of the photographer. Actress Lily Langtry, for instance—to whom Sarony paid $5,000 for exclusive rights to her image—would not be melded into the photographer's interpretation of her, and she was reputed to have uncooperatively asserted her own vision during sittings.[109]

We still need to comprehend the potency of the ideology of authorship, which, after dismissing the challenge posed by a technology that re-created the world, would successfully assert itself over the evidence made visible on the face and surface of the work itself. While the subject-sitter posed the greatest threat to the fatherhood and legal subjecthood of the artist, the power relations between the two could be adjusted in favor of the artist by means of the contract. And in their indifference to *similarities* between works, both aesthetic theory and intellectual property doctrine have ignored generic or conventional features in favor of *differences* between works, distinguishing marks that could be attributed to an artist-originator. By the next century, intellectual property doctrine would become so accustomed to similarity that it would pretend less and less to find distinctions in the work and would be satisfied more and more with the mere fact of origin in the settlement of disputes.

This development should not be surprising, because what the notion of authorship always denies, as Foucault reminds us, is intertextuality, the connections between works.[110] The very concept of authorship overrides the generic and conventional indebtedness that would mark works as the product not so much of individuals as of societies. What the case for authorial copyright in the theatrical portrait must deny is the connection between the photographer's image and theatrical acting styles, the existence of a ready-made character (already invested with meanings), and iconographic conventions (a hybrid mix of high and low art). As in traditional aesthetics, these low origins are denied in the emulation of high art. And in the legal commentary on the Oscar Wilde photograph, the same holds true: Outside allegiances to popular conventions are overruled in favor of commonalities with the style of portrait painting that the photograph emulates.

In the arguments for their authorship of the pose, for instance, photographers Falk and Sarony cannot admit the influence of the traditions of melodramatic acting style, which dictated the fixedness of the actor's body, nor can they acknowledge the theatrical convention of concentrating emotional material in the fixed pose, the better to provide a summary for the audience. And perhaps the characteristic vacant look of the subjects of these photographs (in which we see more eyeball than pupil) may be attributed not only to the bodily rigidity required by the slower camera lenses but also to the tradition of acting as a kind of embodiment in which the physique was puffed up with emotion as a balloon with air.[111] (Hence the hardness and the absolute solidity of these bodies before Sarony's camera.) And perhaps it was the Delsartian method of acting, so popular at the time, that made each pose equal to an entire separate emotion, so that in this hieroglyphic language each stance was eloquent and complete unto itself.[112]

Most of all, though, there is in Sarony's work from this period the unmistakable echo of the theatrical poster—that vehicle for publicizing popular amusement that tended toward the hyperbolic—its imagery bulging with connotations. In Sarony as well there is a strong tendency toward the broad and the overblown in his more intimate portraits, many of which would have been sold outside theaters as companion pieces to the theatrical poster. In both works, the uses of costume and props (accessories) depend upon the widest knowledge of social types. The circus performer is summarized with the trapeze and the strong man with a leopard skin, the actress playing Lady Teazle in *The School for Scandal* is more powdered wig than face, the Shakespearean actor sits in a sixteenth-century chair, the actress in Greek dramas is photographed beside ivy-entwined columns, and the poet Wilde holds a leather-bound volume. Typification may speak more loudly than individuation (as it characteristically does in popular forms), and it is no wonder that we see the broad gesture and the emblematic accessory in the photographic portraits of Napoleon Sarony, who in his earlier lithographic work, in fact, helped to define the aesthetic of the theatrical poster in the U.S.![113]

But there was no ready-made discourse of prestige or property attached to Sarony's skill as a showman or his success as a mass producer. For the prestige that went with it, he increasingly identified himself, even as he brought suit against Burrow-Giles, with the Aesthetic Movement in photography. His homage to the full-length portrait in the style of Sir Joshua Reynolds and Thomas Gainsborough was certainly in the spirit of the

Pictorialist emulation of the old masters. And in 1870 he was, in fact, compared to Rembrandt:

> Discarding those few formal poses so familiar and so oppressive in photographs, he is able to make true and characteristic portraits in positions so various and so free that they rival not only those of the portrait painters, but those in which figures are represented in *genre* or historical paintings. He is master of light and shade, and produces heads which repeat the startling effects of Rembrandt's etchings with a truthfulness to the facts of nature that Rembrandt in the attainment of his effect sometimes disregarded.[114]

The rhetoric of Henry P. Robinson's *Pictorial Effect in Photography* (1869) was available at the time, and Sarony's work went on to follow the pattern set by those Pictorialists who transcended photography by reworking the mechanically produced image by hand as though it were a drawing or a painting.[115] Although much of Robinson's unusual work was created by exploring the technology—by rephotographing and reprocessing—Sarony preferred "photo-painting"—elaborate hand-coloring and retouching.[116] Two years before he died in 1896, he published the portfolio *Sarony's Living Pictures*, which was considered superior to his theatrical portraits—but as much because of the classical subject as his own hand-painting technique.[117] Finally, Sarony's own tortured outbursts attest to the degree to which the photographer must have been fatally summoned by the discourses on art circulated by the Pictorialists of his time:

> Think what I must suffer . . . fancy my despair. All day long I must pose and arrange for those eternal photographs. They *will* have me. Nobody but me will do; while I burn, I ache, I die, for something that is truly art. All my art in the photograph I value as nothing. I want to make pictures out of myself, to group a thousand shapes that crowd my imagination. This relieves me, the other oppresses me.[118]

The courts may have technically settled the question of artistry in the photograph, but the aesthetic debates in both Europe and the U.S. would continue for almost a century, "devious and confused," as Walter Benjamin has described them.[119] In arguing for the analogy between the photograph and the painting, in attempting to establish photography as an art form, early theorists of the photograph made a strategic but predictable error. As Benjamin points out, their position was doomed from the

outset, "for they undertook nothing less than to legitimize the photographer before the very tribunal he was in the process of overturning."[120]

Sandwich Man for Authors' Rights

More than a century after *Burrow-Giles*, what strikes us first about
the portrait of Oscar Wilde, as I have said, is the cardboard pose he
assumes. We now know that the argument for authorship in the image
hinged on Sarony's "posing the said Oscar Wilde" as well as his "disposing the light and shade." Such findings led the Supreme Court to conclude
that the image of Oscar Wilde was an "original work of art," the product
of Sarony's "intellectual invention" in a category in which he could claim
exclusive right. But what also strikes us more than a century later is that
while "Oscar Wilde" is represented by his photographic image, the photographer is represented by the signature "Sarony" in the lower left-hand
corner. What does the one author have to do with the other? Both
subjects have by now vacated the image itself as well as the right to it, so
why is it, then, that this particular photograph should still stand for
ownership in the image? Why is it reproduced on a full page as an
illustration accompanying the text of *Burrow-Giles* in the leading law
school casebook on U.S. entertainment litigation?[121] The answer is in the
posture, the position, the pose.

It is well known that Oscar Wilde's famed 1882 lecture tour of the U.S.
grew out of producer D'Oyly Carte's use of him to promote the New York
production of Gilbert and Sullivan's *Patience*. London theatergoers would
have known that the Reginald Bunthorne character in the play was a
caricature satirizing Whistler and Wilde as representatives of the excesses
of the new Aesthetic Movement. But since the debates that inspired the
mockery were unfamiliar to Americans, Wilde's tour was devised to
supplement their knowledge, if not to pique their interest in cultural
diversions imported from Britain by introducing them to Wilde as entertainment in and of himself. The British press may have lampooned D'Oyly
Carte's intention to use Wilde as "a sandwich man for 'Patience,'"[122] but
one account of the tour suggests that D'Oyly Carte's sponsorship of
Wilde helped to reinforce the producer's ownership in the Gilbert and
Sullivan property in the absence of American recognition of his copyright.
Wilde was positioned to guarantee the originality of the Carte production
against the pirated versions that were inevitabilities in New York.[123]

But if Wilde's pose was a front for Carte's theatrical copyright, in another way it was a promotion for Sarony's photographic copyright, and in this it functioned as an advertisement for authorship in the work. And it is in this sense that we might say that Wilde was a "sandwich man for authors' rights." Wilde's lecture tour is a remarkable example not only of how elite culture discourses on authorship depend upon the discourses of the popular but also of how the very circulation of elite culture en masse threatens to turn it into its opposite. For as Wilde took the attitudes of elite culture to American town halls and literary societies, he became the subject of parody in the local press, where cartoonists produced the long hair, velvet jacket, knee breeches, silk stockings, and lilies as popular signs of "affectation." At least three popular songs were written about him, and his poems were pirated and sold for ten cents a copy.[124] From the moment he arrived in New York and announced to the customs officer, "I have nothing to declare but my genius," he began to produce signs that could be doubly inflected as either a proclamation of intellectual superiority or a caricature of that proclamation. Wilde encouraged the production of the literary figure as celebrity in his remarks about the requests for autographs and locks of his hair,[125] and his dedication to "assuming a pose" tells us that he constructed *himself* as a "work."[126] But my main point is that Wilde could not have been thus constructed without the public articulation of the eccentric artist-type that preceded him. The 85,000 unauthorized photographs in circulation actually advanced not only Wilde's cause but also Sarony's in the long run, because they helped to popularize a paradigm: the opposition between the original and its copy. Wilde was the original for the Bunthorne "copy" of himself and for all those popular parodic copies of the artist type. He was also the source of "original" ideas and sayings that no other man or woman could utter without laying himself or herself open to the charge of having copied Wilde. And finally, Oscar Wilde is aligned with the original negative from which thousands of copies were printed—some of which became the "originals" from which the 85,000 infringing copies were produced.

But that is not all. The existence of a property to be exchanged requires a subject in law. An object is not property unless it is produced by a (creative) subject—by an author who intervenes in the mechanical-industrial production of the photograph, who "invests" his personality in the real before the camera. Without this "investment," the product of nature and the machine could not be claimed as private property. And although property in the self can be transferred to another party via a contract (so that the facial image may be owned by a second legal entity), the legal subjecthood of the person in the image still stands as a guarantee of personal property right in the abstract. In Edelman's theorization, because both photographer and photographed are in possession of themselves (and can sell their labor power), each can claim property in the image that contains "personality." As Kingdom and Hirst comment on the paradox: "The logic of the right of the photographer over his photograph also sanctions the right of the photographed over *his* image. In both cases the right derives from the subject being always-already possessor of itself and its attributes."[127] The author-subject in law, in other words, is a position-holder who makes ownership possible. So it is that Oscar Wilde's own subjecthood in the photograph secures Sarony's copyright in the photograph because they both inhabit identical positions as subjects in law.

But in American copyright doctrine, this legal position-holder produces its antithesis: the author-subject is evacuated from his privileged position in relation to his product. The photographic image may be owned by a second, succeeding party by virtue of the property-producing individuality of the first. There is a contradiction lurking in this formula, and we glimpse it in the foreseeable possibility that the creator might sell an "original work" and then try to reclaim it on the basis that it was *his* personality that made the work protectable in the first place. This hypothetical scenario, in fact, was tested in a 1914 copyright dispute that confirmed ownership over authorship in the photograph in U.S. intellectual property doctrine. In *Gross v. Seligman*, the photographer-artist Rochlitz posed a nude model sitting in profile with her arms around her knees. He sold the rights to this photograph, which he called "Grace of Youth," and it subsequently became popular. Two years after he took the first photograph, the artist produced a second photo, "Cherry Red," using the same model in a similar pose, but this time she held the stem of a cherry in her mouth. The owner of the "Grace of Youth" copyright sued the publisher of "Cherry Red" for infringing his right, arguing that the second photograph was not a new and original conception, but rather a copy of the first. The appeals court upheld the owner's argument.[128]

The court's decision was based on the premise that the photographer did not create a new image but copied one that no longer belonged to him, even though it was originally his own creation. To quote the court, "The identity of the artist and the many close identities of pose, light, and shade, etc., indicates very strongly that the first picture was used to produce the second."[129] The same signs of artistic conception (posing, the arrangement of "light and shade") used in *Burrow-Giles* to argue for the creativity of the photographic work are used to prove "copying." Here originality is suddenly turned against the originator. The artist's first exercise of individuality (the wedge into the work that makes it possible for the owner to charge the artist with infringement) makes it impossible for the artist either to produce or to reproduce the second original conception.[130]

From the point of view of Edelman's theory, then, the "Oscar Wilde" before the camera inhabited a cardboard position: the subject in law. Because his right to property in himself mirrors the photographer's right to property in his product, Oscar Wilde, too, is a place-holder for capital. Now the most difficult question of all: To what degree does this category of legal subjectivity impinge upon other categories of subject construction outside the law? What, for instance, does it have to do with the position constructed for the ideal subject viewer in representation? And what, if anything at all, does this have to do with what has been called the deconstructive turn of the gay sensibility and the transgressive edge of Wilde's fiction as well as his criticism, asserted with even more radical significance in his outrageously unconventional life-as-work than in his "life's work"? Does Wilde's embrace of the "pose" as a way of life and as a critical category suggest a detachability from legal categories as well as from the categories of "masculinity" and "femininity" proposed for us, to us, in representation?[131] Is it possible that we may be more thoroughly inscribed in and through one kind of position than in and through another? That whereas (because of the distanciation of a gay sensibility) one might refuse the culture's proffered positions of sexual difference, one might still be repositioned as a legal subject whose separate self-possession is requisite to the functioning of not only the legal system but the capitalist state itself? Aesthetic and legal discourses meet again and again in the photograph at different historical junctures. Do they confirm or undo one another? At the same time that the photographic portrait appears as the fundamental confirmation of self-possession (the proud banner and badge of property in the self), do the multiple selves we have via the photographic image destroy the old self-containment of the (humanist) self we thought we had?

CHAPTER THREE

Dead Ringer

JACQUELINE ONASSIS AND THE LOOK-ALIKE

In *Ownership of the Image*, Bernard Edelman shows how nineteenth-century French law originally would not extend legal protection to the photograph because it was machine-produced, thus denying it protection as the work of an author-creator, and how the law later reversed its position, maintaining that the photographer *did* have an author's right in the photograph. But the author was admitted at this stage, Edelman says, on condition that he not merely "reproduce" the "real" before the camera but actually "produce" it.[1] He must become a creator of it. Much of Edelman's argument has to do with showing how the creative subject inserted between the world before the camera and the machine itself is that legal subject who has been historically constructed as holding rights. This notion of the subject endowed with rights in turn depends upon an earlier Hegelian sense of the free subject who possesses both himself and his attributes or characteristics.[2]

But what if the real (before the camera) is neither municipal building nor landscape scene, which as public domain belong to everyone, but instead is the face and figure of another person who, by the same basic principle, already owns the real that the photographer appropriates? As Edelman theorizes this issue: "The subject makes 'his' a real which also belongs to the 'other.' In the very moment they invest the real with their personality, the photographer and the film-maker apprehend the property of the other—his image, his movement, and sometimes 'his private life'— in their 'object-glass,' in their lens."[3] It is, as it happens, this same subject thus apprehended who, by virtue of the possession of himself and his attributes, lays claim to the image of himself in the photograph. Thus it is
84 that, as Edelman points out, two contradictory claims can be advanced

over the same object before the camera, both with their basis in a culturally secured notion of personhood and personality.

I want to move from Edelman's point about the intervention of the
photographer as creative subject in the act of picture-taking to concentrate on the construction of the legal real on the other side of the camera,
so to speak, taking with me Edelman's concept of the insertion of the legal
subject. For it seems to me that there is a kind of symmetry in the way the
photographer-subject stands in relation to the mechanical act and the way
the photographed-subject stands (on the other side, now) in relation to
the natural body before the camera. What I want to consider next is how it
is that the law deals with conflicting claims advanced by two different legal
subjects who assert proprietorship over the same photographic likeness,
on the basis that they are both entitled to "authorize" the use of their own
images. The notion of "authorization" importantly emphasizes the symmetry of the photographer and the photographed, both of whom assert
"something irreducibly" their own,[4] something unique, that no one else
could possibly assert in the identical way. The photographer and the
photographed might also be seen as having a parallel material-mechanical
connection with the photographic act, the one having clicked the shutter
(and in French law thus having effected the "imprint of personality")[5] and
the other having left an imprint on the chemically sensitive surface of the
photographic film or plate effected by light reflected from her own bodily
presence. It hardly needs repeating that in both cases the claim of the
subject is based on the notion that even though this is the act of a machine,
the contribution of the personality outweighs what might be considered
purely mechanical functions.

The right of the photographer is also similar to the right of the photographed because of an underlying deference to "origin" in Anglo-
American law. Authorship in copyright law, as I discussed in chapter 2, is
understood as meaning "originating" as much as or more than "originality" in the sense of uniqueness. The human subject before the camera
could, in some senses, be seen as the origin of the photographic image:
that is, following the cause-and-effect version of how photography works,
the subject's physical presence creates the image-impression. This version
of the process might correspond to Charles Sanders Peirce's concept of the
indexical relation between the sign (the photograph) and the referent (the
subject before the camera), in which case the subject is a kind of origina-

tor. The subject as the originating source stands in relation to his photo-graph as, for instance, Christopher Wren stood in relation to the form of the death mask produced by his facial features.[6]

Where the subject behind the camera (the photographer) differs from the subject before the camera is in the advantage the latter enjoys by virtue of a onetime appearance as "reality." However fleeting the fraction of a second before the camera, early attempts to theorize photography and motion pictures gave significant weight to that fraction of experience. Not only could the photograph testify to the existence of an empirical world, but it was itself a kind of translucent "skin" of that real.[7] Although contemporary theories of film and photography have been dedicated to showing up the fallacy of the claims to truth status made by and for photographic signs, common sense persists in granting this special status to these images. And it is this commonsense assumption about the empiri-cal real and its evidence (which tempts even the most sophisticated of theorists in their everyday lives) that is often, though not always, at work in the legal decisions that interest me here.

For instance, as I will show in chapter 6, privacy doctrine and the publicity right that has evolved out of it (as they have dealt with issues regarding celebrity images), depend upon an unexamined assumption that the unauthorized use of a photograph is an appropriation of the identity of the person photographed.[8] The authority of the real here is seen in the way the photographic image serves as the support for the reassertion of the rights of the subject photographed, assumed to be the same subject whose resemblance is, so to speak, "captured" in the image. We will later see how in a 1972 California trial involving a dispute over the image of Bela Lugosi in the role of Dracula, the judge found that Lugosi's right of privacy did survive him, resulting in a decision in favor of the Lugosi family over the actor's former employer, Universal Pictures. Ac-cording to the reasoning of the judge in this first decision, although Lugosi was not alive to object to any invasion of his privacy caused by Universal's use of his photograph in the role of Dracula on T-shirts and swizzle sticks, the photographic "proof" of his existence in the past overwhelmed the portion of the image shared with the fictional character Dracula. Although the California Court of Appeals later reversed this decision and the state supreme court finally upheld the appellate reversal in 1979, the point is that *Lugosi v. Universal Pictures, Inc.*, suggests the threat posed to the law by the return of the referent. Bela Lugosi, a person no longer alive and thus not able to assert a right of privacy, still asserts a presence more potent (although with fewer legal teeth) than the character of the Count, which is still protected by the Universal Pictures copyright in the motion picture *Dracula* (1931). The presence of Bela Lugosi's body (before the camera) in the past, preserved intact in the image in the present, threatens to displace the right to Bela Lugosi as Dracula that Universal Pictures argued that it held in perpetuity.[9]

What, however, does the law do with a photographic likeness of a living celebrity that has not been created in the past by that celebrity's physical presence but has its origins in the empirical body of a second person before the camera? According to the spirit of privacy doctrine, which assumes an identity between the photographic sign and its referent, the person to whom the photographic image "belongs" is the person ultimately concerned with the use of the image. It would seem that the owner of the body before the camera is the legal subject whose publicity right is at stake and who is negotiating the right to have his or her privacy invaded. But the question becomes somewhat different when one legal subject is a celebrity and the other is an ordinary person who has an identity of her own. Whose identity is signified, the identity of the person to whom the body belongs or the identity of the celebrity? Can one body (without the aid of a masquerade) stand for two identities at once?

Onassis v. Dior

Those are the issues raised on appeal in a 1984 right of privacy action heard by the Supreme Court of New York. In this action, Jacqueline Kennedy Onassis brought suit against Christian Dior for use of her image without consent in an advertisement for Dior sportswear. The image of Jackie Onassis appeared in a one-page color photograph portraying the mock wedding of the Diors, a fictional couple created in a series of advertisements photographed by Richard Avedon for J. Walter Thompson's Lansdowne Division (fig. 2). The staged wedding advertisement appeared in the September or October 1983 issues of *Harper's Bazaar*, *Esquire*, *Time*, *The New Yorker*, and *New York* magazines, along with the caption "The wedding of the Diors was everything a wedding should be: no tears, no rice, no in-laws, no smarmy toasts, for once no Mendelssohn. Just a legendary private affair."[10] To suggest the social prominence of the fictional Diors, actresses Ruth Gordon and Shari Belafonte and television film reviewer Gene Shalit were represented along with Jacqueline Onassis in the crowd watching the bride throw the customary bouquet.

Onassis brought suit against Dior on the basis of a violation of her right of privacy granted by sections 50 and 51 of the New York civil rights law, which prohibit the commercial use of the portrait of a living person without consent.[11] To knowingly use for trade purposes the "name, portrait, or picture" of any living person without written consent gives rise to criminal and civil liability. The injured party is entitled to recovery of damages and the right to injunction. Onassis, who sought an injunction on the basis that she had suffered irreparable injury, maintained in an affidavit that she did not give consent for the use of her image in the Dior campaign and that she had never allowed her name or her picture to be used in conjunction with advertisements for commercial products. Only in a very few instances had she given consent for the use of her name in connection with the arts, education, or civic causes with which she was affiliated.[12]

The defendant's argument in this case was that the New York law of privacy had not been violated. The woman in the photograph was not, after all, Jacqueline Kennedy Onassis, but Barbara Reynolds, a Washington secretary hired by Dior as a model for the advertisement. Dior's position was based on the fact that the person photographed was Barbara Reynolds and that it was her identity that had been used, with her permission. The Dior lawyers argued that Onassis sought to prohibit Reynolds from using what was, after all, Reynolds's own image. Or, as Judge Edward J. Greenfield phrased this issue, "[C]an one person enjoin the use of someone else's face?"[13]

Barbara Reynolds was described in the case headnote as "masquerading" as Jacqueline Onassis, and the judge stated that she had "misappropriated" Onassis's identity. But what must be understood immediately is that Barbara Reynolds did not disguise herself with the aid of props, costumes, or special makeup, which would indicate that she has assumed a false identity. Neither was she an actress playing the role of the famous wife of the former president. If she was not disguised and if she did not use an actor's skills of impersonation, how is it that she was seen as someone else? Barbara Reynolds was taken to be Jacqueline Onassis because, colloquially, she "looks like" Jacqueline Onassis—so much so, in fact, that she worked part-time for the Los Angeles firm Ron

The wedding of the Diors was everything a wedding should be: no tears, no rice, no in-laws, no smarmy toasts, for once no Mendelssohn. Just a legendary private affair.

Jacqueline Onassis Look-alike (From an advertisement in the *New Yorker,* 10 October 1983)

Smith Celebrity Look-Alikes, making appearances as Jacqueline Kennedy Onassis.

The Legal Real

In criminal cases the law tends to regard the camera as witness and the photograph as empirical proof of events in the real world. When it comes to cases of image appropriation, which are usually taken up in terms of the "likeness," the emphasis upon identification and recognizability suggests that legal practice has again constructed the representational image as transparent. The question of recognition becomes, "Could one see the person in the likeness?" In its discussion of the Dracula image, the California Supreme Court made a distinction between the likeness of Lugosi in the portrayal of Dracula and Lugosi's "natural" likeness, but the medium conveying this likeness would seem to have evaporated. Does "natural" likeness in this case refer to a drawing that resembles, to a photographic image of Lugosi himself, or to his real-life physical features?

The point is that privacy law has tended to treat iconic likeness as straightforward and unproblematic: A likeness is that which someone recognizes as someone else. What makes the Onassis case significant is not only that the law is forced to take the conveyors or vehicles of likeness into consideration in its decision but also, in deciding whether or not the image of Jacqueline Onassis had been appropriated by Dior, the law had to construct the legal real. By "legal real" I do not mean a real that operates only within the closed system of Anglo-American law, since, because of the relation between law and society, the construction will have ramifications elsewhere. Suggesting the way this concept works, Paul Hirst and Elizabeth Kingdom say, "Law both 'imaginadely' fixes and sanctions social relations. It compels things to be as it recognizes they are."[14] What *Onassis v. Dior* shows is that the real we would have expected the law to recognize does not turn out to be the final real. If the law of privacy were interested in the empirical evidence offered by the photograph, there would be no doubt that the image in question belonged to Barbara Reynolds and therefore that Dior had a right to use it. But photographic realism and privacy doctrine in this case want different guarantees. The one defers to a conviction that there is a final, verifiable, empirical real, and the other defers to a construction of personhood that does not necessarily require the existence of a real body (whether in the past or the present) as its support.

Photographic realism, with its empirical stance, asks, "Who is the real referent?" But privacy law is finally not interested in this question. First of all, let's look at how the judge in *Onassis v. Dior* got around the issue of the empirical evidence of the photograph. In his ruling, Judge Greenfield aligned the case with precedents based on the problem of appropriation of the image without authorization in a wide range of media—from sound recording to literary fiction. The "truth" status of the photographic image was thus circumvented by the court's interpretation of the New York Civil Code's "portrait or picture" in the widest possible way as "a representation which conveys the essence and likeness of an individual, not only actuality, but the close and purposeful resemblance to reality."[15] In other words, Dior may not have appropriated Jacqueline Onassis's *photograph*, but it used her "portrait or picture" without permission. And thus the court declared that for legal purposes, Barbara Reynolds's photo was Jacqueline Onassis's "portrait or picture."

In arguing that it does not matter whether resemblance is created with recorded sound, photography, drawing, or word portrait, the law whisks away any privileged relation between the subject before the camera and the photograph. Essentially, then, what the Onassis decision did was to skip over the photographic signifier medium and to consider only the look-alike body as medium, the signifier whose signified is "Jacqueline Onassis."

The legal problem posed by the look-alike returns us to the epistemological issues raised by the iconic sign. We are again faced with Umberto Eco's "mysterious phenomenon of the image which 'resembles'" and which is commonly thought to deliver the world to us in some way, whether by capturing some part of it or by reflecting it back.[16] And if we stop at the photographic sign, that is just what we have before us—an image of the wife of the former president. Except that the image in question is not the photographic image of Jacqueline Onassis. We are dealing not just with an image that resembles but rather with an image of a person who resembles. And if the iconicity of the photographic sign has made it susceptible to transparency, to our seeing through it, then how do we consider the iconicity of the look-alike, which is transparent only if we actually mistake her for the celebrity referent? And if we don't mistake her for the celebrity, but take the person to be herself, then the look-alike in this case is not operating as a sign, since something cannot stand in for or represent something with which it is identical.

The perversity of the look-alike phenomenon is that we *are* tempted to say, "But the woman in the photograph really *is* Barbara Reynolds," and for a moment we are returned to the stage in the theorization of iconic signs at which these illusive signifiers seemed to have successfully eluded systematic analysis. We rehearse the dilemma of the semiotician's approach to photography, cinema, and television, those mimetic technologies that mass-produce look-alike signs. We understand again the legacy of the false start in this field—Roland Barthes's declaration that the photograph was a message without a code.[17] And we realize how very little theoretical help we have (as well as very little confirmation of what we see as astonishing similarity) in Eco's correction of Barthes: If the only thing that the iconic sign has in common with its referent is the perceptual habituation of the viewer who confronts two similar visual patterns, then why are we so impressed with and so susceptible to being convinced by look-alike signs?[18]

It might at this time be useful to say that the frustration with the iconic sign is entirely a poststructuralist condition. In a way, then, the Onassis case confirms the poststructuralist insight about the way signification works, since we have in the legal dilemma an admission that the meaning of the figure in the Dior ad is indeterminable, or at least put off indefinitely. It even seems that we have nabbed the discourse of advertising in the very act of creating the postmodern aesthetic, in Jean Baudrillard's words, "the virtual and irreversible confusion of images and the sphere of a reality, whose principle we can grasp less and less."[19] The admitted goal of the creators of the campaign featuring a semiscandalous ménage à trois in the style of the film *Design for Living* was, after all, "to specify nothing but suggest everything."[20] But it would seem that it is the Onassis and not the Dior argument that is aligned with postmodernism and poststructuralism. While Dior's argument about the photograph is in essence, "it is what it *is*," the Onassis argument, "it is what it *says* it is," comes down on the side of the reader.[21] It appears, then, that since the law doesn't hold the photographic sign at its word, it is just as well that we no longer consider that sign able to access the real world, and therefore we cannot expect it to take any responsibility for what happens in that world.

Isn't that, after all, the conclusion that feminist film theory came to in regard to the cinematic representation of the female body? In our earliest formulations, commercial cinema used her body decoratively, negating "woman," who as "woman" could never be grasped or signified by patriarchal discourses.[22] Later, the argument was advanced that not only was she not really present in representation but her femininity was itself a masquerade.[23] Even the documentary film that featured women's struggles in the workplace (showing their real relations to production) could not be said to deliver the "truth" of their oppressive circumstances or the analysis of the economic conditions that maintained these circumstances.[24] There were, after all, no real bodies or actual lives that we could hope to know about in any other way except via the photographic, linguistic, and electronic signs that delivered them to us. Is Barbara Reynolds, then, part of this long legacy of female body signs fitted up as models and actresses in magazine advertising, television drama, and fiction film, drained of meaning and stripped of identity in order to serve as vehicles for the discourses of commerce?

But isn't there something slightly different about the Barbara Reynolds case? One could say that the law is on some level concerned about the commercial appropriation of bodies and that it was deployed as an objection on behalf of society to the way Dior emptied Barbara Reynolds's body in order to fill it with the connotation "Jacqueline Onassis." The judge's concerns were stated in terms of the theft of the celebrity's identity, but he also asked what should be done with the identity claim of the noncelebrity as he returned to the issue: "[C]an one person enjoin the use of someone else's face?" From my point of view, the significance of the Onassis case *is* the stand it took against "theft" of identity as well as against the "confusion" of identities. At this point, however, my argument will swerve away from the concerns of feminist film theory. Therefore, I will not be objecting to the commercial uses of the female body. I have a different interest in "theft" and "confusion," terms that open out onto legal issues that I will consider in the following chapter on unfair competition law and that thus lead in another direction. In the end, protection of personhood, difficult to fault from a humanistic point of view, turns into something quite different as it contributes (incrementally and almost imperceptibly) to the creation of a new legal entity. That entity (which I have not yet identified) is one and the same as the "legal real" to which Judge Greenfield defers and which wins out over the photographic real and its claim.

While the law in *Onassis v. Dior* appeared to be concerned only with personal injury and unauthorized appropriation, it was equally concerned with other principles signaled by the references to "theft" and "confusion." In order to show up the double development whereby it becomes possible to engage sympathy for prohibiting injury to one's feelings in support of prohibiting injury to one's commercial value (a distinctly different kind of offense), I need to refer back briefly to the origins of privacy law in New York. The issues that are primary in *Onassis* were first raised in *Roberson v. Rochester Folding Box Co.* (1902), in which Abigail Roberson objected to the unauthorized use of her photographic image on a flour-mill-company advertising poster placed in warehouses, saloons, and other public places. Roberson was denied relief in this case, but the public outcry in response to the outcome encouraged the legislature to enact a statute prohibiting the use of a person's name, portrait, or picture for trade without his or her consent.[25] The original spirit of sections 50 and 51 of the 1903 New York Civil Rights Act was, as one would expect, maintained in Judge Greenfield's language in *Onassis*:

> If we truly value the right of privacy in a world of exploitation, where every mark of distinctiveness becomes grist for the mills of publicity, then we must give it more than lip service and grudging recognition. Let the word go forth—there is no free ride. The commercial hitchhiker seeking to travel on the fame of another will have to learn to pay the fare or stand on his own two feet.[26]

Privacy, the umbrella doctrine encoded in sections 50 and 51, and at issue in *Roberson* and later *Onassis*, does not, however, have its origins in protection against marketplace exploitation. Neither does it derive from a concept of defamation, as one might expect. The branch of American law referred to as "privacy" has its historical origins in a particular idea of a right to seclusion from the public eye, which I will deal with at length in chapter 6. Paradoxically, over the course of this century, the same doctrine that promised to shelter private persons from the public circulation of their names and likenesses (an inevitability produced by the development of mass information technologies) has come to allow the reverse. Privacy law as it becomes publicity law makes it possible for celebrities to circulate their images in public without fear of commercial piracy.[27]

There is an equally important question that suggests a historical parallel with the development of "privacy" into "publicity," and it is worth a digression here to fill out this perspective. The question is this: Why is it that the public circulation of a person's photographic likeness should be analogous to intrusion into one's private life, analogous even to the public exposure of inner thoughts and feelings? Social historians have shown that the notion of the body as somehow synonymous with selfhood is a modern concept. The contemporary sense we have of the body as expressive of the notion of a "personality," evidenced on it through gesture and expression, almost as an involuntary symptom, is as recent as the turn of the century.[28] But whereas one might think that the use of a mechanical instrument would interfere with the pure essence of the person before the camera (as it had negated the unique touch of the photographer-creator in French legal history), portrait photography was thought to investigate scientifically, to probe the "inner" character, more and more thought to be the "true" person.[29] Why is it that two layers of mediation (the face as medium in addition to the photograph), rather than distancing or distorting, are thought to render the "real" person more immediate?

Film theorists from Béla Balázs to Roland Barthes and Gilles Deleuze have considered the language of the motion picture close-up, which seems to have ratified the contemporary currency of and the recent fascination with the face. Although early critics argued that the close-up was a kind of disorienting dismemberment, Balázs would argue that it was not a part but had come to assume the proportions and the significance of a self-sufficient whole.[30] Deleuze would take Balázs a step further and suggest that the image of the face in close-up (the affection-image) is a "component of all images" and a quality ("faceicity") transferrable to representations of other parts of the body and even to other objects.[31] The question arises as to why the face would fuse so easily with the forms produced by new mechanical and electronic technologies. And why, further, in the face (so to speak) of the potential of mass replication, would the face in close-up still stand for the individual, one-of-a-kind personality? It is almost as though the Romantic ideal of humanness, developed as a countervaluation against the institution of "the market," had persistently planted itself right where it had been permanently obliterated—in the reproducible image of the human face. If the face were unreadable and unfathomable, epitomized by the image of Garbo, which, Barthes says, "plunged audiences into the deepest ecstasy,"[32] why would the image-visage still be a means of identification, based on its readability? At some point, Deleuze says, when the close-up is taken to the limit, as in Ingmar Bergman's modernist moments when the depths of the face engulf us in nothingness, individuation is "suspended."[33] Andy Warhol's postmodern postage-stamp portraits of Liz Taylor, Elvis Presley, and Marilyn Monroe make this clear: Individuation is stamped-out, mass-produced. So why the insistence that the photographic portrait is one's identity when by now it should be clear that the image has undergone a thorough transformation and even devaluation in this regard?

Onassis v. Dior asserted the opposite, that is, that in the contemporary world the face has come to stand for the honor and integrity of the individual. Judge Greenfield advanced the position that the facial image had superseded the name, which was once thought to be personhood's nugget of value. After citing Shakespeare on how for men and women the good name is "the immediate jewel of their souls,"[34] the judge went on, "In those days, as the touchstone of recognition, name was all, conveyed in writing or by word of mouth. Today, the visual have superseded the verbal arts, and news photography, television, and motion pictures can accord instant world-wide recognition to a face. For some people, even without their American Express cards, the face is total identification, more than a signature or a coat of arms."[35] The judge further asked why it was that, since the image was "total recognition," the unauthorized use of it was not treated as similar to the use of a person's signature: "The unauthorized use of a person's signature would not pass muster under the statute because it was claimed merely to be a facsimile. Is a picture or a portrait intended to look like someone not that person's picture if it is similarly a facsimile or a simulation?"[36]

The emphasis on facsimile is finally telling in another way. As we have seen, for privacy law, the "real" is not the natural world. This law is finally not interested in what is commonly thought to be a natural bond between the body and the self, summarized in the idea of proper name, personal image, and the self-evidence of the identity between the body and the person, which tautologically becomes "proof of identity." Privacy law is no longer, if it ever was, about personal offense and affrontery. In *Onassis v. Dior*, it is structured along lines of copyright law, which asks questions about authorial creativity in order to determine whether or not there has been theft of a work. In a way, this explains the jaded attitude the decision takes toward look-alikeness. Copyright law, having seen so much of similarity, is unimpressed with it, and thus returns some sanity to the iconic sign. In this regard, I like what W. T. J. Mitchell has said about the problem semiotics has had with systematizing analogical representation.

Iconicity, it seems, is everywhere: "One reason the icon has proved so difficult for semiotics to define is that similarity is such a capacious relationship that almost anything can be assimilated into it. Everything in the world is similar to everything else in some respects."[37] Copyright law, then, cannot be based on the commonsense notion of absolute uniqueness or a one-of-a-kind ideal. It recognizes claims based on firstness in order to break ties when two objects of culture appear to be identical or, in legal terms, "substantially similar."[38] In order to dismiss Dior's claim that Barbara Reynolds had a right to use her image as she saw fit, the judge constructed the Dior ad as similar to an act of plagiarism, a substitution of a copy for the real: "The juxtaposition of the counterfeit figure just behind the real-life figures of a veteran actress, a television personality, and a well-known model lends to the whole ensemble an air of verisimilitude and accentuates the grievance, for it imparts an aura of authenticity to the trumped-up tableau."[39] Further, the judge's remarks echoed the terms of the Romantics' disdain for imitation, now become the commonsense wisdom of the elementary school science lesson: "While some imitators may employ artistry in the use of voice, gesture and facial expression, a mere similarity of features is no more artistry than the mimicry of the Monarch butterfly by its look alike, the Viceroy butterfly. To paint a portrait of Jacqueline Kennedy Onassis is to create a work of art; to look like Jacqueline Kennedy Onassis is not."[40] Theoretically, then, would copyright law defer to Barbara Reynolds's claim if she had impersonated Jacqueline Onassis or if she had painted her picture? If Reynolds had performed a parodic interpretation of Onassis, U.S. copyright law would have protected that expression. Or, if the model had painted the image of Onassis, it would have been protectable as an "original work of authorship." However, Barbara Reynolds cannot just "be herself" and advance any claim to the "portrait" of Jacqueline Onassis that her face and body effortlessly make. She must produce this likeness.[41] We come around again to Edelman, and although still on the other side of the camera, we note the remarkable symmetry in these two problems in the production of the real. Just as French law would not defer to the claim of the photographer without first seeing his human hand at work "producing" the real, so the look-alike cannot by nature and sheer existence be the image of a celebrity, but must "produce" that likeness as a fine artist. Neither the mechanical act nor the fluke of nature is protectable without the intervention of the authorial hand of the creative subject. The body of Barbara

Reynolds is a mere copy of the body of Jacqueline Onassis produced by no one (and here it is clear that the divine hand has no legal subjecthood); a sketch, the judge called Barbara Reynolds's body—a sketch evidencing neither "creativity" nor "originality." According to this interpretation, although one can "authorize" the use of one's image, one cannot "author" one's physiognomy.[42] An actor or actress may use the "raw material" of his or her own physical features and bodily endowments as ingredients in a star image, but he or she must create a public persona, and with that a secondary meaning (requiring public recognition), in order to have a fully protectable image-property.[43] This is yet another reminder that the "real" to which privacy law defers (and that it has itself created) is not the empirical real (as we would have thought). What, then, is this real, reconstituted, as Edelman says, as a legal object "susceptible to appropriation, sale, and contracts?"[44]

I have argued thus far that the Onassis case shows that privacy law, contrary to our expectations, does not automatically defer to the authority of a real tangible presence backing up the photographic image and neither does it hold that the signifier is bound to its real-world referent. The "real" that is signified, although intangible, is nevertheless constituted by the law as its "real." The law does not always match up rights with empirical bodies, as we know from the struggles of the women's movement to assert the right to abortion as a woman's right to control her own body. Rather, the law respects rights in the "real" that it constructs. It is a characteristic of law, says Edelman, to recognize reciprocally through legal mechanisms the very legal subject that it has constituted.[45] And that is what the law did in *Onassis v. Dior.* Dior came up against a "real" that was already the property of another subject, an intangible property (the image), but nonetheless a property and nonetheless constituted as more "real" than a body before a camera. The question "[C]an one person enjoin the use of another person's face?" might then mean that the judge did not deny Barbara Reynolds's property in her own face. In legal terms, two rights were asserted that matched up with two property-images. One way that the judge could then find for one property over another would be to argue that one of the two properties had been "stolen" on the analogy of infringement in copyright law. Thus the objection to the Dior advertisement was that using the natural body of the look-alike was copying the original, protected body. But the final concern, and, in my analysis, the unacknowledged issue upon which the outcome of the case rested, was not copying but the "confusion" of the copy with the original. To quote Judge Greenfield: "No one has an inherent or constitutional right to pass himself off for what he is not."[46] "Passing off" and "likelihood of confusion," of course, are tests of trademark violation, not copyright infringement.[47] Trademark, a branch of unfair competition law, regulates the marketplace by upholding clarity of delineation between products and consistency in the indication of commercial sources standing behind consumer goods. This law stands against the attempt to confuse the consumer and the attempt to misrepresent or pass off the goods of one merchant as the goods of another. The "passing off" argument in *Onassis v. Dior* indicates a parallel development in privacy law, which is nowhere more clearly seen than in the right of publicity, affirmed in state statutes in the later half of the eighties. What we see in *Onassis* is that the image is, as it were, more protectable on the analogy with commercial property than it is on the analogy with the person who experiences injury to feelings, the older basis of privacy. This also means that if the judge was ultimately concerned about "passing off," then the decision in favor of Onassis was not a decision *for* the multiplicity of meaning but against it. And therefore those who view postmodern culture with alarm should not be concerned. U.S. courts, as they resolve disputes in terms of "passing off," are holding the line against massive slippage.

Dior, then, attempted to appropriate intangible private property—the image of Jacqueline Kennedy Onassis. And Dior lost the suit. The judge's assertion that the image of the wife of a former president was protectable private property has ramifications beyond the publication of one advertisement that ran in several upscale magazines in 1983. Because of its status as private property, if it appears as an illustration within a scholarly publication it is at the risk of being enjoined.[48] For the entire text of the advertising copy in question is now placed in a kind of authorial limbo. If, as the answer to my request for permission to reprint the advertising copy suggests, Christian Dior–New York, Incorporated, is not "at liberty" to authorize the reproduction of this text, the question remains whether Jacqueline Onassis is "at liberty" to authorize the use of Barbara Reynolds's face, as she could encounter, in reverse, the private property "real" of the other woman's image. This problem in the circulation of texts that are at once shared culture and private property lurks in every public use of such protected discourse. I am reminded of Judge Learned Hand's description of the ordinary sign that achieves secondary meaning and thus protected trademark status as wearing its protection as a "penumbra" or fringe.[49] And culture that is widely circulated yet tightly held as private property is similarly edged or bordered on all sides.

The Semiotics Lesson

Does *Onassis v. Dior* then have implications for other scholarly endeavors? I am thinking of the elementary semiotics lesson, which features a comparison between two versions of Jacqueline Kennedy's 1967 trip to Cambodia based on a close analysis of an American and a French magazine cover. As the *Life* cover has coded her, Onassis is apparently only vacationing, but on the cover of *Paris-Match*, she is part of the ritual afforded royalty. In Guy Gauthier's "The Semiology of the Image," these two photographs are constituted as an object of study, examples of the codes of culture that students are led to analyze in terms of the dress and posture of the president's wife, her relation to other figures in the frame, the style of the photographs, and the linguistic text accompanying them.[50] Gauthier's "Initiation à la semiologie de l'image," translated and published by the British Film Institute in 1976 as a study unit complete with slides and still widely used in film studies courses in Britain and the United States, is an introduction to the politics of the image. And what is most political about the "publicity image," as John Berger dubbed the photographic product of consumer culture, is that which is seemingly absent from the image we perceive.[51] In our teaching we tease out the cultural knowledge backing up the taken-for-granted codes of the world that stood before the camera, and we stress the stages and conditions of the material production of glossy advertising images. But we do not ask about the conditions that determine whether such images as those of Jacqueline Kennedy, Adolf Hitler, George Wallace, and Mary Ann Vecchio (the runaway who became the national symbol of the Kent State tragedy) could be reproduced as covers of *Life*, *Paris-Match*, *Der Spiegel*, and *Newsweek*, and reproduced again as classroom texts. Each case is slightly different. The image of Adolf Hitler, for instance, is produced by an anonymous defacing of the image of George Wallace. One would think this a clear case of a caricature that belongs to the world, except that it appears on the cover of a German magazine and would be protected by its copyright. The right of the publisher is also asserted in the boldface

Newsweek logo crowning the famous Pieta-like pose of Mary Ann Vecchio, now rephotographed from the original, retouched and reprocessed until it emerges as the emblem of the Kent State deaths.

But the subject of my inquiry is as much the more problematic commercial use of the celebrity image, a use that U.S. courts do not exempt as either cultural heritage or news even when the life of the person photographed is newsworthy. These are the images in which the emergent publicity right of the person photographed can displace the right of photographer, publisher, and employer. The marks of labor are effaced in these images by the deep impression of ownership, which often involves no labor whatsoever. This impression is the stamp of the face itself. Both residue of real person and effective mark of trade, the face fully determines the proprietary status of the image while leaving neither trace nor clue of this mark, the epitome of self-effacement. In the classic cases of commercial image appropriation involving Cary Grant, Cher Bono, and Clint Eastwood, not to mention Bela Lugosi, we have an inkling of what Deleuze means when he says that it is the face that is the vampire.[52] Since the ideology of private property (the assumption that everything in the world is privately owned by someone) diverts us from the question of protection and reproducibility, we are not inclined to think of the meaning of the image as related in any way to the proprietary attachments on it. If the question comes up at all, we generally take it up with reference to the polite concept "permission." Why? Do we in fact also take for granted that if an image is mechanically produced it is therefore meant to be unproblematically "seen"? This question has to do with private as opposed to public looking—a whole new problem that invites consideration.

And what would seem to be more unproblematically public than the events surrounding the Kent State tragedy and the presidential visit to Cambodia? Those events are newsworthy and historically significant. U.S. copyright law, of course, provides for the public interest in the doctrine of "fair use," which expresses a commitment to free dissemination of ideas as an exception to private right restrictions on the circulation of reproducible culture. Furthermore, it is customary for the law to exempt celebrity images constructed as "political speech" from such protection as would curtail free circulation of such expression.[53] In cases early in the century, it was established that news could not be copyrighted.[54] Likewise, it is generally held that history cannot be copyrighted.[55] But a closer examination of the common law relevant to intellectual property suggests that the proprietary status of information is a matter of constant contestation and that the private claims on what we thought was our cultural heritage are often asserted with success. As we have seen in *Onassis v. Dior*, private claims do effectively attach themselves to discourses that have cultural and historical significance.

For if we can agree on nothing else, we can agree that information about a former first lady is newsworthy. The fact that the everyday life of Jacqueline Kennedy Onassis is news has even been legally confirmed, in *Onassis v. Galella*, in which the self-admitted paparazzo was not denied the right to photograph the widow of the former president, although he was required to remain at a specified distance from Onassis and her children, stipulated in number of feet.[56] But why isn't Dior's visual reference to Onassis excluded from private protection on the basis of its status as news or even political enunciation? If her image is news, why isn't it also a part of our shared culture? I will put it bluntly. The issue is no longer whether one person can enjoin the use of another's face or whether another person can use her own body to usurp the identity of another. The question is, "Who owns our cultural heritage?" In order to underscore how the logic of United States intellectual property law structures the ambiguity that invites the question of the ownership of our common heritage, I turn to *Six Seconds in Dallas*.

Six Seconds in Dallas

First we need to consider the relationship between the Super 8 mm color motion picture footage shot with a telephoto lens at normal speed by the Dallas dress manufacturer Abraham Zapruder and the "real" before the camera—the assassination of John F. Kennedy on 22 November 1963. The 480 frames of the Zapruder film, 40 of which show some details of the shooting, are the fullest existing visual record of the events in Dallas. As such, the Warren Commission employed the footage as evidence in its investigation. But of more significance to us, three days after the shooting, Time Inc. began to negotiate the purchase of the footage. The original and the three existing copies of the footage were eventually purchased from Zapruder for $150,000. *Life* magazine reproduced thirty of the frames a week after the assassination, and in the December issue

nine frames were featured, enlarged and in color. A third issue the follow-
ing October reproduced five color frames on the cover, and another eight
inside accompanied reprinted portions of the Warren Commission report.
All of the issues of the magazine were copyrighted, and, in addition, in
May 1967, *Life* registered the motion picture footage with the United
States copyright office.[57]

The status of the motion picture record of the historical events of 22
November 1963 becomes a question because Bernard Geis Associates,
publishers of Joshua Thompson's *Six Seconds in Dallas* (1967), ap-
proached *Life* with a request to reprint some of the Zapruder frames in
Thompson's book, a journalistic history and analysis of the assassination.
Denied permission to copy the frames, Geis employed an artist to produce
charcoal sketches of parts of twenty-two of the frames; these sketches were
then reproduced in Thompson's book.[58] Time Inc. sought a judgment
against Geis for infringement of copyright, and although the United
States District Court of New York ruled in favor of Geis and Thompson
on the basis of "fair use," what concerns me is not the outcome of the case
but the possibility entertained by Judge Wyatt that history might be
protectable private property. For what he maintained on *this* issue was
that although history itself was not subject to copyright, the "form of
expression" of the events of the past was, and thus *Life* could claim to own
the motion picture "expression" of the assassination.[59]

There is no doubt that this theory flies in the face of the most basic
lessons of poststructuralism.[60] How else is history conveyed to us if not
via some form of expression?[61] *Life* argued, and Judge Wyatt upheld the
claim that it had no copyright in the actual events of November 1963:
"They can be freely set forth in speech, in books, in pictures, in music, and
in every other form of expression."[62] These, of course, are also forms
subject to copyright, and one wonders how we are ever to reproduce and
make available the scenes of the past without recourse to forms. How do
we disseminate "the facts" regarding the past without first converting
them into some reproducible medium of expression?

Lest we get too alarmed over this aspect of *Time Inc. v. Geis* (as Bernard
Edelman seems to have done),[63] let me say that the emphasis on "forms of
expression" is nothing more than a restatement of the expression/ideas
dichotomy basic to United States intellectual property doctrine—in essence, an attempt to free up underlying ideas so that they may become
available to the public. Recall from my discussion of copyright in the

photograph that expression, the materiality that conveys these ideas, or the form they take upon publication, can enjoy copyright's limited monopoly. It seems likely that the expression/ideas distinction will require some reformulation in the near future because the protection of the computer program, a system that cannot be used without copying, renders the division more and more untenable. Some have already argued that the merger of ideas and expression in the iconic sign makes the arbitrariness of the distinction all too evident.[64] We see this in the case of the image of Jacqueline Onassis. If we consider, as Norman Mailer has, that the woman is no longer a celebrity but has become a "historic archetype,"[65] she is analogous to the character typeage that United States courts have understood as comparable to "underlying ideas."[66] And if Jacqueline Onassis is an underlying type, she is an idea that cannot be reserved, a type that informs and fills out the "trend-setting socialite" character stereotype constructed in the Dior wedding tableau; as such an idea, she is a part of the materials of culture, which intellectual property law holds should be available to all artists. *Onassis v. Dior* has shown us the inseparability of expression and ideas. But in the end, for the judge, it did not matter what form the expression took, whether "Jacqueline Onassis" was signified by an image produced by her own body or the body of another person. "Jacqueline Kennedy Onassis" in any form is potentially protected private property.

But this application of privacy law also has its other side, which as it mirrors the principle behind copyright law's circulation/restriction and ideas/expression dichotomies, leaves underlying ideas as a cultural preserve. As the *Onassis* judge stated, Ron Smith Celebrity Look-Alikes can "market its clients for fun and profit," and Barbara Reynolds can "capitalize" on her resemblance at parties and even on television.[67] We are free to wear our hair as Jacqueline does, to dress up, and to try our hand at impersonation. Even Australian Leigh Raymond, whose hobby is crashing parties by rushing into a room wearing a pillbox hat and a pink polyester suit covered with red dye, is completely free to entertain his friends.

 "These Boots Are Made for Walkin'"

NANCY SINATRA AND THE GOODYEAR TIRE

SOUND-ALIKE

As I have shown in the previous discussion of the look-alike, American law has some difficulty fitting the products of mechanically made culture to older notions of "copying" and "privacy." Although in the *Onassis* case the court held that the former first lady could claim control over her representational image, the person whose actual body had produced the representation could make no equivalent claim. In *Onassis v. Dior*, Barbara Reynolds's empirical body was no legal match for the constructed persona of Jacqueline Onassis. It would seem from this case that the law defers to connotative signifieds ("Jacqueline Onassis") and is indifferent to signifiers, the concrete vehicles of meaning (the body of Barbara Reynolds). Although other branches of the law may show a clear preference for the empirical and the evidentiary, unfair competition law (especially in cases concerned with public "recognition") deals with socially constructed knowledges. The empirical is moot in unfair competition cases, and there is no better illustration of this than the infringing sound-alike. With the sound-alike, as with the look-alike, the courts are finally not interested in asking questions about who is "really" producing the sound or the image.

In the last chapter I argued that although Jacqueline Kennedy Onassis is not a commercial entity, the court framed the issues in *Onassis v. Dior* in terms of unfair competition law as much as in terms of privacy law. 105

Branches of the law that are apparently removed from the world of commerce, then, have been increasingly "assimilated to the terms of the developing market," to quote Raymond Williams.[1] My point about the pattern of assimilation to the market should become more clear in this chapter, within which I lay out the basic unfair competition paradigm as I did with the copyright paradigm in chapter 2.

Looking at unfair competition doctrine as it is relevant to sound-alike cases, I take up the theory of secondary meaning and the tort or injury of "passing off." As unfair competition lawyers know, secondary meaning opens the door to a consideration of property rights. The establishment of such a new commercial meaning in a word, a representational image, or an abstract design would give a merchant a defense against infringers; he has a proprietal right much like the copyright owner's enforceable right. But it is not so simple in the cases I will discuss. The phenomenon for which the plaintiffs seek protection is "sound," and there is a built-in incompatibility between "sound" and property rights. This incompatibility works to my advantage as it shows up the flaws in the premises of unfair competition. Applied to something as illusive and ineffable as sound, the operative principles behind secondary meaning and "passing off" are revealed in a different light as they are stretched to meet new (perhaps impossible) tests.

For unfair competition law, the sound-alike, just as the look-alike, represents a potential question of appropriation by "imitation." Here the law is interested only in imitation that produces the perception of similarity for most listeners. I should emphasize that imitation and the consequent confusion it produces is not always a potentially illegal use. Sound-alikes as well as look-alikes *can* be noninfringing and thus perfectly legal. Humorous parodies, satires, and a comic's vocal impressions do not raise the issues that push either unfair competition or copyright doctrine to the point of revealing legal inconsistencies. But it isn't only the inconsistency of intellectual property law that concerns me. Mass culture criticism has also had difficulty theorizing sound, and the problems shared by these different attempts to encode the same phenomenon tell us something about the cultural construction of sound.

To say that intellectual property law attempts to encode, however, does not mean to imply that it determines either the formal properties or the content of mass culture. Hirst and Kingdom refer to the law as securing the "conditions of existence" for the relations of production.[2] It seems to

me, however, that intellectual property doctrine is only one of the conditions of possibility, only one of the formations upon which mechanically
produced culture is contingent. And we still need to know whether it is as
institutional practice or as ideological configuration that intellectual property secures these conditions, perhaps the most difficult question of all for
a Marxist theory of culture.

Although I do not propose to answer this question, I can report a
tendency in American intellectual property to expand and stretch, to
enlarge the domain of protectable culture and to extend the duration of
the monopoly grant to owners. Intellectual property law achieves this
expansion by means of one simple rhetorical device: It makes rough
analogies between different cultural forms. (Photography is a "writing,"
the image is more personal than the voice, performance is not a "writing,"
etc.) The law constitutes itself by this process of stretching new forms to
fit older categories. Herein lies the trouble it has had with sound. But
historically, U.S. unfair competition law has shown more tolerance for
sound-alikeness than for look-alikeness. What does this legal tendency tell
us about the epistemological status of sound? What does it tell us about
the structural difference between phonic signs and iconic signs? How has
new recording technology reconstructed sound over the last eighty years?
Reviewing the decisions on sound-alikeness in the context of his overview
of privacy and publicity, J. Thomas McCarthy observes that the general
drift of these cases would lead one to conclude that "so far the judges seem
to have a 'tin ear.'" And further, he asserts, "[t]here is no inherent reason
why the public cannot identify the persona of a person with the ears as
well as the eyes."[3] And yet there is.

Passing Off the Anonymous Singer

Such an example of McCarthy's "tin ear" theory was the 1970
case in which Nancy Sinatra sought to enjoin Goodyear Tire and Rubber
Company from using an imitative version of the song she popularized,
"These Boots Are Made for Walkin'." The codefendant in the suit, Young
and Rubicam Advertising Agency, designed an advertising campaign
around the theme of "wide boots," incorporating a new style of tire into
the imagery of the song. In four television spots, a male voice delivered
the commercial commentary over the image of four women costumed in

late-sixties "mod" fashion—short skirts and high boots—while a female voice sang, "These boots . . . " in the style of Nancy Sinatra. Two radio commercials featured the same arrangement, with the same female singing voice and a male voice-over. Before the production of the commercials, Young and Rubicam had contacted Sinatra's agent in an effort to engage the singer's services, but since the parties did not reach an agreement, the advertising agency proceeded with its idea and, admittedly, hired a vocalist to imitate the popular singer.[4]

Sinatra v. Goodyear Tire & Rubber Co. (1970), heard before the U.S. Court of Appeals for the Ninth Circuit, raised issues of federal preemption of state law and the relation between the copyrighted song and its performance, as well as unfair competition issues covered by the California Civil Code, section 3369. The singer complained that the Goodyear commercial intentionally imitated her style and voice. Not only did the dancers in the television version of the advertisement assume the dress and the mannerisms that were associated with her performance style, but the singer's vocal qualities and musical rendition of the song were clearly imitative. Sinatra further charged that the use of an imitation deceived the public into thinking that she had participated in the production of the Goodyear commercials. She therefore argued that she was entitled to damages, royalties on the use of the advertisements during the period in which they were aired, and a restraining injunction on any further broadcast.

As first posed at the district court level, the legal question was whether or not Goodyear's admitted use of a Sinatra imitation constituted unfair competition, and if so did it meet the test of "passing off"? The court of appeals confirmed the lower court's conclusion that the use of the soundalike was *not* unfair competition, because, to quote the earlier decision, "Defendants did not pass-off; that is, they did not mislead the public into thinking their commercials were the product of plaintiff or anyone else. Imitation alone does not give rise to a cause of action."[5] There are two issues here. First, because the stated interest in this branch of the law is primarily one of policing markets, it is basic to a "passing off" cause of action that competition exist between two parties. Commercial imitation, for instance, is of no legal moment if businesses are geographically separate or if they are not in the same competitive market. Thus if one merchant adopts a familiar product trade name for his completely dissimilar product, the merchant who has been imitated has no cause for complaint.[6] Following this line of reasoning, the appellate court judge in *Sinatra* stated that he could not consider the case in unfair competition terms since, given the difference between record company and automotive tire markets, there was no competition to speak of between Goodyear Tire and Nancy Sinatra.

Second, under unfair competition doctrine (and in this case in particular), imitation—whether performance, packaging, or linguistic similarity—is recast in terms of the question of "passing off." Or, did one merchant represent his goods as coming from another merchant? The "passing off" tort or injury is a more modern synonym for "palming off," a concept that still carries the connotations of hucksterism and quackery, of snake oil and medicine shows. Passing off is not an unusual commercial injury or a rare kind of fraud codified in a seldom-invoked piece of legislation. It is the common concept around which issues are framed in Anglo-American unfair competition litigation.[7]

As William Prosser summarizes the test for passing off, it hinges on the determination of "whether the resemblance is so great as to deceive the ordinary customer."[8] Sinatra claimed that the use of her singing style was an "incidental or secondary passing off." That is, although the professional entertainer was not misrepresented as the source of the Goodyear tire voice, many people would still hear the voice in the television and radio commercials and mistakenly conclude that it was hers. Since the real singer was not identified and the connection with Sinatra was not disclaimed, Judge Trask found no technical misrepresentation. As he concluded for the majority, "[T]here [was] no audio or visual representation, holding out, or inference that any of the commercials embody the performance or voice of any particular individual or individuals." There was no passing off. The public was not deceived.

But in the 1962 Bert Lahr sound-alike case the court heard something different in the anonymous voice. In the offending television commercial for the household cleaning product Lestoil, Adell Chemical Company used the voice of an actor who specialized in Bert Lahr imitations over the cartoon image of a duck. In *Lahr v. Adell Chemical Co.* (1962), Judge Aldrich for the Court of Appeals of the First Circuit ruled that Lestoil's use of a sound-alike was "passing off."[9] Although Lahr did not, in the majority opinion, "show any 'property' interest entitled to copyright protection," he did have a "unique," even a "peculiar" style of performance.[10] *Lahr* recognized a property claim in "individual vocal characteristics." And, crucial to Sinatra's later citation of *Lahr* as precedent, the court recognized the actor's claim of secondary meaning in "pure sound." Following *Lahr*, in *Sinatra* the popular singer argued that she had acquired a secondary meaning in both the song as she performed it and in her stylistic arrangement of it.[11]

Secondary Meaning and the Market of Signs

But what is secondary meaning? And why did Sinatra want to claim it for her singing style? Secondary meaning is the claim of one cultural sign to a special status vis-à-vis other, competing signs; it is the legal recognition of the process by which ordinary words, proper names, shapes, symbols, containers, designs, faces, and bodies become popularly recognized within the culture. Technically, secondary meaning is a doctrine rooted in trademark law. However, it is loosely applied as a test of the public recognition of a celebrity in unfair competition disputes. It is also pertinent in right of privacy disputes, in which a celebrity might not necessarily want to claim trademark status for his or her popular image, but in which the work of promotion has produced wide recognition. The development of this legal doctrine, especially since the middle of the century, tells us much about the goals and the effectiveness of commercial advertising and corporate public relations in recent decades.

Although secondary meaning now covers iconic signs as well as linguistic signs, originally the doctrine applied only to words that marked goods and services—a linguistic bias still evident in the basic secondary meaning paradigm: the dichotomy between "descriptive" and "distinctive." Indeed, this dichotomy is itself quite simply based on the difference between the dictionary meaning of a word and a meaning acquired secondarily or later in time. A trademark's *primary meaning*, in other words, is the dictionary definition, and its *secondary meaning* is any new, culturally acquired connotation. Moreover, it is only if a sign is borrowed from an existing language that a merchant may claim that his use has given it a special, *distinctive* meaning.[12] Not surprisingly, then, secondary meaning is not a consideration if a merchant has adopted a commercial symbol that is specially "coined" and has no other utility in everyday discourse.

One of the best examples of this is the coined word "kodak." This nonsense word was George Eastman's choice for his camera company because it was "short, pronounceable in any language, distinctive, easily remembered," and as fundamental "as the baby's first 'goo.'"[13] Joining "kodak" later as some of the most successful random recombinations of letters in the English alphabet—and taking advantage of the seldom-used letter *x*—were "clorox," "chemex," "xerox," and "exxon."[14] U.S. trademark law calls such words "fanciful" or "arbitrary," and some sense of the fantasy nature of such made-up signs is underscored by the equivalent concept in Italian law, where the comparison is between not "descriptive" and "fanciful" but "descriptive" and "fantastic."[15]

Our concern, however, is not with those signs that unfair competition law sees as already or "inherently" (and thus unproblematically) "distinctive" ("exxon," "kodak"). Instead, it is with those "descriptive" words that must transcend their ordinary signifying function to take on commercial (secondary) meaning, which eclipses the primary meaning in the minds of consumers. So it is that the ordinary descriptive words "camel," "shell," and "tide" acquire the commercial connotations that elevate them to CAMEL cigarettes, SHELL oil, and TIDE soap.[16] And ultimately our concern is with how this same notion of acquired distinctiveness in the linguistic realm applies to the signs of personhood (face, name, voice).

One standard legal text gives as an example of the loss of descriptiveness and the acquisition of distinctiveness the word "apple"—a sign that, although it does distinguish one computer manufacturer from the rest (APPLE), cannot distinguish one fruit producer from another because it only "describes" the product itself. And the same problem, of course, would apply to the use of "red" as a distinguishing mark for such produce because it runs the risk of describing all apples rather than those marketed by a particular producer.[17]

This explanation by example scarcely begins to illuminate the legal significance of the doctrine of secondary meaning, which assumes the existence of competition so close (and the number of familiar symbols so limited) that entrepreneurs will not only cut into each other's business but will in fact become parasitic on the commercial messages of one another. Semiotic theory sees this phenomenon as nothing more nor less than cultural buildup, the "transformation of denotations into new connotations."[18] Legal theory, however, understands secondary meaning above all in terms of potential unfair competition within markets and territories. There is much at stake. If the producer of popular (secondary) meaning can claim "ownership" in a meaning that would exclude others (presumably competitors) from using the same and even similar signs, then parody, imitation, recombination, and wordplay may be judged as attempts to "hitch a free ride" on the familiar symbology of a competitor.[19] They may be seen, in short, as unfair competition.

Supreme court justice Frankfurter's statement in *Mishawaka Rubber & Wollen Mfg. v. S. S. Kresge Co.* (1942) suggests what is at stake here and how individual capitals operate within this semiotic force field of buyer recognition: "The protection of trademarks is the law's recognition of the psychological function of symbols. If it is true that we live by symbols, it is no less true that we purchase goods by them. . . . The owner of a mark exploits this human propensity by making every effort to impregnate the atmosphere of the market with the drawing power of a congenial symbol. . . . If another poaches upon the commercial magnetism of the symbol he has created, the owner can obtain legal redress."[20] On first consideration, it seems that the law of unfair competition, at least in this instance, has a limited understanding of "meaning," since it insists on translating meaning into buyer association or recognition of a product. And it also seems to be predicated on a moment of identification in a supermarket, an act of meaning conflated with an act of purchase. And yet unfair competition law has a sophisticated grasp of the meaning of commercial symbols as relational.

The basic intellectual property text that I have been quoting states, in fact, that secondary meaning must be understood in relation to its specific context: "[T]he acquisition of secondary meaning is of basic and primary importance in determining whether rights exist. Secondary meaning is actually the primary meaning and, within the particular trade and market, secondary meaning is the *natural* meaning of the mark."[21] We might understandably ask here, Natural to whom?, particularly since the next sentence of this text asserts that secondary meaning is "acquired" and not "inherent." I can hardly think of a better illustration of Roland Barthes's conception of the ideological sign as "passing itself off" as natural.[22] Does this mean that as the new, second-in-time meaning becomes "naturalized," it is *no longer seen* as acquired, and thus, as poststructuralism tells us, it is *no longer seen* at all?

While I would not want to attribute poststructuralist philosophical insight to trademark theory, I would suggest that this theory is valuable as a description of semiotic operations within a circumscribed system of commercial signs, not least of all because it grows out of direct participa-

tion in the practices of commercial meaning-making. Consider, for instance, the contemporary evolution of the doctrine of secondary meaning.[23] It is clear that, since the World War II, trademark law has shifted
from its original mission—to protect consumers from merchant fraud—
and has instead been increasingly enlisted to protect commercial investment.[24] As commercial activity has become intensified and concentrated
in particular areas, and as competitors have engaged more and more in a
kind of semiotic encroachment upon each other's domains, trademark
theory has responded to changing commercial conditions by altering its
conception of how a primary sign comes to take on secondary distinctiveness. Increasingly, trademark theory has focused on the status of the
commercial sign both *within* its own sphere and relationally, *against* other
signs within a competitive market or field. The signifying "use" of a mark's
secondary meaning is now determined as much by evidence of advertising
and investment as by consumer recognition, as if to say that it is circulation, as much as or more than reception that counts. Unfair competition
doctrine tells us that secondary meaning is "developed in the marketplace
through use that makes the mark distinctive of the owner's goods or
services."[25] To put it another way, trademark theory shows us that we
can't exactly equate "use" with the semiotic practices of consumers. In
short, secondary meaning is understood in legal terms as positional; it tells
us that meaning is *not* coincident with the sign-vehicle that carries it. In
almost uncanny confirmation of Saussurian linguistics, trademark theory
conceptualizes a market field of differential positions that determine the
semiotic content of the signs within it.[26]

Curiously, in the descriptive-distinctive dichotomy that underlies the
doctrine of secondary meaning, we see the double movement of circulation-restriction to which I have already referred. It appears here as a
double rationale—it restricts the *use* of a bona fide distinctive mark at the
same time that it circulates merely descriptive marks. Circulation, in
secondary-meaning doctrine, amounts to a prohibition against proprie-
torial claims on generic and "descriptive" terms that are kept available for
competitors to share. Ostensibly, if one producer were to tie up the
generic terms and symbols that all other producers needed, then there
would be no competition. So it is that the two-tiered first order of
meaning is designed to prevent the monopolization of signs.

I need to digress here to offer a perspective on the significance of the
development of secondary meaning for a historical and political analysis of

American law. Kenneth Vandevelde, in his article "The New Property," discusses trademarks along with trade secrets and business goodwill as indexes of a twentieth-century development that he calls the "dephysicalization" of property. Since the turn of the century, Vandevelde says, American courts have "increasingly sought to protect valuable interests as property even though no thing was involved." Not surprisingly, this tendency has resulted in the expansion of the legal category of property.[27] One landmark case he cites is the 1899 "Waltham" case in which the watch manufacturers claimed a secondary meaning in "Waltham," even though it was also the name of a Massachusetts town.[28] It became clear from the outcome of this case that the principle of secondary meaning could extend to any trade symbol deemed valuable. Just to suggest the implications for manufacturers who increasingly saw trademarks as assets, let me quote from the 1917 *Trademark Advertising as Investment*: "Should the manufacturers of IVORY SOAP lose everything they possess in tangible assets by fire overnight, while totally uninsured, the brand name alone could be recapitalized for many millions of dollars within a week."[29] According to Vandevelde, common law responded to the problem involved in such a blanket extension of property rights by creating a continuum of categories of protection based upon the descriptive-distinctive range of possibilities. The degree of legal protection began to vary in accordance with the difference between the classic trademark (the truly distinctive, e.g., KODAK), the descriptive that achieves secondary meaning, and the merely descriptive.[30] But, as Vandevelde argues, the expansion of the category of property within legal doctrine meant that "property" threatened to completely lose its significance as a distinct legal category.[31] For to admit that there were various kinds of property, not all equally protected, meant that "the designation of an interest as property no longer provided a premise from which legal rights could be automatically deduced."[32]

Clearly, this expansion and disruption of the meaning of property poses a challenge to legal doctrine because the courts are under some obligation to produce a coherent law. From this vantage, we could view the Sinatra court's reluctance to award the singer a secondary meaning in her voice as a judicial attempt to preserve internal consistency. The court, we might say, was holding the line against the inflation of the category "property."

My contention is that the reluctance to extend protection to the performer's voice (what McCarthy diagnoses as the "tin ear" of many judges) has something to do in part with this basic concern about potential monopolies. It is a sign of legal largess, one that we can read as the law's reluctance to continue on its current course, its apprehension about turning elements of free-flowing culture to commercial stone. However, we must not be too quick to interpret this unclaimed cultural territory as a public domain for "the people." This territory is also "free" to corporate users like Goodyear Tire.

The court's reluctance to protect the performer's voice has to do less with legal magnanimity than with a cultural perception of sound as unprotectable because of its essential "propertyless" condition. For in order to establish secondary meaning in one sound, a proprietor must establish its distinctiveness from other sounds. Or, to go the other route and attempt to establish a copyright claim, a proprietor must distinguish the performer's contribution from those of composers, lyricists, instrumentalists, arrangers, and authors. These problems of audio distinguishability will bring us eventually to the question of the physics and the ontology of sound. But the question for now is this: Why has sound historically resisted the transformation into property, especially given the possibilities of intangible "new property" to which Vandevelde refers?

These particular issues of property in the voice came to a head again in *Booth v. Colgate-Palmolive* (1973), heard before the U.S. District Court of New York three years after *Sinatra*. *Booth* also declined to recognize a property right in the voice. Actress Shirley Booth, who had starred in the successful "Hazel" series broadcast from 1961 to 1966, objected to the use of an anonymous voice that imitated her character, over a commercial, aired in 1971, for Colgate-Palmolive's detergent Burst. The producers had secured permission from author-creator Ted Key to use his copyrighted cartoon character Hazel in the commercial, and he was credited accordingly. But out of Hazel's mouth came the voice of actress Ruth Holden imitating the voice of Shirley Booth. Lawyers for Booth charged the soap manufacturers and Ted Bates, the advertising agency, with violation of the actress's right of publicity, with theft of secondary meaning, and with defamation as well as unfair competition. Judge Bonsal found that there was no unfair competition under the Lanham Act, because the "voice does not function as a trademark or tradename."[33] Taken together, *Sinatra* and *Booth* raise similar questions about the protectability of the voice. But whereas *Sinatra* requires us to think about singing style, *Booth* confronts us with the deeper dilemma of the production of social hearing. We could explain Nancy Sinatra's failure to argue successfully that her singing style was protectable as a problem of the inextricability of the rendition of the song and the underlying copyrighted music. But Shirley Booth's inability to protect her style of speaking (separate from either a musical composition or a copyrighted character), suggests that the elusive and disputed problem signifier here is the voice itself. At this time in history, the voice cannot be transformed into a trademark; it cannot stand in place of the maker behind the goods. The history of American intellectual property as it relates to sound, however, suggests that it is only a matter of time before the signature tune and the celebrity voice will function like (if not actually *become*) trademarks.

The Immateriality of Sound

Sound, that elusive signifier, has historically presented a problem for aesthetic theory as well as for legal theory. In cultural studies, one hears a frequent lament that sound has been incompletely grasped and under-theorized, especially in comparison with the sophisticated and abundant work on the photographic image produced since the seventies. Likewise, in the scholarship on entertainment law, there is a general complaint that, in comparison with the image and the name of the performer, the voice of the performer is a problem area. The legal question of the voice starts with the phenomenological problem of sound, a problem signaled in the *Sinatra* and *Booth* cases' references to the "anonymity" of the voices heard in the television commercials.

Judge Trask in *Sinatra*, for instance, asserted that the anonymous expression on the sound track had "no audio or visual representation, holding out, or inference that any of the commercials embody the performance or voice of any particular individual(s)."[34] But although singer Sue Raney, the producer of the anonymous voice, was not identified within the commercials, the voice was, as Goodyear hoped, "identifiable" as the voice of Nancy Sinatra. What Judge Trask's reference to "embodiment" suggests, then, is that the voice needed a body of some kind as protection against unauthorized uses. If the anonymous voice were to gain a body, it would no longer float in this authorless state, susceptible to appropriation.

The problem that sound poses for the law in these cases may be better understood if we begin with the physics of the sound wave as seen by semiotics. We find that the soundwave gives us very little materiality to grasp. It is nothing more (nor less) than a vibration, which gradually ceases to exist just as we have apprehended it.[35] The semiotics of this phenomenon, as Régis Durand describes it, is the experience of something that immediately "[vanishes] in thin air leaving no trace of signifiers behind, no *body*, leaving us in the immediate presence of the signified."[36] But, if we follow Roland Barthes's argument that sound is a kind of "*signifiance*," even before it coheres into meaning, then we are left with even less than the signified.[37] We are left, in short, with nothing at all but affect.[38] Surely (this time) we are talking about a phenomenon that has been more successful than the photographic image at eluding cultural codification. But it scarcely escapes culture. Close upon the heels of its production, sound is on its way to meaning.

In several senses, music gives us a model with which to understand sound without voice and voice without speech. Music seems to arise directly out of the unconscious of the producer, and it seems to access the unconscious of the listener just as immediately.[39] Produced and picked up, "played" and heard with such apparent effortlessness, this presignifying stream of musical sound seems not only unmediated by culture but unshaped by the apparatus through which it flows. And finally, not only does sound or music "leave no body," but it refers to no body outside of itself. As Claudia Gorbman describes music, it is "a discourse without a clear referent."[40] With no grounding in the physical world, and no clear test of truth to which it is tied, sound (at least for the untrained ear) is always received as an approximation.

Moreover, sound similarity, the acoustic déjà vu produced by imitation, also depends on undependable memory. Since the recognition of sound likeness is a kind of reminiscence, it is difficult to speak of a "positive identification" of a person's voice.[41] Certainly we wouldn't speak of voice identification in the same way as identification of a person by his or her photographic image. This is not to suggest that there isn't an equivalent fuzziness in the process of seeing similarity in visual patterns. But because we are so accustomed to filling in as we hear, while we require our seeing to be already full and complete in information, we may be more inclined to see (and enjoy) visual variation and less inclined to want to hear and consequently to actually *make* acoustical distinctions. In fact, human hearing works by cutting off the waves at either end of the sound spectrum, by reducing differences; hearing constitutes a drive toward sound sameness, which no doubt increases over the course of a lifetime with gradual hearing loss.[42] The immateriality of sound presents the law with different questions of definition and delineation. Could it be that the "trouble" with sound (if that is what it is), is that it lends itself so easily to whatever we want to make of it?

To begin with, sound is an epistemological paradox, one exemplified by the fact that reproducible sound is held to be a greater measure of the real than the visual image at the same time that it is understood as a lesser measure of veracity. Judge Trask in *Sinatra* held that a disembodied voice offers us no way of telling who is speaking. Contradicting him, Judge Noonan in *Midler v. Ford Motor Co.* (1988) argued that we easily identify telephone voices with familiar speakers. Mary Ann Doane, in her important article on sound mixing, comments on this apparent inconsistency. As she explains sound technology, it is the "ineffable, intangible quality of sound—its lack of concreteness which is conducive to an ideology of empiricism."[43] I would put this same idea a little differently. It is the ineffability of sound that makes it so ideologically malleable, so responsive to the shape we want to give it; thus it is empirical proof at the same time that it is uncertainty and ambiguity. The sound-alike voice-overs are anonymous at the same time that they are nameable. There is something that is not only confusing but disturbing about the anonymous voice.

The voice without the body is strange, uncanny, and sometimes frightening. "Is it because the voice gives us nothing to *see*, because it has no mirror-image?" asks Durand.[44] The subjectivity of hearing associates voices with the supernatural. It is this mystery surrounding the invisible wave, the very mystery that produces the fascination of the ventriloquist's trick, that makes voice imitation legally problematic.

If this is the case with bodily and instrumentally produced, "promicrophonic" sound, what of new sound technologies that accentuate the elusive strangeness of sound in their capacity to bounce, envelop, and re-echo it?[45] Considering that the voice imitating Nancy Sinatra probably *did* deceive many listeners, we might regard "passing off" as not only an unfair competition claim, but as a redundant description of a commonplace electronic communications phenomenon. After all, drama on radio (a totally "blind medium") is completely organized around passing off one voice as the voice of another.[46]

New sound technologies—the phonograph, the telephone, the radio, the tape recorder-player, the television set—may accentuate the phantasmic sense of the voice, especially if it is heard separate from an originating body. In the "record" mode, these technologies suck sound from its source and molecularly break it down. In the "playback" mode, the reconstituted sound becomes an audible check, a verification. In the record mode, sound technologies produce the ephemeral and intangible as tangible and fixed. These technologies produce and replay sound scientifically so that at once the mysterious is probed and explained. Consider the magnetism of magnetic recording tape, which mysteriously, through the all-hearing medium of the sensitive microphone, attracts sound ions and stores them (unseen) in another form, which can retain them until they are reconverted and restored to us as "the sound itself."

Legal attempts to turn the voice into property confirm something about the relationship between voice and personhood that helps us to understand the cultural construction of sound in a new way. There is no doubt that the increased scientific precision as well as the increased availability and prevalence of audio recording and transmitting devices have produced the voice as something susceptible to proprietal claims because it is less and less immaterial illusion and more and more material attribute. What we are seeing *is* the development of that voice into a protectable property-appendage.

I want to explain before I go much further about what is generally meant by a copyright in music. In my discussion, I will make distinctions between *musical composition*, *musical performance*, and the *recording* of musical performance. Although musical copyright is also concerned with plagiarism (yet another type of copying), I will not deal with that kind of theft since it takes us too far afield from the problem at hand: mechanical reproduction. Significantly, the issues raised in *Sinatra* arise because sound recording and bodily performance are both potential producers of sound-alike signs. Although sound recording and musical performance are similar enough to be confused in legal terms, each has a different legal status and a separate intellectual property history. Because musical composition has been copyrightable in the U.S. since 1831, the law, by habit, has dealt with sound technologies on the model of the protection and registration of the written score.[47]

The first significant adjustment in copyright law as it pertains to music was made to accommodate performance. In 1856 and 1859, the U.S. copyright statutes were amended to include protection of the rights of performance. At that time, "performance right" referred to the protection of theatrical work and the musical composition as performed publicly by actors and played by instrumentalists.[48] These amendments were a crucial break out of the musical score mold. Now it was possible to consider the activation of written sound notations as protectable. Mechanical sound recording as a form of performance, of course, was not in the conceivable future. Historically, the right to reproduce in phonorecord or piano roll accompanied the copyright in the musical composition as codified in the 1909 copyright revision, which repealed all prior laws.[49] Essentially, this provision gave the composer or owner the first right to reproduce as an extension of the right to perform. Sound reproduction, then, was defined in terms of the performance paradigm and remained so until the 1971 amendment to the 1909 U.S. Copyright Act.[50] The new 1976 act confirmed that record producers had the right to reproduce sound recordings, but these manufacturers were not given rights to royalties from public "performances" of tapes and records.[51] In retrospect members of the Recording Industry Association of America would be sorry that they hadn't pushed harder for such royalties in the debates over the 1976 revision, especially when the Motion Picture Producers of America had organized such an impressive campaign for royalties on videotaping when the issues arose around *Sony Corporation of America v. Universal City Studios, Inc.* (1984).[52]

The key to understanding the law's reluctance to see sound recording as a copyrightable form in and of itself is the premium placed on authorship and its legal extension, ownership. Since copyright in musical composition was based on the analogy with literary property, it was also presumed that music was a "writing," a "work of authorship" that had its form in either a notational system or a performance. While one could "author" a musical composition, one could not "author" a mechanical reproduction of sound. One could have ownership in a musical composition or its performance, but no parallel property claim on the mechanical reproduction of that music. Ownership in mechanical reproduction was finally introduced into American copyright law in 1971, not to restore rights to producers or authors but to curb an epidemic. As an amendment to the Copyright Act of 1909, the Sound Recording Act of 1971 was designed to discourage sound piracy. As in *Burrow-Giles v. Sarony* (1884), copyright law was used to regulate the market.

I want to emphasize this point by paralleling the histories of copyright in the photographic still and magnetic tape technologies.[53] Around 1900, the flat, grooved phonorecord replaced the sound cylinder. But even with its tremendous popularity, this new sound-preserving technology did not initiate the change in sound reproduction that parallels the 1882 photographic copyright infringement epidemic. The technology for printing records in 1900 was still so elaborate and expensive that it discouraged fly-by-night piratical operations. A much simpler and cheaper technology would later invite epidemic infringement: magnetic tape.

The spread of magnetic tape technology was not encumbered by binding patents because it was literally confiscated as the spoils of war from the Germans after World War II. It was a pirate's dream because it required nothing more than two reel-to-reel tape recorders.[54] By the sixties, inexpensive plastic cassettes began to change modes of listening and recreational habits. In the seventies, it was estimated that 60 percent of the tapes and records sold in New York City were pirated versions.[55]

By constructing sound recording as a "work of authorship" separate from the musical composition, the 1971 amendment to the 1909 U.S. Copyright Act gave record producers enforceable rights against infringers. Significantly, the copyright in sound recording did *not* include a prohibition against an imitation of recorded sounds. And it is this distinction—between *duplication* (which requires two machines) and *imitation* (which requires two performers)—that is the crucial one for us. It is in this gray band in the concept of copying that sound-alike imitators will be heard.

It is important to be clear, in other words, that it is neither copyright in the composition nor in the performance of that composition with which we are concerned in the *Sinatra* case. The issues in *Sinatra* pertain exclusively to the style of interpretative performance. And it is musical performance style that to this day is *not* protected by federal statute. It therefore has become a sensitive area and a point of contention for popular vocalists like Sinatra.

Broadcasting the Voice

Let us put aside *imitation* for a moment while we consider the problem of *duplication*. For we need to see how audio technologies—phonography, radio, and television—all contribute to the material conditions that produce the legal possibility of infringing sound-alikes. First of all, intellectual property doctrine has historically constructed sound emissions as unfixed, as opposed to fixed (a paradigm that has no equivalent in the history of copyright in the photographic portrait). The easy way of understanding the unfixed-fixed paradigm would be to interpret it as an evolution from immaterial to material form. Such a hypothetical overview, albeit a reductive history, would begin with the Copyright Act of 1909—which left phonorecords as unfixed, transitory "performances"— and would see its key moment in the 1971 amendment recognizing sound recording as a separate work. And finally, it would culminate in the 1976 copyright revision, which redefined "publication" of a musical performance as the occasion of its "fixation" in phonograph record or magnetic tape. Such a review would conclude, in short, that technological developments in this century produced ephemeral talking voices and moving bodies that are (at least in legal terms) progressively solidified and increasingly "stable."[56] And on the basis of this hypothetical overview, one would be tempted to make a generalization that is nothing more than this: There is a connection between technological materialization and increased statutory protection.

From this oversimplified history, it would also be tempting to draw conclusions about the commodification of voiced and instrumental sound in contemporary culture. But surely the analysis of consumer culture as "commodified" is by now bankrupt as a paradigm. It may identify a *gradual petrification* of daily life in Western culture, but it simply does not explain the features of contemporary existence in their complexity. To put it another way, it is no longer enough to say that cultural forms have become reified without showing *where* and *how* they are reified. And a thoroughly systematic analysis of such forms would surely show that reification is uneven.[57] Certainly there are ways in which copyright protection and its accompanying property rights *do* commodify, solidify, and tie up elements of culture. But there are also ways in which legal protection facilitates cultural circulation. Copyright's monopoly grant, whether we like it or not, *does* work as an incentive to publish and consequently to disseminate. Copyright *protection* is always and at the same time circulation and restriction.

It would make things tidy if the circulation-restriction paradigm corresponded with copyright's unfixed-fixed continuum for sound recording and performance rights. But it does not. Some unfixed signs may be protected, and some fixed signs may circulate unprotected. Because of differences in state and federal laws and in the principles of copyright and trademark, we can't understand the protection of sound as simply the commodification of sound. For the history of the legal protection of sound presents us with too many exceptions: the state-level "common law copyright" in performed (unfixed) work, which allows a perpetual monopoly;[58] singing style in which there is no secondary meaning but in which there may be a property interest; the celebrity voice, which cannot be copyrighted (because sounds are unfixed) but which is inheritable property in several states, and so on.[59]

This irregular pattern tells us that the differences between state and federal law produce contradictions. Under state common law, unfixed sound may be a property, and one may even have a perpetual monopoly in it. (Think of a musical composition that is continually performed but never "published" in either sheet music or recorded form.) Under federal copyright law, a performance style, although fixed in record, tape, or disk, may be available for others to use. (Think of Nancy Sinatra's recording of "These Boots Are Made for Walkin'," Glenn Miller's recording of "Moonlight Serenade," and the Fifth Dimension's recording of "Up, Up, and Away.") These inconsistencies tell us, in short, that we can neither characterize sound as a "holdout" from consumer culture nor see it as thoroughly commodified.

To return, then, to the question of imitation. Even though the voice is unfixed, it lends itself to empirical claims (the spoken confession, Freud's "talking cure," the voiceprint). However, arguments for the voice as property have not borrowed the logic of empiricism—the logic we saw in the image-as-property argument, which is based upon the premise that a real person is injured and a genuine life is somehow touched by commercial appropriation. There are no right of privacy voice claims upon which to build a claim to property rights in the voice (on the analogy with privacy doctrine's property in the facial image), and there is no equivalent history of voice appropriation that builds on privacy invasion. The privacy of a real person, in other words, is not invaded by the commercial use of his or her empirical voice. Furthermore, in practical terms, the surreptitiously recorded voices of real persons are rarely used in this manner, and commercial appropriators, after all, do not need to "steal" celebrity voices when they can "construct" them with the voice of an anonymous actor. It would seem, then, that the voice-body disjuncture complicates the claim to personal property in the voice.

And that claim is further complicated by the fact that a part of a recording that is a performed "imitation" of prerecorded sound is *not* protectable. For intellectual property doctrine, this "imitation" is drawn not from the actor's repertoire but from a reservoir of culture containing styles, gestures, types, and genres out of which all performers must draw. The often-repeated statement of this position is Judge Bonsal's opinion in *Booth v. Colgate-Palmolive*: "[T]o grant . . . a performance right monopoly . . . [and thus] prevent others from imitating posture, gestures, voices, sounds, mannerisms may impede rather than 'promote the progress of the useful arts.'"[60] Since the legal fear is of a performance right monopoly, copyright law's reluctance to protect individual voice and gesture theoretically keeps performance signs available to the culture at large. But legal doctrine seeks to strike a balance by protecting sound recording instead. The use of the fixed materiality of the musical composition, its recording, and its performance is restricted. But the musician's *rendition* and the performer's style of playing or singing are "there for the taking." In the cases I have been discussing, it is clear that neither unfair competition doctrine nor copyright law offers a solution to the performer whose style is unprotected by common or statutory law. To gain such protection, a new legal celebrity subject would have to be constituted, one for whom the appropriation of the voice would be a "loss" of a valuable property.

There is a condition that we can't leave out of the history of intellectual property law and the protectability of sound. Let's call this a precondition for celebrity voice recognition: the construction of listeners. The listener, after all, is the objective of broadcast repetition, which is aimed at building sound familiarity and recognition. In these terms, one might ask why these issues of voice protection did not arise immediately after the development of the gramophone. After all, image protection issues arose coincident with the mass reproducibility of the physical likeness by photography, lithography, and mass circulation newspapers and tabloids. So why did the economic success of the 1904–6 Victor Phonograph recordings of Caruso not produce a popular recognition of the great baritone's voice on a mass scale? Why was Caruso's voice not the equivalent of the *carte de visite* image of Lily Langtry?[61] The answer, I think, is that the celebrity claim to property in a voice awaited the household familiarity produced by commercial radio broadcasting in the twenties.

In 1945, Theodor Adorno wrote that music broadcast on the radio produced "commodity listening." As Adorno characterized this sound:

"It is the ideal of Aunt Jemima's ready-mix pancakes extended to the field of music. The listener suspends all intellectual activity when dealing with music and is content with consuming and evaluating its gustatory qualities—just as if the music which tastes best were also the best music possible."[62] Adorno might also consider that it was the "imprint of profit" on the spoken word that produced the voice of Aunt Jemima as commercially appropriable.[63] Actually, one of the first sound-alike cases arose because of a voice imitation of an actress famous for her personification of Aunt Jemima. *Gardella v. Log Cabin Products, Inc.* (1937), cited as precedent in *Sinatra*, arose from the commercial radio broadcast use of the voice of Tess Gardella, an actress of Italian descent who had adopted the theatrical persona of the Black folk figure. Here, the actress was unable to secure a judgment against Log Cabin/Quaker Oats on the theory that the company had engaged in unfair competition.[64]

Nevertheless, we can see in this case the foothold for an argument for secondary meaning in the voice, one directly related to the fact that sponsored advertising had begun to produce an increasingly wider audience recognition of voices. While the courts since *Gardella* have held out against seeing any secondary meaning in voice or singing style, entertainment law scholars give the impression that it is an inevitability. For them, the "distinctive" commercial broadcast voice could easily meet trademark doctrine's test of acquired "distinctiveness," which raises the ordinary sign to another power—property status.

The value of trademark law's property-building provision is that it adds another dimension to the observation that theorists in cultural studies have recently made about the way television constructs its listener. Television theory asks: Do the distinctive sounds of auditory stereotypeage construct the inattentive viewer as attentive? The argument is sometimes made that the voice is more resistant to commodification than the face. As Kaja Silverman observes, the voice, because of its distinctive "texture" or "flavor," is "never completely standardized."[65] But one-of-a-kindness, based upon a notion of the infinitude of natural variation, does not necessarily produce holdouts from consumer culture. In fact, as I argued in chapter 2, the Romantic ideal of originality and singularity is the very foothold for the concept of property.

In another version of the Romantic characterization of the voice, Amy Lawrence, from a Derridian perspective, contends that the voice is relatively difficult to commodify because it is "more deeply personal."[66] Not only is it thoroughly individualized, it bears an even closer relation to the soul than the face, coming as it does out of the secret recesses of the body. But Jacques Derrida's insight about the voice as direct line to the soul and hence measure of authenticity and veracity works only in relation to a writing/speech dichotomy in which writing plays the secondary, supporting role. The sound/image dichotomy that informs the development of mimetic technologies in Western culture, however, is not a relation of surrogacy but one of a hierarchy defined by the model of the socialized body. In this hierarchy, eye is over ear and the body is higher than the voice.

The sound/image hierarchy may of course be seen as evolving and changing in relation to the development of mechanical and electronic technologies. But a reductive notion that sound has become increasingly commodified does not help us produce the more detailed picture we need. More than any other theorist of music in the industrial age, Theodor Adorno is allied with the concept of sound as progressively commodified. Ironically, though, the book on motion picture music that he wrote with Hanns Eisler offers other, more subtle critical models. Adorno and Eisler imply that hearing, because it is relatively "archaic," is not, as yet, thoroughly commodified. Their discussion of the ear versus the eye suggests that this is a matter of historical development and emphasis, of bourgeois society's establishment of "the real" as the concrete commodity-object, which required the development of an eye that could make distinctions quickly. Thus industrial society was organized around the regime of sight. Listening, in contrast, remained passive rather than active, unable to make the sharper distinctions and identifications of sight. For Adorno and Eisler, listening is potentially subversive: "[O]ne could say that to react primarily with the unselfconscious ear rather than with the alert eye is, in a certain sense, to contradict the later industrial age and its anthropology."[67]

But further, and I think more significantly, Adorno and Eisler associate hearing with a "pre-individualistic collectivity," which eludes the organizational structure of commodity culture.[68] Following Adorno and Eisler, we could say that it is this capacity of sound to disseminate, to fill space, to cross distance and time, that makes it potentially oppositional—not its source in personhood. The tendency of sound is to spread out; it seems to belong to everyone. Sound is an unsettling problem for industrial culture, which wants to fix, to privatize, to isolate it. If the still image hands itself over easily to individualistic privacy and property, sound, in its collectivity, must be specially packaged as exclusive and personal.

Phonograph records and magnetic tape have to some degree solved the problem of how to fix and package sound; earphones and individual record-playback units have made it private. Sound imagery, however, still remains largely "unapprehended," in contrast to the visual imagery on which consumer culture has banked so much, and to which we therefore attend with such expertise. Acoustic apprehension remains relatively undiscriminating and lazy. And I would surmise that it is because of our relative auditory lethargy that mimetic technologies have had to construct us as more discriminating sound consumers.

Consider, for example, the relationship between sound and image in audiovisual entertainment technologies. Sound, the subordinate partner in motion pictures, has become dominant in television, where it commands the attention of the viewer while the image performs merely an illustrative function. As John Ellis theorizes this reversal, which he finds especially pronounced in comedy genres and in commercials, it is sound that supplies the coherence from image to image, the detail and nuance that is now missing from the visually barren television image.[69] More and more, sound compensates for our indifference to the image, to which viewers do not necessarily attend in the home environment. As Rick Altman describes it, in the contemporary living room, television "competes with surrounding objects"; like an auditory advertiser, television sound is used to "call the intermittent spectator back to the set."[70] While the picture is limited to the screen, it is the very capacity of sound to "radiate in all directions" that defines it as the preferred carrier medium for the televisual message.[71]

Given the conditions of television viewing, then, the phenomenon of the signature voice (as well as the signature tune), is a fairly predictable commercio-aesthetic development. To some degree, the musical jingle, the disembodied voice, and the comic sound effect are legacies of radio. But what is significantly different about the ascendancy of television sound is that it carries with it the expectation of a coordinated, matching body. Television sound promises visual verification and explanation of its source, generating what Altman calls a "sound hermeneutic," which leads the viewer into a quest for the sound's source in the image.[72] And television sound is all the more effective when it sets up the expectation of visual completion and confirmation of a familiar image. As Altman puts it,

"When we hear the voice of a favorite star, we turn toward the screen to complete our sense of the star's presence."[73]

The sound-alike is a supremely logical outcome of these aesthetic conditions. Given the hermeneutic that Altman describes, viewers may develop a new "sense" of what was or was not "on" television, regardless of what they actually did or did not view. The notion of having "been on" television does not differentiate between an appearance as voice on the track or as image on the screen. The "viewer" washing the dinner dishes in the kitchen may claim to have heard Nancy Sinatra sing "These Boots Are Made for Walkin'" and might then deduce that the singer had "appeared" on television in a commercial for Goodyear Tire. In a sense, the viewer's notion of what was or was not "on" television may be quite correct, because television, after all, delivers image samplings and sound impressions, selective portions of the original visual and acoustic events they represent.

We could argue, then, that the sound-alike phenomenon takes advantage of television's selective aesthetic and the viewer's sloppy hearing to pass off one voice as that of another. But there is another way of understanding this phenomenon, one indicated by the number of sound-alike cases that have raised identical issues in the last twenty years. From the legal perspective, we can see sound imitation developing in an uncultivated band of culture that as yet has not been identified by copyright law as a "work of authorship."

The Acoustic Territory of Contemporary Music

Since the 1888 invention of the gramophone, "promicrophonic" sounds have become relatively easy to capture, play back, or transmit. We now enjoy the relative easiness of catching sounds and turning them loose into the atmosphere. Enthusiasm for this technological magic has produced an acoustically transformed social space. The "free-for-all" radiating capacity of sound production (recorded "live") lends itself to use and re-use, imitation, and re-creation. Popular music will inevitably be heard, it will be circulated, and, as I have been arguing, it will spread out democratically. To some degree this inevitability is already prefigured by the body's own sound collection and reproduction apparatus, the prototype for the mechanical and electronic record/store/playback functions: listening, remembering, speaking, or singing.

The trouble with sound begins with listening, or what Barthes calls "trapping signifiers." As acoustic interlopers, the ears indiscriminately "pick up" noise, musical harmonies, tonal qualities, melodic phrases. The body's vocal production box can immediately "play back" what is heard. This is, after all, a replay of how language is learned—by imitation and repetition. So close is the record to the playback device in the body that it is almost as though "listening speaks." But this is an active, interpretative, collaborative listening, a "free listening . . . which circulates, which permutates, which disaggregates, by its mobility, the fixed network of the roles of speech."[74] If "listening speaks," the speaking voice "hears" (itself) and other sounds as it is voiced.

To Barthes's theorization of the phenomenon of producing and hearing sound, we should add the dimension of industrial reconstruction. Rock music historians describe the contemporary environment as a post-sixties phenomenon made possible by the "industrialization" of music. These historians see the industrialization of music as having altered the acoustic space within which we have been living since midcentury in such a way that our social movements are always accompanied by recorded music. Describing the youth culture participant who lives most thoroughly in and through contemporary music, Lawrence Grossberg says: "Music's sensuous materiality transforms reception into active production. Music surrounds and invades the body of its listeners, incorporating them into its spaces and making them a part of the musical event itself. The listener becomes a producer in real and complex ways."[75] The professional musician perfects this possibility of sound collection and dissemination as a supertransmitter with the help of instrumentation. He or she does this with the aid of the new technologies of sound, which pipe in, feed in, reverberate, throw, break down, and reconstitute, thus magnifying existing musical-acoustic properties and tendencies. It is as though, as Felix Guattari puts it, "the abstract machines of music [are] . . . the most nonsignifying and de-territorializing of all."[76]

The history of copyright law in relation to sound recording reveals the difficulty of reshaping legal discourse that defines sound software on the model of musical notation systems. Sound presents special problems because of the immateriality of the form, the confusion of the ear, and now the democratization of acoustic space. We might say that the 1976 Copyright Act's section 114(a) yields to the problem of sound and its producing and trapping technologies. After all, the statute allows the commercial imitation and simulation of recorded sounds that are *already protected*. To some degree the 1976 act acknowledges that sound-alikeness will inevitably be produced by voices and instruments.[77] It defers to the fact that sound is no respecter of territory.

As I have been arguing, the history of Anglo-American copyright as it has dealt with developing communications technologies *does* reveal a pattern: from the circulation and availability of signs to private property restriction. And yet it is an uneasy course, made difficult by the cumbersome problem of translating political policy into questions of cultural form. I want to look back now at the political and economic coordinates of circulation and restriction.

The Legal Construction of Sound Recording

What is striking about the history of U.S. copyright in recorded sound is that for roughly sixty years, the status of recorded sounds under federal statute was significantly different from that of other mechanically and electronically produced objects of culture. The comparison is most often made between sound recording and the motion picture, which has been fully protected since 1912. However, I have been more interested in contrasting sound recording with photography because the juxtaposition raises issues that form the basis of a more thoroughgoing critique of intellectual property. For my purposes, the two comparable Supreme Court cases regarding copyrightability are *Burrow-Giles* and *White-Smith Music Co. v. Apollo Co.* (1908). In *White-Smith*, the U.S. Supreme Court decided on the copyrightability of mechanically reproduced sound based on the case of the player piano roll. In this case, the court concluded that the player piano roll was not a "copy" of the underlying musical composition and therefore that it could not be considered a protectable "work."[78]

It is tempting to seize upon the fact that the court based its conclusion in regard to the status of the perforated piano roll on the basis that "[t]hese musical tones are not a copy which appeals to the eye." Justice Day, for the majority, went on: "A musical composition is an intellectual creation which first exists in the mind of the composer; he may play it for the first time upon an instrument. It is not susceptible of being copied until it has been put in a form which others can see and read." The analogy between sheet music and piano roll shaped the court's conclusion that whereas the former was perceived directly by the eye, the latter was "read" with the help of a machine. In this case, the perforated roll was, in fact, "part of the machine."[79] Later, this analogy would be extended to phono-records, which also had to be "read" by a machine (in this case a gram-ophone or phonograph player) and which were therefore not "copies" of the musical composition either. But if the piano roll and the phonorecord were not "copies" of the composition that listeners heard when these items were played by machines, then what were they? For legal purposes, they were, until the 1971 amendment, "performances" of a composi-tion.[80]

The debates over whether a sound recording is or is not a "copy" will have a familiar ring to the film scholar. The question arises as to whether the court in *White-Smith* held the same notion of sound as contemporary French critics such as Christian Metz. Recently Metz and others have been criticized for lapsing into an idealism with regard to the relative "real" of sound recording, a position that these critics would never have subscribed to for the visual image.[81] The position amounted to an assertion that although the motion picture image is a selective "copy" of the real, sound recording produced acoustic reality rather than a "copy" of that reality. To quote Jean-Louis Baudry, "[I]n the case of all talking machines—one does not hear an image of the sounds but the sounds themselves."[82] In response to this, certainly in the wake of poststructuralism, there isn't the insistence that mechanically produced sound is not the same as the sound itself. While sound recording is certainly mechanical or electronic "copy-ing," it produces neither a "copy" of the acoustic event nor a "copy" of the notational system in which the underlying composition has been en-coded. It is more likely a "sample" of an acoustic event stored in another form such as paper roll, magnetic tape, pressed vinyl, or compact disc.[83]

But the problematic of film theory here is really quite different from that of intellectual property. In arguing that piano rolls were neither copies of musical sound nor copies of the musical composition, the *White-Smith* majority was not arguing that this early sound software was "the sound itself." *White-Smith* asserted that the piano roll (precursor of mag-netic tape) was a "performance" of the composition rather than a "copy" of it. What is significant for intellectual property law here is this: To construct the means for sound production as "performance" is to construct it as ephemeral and unfixed. Note that the intellectual property paradigm (fixed-unfixed) is significantly different from the constructed-real paradigm of film and television studies.[84]

By now it should be occurring to the reader that the intellectual property conception of the "copy" is as ambiguous as the term "originality," which I considered in chapter 2. In intellectual property doctrine, a "copy" is really another *form* of the "work." To copy singly in disregard for the owner's right is plagiarism; to copy multiply is infringement. We are only just now realizing the kind of cultural upheaval threatened by the reconception of audiovisual recording technologies—from the VCR to the DAT (digital audiotape). In the area of sound recording, the difference between the original and the copy has essentially been obliterated within the last few years by the development of the superior sound of DAT. "Everyone may produce an original," says Andrew Goodwin, describing the newest in professional audio technology.[85] But the magnitude of the problems raised by copying in the industrial age is very simply explained by the fact that industrial production is predicated upon copying.[86] And it is my impression that the confusion one reads in the history of American intellectual property stems from the difficulty of regulating new mechanical and electronic technologies with the use of three basic terms: copy, work, and writings.

In answer to the dilemma "What is copying?" there is nothing more calming than Raymond Williams's fundamental statement on cultural production: "A form is inherently reproducible—that is its necessary definition as a form."[87] If we consider a "copy" as just another form of a work, then we circumvent the semiotics of similitude since, in intellectual property doctrine, copying does not imply linguistic, phonic, or iconic similarity. But copying by machine is constantly conflated with all manner of replication, simulation, and, in our case, imitation. Thus it is that we have the potential confusion in *Sinatra* as to whether the right to prohibit others from copying a sound reproduction (duping) is also a right to prohibit others from copying a sound reproduction (imitation by performance).

I don't want to give the impression that American copyright law gave a particular shape to new technologies because it could not comprehend them. A closer look at *White-Smith v. Apollo* against the political and economic backdrop of 1908 tells us something else. Although intellectual property at times may seem to be rife with the most commonsensical notions of "how things are" (of what constitutes an identity, a name, a face), it always has a reason. Sometimes these assumptions are clearly political; at other times the political goal is submerged.[88] At the level of Supreme Court rulings and federal statutory developments, the connection between a political goal and an aesthetic form often *appears* to be one of causality. We can almost see forms of culture taking their odd shapes in conformation with national policy. But it is not enough to see these federal rulings as producing "effects." They also summarize ideological conflicts. As Maureen Cain and Alan Hunt put it in their comment on Marx's reading of the relationship between history and legislation in the fifteenth through the nineteenth centuries, "Legislation is both an active agency in historical processes and, at the same time, it records and encapsulates the balance between social forces at particular historical moments and the ideological forms in which these struggles are fought."[89]

Taken together, *White-Smith v. Apollo* and the Copyright Act of 1909 encapsulate U.S. ambivalence about monopoly and its relation to the problem of the "copy." Where the Supreme Court case took the hard line against monopoly, the legislative reform gave a new, modified monopoly back to composers in the form of restrictions on use of their work by others. But in *White-Smith*, the Supreme Court's conclusion that piano rolls were not "copies" of the musical composition was an attempt to stave off a developing monopoly.

What exactly did the Supreme Court seek to achieve by deciding that the perforated rolls within which music was encoded were not copies and therefore were not copyrightable?[90] The court was aiming for that balance between circulation and restriction that was thrown off by either monopoly concentration or rampant piracy. In both the 1908 case and the 1909 act, the refusal to grant copyright reflected a concern about concentrated monopoly—the fear, in this instance, that the Apollo Company would dominate the player piano market by manufacturing software as well as hardware, piano rolls as well as pianos. The situation was reversed, however, sixty years later during a period characterized by a relative political indifference to monopoly growth. In the 1971 amendment, copyright recognition reflected instead political concern about the worldwide piracy of U.S.-produced sound recordings.

This historical seesawing between circulation and restriction is in turn underwritten by the contradictory principles behind the justification for copyright: Whereas legal restriction is supposed to encourage creativity (by securing the fruits of the author's labor for a limited period), circulation is supposed to make creativity possible by freeing up cultural raw materials. But once these materials are freed up, more works are produced for which author-proprietors want protection. And the restriction on the use of these works, in turn, takes them out of circulation.

There is one more aspect of *White-Smith* that I want to examine, since it is so relevant to the commercial effort to transform the immaterial into the material by means of a *right*. In copyright law, the right to prohibit constantly threatens to turn into the right to possess an object. Justice Holmes spoke to this tendency in his dissenting *White-Smith* opinion: "The right to exclude is not directed to an object in possession or owned, but is *in vacuo*, so to speak." Further, "It is a prohibition of conduct remote from the persons or tangibles of the party having the right." And finally:

> The ground of this extraordinary right is that the person to whom it is given has invented some new collocation of visible or audible points—of lines, colors, sounds, or words. The restraint is directed against reproducing this collocation, although but for the invention and the statute anyone would be free to combine the contents of the dictionary, the elements of the spectrum, or the notes of the gamut in any way that he had the wit to devise.[91]

For the producers of "new collocation[s] of visible or audible points," it is difficult to think that they have nothing in hand. Holmes's notion of a possession *in vacuo* brings to mind R. F. Whale's dramatization of the difference between the thing itself and the right to copy it, the life and death of the painting and its copyrighted reproduction. The painting might be consumed in a fire, but it is survived by the right to copy it. After the painting is destroyed, the reproduced work "takes on its own 'life.' "[92] Indeed, this is borne out in Vandevelde's overview of U.S. unfair competition law since the turn of the century; what Justice Holmes saw as the protection of a valuable interest has become an argument for the existence of a new property. More and more cultural phenomena, which are often unpropertylike to begin with, come to have this legal designation, which, for the parties interested in these values, produces the voice and the face as self-expanding capital. Such is the case with the argument for the protection of singing style.

What Is Singing Style?

If sound, the immediately evaporating signifier, eludes aesthetic definition, what do we do with sound "style"? Historically, style has a reputation for being inconsequential and only ornamental. If musical *sound* is not heard as such, neither is *style*, that decorative particularity that often goes unnoticed unless it announces itself *as such*. For an author, style provides an edge of distinctiveness over other authors. But this excess, while it may be real to authors and apparent to critics, may be totally invisible to audiences. While the connotations of style may "reach" audiences, they may not see or hear the twist, the inflection, or the nuance that carries as well as constitutes this something extra.[93]

A case for the protectability of style, then, contends with the aesthetic reception of stylistic coding in the various worlds of arts and culture. This invisibility and inaudibility of style presents special problems for any movement aimed at instituting its copyright protection. A further disadvantage for proponents of a copyright in artistic "style" is that performers (both actors and musicians) have been historically excluded from the benefit of the protection that is afforded other culture workers, such as painters and writers. For the performer, the problem is one of securing rights to (and thus royalties on) the *interpretation* of works rather than the works themselves.

Advocates of the existence of "rights" in an interpretative performance have seen the development of mechanical technologies as an opportunity for artists at last to "secure" the expression that had been easily appropriable before new material forms gave it concrete existence. In 1934, for instance, Robert Homburg, writing from the point of view of French law, argued that "scientific progress separates the intellectual part from the material part of the artist's activity."[94] Reviewing the proceedings of the 1928 meetings held to revise the Berne Convention, Homburg plainly summarized the position of the convention: "[A] performer is not an author." The International Union of Artists agreed, but added that the performer should have international protection when his performance was "creative." This "part of the artist," the report continued, had become unmistakable with the advent of radio, phonography, and motion pictures: "The 'form' until then crystallized in books or scores where only the work of the writer or of the composer was apparent became condensed in reels of film and phonograph records which brought out the creative part of the interpreter."[95] But while this new hard "evidence" of the performer's interpretative style, this condensation in reels and records, has historically made the case for performers in Europe, in the U.S. this performance right has not materialized for musicians or actors.[96]

To some degree, however, the "fact" that American copyright law isn't cognizant of a performance right is misleading. The charge that artists are denied "rights" in their interpretative work is often cast to imply that they are utterly defenseless against unauthorized "taking" or misconstrual. To a degree, the nonexistence of a performance right in the U.S. *is* a denial (at the level of federal statute) of the labor of the artistic worker. But what the property right argument so often eclipses is the possibility of what the law euphemistically calls other legal "remedies," many of them available at the state level: defamation, misappropriation, and right of privacy as well as right of publicity.

In the sound-alike cases, between *Gardella* in 1937 and *Midler* in 1988 there is a clear movement from an argument against deception to an argument for some kind of property right in a characteristic sound. In *Midler*, the problem of guarding against sound imitations is resolved not with an argument for protecting performance but rather with an argument for property in personhood—ostensibly something more valuable and inviolate than interpretative performance style.[97]

This is not to say that there has never been a systematic attempt to produce "style" as artistic property. Between 1937 and 1988, the various arguments made on behalf of the concretization of style have tried to separate the work of performance from the already secure underlying musical work. Like the case made on behalf of artistry in the photograph, the argument here is that something exists that has previously gone unrecognized, something that the law needs to "bring out." Is the work of performance, then, there to be discovered, or is it instead created only as it is legally recognized? Unlike the "work of authorship" argument on behalf of the photographer, this strategy insists on the preexistence of a *work*, not the presence of the *author* in the *work*.

But the legal attempt to find an "artistic property" in style by turning style into a "work" depends upon the question of whether or not it is a "writing." If it is a writing, as the argument goes, copyright protection should be available.[98] Or in yet another strategy, style may be seen as a *derivative work*, subject to the copyright provision that allows for the adaptation of an "original" work in an "original" way into other media (as in, for instance, the transposition of a novel into a motion picture narrative). For this strategy, what is required is that the adaptation be a "distinguishable variation."[99] From this vantage, one legal commentator has argued that in *Sinatra* and *Booth* the "stylistic contributions" do not touch the property rights in the underlying compositions upon which the performances are based.[100] In this line of thinking, in other words, the song is separable from its "distinctive expression," ample evidence of which is provided by the thirty distinct recorded versions of "Up, Up, and Away," each different from the one popularized by the Fifth Dimension.[101]

But the issue of the separability of the singing style from the song itself cuts both ways. In *Sinatra*, Judge Trask's decision turned on the fact that while Nancy Sinatra's vocal rendition was not hers to claim, what mattered was the musical copyright in the song, for which Goodyear secured permission from composer Lee Hazelwood before the commercials were telecast. In so ruling, the court attempted to forestall the possibility of multiple claims; had Sinatra's style become attached to the composition, it would make the use of the song by others prohibitively expensive. Future artists would face a nightmare of negotiations with singer as well as composer. Judge Trask presented a vision of future licensees of the musical composition having to secure releases from musicians as well as from Sinatra herself for every use of "These Boots Are Made for Walkin'."[102] And American entertainment law in general has vacillated between following Judge Trask and understanding style as protectable work, between seeing style as an expression that circulates and seeing it as a work that doesn't.

Presented with the same question of the separability of the song and the style of singing, the semiotics of musical performance shows the same sort of ambivalence. It sees the popular singer's mode of shaping the melody and lyrics as something that significantly reforms the music that she uses for her own purposes. The singer's voice, like interpretative work on products of culture, rewrites the song, and a popular rendition such as Sinatra's will never leave the underlying composition exactly where it found it.[103] There will be lingering connotative echoes and accents. But the music will still be a freestanding set of signs available to the next singer, or for the next instrumental arrangement. This possibility that the popular singer's style is both permanently intertwined with and ultimately separable from the composition seems at first an enigma. Is the musical composition (like the dramatist's written scene) delivered through the voice-body medium of the actor? Is musical performance akin to what Tony Bennett calls the "activation" of the literary text?[104] What is the relationship between the latent words on the book page or the notes on the score and what might be called the performative reader?

From the existing theorization of the relationship between music, language, and the singing voice, we have some help with this question. Existing theory gives us an image of singing style as the product of this very interrelation. That is, the manner in which music and language come together is itself the stylistic measure. In "Music, Voice, Language," Barthes gives us the beginnings of a theory in his distinction between pronunciation and articulation in the singing voice. Whereas the former is rather more respectful of the music in its maintenance of balance between the phraseological "line of meaning" and the melodic "line of music," articulation does some violence to music. Pronunciation, rather than intrusively entering language where it is unwelcome, finds the music that is already there in language, finds what is "amorous" in voiced words. But articulation, says Barthes, "explodes into the music and deranges it . . . thrusts itself forward." It is the "intruder, the nuisance of music."[105] Here Barthes is using concepts derived from a particular school of French vocal training not necessarily generalizable to other genres of singing (each of which has its own stylistic requirements). But his critique *does* make us think of singing, as vocalists do, as the rush of air that becomes speech or musical tone *in the mouth*. Music locates the rhythms and pitches, the resonances and beats already in language and recognizes them as its own. The discourse of vocal music is not foreign to the body as is the written word. The voice, to paraphrase Barthes, is the place where the body meets discourse.[106] The body, in a sense, is always *in* the voice. We hear it, as he is so often quoted as saying, in the "grain" of the voice.[107] As Caruso's physician tells us, it was the configuration of the internal cavities and the resonant bones that really produced *that* amazing voice.[108] So the body produces vocal distinctiveness, and it is the body that is heard in the voice.

This line of reasoning suggests that the voice is as distinctively "printed" with the identity of the singer as the photograph is with the facial identity. Clearly, here is an observation that would help any argument for a right of publicity in the voice. But what happens when that voice (like Nancy Sinatra's) is also delivered to us via a song? Is the singing voice fitted to the

rhythms and the tonality of the musical form? And is it therefore significantly altered by the written notes on the score? Again, we are faced not
only with the question of the total performance style but also with the
problem of musical genre.

If style is difficult to pinpoint, and sound recording is troublesome,
music itself represents an even more vexing problem for the student of
cultural meaning. Music is not a sign system that lends itself to study on
the linguistic model. What it gains from its capacity to retain everything
that language cannot express, it seems to lose in the fact that it is at once
articulate and inarticulate. The piano, Barthes writes, "speaks without
saying anything." Music is neither ideas nor meanings, but signification
on the verge of meaning;[109] rather than a system of signs, it is a "field of
signifying," a dispersed "shimmering."[110]

If semiotic theory finds musical composition perplexing, what does
copyright doctrine do with claims of substantial similarity in sound?[111] In
fact, the issue of "What is music?" arises only when a court has to analyze
two musical pieces to decide if one composer copied another when there is
no evidence that one had had direct access to the other's music.[112] Since
music, according to legal commentators, does not "communicate ideas"
in the way that literature does, the burden of proving copying is placed
directly upon comparison of the two "expressions," or the musicological
elements in the compositions.[113]

Despite the existence of rough tests devised within copyright law that
could take account of musical structures, the history of case law suggests
that in copyright law music is synonymous with melody only. And if
copyright law has historically "heard" musical compositions in terms of
their melodies alone, to the exclusion of chord structure and harmonics, is
it any wonder that musical "style" has historically continued to evaporate
in the law?[114] And is it any wonder that imitation and duplication as well
as re-performance and re-recording are confused? Both recording and
performing are always in danger of disappearing as specific labors, which
explains the commercial feasibility of sound stand-ins and the effectiveness of the machines of invisibility (orchestra, recording session, audiotape deck) that produce them. Although neither seen nor heard in legal
terms, however, stylistic signifiers are the basis for audience "recognition."[115]

Rock singing presents us with a particular problem in stylistic apprehension, for one could argue that rock singing style is inseparable from the persona of the singer. One recent rock critic has adapted film criticism's distinction between the *auteur* and the *metteur en scène* to make the point about the singer:

> The musical equivalent of the *metteur en scène* is the performer who regards a song as an actor does his part—as something to be expressed, something to get across. His aim is to render the lyric faithfully. The vocal style of the singer is determined almost entirely by the emotional connotations of the words. The approach of the rock *auteur* however, is determined not by the unique features of the song but by his personal style, the ensemble of vocal effects that characterize the whole body of his work.[116]

But the question, of course, is this: Why do the musical conventions of pop—especially rock—require the foregrounding of the singer-persona, who no longer effaces himself or herself in deference to an author's message? In his discussion of the way lyrics are delivered in popular songs, Simon Frith writes, as if in response: "In songs, words are the sign of a voice. A song is always a performance and song words are always spoken out, heard in someone's accent. Songs are more likely plays than poems; song words work as speech and speech acts, bearing meaning not just semantically, but also as structures of sound that are direct signs of emotion and marks of character."[117] Frith goes on to suggest how singers perform songs nonverbally, through tone and tempo changes, emphases and accents, but also through the *signifiance* of sighs, pleas, sneers, and commands. As Frith suggests, such presignifying utterances are part of the language of music, even if they are not (as yet) the formalized language of the lyrics. Rooted as it is in the American blues tradition, does rock carry the resonances of an oral culture's closer physical involvement with the environment?[118] And can one describe the physicality of the blues idiom (carried over into rock, but diminished in the long cultural crossover) in terms of emotional signs that are somehow melded into instrumentation or vocalization? Such a description might help us account for the distinctiveness of the angry thumping of Nancy Sinatra's version of "These Boots Are Made for Walkin'." In her performance, she brought to the musical composition a new role: the tough female "love trucker" who ("Are you ready, boots?") kicked her man and stomped away.[119]

Bette Midler and Property in the Voice

I am surprised that it has taken so much historical and political background to explain why, in 1970, Nancy Sinatra could not win a judgment against Goodyear Tire's appropriation of her singing style. The simple explanation for the outcome in *Sinatra* is that at that time in history, American copyright law did not protect a recording that was a performed "imitation" of prerecorded sound. And so styles of singing were treated as performance signs that were left "available" for others to use. But why, in 1988, was Bette Midler able to win a judgment from the California Court of Appeals against Ford Motor Company for using a sound-alike to imitate her voice in a television commercial? Given that the facts in the cases are almost identical, how can we account for the completely different outcomes? Both singers developed bold vocal styles and unmistakable personas. In both cases, Young and Rubicam Advertising Agency hired other singers to create the impression that Sinatra and Midler were actually singing over the images in the televised advertisements. In both cases, aspects of these star personas were borrowed without permission or attribution. But Nancy Sinatra did *not* secure a verdict against the company and the advertising agency, and Bette Midler *did*.

If we examine the two cases internally, we find that the *Midler* court, in reversing the district court decision, adhered to existing principles that evolved through the other cases we have discussed. Judge Noonan asserted again that "mere imitation" of sound recording was not an infringement and that the voice itself was not copyrightable. The opinion was thus linked to precedent, and it therefore contributed to the coherence of an evolving doctrine. But the crucial difference in *Midler* was the reference to section 990(b), a 1985 amendment to the California Civil Code that offers statutory protection to the voice, signature, photograph, or likeness of a deceased celebrity. Section 990(b) provides rights to these attributes as "property rights."[120] What Midler therefore had was a "proprietary interest" in her identity, the judge reasoned. The "proprietary interest in identity" introduces two new categories into a sound-alike case that we have not seen featured until now: personal identity and property value in the voice.

First, Judge Noonan asked: "Why did the defendant ask Midler to sing if her voice was not of value to them?" And second, he went on to establish the connection between voice and personal identity. "A voice," he said, "is as distinctive and personal as a face." In conclusion, Noonan argued, "A fortiori, these observations hold true of singing, especially singing by a singer of renown. To impersonate her voice is to pirate her identity."[121]

Midler signaled a new development in intellectual property law, one that had been evolving since the fifties but that was not recognized in common law until the early seventies: the introduction of the right of publicity paradigm.[122] By the eighties, the right of publicity would become part of the civil code in a number of states, and this meant that the celebrity performer could now meet the problem of the infringing sound-alike by legal recourse to "personhood" and "property." In short, intellectual property law moved to reinsert the legal subject and its rights squarely into the work. Nancy Sinatra argued only that she had produced a secondary meaning in her product, that is, her *style of singing*. Bette Midler's complaint was that her very identity-property had been stolen.

Thus far I have considered only the issues arising from the appropriation of the voice and the face where the parties in conflict are the celebrity who is imitated and the infringer who employs the sound-alike or the look-alike without consent. In the course of performing for those technologies that record and preserve the voice and the face, however, the celebrity *does* give over, by contract, these aspects of personhood to other parties. But how are the voice and the face "given over" without being lost forever to the performer?[123]

What we have seen so far is that a body of case law accumulates around difficult areas in the law. There is a kind of case law accretion that builds up around legal ambiguities. These ambiguities are in turn often signs of an ambivalence in the wider culture. In entertainment law, it is generally held that the purpose of a contract is to clarify and ensure. But what I want to consider in the next two chapters is how the entertainment industry's personal services contract has instead historically constructed an area of legal ambiguity concerning the rights to the name, likeness, and voice. This ambiguity would in time give rise to a body of case law in which the families of celebrities who had signed away the rights to their personal attributes began to assert "personhood" and "property" claims in the name of the deceased.

CHAPTER FIVE

Reading Star Contracts

How are wastepaper baskets and lunch boxes like music videos? Let me answer this with a discussion of a recent entertainment industry arbitration as it pertains to motion picture exploitation.

In June 1986, Joseph F. Gentile, arbitrator in a labor dispute between the Screen Actors Guild and major Hollywood producers (Columbia Pictures, Metro-Goldwyn-Mayer/United Artists, Orion Pictures, Paramount Pictures, Twentieth-Century Fox Film, Universal City Studios, and Warner Brothers) was asked to decide whether the use of a film clip of a motion picture in a music video constituted a "reuse." If the producers of the more than two hundred music videos made since the first of these videos (*War Games* in 1983) had reused motion picture clips featuring SAG members, then they were in violation of the SAG basic agreement. Where the producers might be considered in violation of the SAG agreement was in their failure to bargain with the actors involved. If Gentile defined music videos in terms of the contractually established uses of the employed actor's image, then the motion picture producers would be "contractually excused" from the requirement that they negotiate the employment provisions of this new use with the Screen Actors Guild.[1] What was at stake? On the one hand, SAG saw that motion picture actors might be paid additionally for the use of their images in clips constituting the music video if the new form could be established as a particular type of use. On the other hand, the producers wanted to treat music videos as an extension of their traditional right to use actors' images as part of their marketing campaigns.

As the 1960 SAG contract defined the producer's entitlement: "This provision shall not limit Producer's right to use photography or sound track in exploiting the picture, or in trailers or in advertising, as provided in the Basic Agreement."[2] The operative principle here has to do with the distinction between the motion picture itself and the promotion that launches it, the history of which I have already touched upon. And here it is in the producer's interests to contractually secure the right to reproduce (reuse) the image and voice of the actor in scenes from the motion picture in a variety of promotional forms. In the contemporary period, new sites of promotion have been increasingly brought within the terms of labor relations as contractual issues. By 1983, in addition to exploitation, trailers, and advertising, promotional films, news programs, and award programs had been added to the list of reuses covered in the SAG basic agreement.[3] In that contract, different provisions are laid out for each of these categories of reuse.

Although the real issue was actor compensation, the 1986 arbitration report is phrased in such a way that it would appear that the dispute was decided in terms of the relation between the new form (music video) and existing industry practices. The producers tried to establish that, of all of the categories of reuse provided for in the contract, the music video was most like a preview of coming attractions, or "trailer." If the music video could be defined as a "trailer," actors did not need to be compensated, even for the reuse of behind-the-scenes shots photographed with separate cameras. SAG, in contrast to the producers, preferred to see music videos as "promotional films" (defined as those short films that use behind-the-scenes shots to "illustrate the 'making of' the motion pictures"). This type of reuse required individual bargaining with those actors who were paid $25,000 or more for their work on the motion picture.[4] In other words, actors would be more likely to be compensated for the reuse of their images if the arbitrator decided that music videos were promotional films than if he decided that they were trailers.

The arbitrator, however, finally decided for the producers. But in his decision he dismissed the producers' "trailer" analogy. Although the music video and the trailer were both a kind of "teaser," he reasoned, in the context of promotion for a theatrical release, the industry's definition of "trailer" could not be stretched to fit the music video.[5] What *was* the music video then? Gentile concluded that the music video "met the test" of exploitation, which was defined in the 1960 SAG basic contract as "taking advantage of a situation in order to promote and publicize a theatrical motion picture to enhance the profits to be gained from its release."[6] How did he determine this? In his decision, Gentile relied most heavily on the testimony of publicity department personnel, who described the production of music videos as part of current motion picture marketing strategy.[7] Not only were the videos distributed through marketing and publicity departments, but they were financed through them as well. Moreover, the producers' publicity departments were involved in coproduction with music video–making companies, which were supplied with the clips and the key art from the film. As promotion, music video distribution was handled like a single from the film sound track: The video went to outlets such as MTV free of charge. Also, like the traditional motion picture advertising campaign, this kind of promotion was packaged and positioned to appear in the four-to-six-week pre-release "window period."[8]

Although the 1986 arbitration report did not attempt to answer the question of whether the music video is actually a new form of entertainment, that issue is alluded to in the concluding paragraphs: "This case raises a difficult and complex problem. A movie music video may leave the primary orbit of "exploitation" of a theatrical motion picture and gain an overriding independence as it moves into the 'secondary market.'"[9] Contrary to Gentile's conclusion, then, the motion picture music video may not be understood strictly as exploitation for a soon-to-be-released film. But what *does* the music video become as it moves into this secondary market? Is it a new form in and of itself, as opposed to a parasitical promotional form? Legal thinking, as we should remember, tackles problems of aesthetic form by analogizing from existing categories. At the same time, however, in its distinction between restriction and circulation, intellectual property law cuts culture up into protected and unprotected, exclusive and nonexclusive zones.

From the producer's point of view, the law establishes what might be called free zones and toll zones, spheres of circulation within which the producer does or doesn't pay the actor for his or her photographic likeness. In regard to the likeness of the actor, then, the contract maps out the free and toll zones of representation. From another vantage, we can "read" in the contract's handling of image reproduction something significant about the history of labor relations in the American film and television industry. But this less familiar history is also a history of production and distribution, one that must be told in somewhat different terms, since it is about how transfer of rights and control of labor become control of image property. To read that history, we need to investigate the legal ancestry of the music video decision in the "results and proceeds" section of the studio term contract, which began to take shape in 1927 after the advent of sound.

Background

Thus far, we have been considering the provisions of a basic union contract, employment stipulations that would apply to all members of the Screen Actors Guild, no matter how well paid they were. More powerful actors, of course, negotiate special conditions on top of the basic agreement, and what I want to consider are the features of these star term contracts, which bound studio employees even in the years *after* the Screen Actors Guild became the chief bargaining agent for industry actors.

First, we need to separate the standard features of the personal services contract from the exceptional features written in such agreements. For example, the "act of God" (or *force majeure*) clause and the "morality clause" are both standard in most employment contracts of this type.[10] Nevertheless, during the studio era, when the producing company was all-powerful, these contracts sometimes became the focus of exceptional power battles, which held potential interest for the public. Richard Griffith exaggerates somewhat but captures a sense of how the contract disputes were made relevant to fans: "The studio contract system and the contracts themselves, right down to the 'acts of God' and the 'morality clauses' in the fine print, were of greater interest than the plots of current pictures."[11] Possible discharge for gross immorality or "misconduct in the course of service" or, again, the negotiation of unusual provisions written in "fine print" could be reproduced as gripping narratives. In Jack Warner's disputes with George Raft, James Garner, Errol Flynn, James Cagney, Olivia De Havilland, and Bette Davis, contract issues came to life for fans who followed these legal dramas.

The star contract in the studio period represented a complicated convergence of several legal entities. The first convergence has to do with the way the "private" person meets the star image in the contract. The contract may be a meeting place for two legal entities, but it is also the place where the person can be seen to escape from the image.[12] As one sign of the star, the studio term contract has some advantages over other signs (personal appearances, newspaper interviews, photographs), which promise indexicality but deliver only myth. The contract has a truth status because it bears the notarized signature of the actor, divulges his or her legal name, and contains confidential information about the real conditions under which the star works—including information about his or her salary. As an icon and a fetish, however, the star contract bears comparison with the photograph. (Consider, for instance, the remarkable sale in 1975 of Rudolph Valentino's contract for *The Sheik* [1921], which, mounted along with his sepia-tinted portrait, sold for $7,500.)[13] But more serious leakage of the real from the image is produced in a second convergence—the contractual convergence of the star and the studio. For it is often within and around the contract that antagonisms surface and potential clashes erupt into litigation.

Star contract negotiations had significant publicity value during the studio era for what they appeared to "betray" about the stars, as I have said. But just as information appeared, it had to be interpreted and managed, in part by translating it into the lives of the star's fans. Most of the translation and interpretation of the "fine print" features of the star contract went on in mass circulation publications, such as newspapers and fan magazines.

"Crazy Contracts of the Stars," a typical article that appeared in *Motion Picture* in 1943, featured the more unusual provisions of these contracts.[14] First, I want to deal with the way the article constructs its reader; and second, I want to consider its attempt to translate the star contract provisions in a particular way. Relevant here is Richard Dyer's observation that some stars more than others embody an ordinary-extraordinary dialectic, which synthesizes a general condition of American stardom best summed up in the "rare as gold and common as bread" syndrome identified by Edgar Morin.[15] This dialectic, in turn, works ideologically as it is able to articulate and yet contain competing values within the culture by unifying them as the "traits" of a single star image.[16] Implicit in the ordinary-extraordinary dialectic is a hint of the connection between the star and the ordinary person whose fantasy depends upon the unity-in-difference of these two possibilities. Finally, the dialectic helps to wish away the economic and social distance between the ordinary fan (usually female) and the exotic star.

"Crazy Contracts of the Stars" then bridges the gap between the life of the star and the life of the fan and at the same time holds out the star's exoticism and specialness, without which there would be no justification for the institution of stardom. But if the article characterizes the star as eccentric and subject to what it calls "screwballitis," then how is it to make the female fan similar to the star? The author begins by asking, "Have you a little private superstition? Are you 'tetched' in the head? Do you fear something that would jinx you if it came up in your job? Or is there something that you feel would bring you luck if you could make it a condition of your work?"[17] The article adroitly constructs the reader as both superior to and equal to the star. She is able to excuse and understand the star's eccentricities and superstitions, but only because she is a normal, sensible person. She too has eccentricities and superstitions, but they are only "little, private" ones.[18]

Clearly, the emphasis on luck and superstition here deflects attention from the real issue of employment conditions and redirects it toward the inexplicability of human behavior. Still, the material in the article is drawn directly from the basic employment concerns of actors and actresses who worked under term contracts during the studio period, and the article's examples of "quirkiness," in fact, all fit in three areas of particular sensitivity: support staff and personnel issues, work conditions, and control of one's image. And we should remember that the article's ostensible topic, the term contract, was a major means for working out conflicts between studio and star over the interpretation of the star image. Male stars, in particular, attempted to ensure the construction of their own versions of masculinity through contract stipulations. Gene Kelly's contract clause forbidding the studio to make up or retouch his facial scar was a well-known case, and "Crazy Contracts," with muted cattiness, congratulates Tyrone Power for his successful negotiation with Twentieth-Century Fox, which gave him the right to mark his own photographs for retouching: "His precaution has kept the re-touchers from turning him into the pretty-boy type, a metamorphosis that at various times has threatened to ruin several handsome Hollywood leading men."[19] Female stars, the article goes on, are concerned about both their costuming and the images constructed for them by the publicity departments. Eleanor Powell's contract, for instance, contained a clause ensuring that she would not be required either to wear anklet socks or to appear with bare legs without tights or hose. And Ann Sheridan, in an attempt to control her image at the level of publicity discourse, asked Warner Brothers for approval of all "descriptive phrases"—a retaliation against the studio's attempt to promote her as the "Oomph" girl.[20]

But whereas the star wanted some control over self-definition, the studio wanted image insurance. Sydney Greenstreet's contract, for example, included the agreement that he not let his weight fall below 250 pounds.[21] And it was often rumored that Buster Keaton was required by contract not to laugh in public. Thus continuity within the film from shot to shot as well as on-screen and off-screen consistency of character type would be backed up by written contract. The studio used the contract to secure on-screen continuity through provisions for illness and vacations, wardrobe fittings, tardiness on the set, absences, photographic sittings and retakes. But while the studio tried to guarantee continuity, stars with demands represented the threat of discontinuity in the eyes of their employers. Stars retaliated with riders modifying wardrobe requirements, stipulating screen billing order and typeface size on the credits, and mandating the number of close-ups per picture. It was also common practice for the stars to write requests for particular designers, hairdressers, and cinematographers into their studio contracts. Again, such demands were an attempt on their part to control the manufacture of their own images within the constraints of the studio system.

But the written contracts also testify to the stars' concern about securing an environment conducive to producing their best work. In the struggle between studio and employee over the contents of the star image, it was clear that the industry did not want actors to operate in competition with producers. Thus one of the recurring points of studio-star contention understandably had to do with the employment of outside press agents. The studios took a firm stand against the star's use of such image industry middlemen, and in the thirties even moved to require that all agents be licensed by producers, a proposal opposed by the Screen Actors Guild.[22]

How, then, do we move from this local struggle over the image to the structure of monopoly capital? In one of the few overviews of economic theory as it relates to the star system during the studio era, Gorham Kindem dismisses the attempts of traditional economics to understand the star phenomenon. Paul Samuelson, for instance, has argued for understanding stars in terms of the "pure economic rent" they can extract as their box office value increases, much as land value fluctuates with the demand for grain. Or, again, Sidney Finkle and Vincent Tarascio argue that stars, like professional athletes, are "individual monopolies" who can ask for high salaries because competing products cannot meet the fans' demands for specific star idols. Kindem takes issue with that view, stating that these theories, based as they are on the neoclassical understanding of supply and demand, do not take account of the oligopoly (noncompetitive) market within which producers who bought the labor of the stars used monopsony (single-buyer) control.[23]

The star phenomenon also offers at least two problems for the classic Marxist model of economics, Kindem continues: There is no traditional class conflict here, and the star is not an anonymous worker. Instead, the star is part of the product.[24] But despite the apparent irrelevance of a theory of class to the star phenomenon, some critics have productively used the theory to analyze the novelty of these economic relations. Barry King, for instance, sees the star as "ambiguously" situated halfway between labor and capital.[25] I would agree with King's theorization, but would go on to point out that the star is not only thus ambiguously situated, but has historically vacillated between labor and capital. In the twenties, for instance, the big box office stars such as Mary Pickford received a percentage of the studio profit.[26] But those conditions changed in the financially rough thirties, when government-mandated industry cuts were threatened, and screen actors began to see themselves increasingly as labor. During the thirties, the seven-year term contract with its unfair provisions for suspension (as I will show) was, in fact, emblematic of exploitative studio work conditions.[27]

What, then, about the labor union function of the Screen Actors Guild in relation to worker-employee antagonism? SAG was formed in 1933 as a protest against the announced 50 percent pay cut for actors that had been mandated by the National Recovery Act.[28] The cut was subsequently withdrawn, but the union continued to function on the margins of the industry until Louis B. Mayer finally recognized it as the actors' official bargaining agent in 1937.[29] The few published histories of the Screen Actors Guild characterize the group as more cooperative than antagonistic to industry management and even portray it as instrumental in maintaining the extreme stratification within the acting profession.[30] But again, it is a matter of historical shift. As Danae Clark argues, when actors supported the studio's "discourse of industrial unity," they were seen as part of the "Hollywood community." But when they openly opposed the studio, as they did in the thirties, they were characterized as "workers."[31] Still, it is difficult to see even the more outspoken star actors instrumental in founding the SAG (Robert Montgomery, James Cagney, Eddie Cantor, Paul Muni, George Raft, Fredric March, Groucho Marx, to name a few) as worker-activists in the traditional sense.

But even if actors were categorically sometimes like labor in the thirties, they were more and more like capital following the industry changes of the late forties. First, after the 1948 Paramount decrees and the consequent demise of the studio with its stable of stars, the seven-year term contract was replaced by the contract on a per-picture basis.[32] In 1950, for example, actor James Stewart negotiated a percentage of the profits on the film *Winchester 73* with MGM, and thereafter more stars successfully made such arrangements with producers.[33] Not only did star actors increasingly operate as independent businesses in regard to motion picture production, but more and more they began to form businesses to market their own images. And once they gained some control of their own image capital, actors were in direct competition with the studios.

When television finally appeared, the serial form and commercial sponsorship structure that immediately defined the new industry altered management-labor relations significantly. Actors became more clearly like "workers" in the struggle to define the new medium. Bargaining was characterized by an escalation of disputes over the division of profits in new television-produced markets—especially in commercial advertisements and program syndication.[34] To some degree, the film studios first perceived the new medium as a "secondary market" outside the "primary orbit" of the motion picture.[35] But networks were leery of the motion picture industry, and both NBC and CBS originated their own programming in an attempt to keep from becoming mere "time-sellers" to the feature film industry.[36] The early "telefilm syndicators" who did show motion pictures were given time slots that attracted relatively small audiences, and the more popular genre films (such as westerns and gangster pictures) were recut by the networks and relegated to the margins of the schedule.[37] Through that approach, NBC and CBS maintained control of prime time.

If the networks thought that the film industry perceived television as a channel for promoting existing motion picture product, they were right. When, in 1954, the motion picture industry *did* secure prime time on the newest network, ABC, they still conceived of this programming as secondary to the *real* entertainment product. For instance, one-third of ABC's "Disneyland" was devoted to studio publicity and following its success, "Warner Brothers Presents" was initially conceived in a similar way.[38] The idea was to isolate three series based on Warner Brothers properties (*Casablanca*, *King's Row*, and *Cheyenne*) and then to include in each hour-long program a ten-minute Warner Brothers promotional film, *Behind the Cameras*. Although the formula for the 1955–56 season was not necessarily successful, "Cheyenne" ran for seven years and provided the model for "Maverick," "Lawman," "Sugarfoot," and "Colt 45."[39] These programs, like other successful series in the mid-fifties, spawned television's own new "secondary markets" in foreign and domestic syndication and merchandising.[40] In a way, the motion picture actor in the fifties was in a position similar to that of his or her counterpart, for whom music video made a difference in 1986. The actor was faced with a situation in which producers had found a new use for an image not covered by an existing contract.

The Studio Term Contract

Harry Braverman's model of the control of production under monopoly capital—with its division of labor, its centralization of employment, and its "scientific management"—usefully describes the efficient organization of the studio under the star system.[41] Producers used the seven-year contract to those ends, and in the process they stratified the work force and created the available pool of actors and actresses. An especially ingenious example of such a strategy was the management of the actor work force by what might be called cost-effective "miscasting." Studio head Jack Warner was particularly adept at using this technique in conjunction with the contractual provision for suspension as a means of keeping costs down. Warner would assign a high-salaried actor an unsuitable role, and when the actor refused it, the producer would suspend the actor without pay, thus cutting his own costs.[42] But the studio's interpretation of the suspension provision put actors in a position in which they thought of themselves as workers. Suspension effectively stopped the seven-year contract clock, thus adding more time to the actor's required employment for every day he or she was laid off. Actors who wanted to be free to work for other studios on scripts of their own choice felt trapped by the compulsory extension of their contracts. When actress Olivia De Havilland decided to challenge Warner Brothers in court, her contract had been stretched to nine years—two past the legal seven.[43] In that case, the actress successfully sued the studio for using suspensions to try to extend her obligation beyond the legal limit. As a result of *De Havilland v. Warner Bros. Pictures* (1944), the studios could no longer enforce the seven-year contract after seven calendar years had elapsed.[44]

Enforceability continues to be a basic issue in film and television industry contract disputes, which today center on the "standard agreement" (technically, a personal services contract). But there is more at stake in the enforcement of a personal services contract in the entertainment industry than in other fields of employment because the entertainer *is* the product. Without the musical or theatrical talent, there is often no music concert, no television program, and no motion picture.[45] At the same time, however, the performer is *not* a product. He or she cannot legally be forced to work, since to force an employee to work is a violation of the involuntary servitude clause of the Thirteenth Amendment to the U.S. Constitution. Faced with the problem of a celebrity under contract who will not work, entertainment industry employers have historically enforced the contract's *negative services covenant*, which stipulates that the employee must not work for anyone else during the term of the contract. If the employee takes another job, he or she can be sued for breach of contract. The ability to secure an injunction for such a breach depends upon two showings, which might be said to define the legal conditions of stardom. First, the employer must show that the services of the actor or actress are entirely extraordinary and unique. And second, he must show that without the services of *this* creative person, for whom no other could be substituted, he would suffer losses for which damages could not compensate him.[46] The legal conditions of stardom, from the employer's point of view, then, are predicated on the condition of exclusivity.

This condition is well illustrated in *Warner Brothers Pictures, Inc. v. Nelson* (1936), the case in which the studio successfully enjoined Bette Davis from appearing in a motion picture produced in England.[47] Some months before Davis left in anger for England, Warner Brothers had refused to loan the actress to RKO for the lead in *Mary, Queen of Scots*, and in retaliation she asked the studio for a new contract. In four years under contract to Warner Brothers, Davis had produced twenty-three films, six in 1935 alone, and she wanted a guarantee that she would have to do only four each year. In addition to a proper loan-out clause, she requested a salary escalation, a three-month vacation, her choice of cameramen, and a five-year—instead of a seven-year—contract. When Davis refused to accept the role she was assigned in *God's Country and the Woman* without a new contract, the studio suspended her. After months of negotiation, the studio made no attempt to meet her requests halfway, and Davis left the country to make a film in England with an independent company.[48]

Consequently, the studio sued Davis for breach of contract, filing its suit against her in London, where she was working at the time. There, the negative services provision in the actress's Warner Brothers contract was upheld by a British court, which was largely persuaded by two of the producer's arguments. The court agreed that injury to the studio was out of proportion to any amount that could be assessed in damages. But the court was particularly impressed by Warner Brothers' argument that Davis would still be appearing in films that she had produced earlier for the U.S. studio. As the court saw it, any independently produced Bette Davis film would be in competition with the films the actress had already made for Warner Brothers.

The Davis litigation illustrates as well the critical legal studies critique of contract law observing that as courts enforce contracts, they are indifferent to differences between the parties entering into the bargain. Or, as I discussed earlier, the contract produces unequals as equals.[49] Courts assume that the existence of an agreement signed and entered into freely by two parties is a sign of a fair bargain, but in fact, the actual fairness of the agreement is no longer even a consideration in Anglo-American law.[50] In the Davis case, for instance, the imbalance of the two parties (the corporation versus the employee) is masked by the implication that Davis had a power equal to that of her employer because her failure to perform contracted services for Warner Brothers could cause the company irreparable financial injury. But that equality, of course, is only imaginary, and in a contract dispute, "contracts of service" (and the equality they presuppose) may be challenged as "contracts of slavery," much as they were in *Warner Brothers v. Nelson*.[51]

The contract is magical not only in its facilitation of "imaginary relations" between parties but also in its capacity to transform and transfer the labor, rights, and property that the society holds to be inalienable.[52] Transferability, as Pashukanis puts it, is nothing more or less than the alienation of one's labor, which is characteristic of capitalist productive relations in general. "Capitalist property," he writes, "is basically the freedom to transform capital from one form to another, the transfer of capital from one sphere to another for the purpose of gaining the highest possible unearned income."[53] Another way of explaining the ease with which one form becomes another is by means of the concept of commodity fetishism. In the classic theorization in *Capital*, commodity fetishism is a condition produced in the entire society and arising out of the way the product of labor appears to the worker as something other than the result of his own work. The fetish aspect is important to retain here because of the features of unrecognizability, potency, and the creation of value.[54] It is the worker's own labor that creates value and is unrecognizable to him. At first it would seem that such a theory could not apply to the screen actor's performance. How could one mistake one's own image? To some degree, the transfer of his product from sphere to sphere explains something about this misrecognition. The further the product is removed from the worker, the less he sees it as his product. But that happens also because the transfer of rights in the image means that as it is transferred to second and third parties it is divided and split. It is reworked by other labors—the labors of editors, graphic artists, advertising directors, publicists, and photographers.

And it is the transferability of rights that is the basis of the mass marketing of the human image and the human voice in the communications industries. The basic film and television talent contract is markedly different from the employment contract in other industries (in which one agrees to be separated from one's labor power for the duration of the employment) because of what it is that the actor leaves with the employer. It is not exactly as though the actor leaves inventions or ideas with the employer.[55] In contrast with the ordinary worker, who leaves the proceeds of his work with his employer, the screen actor may be permanently separated from tangible aspects of personhood—his or her voice and photographic likeness. And since photographic and electronic technologies do, in fact, preserve the actor in time, the legal question becomes, Can the actor regain control of his or her image after the expiration of the term contract? Can these aspects of personhood, once they are embalmed in celluloid or stored on magnetic tape, ever be reclaimed by the actor? These and other questions not necessarily anticipated at the outset, have had to be resolved by rereading actor contracts from the studio years.

The "Results and Proceeds" Clauses

The section of the entertainment industry personal service contract that marks the boundaries of the image property is called the "grant of proceeds," the "grant of rights," or sometimes (in reference to the producer's profits and benefits) the "results and proceeds" clauses.[56] What one notices immediately in reading these sections is the redundancy of the phraseology that pertains to exclusivity. Not only does the artist "give and grant to the producer the sole and exclusive right to photograph any and all of her acts" (with "sole and exclusive" repeated as often as four times within the grant of proceeds section), but the same obligation is also stated as a negative provision: "[T]he artist shall at no time during said term grant the right to, authorize or willingly permit any person, firm or corporation other than the producer to make use of her name." In this case, however, exclusivity does not really mean the total prohibition of use by others (as it did in my earlier discussion of the negative services covenant). Here, the principle of exclusivity actually facilitates the transfer of rights in the image to a third party by binding up the grant so that no stray right or unforeseen use is lost in the process. The "sole and exclusive right" granted in the term contract means that only the studio may "allow others to make use of [the actress's] name for advertising, commercial and/or publicity purposes (other than in connection with the acts, poses, plays and appearances of the artist hereunder)."

But it was not only the actor's name and likeness that was governed by the "results and proceeds" clauses. After the advent of sound, the voice was added as well. In contractual terms, the coming of sound represented an unprecedented expansion of the producer's rights. With one new technology, studios not only cornered new markets but also acquired new acoustic properties. And they did so without having to finance the venture, simply because they acquired the vocal assets of the talent they already had under contract. Suddenly, the actor as legal subject had to be redrafted as a speaking entity as well as a bodily one.

Not surprisingly, contracts from the silent film period before 1930 conceive of the actor as voiceless and without any capabilities for producing either music or sound effects. But the industry's tendency to privilege the image over the voice has historically produced a contractual blind spot, and to this day, the legal provisions meant to pin down every conceivable element of the actor's persona may still omit the voice. In 1930, however, Warner Brothers was particularly enamored of sound, and the difference in Loretta Young's 1927 and 1930 contracts reflects that preoccupation.[57] The earlier contract stakes out only the studio's entitlement to "acts, poses, plays, appearances" (as well as "name of the artist, and pictures or other reproductions of the artist's physical likeness"), but the later contract discovers the actress as a simultaneous producer of sound.[58] The new wording in the "results and proceeds" section of Young's contract now acknowledges the studio's proprietal interest in the "voice and all instrumental, musical, and other sound effects produced by her in connection with such acts, poses, plays and appearances."[59] In other words, even if Loretta Young played the saxophone in a film, the music produced and recorded on the sound track would now belong to the studio. Anticipating the later development of the soundtrack album and acknowledging the radio broadcast, the post-sound section also gives the studio the right to "record, reproduce, and/or transmit" the star's sound performance, whether or not in conjunction with the exploitation of a motion picture.[60]

And so we encounter again the important difference between the use of the image for publicity purposes and its embodiment in the form of a motion picture. "Acts, poses, plays, and appearances" came to be interpreted as the *moving picture itself*, while the "name, voice, and likeness" designated commercial and promotional uses. Hence, the actor's image fell into two basic zones of utilization—the product and its exploitation. As embodied in the motion picture itself, the "acts and poses" of the actor belonged unquestionably to the copyright holder of that work of authorship, but the rights in the "name, voice, and likeness" were less clearly defined because of the opportunistic and ambiguous nature of exploitation. Historically, industry convention has held that the right to use the name, voice, and likeness in advertising for the motion picture or television product belonged to the producer, and courts have consistently upheld that view. But as the 1986 music video arbitration shows, exploitation for the entertainment product is a notoriously ambiguous category. To clarify things, the zone of exploitation has sometimes been broken down into *direct* and *indirect* advertising. *Direct* advertising corresponds with more clear-cut practices and forms (trailers, posters, magazine and newspaper copy referring to the film), while *indirect* advertising seems to refer to any opportunistic consumer good tie-up or even to the most tangential and offhand use of the actor's name, voice, and likeness.

The poor reputation of such tangential promotion may be attributed to two of the more historically controversial practices of *indirect* advertising for motion pictures: product licensing and product endorsement. Because of the easy transferability of rights, the likenesses of actors under contract can be recruited for any commercial purpose that suits the studio's fancy. The principle of contemporary product licensing works for the commercial property owner in the same way that tax collecting for the Vatican worked historically. Like the ancient church, the commercial property owner (or the owner's agent) *licenses* a local businessperson for a limited amount of time, to act in the name of the owner. But rather than collecting tax revenue in the name of the licenser, the commercial licensee returns revenue to him in the form of a royalty on consumer goods sold.[61] For example, a small company that manufactures inexpensive knickknacks or clothing will license a popular character, celebrity, or prestige symbol, such as Betty Boop, Michael Jackson, or Calvin Klein, through a licensing agent. The agent, such as United Features, Columbia Pictures Merchandising, or Licensing Corporation of America, acts, in turn, in the name of the owner of the image property.[62] Each licensed toy or greeting card may appear to the buyer with a familiar face, but that familiarity is produced by the radiation of millions of legally protected images issued from a single unseen source.

In this century, the character license was pioneered by Woolworth's dime store, which merchandised "Buster Brown" for shoes and socks. But the Midwestern shirt salesman Herbert "Kay" Kamen is the person remembered as the father of modern merchandising. Kamen had a vision of the world buying Mickey Mouse products, and he successfully persuaded Roy and Walt Disney to sell him their merchandising rights, which he owned until his accidental death; at that time the valuable rights reverted to the Disney corporation.[63] Around the same time, these practices would be extended to Shirley Temple—like Mickey Mouse, another merchandising legend. The character was first licensed to the Ideal Toy Company in order to produce the Shirley Temple doll for the 1934 Christmas season. Shirley's mother, Gertrude Temple, handled the negotiations involving the family, Ideal Toy, and Twentieth-Century Fox (where Shirley was under contract), and she produced an arrangement that would have been the envy of other stars. In the midst of the Depression, the Temples' first royalty check amounted to $70,000.[64]

Theoretically the motion picture studios could license any element in the mise-en-scène for reproduction as a consumer good. But the arrangements were easier to make for inanimate props, place names, abstract designs, and cartoon characters than for actors' faces and bodies. In the case of *Ziegfeld Girl* (1941), for example, hair barrettes and ladies' rayon and silk slips were licensed for tie-ups with the motion picture, and a royalty of several cents was returned to Metro-Goldwyn-Mayer for every ZIEGFELD GIRL item sold. The images of Lana Turner, Judy Garland, and

Hedy Lamarr would also have been available to merchants by the same means, subject to contractual stipulations.[65] But there would also be other considerations. First of all, manufacturers would be interested in licensing only if the image property were extremely popular and widely recognized; it would not be feasible to charge extra per item unless an increase in sales was probable. Second, such arrangements (as in Shirley Temple's case) involved elaborate three-way negotiations, and very few actors had the bargaining power to ensure their own percentage profit on star merchandise.

But studios discovered that they didn't necessarily need to license popular properties for a percentage return on sales when they could secure an equally valuable publicity advantage by means of cooperative advertising. Like product licensing, cooperative advertising was, in publicist's jargon, a "tie-up" or "tie-in," but it was a much less structured agreement between the motion picture studio and a consumer goods advertiser. To suggest how unstructured such a tie-up could be, one might refer to the studio practice of photographing actors with whatever products happened to be in the photographer's studio at the time of the shooting session.[66]

Beginning in the twenties, studios were besieged with requests for star product endorsements, both legitimate and illegitimate. (Actress Dolores Del Rio, according to one report, was asked to endorse a false eyebrow, a shoe polish, a wine tonic, and a line of bath fixtures.)[67] According to Roland Marchand, the popularity of print and radio endorsements in the twenties grew in part from the discovery that the "personal angle" was an effective way to influence potential buyers. For one thing, experts and celebrities, whose personal testimony and photographs appeared in advertisements, functioned, according to Marchand, like an aristocracy.[68] Moreover, the famous J. Walter Thompson philosophy of "testimonial advertising" was based on the idea that advertising messages should be "personified" to take advantage of three basic tendencies in mass society: curiosity about others, the spirit of emulation, and the search for authority.[69] But problems arose when the use of an actor in association with a consumer product implied the actor's approval and recommendation. Although testimonial advertising was quite successful for Thompson and other agencies, the practice fell into disrepute almost as soon as it became popular, amid charges that the statements by experts were fraudulent and that public figures never used the products they raved about.[70] The controversy over the misleading nature of testimonial advertising has continued into the present. To some degree, the 1938 tightening of the Federal Trade Commission advertising regulations protected consumers against "deceptive practices," thus checking the more irresponsible endorsement gimmicks.[71] Finally, in 1980, the FTC issued industry guidelines mandating that a celebrity endorser had to be a "bona fide user" of the product at the time of the endorsement.[72]

But even stiff federal guidelines cannot exactly regulate the principle of recommendation-by-association upon which product endorsement works. In the twenties, manufacturers quickly learned to stop asking celebrities to say that they liked a soap they had never used. Instead, businesses continued to associate the images and names of stars with products more subtly, in a range of contexts—on clothing hangtags, in store windows, and on display counters. It was just such an association that led Fred Astaire to charge *Esquire* magazine with unauthorized use of his image. An advertisement in the January 1936 issue of the magazine pictured Astaire in conjunction with the name of a jewelry company, along with the caption "As inspired by Fred Astaire in *Top Hat.*" The dancer argued that the advertisement created the impression that he wore the company's jewelry and that it therefore "exposed him to ridicule." Astaire won the case and was awarded $25,000 in damages.[73]

But more often than not, stars were stuck with unwanted advertising associations simply because the studio authorized them. In the early contracts, term players, with very few exceptions, had no right to withhold the use of their images from these *indirect* commercial arrangements—especially if the motion picture was mentioned in the advertisement. An actress might be shocked to see her image reproduced in conjunction with products as diverse as Auto-Lite car batteries or Serta mattresses and box springs, but there was little she could do about it. Kay Francis, for example, was surprised to find herself advertising Compco shoe soles in a 1933 issue of *Photoplay* magazine. But when she complained, the publicity department argued that the advertisement was part of an arrangement that would guarantee that her image would be used later on a *Photoplay* cover.[74] Although the studios managed their image properties by trading them and circulating them, often without the actor's knowledge, they also vigilantly policed them so that even if the studio used a star's photograph irresponsibly, the star could be sure that others did not. In 1935, for instance, when a Detroit dentist used Kay Francis's image on a circular advertising both his business and a dental manufacturing company, "Luxine," Warner Brothers took preliminary legal action.[75]

In the forties, stars with bargaining power tried to contractually stipulate that commercial uses of their names and likenesses be restricted to motion picture promotional campaigns. (After all, they could hardly object to advertising that legitimately secured exposure for their own films.) Many stars reserved the right to control their own likenesses out of a desire for privacy and a disdain for commercialism. Others tried to separate motion picture promotion from general commercial uses in an attempt to reserve the right to publicize their personal likenesses either for career advancement or as the basis of their own merchandising ventures.

But the star who successfully reserved the right to negotiate such matters was the exception during this period. More often than not, the studio retained full control of *all* commercial uses of the image. Warner Brothers, for instance, used at will the name and likeness of Bette Davis in magazine stories (notably the *Photoplay* advice column she "wrote" during these years) and, as her contract went on, in "trade papers and newspaper column stories and items, feature stories and items, motion picture production news, radio breaks." Such copy could be illustrated or not with Davis's likeness, within the "sole discretion of the Producer."[76] Crucially, that distinction entitled the producer to use Davis's image aspects *without* any direct ties to the motion pictures in which she might appear. To quote the 1943 contract: "The artist hereby grants to the Producer the right, which shall be sole and exclusive during the full term hereof, to use or make use of and control her name and/or her professional name and to use and/or distribute her pictures, photographs or other reproductions of her physical likeness for advertising, commercial or publicity purposes, *whether or not* in connection with the acts, poses, plays and appearances of the Artist or the advertisement or publicity of the photoplays produced hereunder."[77] In other words, the 1943 contractual agreement that handed to Warner Brothers all rights to the Davis name, voice, and likeness is worded in such a way that the studio can claim "Bette Davis" as its own corporate trademark for seven years. It would seem, then, that Warner Brothers alone authorized the popular discourse on Bette Davis. But, as Barry King has pointed out, Davis, as compared with Joan Crawford, was a relatively independent meaning-making agent in relation to her star image. In his terms, Davis was a *high autonomy* as opposed to a *low autonomy* star, the latter seeking to conform herself to the studio's image and the former to work independent of it.[78] Unlike Crawford, Davis chafed against the advertising tie-up rights in her contract.[79]

But Davis was unable to control, authorize, or initiate the commercial uses of her own image. And what's more, she was given no official right of approval of such uses until her 1949 contract, in which she succeeded in getting the studio to agree that her name and photograph would be used "in a dignified manner."[80] For Davis and other actors, exercising the right of approval over image use became a way of gradually loosening the shackles of the term contract. Increasingly, firms sent release forms to actors through the studio legal departments. And it was in the releases that actors could exercise a small degree of power and influence in shaping their own public personas.

Naturally, "approval" soon became a point of contention. In the "results and proceeds" section of some studio contracts from the mid-forties (and almost all contracts in the fifties) the star had to agree "not to unreasonably withhold such approval."[81] The phrase appears as a rider in Lauren Bacall's 1945 contract, drawing attention to a sore point in the negotiations. At Warner Brothers, the high drama of the clashes over studio uses of the actor's photograph was matched by disputes over motion picture roles. Something of the heat of the conflict is suggested in this portion of a telephone conversation between Jack Warner and Lauren Bacall, which was transcribed and placed in Bacall's personnel file:

Bacall: Well, I want to see it in the script.
Warner: Don't be so clever. Besides, your contract doesn't give you the right to tell us what to do. This is America where people live up to the contracts they sign or stand the consequences. I am sorry this all happened but that's the way of the world.[82]

The producer retaliated in the rider to Bacall's 1945 contract (she would agree "not to unreasonably withhold such approval"), but actors nevertheless registered their protest with clauses like the following, which appeared in Bacall's contract in 1945 (although not in Davis's two years earlier): "[T]he mere use of Artist's name and/or physical likeness in connection with any such tie-up shall not in itself be deemed an endorsement by Artist, express or implied, of such product."[83]

We need to keep in mind, however, that many actors at this time were not opposed to the unchecked uses of their images, particularly at the beginning of a career. Image circulation kept the actor alive in the public consciousness *between* motion picture roles and conveyed a message of popularity and commercial viability to fans as well as to the studio itself. Even Bacall, in the period covered by her 1945 contract, would sign a release giving J. Walter Thompson and Lever Brothers permission to use her "name and/or photograph or portrait" to advertise "Lux Toilet Soap, known in Brazil as Sabonete Lever, and/or Lux Flakes."[84] And in 1947 she signed a release granting "Arnold, Schwinn & Company and/or its advertising agent" the right to use her name and likeness in "magazine advertising, display advertising, and advertising literature" in the publication of the bicycle company's new "Cyclorama" advertising folder.[85] As Lauren Bacall's career testifies, the stars may have objected to such arrangements, but they pursued them nonetheless, for one fundamental reason: Merchandising and advertising helped to underwrite the personal monopoly, which strengthened the actor's bargaining position with the studio.[86] Hence the studio's fear of actors who hired press agents to manage clients' images, the better to consolidate their bargaining power.

For that reason and others, Warner Brothers tried to discourage stars from hiring their own press agents. And in fact the ban on press agents in the thirties was an important part of a broader crackdown on actors. Later, the prohibition became as much a means of controlling the shape of the star image in public as it was a way of protecting the exclusivity for which the studios had bargained so hard. The intent is clear in Bette Davis's 1943 contract; the studio agreed that she could employ a "personal press agent" to help her with her fan mail, *not* "for the purpose of arranging for interviews or giving statements to the press."[87] And the agent was not allowed to publicize production schedules or plans for stories because that was the exclusive right of the producer. By 1949, it appears, the studio began to back off somewhat on the issue of the separate press agent. Although Bette Davis signed away the possibility of employing a "personal press or publicity agent" for the purpose of promoting her motion picture production work, she *was* allowed to engage an agent to arrange and promote her other public activities.[88]

To give one final example, Joan Crawford violated her 1944 contract with Warner Brothers when she retained a press agent during the period of her first three pictures at Warner Brothers. But after the success of *Mildred Pierce* (1945), Crawford was able to negotiate the right to keep a personal agent as long as the extra publicity he generated for her contained only a "minimum reference" to her motion picture work with Warner Brothers. Her 1947 contract for three more pictures stipulated that there should be "as little conflict as possible" between the promotion of her motion picture performance and the promotion of her outside activities.[89] But Crawford, unlike Bette Davis, was more than willing to publicize herself through commercial vehicles throughout her career (from the MGM through the Warner Brothers periods), thus creating a different problem for her employers—the danger of "Joan Crawford" image saturation.[90] The studio, however, was concerned not so much with "allowable outside activities" ("radio, vaudeville, motion pictures, and other fields of entertainment") as with commercial product advertising. Crawford's renewed box office strength enabled her to negotiate the right to use her name, voice, and likeness in commercial advertising tie-ups *outside* the studio's standard right to use her image to advertise its motion pictures. What was at issue was the way the wording allowed Crawford to sign over her image to any other entertainment entity to promote radio shows, vaudeville shows, and even motion pictures produced by other studios. But in 1950 the Warner Brothers legal department would explore ways of interpreting Crawford's contract to the studio's advantage and wanted to draw the line at Crawford's outside use of her image in conjunction with commercial products.[91]

Rogers v. Republic

In the fifties, one of the fears of the studios—that the actor would enter into competition with them for his or her own image revenues—began to be realized. In the past, stars, such as Shirley Temple, who were able to negotiate merchandising arrangements as separate corporations had been the exception, especially if they worked for major studios. But Warner Brothers' concern with Joan Crawford's commercial activities and use of a press agent indicates the view that the star's outside commercial promotions constituted damaging competition. Still, Crawford's contractual arrangements, at least in part, *did* benefit the studio, simply because the publicity that she paid for helped to promote the motion picture product.

In contrast, Roy Rogers's negotiations with Republic Studios were unusual because his 1937 term contract made it possible for him to begin building a parallel company that would compete with the low-budget production house that still employed him. The potential conflict between Rogers and his former employer came to a head only after the actor had left the studio and was devoting full time to his own "Roy Rogers" enterprise. On the face of it, *Rogers v. Republic Pictures* (1952) looks like a dispute over whether or not Republic had the right to televise the star's western films.[92] As it was framed, the point of law had to do with this question: Did broadcasting the films constitute a "use" of them for commercial advertising? More specifically, did the broadcast of the films in conjunction with either the sponsor's message or the station's message produce these western films as advertisements? But there is something more involved here than the right to telecast motion pictures. In 1952 the judge wrestled with the relationship between programming and commercial advertising during a period when television form was still in flux. And in doing so, he addressed another question: "What is television form?"

Roy Rogers started his separate business in 1938, one year after signing his first contract with Republic Studios. The goal of the Rogers company was to commercialize the name, voice, and likeness of the western cowboy and his horse, "Trigger."[93] Republic agreed to an arrangement whereby the "results and proceeds" of the uses of the Rogers image were to go to the actor, who received these rights in lieu of additional salary. In exchange, the studio received the benefit of the extra advertising and publicity produced by Rogers's enterprise.[94] In 1942 the actor officially changed his name from Leonard Slye to Roy Rogers, thus consolidating his assets.[95] And in 1948, he entered into a final contract with Republic that extended the 1937 agreement until 1951 and stipulated that all commercial uses of the image would belong to him after the expiration of that contract—with one exception. Rogers would grant rights to Republic for perpetual use of "Roy Rogers and Trigger," and those rights would be limited to the advertisement of his motion pictures or of the studio itself.[96]

In 1951, however, Republic Productions made arrangements with the Hollywood Television Service to license the eighty-one motion pictures starring Roy Rogers produced between 1938 and 1951. The films were to be cut to fifty-three and a half minutes in order to fit the one-hour broadcast slot, and the image of the western star was to be made available for advertising in newspapers and other media.[97] But Rogers sought to enjoin Republic from licensing the motion pictures for such televisual syndication. Among other facts in the case, Southern California district court judge Hall found that such use would "substantially and irreparably damage" the star's own advertising business. Furthermore, the judge found that the value of his "name, voice or likeness" would be "destroyed or substantially damaged and diluted" if Republic were to air these films. Rogers would not be able to maintain his image because he would have no control over the kind of products sold in conjunction with it.[98] And the result would be damage, Judge Hall argued, to Rogers's present and future licensees, and to all whose reputations stood to gain or lose by association with the name and likeness of "Roy Rogers." Already the Quaker Oats Company, Rogers's radio program sponsor, had broken off negotiations for further radio appearances and a contemplated television program.[99]

To the general public, the image of Roy Rogers—whether it promoted Republic Pictures or Roy Rogers, Incorporated—must have looked essentially the same. But the contractual arrangements between Rogers and Republic suggest that the companies' internal commitments were carefully monitored to orchestrate a single coherent persona, despite the fact that this image was controlled by two separate firms. Roughly, the areas over which the two firms had jurisdiction corresponded with the two zones of utilization I have identified: "motion pictures" or "photoplays" (which the studio claimed) and commercial advertising (which the Roy Rogers company controlled). That division of the image placed special importance on the definition of what constituted "motion pictures." As defined by the 1948 contract, "motion pictures" could have equivalents that were not limited to forms "produced, exhibited and/or transmitted by or with sound and voice recording, reproducing and/or transmitting devices, radio devices, television devices and all other devices and improvements."[100] And it would seem, at least by that definition, that Republic had the right to telecast the Roy Rogers motion pictures. But the question, as we will see, would be complicated by other factors.

Not only the generic form but the character type as well was written into the contract, by means of some of the more unusual stipulations found in contracts from this period. The Roy Rogers 1948 contract contains a clause that had to be written into all licensing agreements to ensure against negative connotations that might accrue to the character in the context of commercial advertising: "The Artist shall not be depicted, described, shown or mentioned, in any form whatsoever, in the character of a villain, thief, or other despicable or derogatory character, or as consuming, dispensing, or handling alcohol . . . or as engaging in any mental or physical dissipation, or in any manner which will appeal to the sensual emotions of the reader."[101] The commercial Roy Rogers, no matter what product he was pitching, could not contradict the on-screen character who behaved in a "decent and virtuous manner" and acted as the "champion of right and the enemy of wrong."[102] As if to make Rogers live up to his commercial imagery, the 1948 contract also contained the standard morals clause, in which the actor agreed that he would not commit any act that would "reasonably tend to degrade him or to bring him into public hatred, contempt, scorn or ridicule, or that will reasonably tend to shock, insult or offend the community or offend public morals or decency, or to prejudice the Producer or the motion picture industry in general."[103] The significance placed upon public appearances in this contract suggests that both producer and star entrepreneur viewed off-screen activities as part of the "Roy Rogers" totality. But the coincidence of on-screen and off-screen personas here is *not* left to publicists to reconstruct through public discourse. It is contractually guaranteed. And not only is a coherent Roy Rogers persona guaranteed; the motion picture fiction is assured as well. To a degree, the on-screen/off-screen relationship here is like that of other stars whose lifestyles replicate their screen existence. The mise-en-scène of the Republic films echoes the ranch life of Roy and his wife, Dale Evans, who, even in their contemporary California "private" lives, are always represented wearing western gear, driving a jeep, or riding horses. What Tony Bennett and Janet Woollacott write of the actors who play James Bond seems also an apt description of Roy and Dale. Their style of living, as well as their personal tastes and attitudes, "have been made to mimic the fictional world . . . in order that that world might appear not entirely fictional. Life is thus modelled on fiction in order that fiction, in appearing to reflect life, might also serve as a model for it."[104]

Hence the importance of the rodeo appearance for Roy Rogers. Between 1938 and 1951, the actor made 640 personal appearances, 242 radio appearances, and 563 rodeo appearances.[105] But of the three kinds of promotion, the actor considered the rodeo so important that he specifically reserved the right to perform in rodeos in the interests of his own Roy Rogers enterprise. Here, as elsewhere, the contract betrays the potential conflict of interest between Roy Rogers the Republic studio employee and Roy Rogers the self-employed cowboy star. The contract requires that the actor consult with Republic when making personal appearances in theaters (the better to coordinate the theatrical exhibition of his films with his appearances). And if the artist is engaged to make such an appearance in a city or town where his films are playing, he must try to appear in the theater that is showing his Republic films rather than in a competing theater.[106] But Rogers did not want too many restrictions placed upon his time or his outside business activity. And his success in negotiating this terrain is evidenced in Republic's agreement that Rogers was not required to make more than one radio appearance for each film the studio produced.[107]

But the serious differences between Rogers and his former employers that planted the seeds of the 1952 legal battle had to do with the use of the star in association with commercial products. Although the "results and proceeds" paragraph of Rogers's contract gave the studio the use of Roy Rogers's "name and/or likeness" in conjunction with "commercial advertising" (or "products other than motion pictures"), that grant was subject to a range of limitations. For instance, the first stricture limited the producer to the use of "Roy Rogers" in conjunction with no more than twenty products per year, and it specified that the actor's name must not be used as a trade name. Nor could the producer use the Rogers name or likeness to imply an endorsement. In a kind of mutual protection compact, the producer and the actor both agreed not to use the image with specific products, among which were "alcoholic beverages, tobacco, laxatives, deodorants, or articles of feminine use." And, above all, no association was to be made that might be "inconsistent with or harmful to his position as a motion picture star, particularly with reference to his youthful fan audience."[108]

Another subsection addressed the eventuality that two companies owning the same product-image might involve third parties in unwanted competition. The producer agreed not to authorize the use of the name or likeness in connection with a "competing product"—one in the same class as a product sold by a firm sponsoring one of the radio programs or with whom the artist was negotiating a commercial tie-up.[109] Such issues conjure up the image of Roy Rogers and Trigger appearing on competitors' cereal packages on the same grocery store aisle—an open admission of the fact that "Roy Rogers" was not one but two commercial entities.

Finally, the 1948 contract reserves for Rogers the right to enter into commercial tie-ups and to transfer that right to ostensible licensees. The section lists "phonograph records, transcriptions . . . publications (including so-called comic books or magazines), guns, shirts, boots, belts, blue jeans, toys, candies and gums."[110] It would seem, then, that Roy Rogers's enterprise was defined largely in terms of the merchandising of these official "Roy Rogers" products in the toy, magazine, and clothing markets for children and adolescents.

Why, then, did Judge Hall, in his 1952 trial court opinion, interpret Republic's proposed broadcast of the Roy Rogers films as analogous to a "commodity tie-up" of the kind reserved exclusively for the actor? In Hall's words, the "telecasting or broadcasting of any one of the eighty-one motion pictures . . . on either a sustaining or commercially sponsored basis . . . to advertise any service or product whatsoever (except only Republic Productions, Inc.) would constitute a use of plaintiff's name, voice or likeness in a 'commercial tie-up' of the type reserved exclusively to plaintiff by the 1948 agreement."[111] In other words, the television sponsor's use of the Rogers image in the motion picture was like other commercial uses of the image to promote guns and shirts, candies and gum. To some degree, the judge's opinion, unexpected as it is, provides a frank interpretation of the function of sponsored television. For the principle of commercial television has historically been to enhance the sponsor's product by associating it with a star or a narrative image.

Because of the mere proximity of program and commercial message, actors feared, perhaps rightly, that their appearance on television drama might be read as an inadvertent endorsement. Did intercutting the program with commercial messages (as well as station identification) imply the dramatic actor's endorsement of either the network itself or the sponsor's product? In a 1955 public forum on television agreements, one of the lawyers for AFTRA (American Federation of Television and Radio Artists) implied that it did; even in the case of the network's "tune-in" self-advertisement, the actor is placed in "juxtaposition to the commercial product."[112]

From this vantage, it should not be surprising that the judge in *Rogers* decided that television *was* purely commercial advertising. During this period, the commercial grammar of television was as yet undefined. But two years later, *Rogers v. Republic* was reversed, essentially on the basis that television was *not* commercial advertising. In *Republic Pictures Corp. v. Rogers* (1954), the appellate court decided the issue as to whether broadcasting Rogers's films would be a use of the name, voice, and likeness in advertising. And in its decision the court confirmed the industry convention of separating rights to the motion picture and rights to the image. Rereading Rogers's contract, Judge Bone concluded that it restricted the studio's use of name, voice, and likeness but *not* its use of acts, plays, poses, and appearances. And since the two categories of rights were distinct, changes in one set of rights could not affect the other.[113] Because Rogers consented to Republic's use of his motion picture image embodiment, he couldn't later claim that the studio was engaging in unfair competition in what Judge Bone saw as a separate zone of utilization.

The significance of the *Rogers* case, as it interpreted preexisting commercial advertising arrangements in relation to emerging television form, becomes more evident when we compare it with a 1954 case in which another cowboy actor also attempted to prohibit the syndication of his films. Like Roy Rogers, former Republic Productions star Gene Autry objected to the studio's reuse of his films from the thirties, but Autry tried a different argument. In *Autry v. Republic Productions, Inc.* (1952), he objected to the recutting, which reduced the films to fifty-three and a half minutes and which allowed seven minutes of advertising within the hour of programming. Like Rogers, Autry had established his own company, but in his case Republic's decision to telecast (and the potential overexposure and consequent devaluation of his image that went with it) was perhaps more disadvantageous, since the Autry company produced films for television.[114] Autry's objection, at least in legal terms, was not so much that the films were to be televised but that they were to be sponsored by a commercial advertiser.[115] In finding for Republic, however, Judge Harrison disagreed with Autry's characterization of television as "commercial advertising." The practice of "punctuating" television with advertising was not, Harrison argued, significantly different from the use of "spot advertising" in motion picture theaters. It was, he went on, self-evident that "pictures intermingled with advertisements flow constantly over the television screen."[116] Republic had as much right, the judge concluded, to broadcast Autry's films on television as to exhibit them in motion picture theaters. But Autry was not satisfied with this outcome.

In *Autry v. Republic Productions* (1954), the actor appealed the 1952 decision, and in doing so he strengthened the moral rights aspect of his argument—so much so that the case has become part of the literature on intellectual property and performance rights. Autry's concern now was that in cutting the films Republic might so "emasculate" them as to significantly alter the artist's product.[117] To some extent, the court agreed that cutting posed problems because programs could be "doctored" in a way that made the artist appear to endorse the sponsor's products.[118] But finally, on the very same day he returned a ruling for Republic in *Republic v. Rogers*, Judge Bone brought down a second verdict for the studio. Autry could not object to this new use since, according to the court's interpretation of his 1938 contract, he, like Rogers, had already signed over to Republic his rights to his acts, poses, plays, and appearances.

Television and Merchandising

As the *Rogers* and *Autry* cases reveal, an actor who was an image entrepreneur undercut the studio's monopoly position and threatened to devalue its property through overexposure.[119] When the star actor became a separate corporation, that corporation could even challenge what was most crucial to the studio: the copyright in the motion picture itself. Clearly television was important to the studios as a "secondary market," but what difference did television itself make in terms of *other* "secondary markets"? To what degree, if at all, was merchandising important to the studios?

The answer to this question is easier to see when we look at Warner Brothers' first agreements with television stars regarding commercial advertising tie-ups. John Russell, the highly paid star of "Lawman," had a clause in his contract stipulating that commercial tie-ups must refer to the program. But Peter Brown—an actor with less bargaining power who played Russell's sidekick—had to agree to let the studio use his image for merchandising.[120] If at all possible, the studio wanted the option to slot actors' images into merchandising arrangements (whether through licensing, product endorsement, or tie-ups of any kind) even if the television program was not mentioned. And with television, the studio began to divide merchandising rights three ways: on the original "Maverick" merchandising contract, for instance, the revenue from sales of comic books, puzzles, hats, and playsuits was split between ABC, sponsor Kaiser Aluminum, and Warner Brothers, with ABC functioning as licensing agent.[121] Surprisingly, through, merchandising for revenue was not the studio's only motivation. Although Howdy Doody reportedly made $1.5 million for the network in merchandising, it is doubtful that either the studios or the networks made consistently impressive profits from the practice during these years.[122]

But it is also important to see merchandising as part of scientific management strategy, in which the principle was simply to turn star property into capital wherever possible. Control of the star image gave studios certain leverage with other industries with which they may have had many other kinds of cooperative arrangements. And in fact, studios even traded star images for free supplies of props such as automobiles, wild animals, and cowboy boots.[123] The Warner Brothers merchandising contract with Acme Boot Company, for instance, gave the studio a $2,500 cash advance and fifty-four dozen pairs of western boots each year for two years in exchange for the use of the stars of "Cheyenne-Sugarfoot," "Lawman," and "Maverick" in their advertising.[124]

Even so, few television actors in the late fifties tried to challenge the producers' rights to the royalties from licensed products, as "Cheyenne" star Clint Walker did. The studio's position, as outlined in a memo from the period, reveals that it clearly saw actors as competitors for this revenue: "[The] . . . theory of the term contract is exclusive right to what is contemplated here and the artist has nothing to say about it . . . the trouble with artists dealing with advertisers directly . . . [is that] they get the idea they don't need us and . . . [an] artist can secure all or part of the revenue we derive from commodity tie-ups, merchandising, endorsements, by-products. . . ."[125]

Since the fifties, more television actors have been able to bargain for some portion of the merchandising business on a program. But the special arrangement that Alan Alda had with Twentieth-Century Fox—for 10 percent of the company's 6 percent of the royalties on the "Mash" licensing (including the famous best-selling "Property of M*A*S*H" T-shirt)—is an exception.[126] Since today's television actors now sign their first contracts even before they audition for the pilot, they are usually only negotiating the standard right of approval for use of name and likeness in conjunction with the advertising for a hypothetical show. And only after a program makes it into syndication does merchandising become viable.[127] At that distant point, actors who years earlier signed a contract giving the producer the right to use their likenesses may be surprised to find their faces reproduced on consumer goods. For example, actors starring in the "Dukes of Hazzard" suddenly discovered their images on lunch boxes and wastepaper baskets.[128] At the height of the program's success, they tried what is known in entertainment law as the "gun to the producer's head" approach—refusal to appear on the show—in order to force renegotiation of merchandising issues in the contracts they had signed long before the show became popular.[129]

What do the "Dukes of Hazzard" lunch boxes and wastepaper baskets have in common with music videos? Since the 1986 SAG arbitration, all such items are part of the producer's free zones of exploitation, within which the actor's physical likeness may be reproduced without his or her approval and without compensation. And the consumer rage for lunch boxes and music videos raises yet another question: What is the final entertainment end product? Is it the program itself or the promotion for the program? In attempting to answer that question, we are forced to acknowledge that consumer culture has again swallowed its own tail. In postmodern culture, we see the interpenetration of forms and the indistinguishability of things that were once strictly separate. Music videos are both exploitation for the real entertainment product (the motion picture) and the product itself. And this confusion is mirrored by another confusion—the apparent indistinguishability of legal relationships and the mode of production, which arises out of the confluence of several ambiguities. What is so remarkable is that these ambiguities are of a different order of things.

The legal confusion here begins with the ambiguity of "exploitation" in entertainment law. It is, to quote the 1960 SAG basic agreement, nothing more specific than "taking advantage of a situation" that might promote the motion picture and ultimately "enhance" profits.[130] In reading star contracts from the studio era, we find the same equivocation regarding the uses of the star image as "exploitation." Sometimes radio appearances are considered as exploitation for a motion picture, and sometimes they aren't. The point is this: Anything that the actor or actress does in any capacity can be construed as constituting exploitation for a motion picture, whether it is a past, current, or future release.

We can't hope to explain this ambiguity by looking only at legal relations. For here it seems to me that a legal practice—the constitution of the zone of exploitation as it relates to the entertainment product as the zone of contest over control of the image—is a condition of the institution of stardom. The institution of stardom itself is deeply ambiguous. Not only is it a phenomenon that is half labor, half capital but, as we will see, it is an entity that is legally a person and yet not a person. In what other industry does the product-agent get up and walk out of the product-narrative and yet remain there in solid state? And where else does the image deposit left by the product-agent remain the same while he or she ages—and is still there, increasing in value, after the death of the actor?

Dracula and the Right of Publicity

In *Lugosi v. Universal Pictures, Inc.*, heard before the California Supreme Court in 1979, Justice Mosk began his opinion in concurrence with the court majority by stating the following: "Factually and legally this is a remarkable case. Factually: not unlike the horror films that brought him fame, Bela Lugosi rises from the grave twenty years after death to haunt his former employer. Legally: his vehicle is a strained adaptation of a common law cause of action heretofore unknown either in a statute or case law in California."[1] In finding for Universal, Lugosi's former employer, the court attempted to nail down the lid of Dracula's coffin by holding that the proprietary right to his image, since it was a personal right, could not be passed on to his heirs. For the legal community, the point of law pertained to the survivability of Lugosi's right of privacy: In this case, it did not descend.

In legal terms, the specter of Lugosi returning from the grave to claim his publicity rights represents the problem of stretching "privacy," an old doctrine, to fit situations rising from twentieth-century developments in mass communications—the social and economic conditions of stardom and the technological reproducibility of the image. For the larger society, however, the issues taken up in *Lugosi v. Universal* represent something more unsettling—a broken taboo. For what the plaintiffs, Lugosi's son and wife, essentially argued was that the Lugosi-as-Dracula image was not interred with the actor's body but survived him as tangible property. An impossible entity—a dead man with "rights"—could become a legal reality.

In *Lugosi*, the complexities of the commodity tie-up are so fully un-folded that a T-shirt will never again seem a trivial thing. Lugosi's 1930 and 1936 contracts with Universal Pictures were first opened up in April   175

1963, in the suit filed against the studio by Bela George Lugosi, Jr., and Lugosi's widow, Hope. In this action, the family sought an injunction against Universal to stop the commercial use of Lugosi's image. Four years after Lugosi's death in 1956, Universal had begun to license the actor's image from its 1931 film *Dracula* for reproduction on merchandise (fig. 3). After the initiation of the licensing program in 1960, the Lugosi image was "rented" to small manufacturers for use on plastic toy pencil sharpeners, plastic model figures, T-shirts and sweatshirts, card games, soap and detergent products, picture puzzles, candy dispensers, masks, kites, belts, belt buckles, and swizzle sticks.[2] Although Lugosi had earned more than a half million dollars in his career, he was destitute when he died, and his heirs viewed Universal's merchandising program as an infringement of a valuable property right that belonged to them.[3] The suit for breach of contract and unjust enrichment, however, was held up for three years while the Lugosi estate was probated. Not until 3 February 1966, after Universal had arranged fifty licensing agreements, was the action that concerns us here officially filed.[4] The California trial court, convening in 1972, decided in favor of the heirs and concluded that although Universal had the right to use Lugosi's likeness in conjunction with advertising for motion pictures, he had not given them the right to use his likeness on licensed products. Furthermore, the court ruled that he had a proprietary right in his own likeness, which, under the common law right of privacy, had passed to his heirs at his death. The plaintiffs were awarded $53,023.23 of the $260,000 that Universal had received in royalties, subject to the statute of limitations.[5]

But the trial court decision was subsequently overturned by the Second District Court of Appeals in 1977, and the appellate court's ruling was upheld by the California Supreme Court in 1979. In a four-to-three decision, the state supreme court rejected the conclusion that the Lugosi name and likeness could be passed on to his heirs. The actor did indeed have a right of publicity, the court ruled, but that right fell under a theory of privacy that, since it was a personal entitlement, was not descendible. The dissenting opinion, written by Chief Justice Rose Bird, however, would become the definitive text on the commercial viability and legal substantiality of a descendible right of publicity. As we have seen in the way the New York Civil Rights Act of 1903 answered *Roberson v. Rochester Folding Box Co.* (1902), and the way the Copyright Act of 1909 adjusted *White-Smith v. Apollo* (1908), statutory law rectifies common law judg-

Bela Lugosi in *Dracula* (Universal Pictures, 1931)

ments. Here, too, *Lugosi* was overruled by statute, and the position of the dissent became the basis for section 990 of the California Civil Code (known as the "Celebrities Rights" act), which took effect 1 January 1985.

What will immediately strike the layperson about the above account of the judicial history of *Lugosi* is the contradiction between the concepts "privacy" and "publicity." How can a person insist, at one and the same time, on a right to be left alone and a right to stake out a claim to a public persona? In judicial practice, the pertinent principles in cases involving commercial appropriation, such as the *Lugosi* case, have been considered part of a kind of family tree of "privacy" law, a tort or injury rule that differs from the law of libel in that the truth status of the injury is not the crucial issue.[6] In deciding common law cases of this kind, judges theoretically connect the issues before them with the related precedents. Thus it is that decisions in contemporary cases involving mass media uses of celebrity imagery have been grafted historically onto an original principle of "privacy" put forth in an influential law treatise in 1890 and sustained in subsequent case law precedents based upon disputes involving calendar art, beer advertisements, televised football, and baseball cards.[7]

Privacy Becomes Publicity

What do we mean by "privacy" in American law, and what could it possibly have to do with the image of Bela Lugosi as it was reproduced on cocktail napkins? First, I should explain that this right is entirely of American derivation. In France every citizen has an undisputed moral right to his or her own likeness. In English law there is neither an equivalent nor any foundation for "privacy" in the common law; correspondingly, there is no British right of publicity.[8] In the U.S., the understanding of "privacy" as a constitutional right, based on an interpretation of either the Ninth or the Fourteenth Amendment, emerged in the sixties. It became a broad concept embracing various rights of citizens to defend themselves against unwarranted government intrusion in their lives. This same constitutional concept of "privacy" was the basis of the majority argument in *Roe v. Wade* that a woman had a right to end her pregnancy.[9]

Common law and statutory law "right of privacy," however, do not belong to the same family tree as the constitutional right. The right with which we will be concerned has a clear, straightforward lineage, traceable to an influential *Harvard Law Review* article written in 1890 by Samuel D. Warren and Louis D. Brandeis.[10] Warren and Brandeis, friends since they graduated together at the top of the Harvard Law School class of 1877, wrote "The Right to Privacy" as retaliation against a scandalmongering Boston press. Over the past one hundred years, several myths have attached themselves to the circumstances surrounding the appearance of this article. It has been said that Warren was motivated by the publication of embarrassing detail regarding the lives of himself and his wife; others have argued as often that it was the coverage of Warren's daughter's society wedding that offended the Boston lawyer.[11] Finally, in 1979, one scholar's search through the issues of the *Boston Saturday Evening Gazette* revealed no evidence of the offensive journalism.[12] But the history of the article reveals only one half of the fallacy. For the Warren and Brandeis article, which is often cited as the single most influential law review piece ever written, proposed a concept that had no basis in existing law. In fact, Ronald Dworkin, in his discussion of legal "mistakes," calls the reputation of the article a "brilliant fraud" because of the authors' success at arguing that the right to privacy had been *demonstrated* in earlier decisions even though it had never been defined.[13] It might be said that Warren and Brandeis invented the right from scratch instead of establishing its preexistence through the careful linkage to precedent dictated by legal convention.

The right advocated by Warren and Brandeis diverged from already established rights that could be protected by the laws of slander and libel. To keep their grievance on an elevated plane, the authors disassociated themselves from these laws, which, they argued, were "in their nature material rather than spiritual."[14] The more "spiritual" right they envisioned was an entitlement that was to have nothing to do with the seedy realm of commerce. It was to rest solely upon the injury to a person's feelings. As one commentator later characterized the lawyers' argument, it had "an air of wounded gentility about it."[15]

The right "to be let alone" looks back to a period before mass society and its information technologies that threatened to burst the bubble of the sheltered life of the upper classes. The development of the right of privacy case law coincided with an evolving notion of what it means to be a person in mass society. The ideal of privacy, as Raymond Williams has discussed it, is "a record of legitimation of a bourgeois view of life: the ultimate generalized privilege, however abstract in practice, or seclusion and protection from others (*the public*); of lack of accountability to 'them'; and of related gains in closeness and comfort of these general kinds."[16] What we witness in the twentieth century is the movement from private life "safe from the public eye" to the notion of the personal. And this movement is both prefigured and summed up in Warren and Brandeis's right of privacy argument that the harm done by exploitative news media is to one's emotional well-being. In Warren and Brandeis, the slightly older private-public opposition is retained, but that dichotomy becomes less and less compelling with the emergence of the private as synonymous with the personal.[17] What happens, in other words, is that the concern about preserving the sanctity of the private bourgeois home gets displaced onto the person, the individual, who then experiences media exposure as personal injury. We can trace this social development in legal terms: Only in the early part of this century did it become possible to make a claim that one had been personally injured by a public intrusion. As soon as this claim was recognized by the courts, however, it began to turn into something else, so that by the middle of this century a privacy claim had little to do with the plaintiff's right "to be let alone."

Privacy, the umbrella cause of action covering the issues raised in *Lugosi*, was divided by William Prosser in 1960 into four separate types of personal invasion: "intrusion on plaintiff's physical solitude or seclusion," "public disclosure of private facts," "false light in the public eye," and "appropriation of plaintiff's name or likeness for defendant's benefit."[18] Already, we can see how the issues addressed by Prosser's principle in cases involving wiretapping, record confidentiality, and computer record storage are far removed from the original concerns of Warren and Brandeis. But Prosser's fourth point has an especially strange relationship with the original concept of privacy right. For it is not just that this fourth privacy tort deals with protection *against* commercial appropriation, but that it has come to function as a mechanism for allowing commercial use of one's identity.

To broaden the context for the moment, we should not be surprised that Anglo-American law contains anachronisms; as one legal historian describes it, the law changes in "piecemeal fashion."[19] Parts of it fall into disuse and remain there to haunt later generations until overturned. Other parts are maintained through the practice of adherence to precedent. Already I have shown in my discussion of "originality" how the common law retains in fossilized form the values of an older, bourgeois society along with its more recent accommodations to the needs of advanced capital. As such, it is also a map of an irrational society. In the case of the "right of privacy," a legal principle persists because of precedent, to be certain. But it also persists, I would argue, because the older value it retains carries with it a certain rhetorical weight. The legal commentary on the 1890 principle of "privacy" from the thirties on, however, is increasingly critical of this legal remnant, which cannot be made to serve emergent commercial needs. Melville Nimmer puts it this way in his textbook on copyright and entertainment law: "Although the concept of privacy which Warren and Brandeis evolved fulfilled the demands of Beacon Street in 1890, it may be seriously doubted that the application of this concept satisfactorily meets the contemporary needs of Broadway and Hollywood."[20]

What, then, do judges do? How can they adhere to the structure of precedent and still meet "contemporary needs"? In answer to this question, Stanley Fish has written, "Paradoxically, one can be faithful to legal history only by revising it, by redescribing it in such a way as to accommodate it and render manageable the issues raised by the present."[21] In the case of the tort law of privacy, one might say that fidelity to the legacy of the right has meant not only that legal history has been accommodated in order to meet the needs of the culture industries, but that "privacy" has been used to secure its opposite. Nimmer and others, in building upon his important 1954 discussion of the right of publicity as it emerges from privacy law, have continued to weave the original concept of privacy back into doctrine, according to legal custom.[22] Although Nimmer continued to argue from 1954 until his death in 1985 that the right of publicity should be a property right rather than a personal right, he could not argue—if he wanted to follow the methods of legal logic—that since the two rights are contradictory, the one must entirely replace the other. To put it bluntly, he cannot throw privacy out altogether, because doing so would call attention to the inconsistency. So privacy and publicity for Nimmer become "two sides of the same coin," or one becomes a "subdivision of the other."[23] As Nimmer's argument testifies, when principles are in complete disharmony, legal reason, often by means of such abstractions and homely metaphors, attempts to dissolve inconsistencies. But at other times, legal commentators will simply express amazement at developments that baldly announce doctrinal conflicts. In his treatise *The Rights of*

Publicity and Privacy, J. Thomas McCarthy, for instance, deals with the contradiction between "publicity" and "privacy" by explaining that the concepts are the same but that the terminology is new. What happens, he says, is that "at some point the labels change and 'privacy' is magically transformed into 'publicity.'"[24]

It is this magical transformation that indicates to me something of the way in which the law manages structural contradictions. Mark Tushnet has remarked that "a full Marxist analysis of law would relate the internal contradictions of the structures and their composition to . . . contradictions in the social relations of capitalist production."[25] It is to that end that we need to examine parallel developments in this century: the growth of the culture industries, the transformation of privacy right into publicity right, and the shift from the class-specific regime of the private to the sense of the personal, which blurs class distinctions. To suggest such parallels from within legal scholarship is, admittedly, to break a rule of classical legal theory that understands the body of law as a coherent, self-contained whole, within which earlier decisions exert influence over later ones. Rather like the text of New Criticism, the body of the law in classical legal theory is sealed from outside influence. But how can the law be sealed off from history and economics and at the same time be expected to respond to the "needs of Broadway and Hollywood"?

If we are to develop a comprehensive theory of the way in which "internal contradictions" within the law relate to contradictions elsewhere, we need to rethink the model of textual contradiction that we already have from aesthetic theory. There, structural faults in the text are often said to be "contained" on the formal level so that the text can accommodate ideologically antithetical positions. In Pierre Macherey's theory of textual "dislocation," the literary text is inherently flawed because it cannot speak these opposite positions at once, and rather than representing one or the other, or their sum, the text finally speaks their "difference, their contrast."[26] In Marxist aesthetics it is as though antithetical forces produce textual form; in what sounds a little like an account of the oyster's production of a pearl, an artistically exquisite object is produced out of the contrast between two irreconcilable positions. There is something of this, for instance, in Theodor Adorno's account of the relation between social contradiction and aesthetic production: "Antagonisms are articulated technically, namely in the internal composition of works of art. This composition is susceptible of interpretation in terms of tensions that exist outside of art. These external tensions are not re-produced or copied in the work of art, and yet they shape it. This is what is meant by the concept of form in aesthetics."[27] The body of the law, too, as argued in chapter 1, does not just carry over or reproduce tensions existent in the social formation. Within the law as well, these tensions will take different shapes, subject to conventions specific to legal discourse. It is safe to assume that they will not take the shape of the exquisite aesthetic object. What shape, then, will they take? Our answer to that question must recognize that one key difference between legal and aesthetic form is the way in which legal form is subject to change. The body of written law is constructed as impervious and self-contained, but it is also subject, at anytime, not only to reinterpretation but also to nullification by the agency of an intervening institution.[28]

Historical and social developments do not have easy equivalents within legal history. Social tensions may be as disguised and as inverted in the law as they are in their other lives—their aesthetic manifestations. We do, however, have some help from critical legal studies scholars toward un-derstanding how legal doctrine manages contradictions. As these scholars have argued, legal reasoning works through accommodation and incor-poration. Rather than overruling and overturning in overtly political ways, the law prefers to graft new decisions onto the relevant branch of the family tree, thus creating the "illusion of legal consistency."[29] Part of this illusion is created by the way legal discourse retells its own history: Through systematic review of precedent and long deferential citation, thoroughly investigating its own legacy, legal discourse attempts to dem-onstrate that it is legitimate.[30] And hence the force of the additive princi-ple of precedent in the development of privacy into publicity. Even though contemporary right of publicity cases such as *Lugosi* have progres-sively less and less to do with privacy's right to seclusion, they proceed, nevertheless, by grafting themselves onto the Warren and Brandeis 1890 precedent. And, as I see it, it is this careful legal grafting that effectively denies logical inconsistency. In any other scheme of things, privacy and publicity would have nothing to do with each other and could go their separate ways. But in legal discourse, as we will see, they are bound together, their differences minimized, and the rift between them recon-ciled. In the textual body of law, as in the aesthetic text, what we see within the codes at work is the binding up, *not* the opening up, of contradiction. The opening up remains for us to do, for, in Macherey's terms, the text is not laid out for us in all of its contradictions. Rather, in the critical act it is "put into contradiction."[31]

Putting legal doctrine into contradiction involves, for one thing, bringing it into contact with other discourses. The cases that follow in the line of Warren and Brandeis's "right to privacy" have a kind of relation to the development, in English language usage, of "private" as Williams traces it: from bourgeois ideal and a sense of class irritation to a new sense—the personal—within which class does not necessarily play a part. After *Roberson v. Rochester Folding Box Co.* (1902) (the case in which a woman's photograph was used on a flour mill calendar advertisement without her approval), New York followed Warren and Brandeis in passing its Civil Rights Laws 50 and 51, which protected persons from injury based on the violation of their right of privacy.[32] And as the history of case law shows, the early uses of the theory successfully defended ordinary people against invasions of privacy, whether by false representation, intrusion, or commercial appropriation. Still, a closer study remains to be done on the correlation between these early cases and the evolution of "the private." What happens? Does privacy dig deeper into the self to emerge as "the personal"? Does the impersonal nature of the mass media exposé (as different from the face-to-face insult of an earlier era) change the character of the offense?

From studies of mass culture, we know that early in the century, both motion pictures and theater produced a new kind of subject with a specially constructed public persona. In chapter 2 I provided some background to the developments in photographic technology and photo processing that transformed the ordinary person into a celebrity and in turn produced the celebrity as common (as seen, for instance, in the way the *carte de visite* produced the image of Prince Albert as a common object immediately following his death). New image technologies in the late nineteenth and early twentieth centuries also constructed a notion of the personal as multiple and mass as well as intimate. And, to a degree, the photograph resolved the dilemma we are describing because of its aesthetics of absent presence.[33] But while mass culture adjusted to the discrepancy between the private person and the public person, U.S. courts took the discrepancy absolutely literally.

It is easier to track the evolution from the private to the personal in privacy doctrine because the model of offense to personal dignity changes markedly within this century. For a short period, U.S. courts followed traditional lines of privacy in protecting the images of ordinary persons from unauthorized commercial use. But in the cases involving celebrities, where a popular personality objected to the commercial appropriation of his or her image, courts consistently decided that the personality had "surrendered" the right of privacy. In *Maxine Martin v. F.I.Y. Theatre Co., Inc.* (1938), for instance, the court ruled that a professional entertainer, by definition, could not complain that publicity, however unwanted, was an invasion of a "right of privacy." Martin, a legitimate stage actress, complained that her photograph, enlarged as a poster, had been exhibited outside the Roxy Theatre in Cleveland along with posters of burlesque actresses in "lewd" poses. Judge Merrick disagreed:

> Persons who expose themselves to public view for hire cannot expect to have the same privacy as the meek, plodding stay-at-home citizen. The glamour, genuine or artificial, of that business removes the participants therein from the realm of the average citizen. . . . An actress of the accomplishments and reputation claimed for this plaintiff is no longer a private individual, but has become a public character and cannot complain that any right of privacy is trespassed upon by the mere unauthorized publication of a photograph.[34]

And in the same year, in *O'Brien v. Pabst*, the court ruled that since O'Brien had been the most publicized football player of the year, he could not complain that his photograph was used in advertising.[35] Here, the defendant stressed the side of "privacy" that referred to the personal, and the action was brought on the basis of a violation of personal liberties above and beyond the publicity issue about which a celebrity could not complain.

By the fifties, it was clear that celebrities could not depend upon the traditional structure of privacy doctrine for relief from commercial appropriation (even though, of course, unfair competition remedies were still available to them). But why, then, did the privacy argument persist, and why did the celebrity's right of publicity evolve out of that particular doctrine? Nothing within the structure of common law dictates that a publicity right had to grow out of privacy doctrine, and over time such protection could conceivably have evolved in copyright terms, or it could have been attached to the unfair competition law theory of passing off. The answer, I think, is that an argument for a celebrity publicity right based on the old "right to privacy" has rhetorical and structural advantages. Since, as Ronald Dworkin tells us, it is finally impossible to tell whether judges have applied legal standards or moral standards in their judgments, it would seem that a tort law appeal based on the mental and emotional distress suffered by a human being would have an advantage over a complaint cast as an unfair competition dispute.[36] Later in entertainment law history—to take only one example—it would become clear that both "Nancy Sinatra" and "Goodyear Tire Company" are, in fact, commercial enterprises with competing economic interests. But even though Sinatra appears on a stage as a star persona, in a courtroom she appears as a natural rights-holding subject. So what I want to emphasize is that the star image industry has a particular investment in privacy doctrine. The advantage the right of privacy has over other causes of action, then, is a "natural" advantage—this right stems from the inviolate right of a natural person. The right to one's personhood and the representation of it, whether in name, physical likeness, or "attribute," is bound up with the subject-holding rights. And on the basis of that legal subjecthood, a celebrity can claim a "personal monopoly" in his or her image. As Barry King describes it, the star persona is a "collective representation that presents/re-presents itself as the private expressivity of a unique individual."[37]

There is a limit, however, to the advantage of the personal right argument from the litigator's point of view, and that is where the contradictions in the society have their inverted form in the law. Historically, the personal right argument worked defensively when the plaintiff wanted legal sanctuary—protection against appropriators in order to withdraw from the public eye. But the right did not offer to the celebrity offensive protection—a shield needed in the marketplace against infringers. One's personal right of privacy could be *defended*, but the integral, private part of one's personhood could not be wrapped up and sold. Theoretically, only the individual whose personhood was violated could undertake the defense against such violation. And since the insult did not extend to anyone else, and the "invasion" did not apply, the protection could not be possessed by anyone else, not even one's heirs. This is precisely what Universal argued in the *Lugosi* case, in which the producers maintained that they could use Lugosi's likeness in their merchandising program because he was no longer alive to claim that his image had been appropriated and that his personal right had been violated. No personal right was violated, they argued, because no person existed. Upholding this position, the California Supreme Court in 1979 confirmed what legal commentators would characterize as the more cautious stance—the principle that personal rights are nonassignable.

But in the aftermath of *Lugosi*, entertainment law commentary on the case was critical of the majority view and overwhelmingly sympathetic with the dissenting view that Lugosi had an inheritable property right in his likeness. The concern with the so-called limitations of the right of privacy expressed in this commentary, however, has less to do with the degree of protection that the right offers to the private individual than with the kind of commercial toughness the right can be shown to have. But how is it that a right originally set out to ward off commerce should now be recruited for aggressive use in the commercial fray? Why, again, the defense of a right instead of a complaint about unfair competition?

Chewing Gum and the Creation of Value

In a remarkable case in 1954, a brand-new right materialized out of the older right of privacy. The new right emerged from a dispute over the images of players on baseball cards issued by chewing gum manufacturers. *Haelan Laboratories, Inc., v. Topps Chewing Gum, Inc.*, unlike the other image property cases I have discussed, did not involve complaints from the persons whose likenesses were commercialized.[38] Their rights were at stake only indirectly. What *Haelan* did do was examine the awkward legal solution of basing commercial protection upon privacy doctrine: The right to be left alone was turned inside out and made into a shield against competitors.

This legal solution came into question only because one chewing gum manufacturer attempted to undercut its competition by invalidating another's contracts with the ballplayers whose likenesses were reproduced on trading cards. The Topps strategy against Haelan Lab's Bowman Gum was to challenge the exclusivity of Bowman's agreements with the players by challenging the issue of the assignability of the right of privacy. Thus, Topps argued, Bowman could not protect or enforce the contracts since they were nothing more than liability releases; they constituted only a player's "non-assignable right not to have his feelings hurt by such a publication of his photograph."[39] Structurally, this argument is similar to Universal's position in *Lugosi* twenty-five years later. The question in both cases is this: How can one's privacy right be transferred to another or left to one's heirs? Ultimately, of course, these disputes are not about protecting feelings but are rather about monopolies based on personhood. Topps, like Universal, challenged personal monopoly based on privacy right at its weakest point, the juncture at which one person's protection against insult is assigned to a second, entirely different entity. If X can establish that Y's right of privacy cannot be assigned, Z does not possess it and cannot protect it; therefore X can use the image commercially—on bath towels, calendars, or baseball cards. The dilemma for the judge in *Haelan* was this: Yes, it would seem that the baseball player's privacy is inviolate, but he has agreed to the use of his photograph on cards included in packages of gum sold to millions of children. Bowman Gum has paid him for something, and if it is not his privacy right, then what is it he has signed over? Traditionally, what was secured in such cases was the right to "invade the privacy" of the celebrity. But *Haelan* significantly rejected this awkward route.[40]

The court's solution in *Haelan* was to invent a new right, one that Judge Jerome Frank called the "right of publicity." I say "invent," but I say it with qualification. What I find in the opinion itself and in the discourse around *Haelan* is not a single rationale for creating this right but rather a number of ways of justifying it, which fall into five general categories: The right of publicity has evolved historically within common law, it is discoverable in economic practices, it is inherent in the person, it is produced by a labor of promotion, *and* it is created by legal mechanisms. How can it be produced by all of these means? I approach this entire discussion with some caution, since rights discourse is notoriously circular.[41] To the outsider it appears that judges often do one of three things when faced with a conflict between two rights-holding parties: They find that one of the two rights existed prior to the other, they invalidate one of the two, or they discover an entirely different right. Judge Frank took the third route. What else could he have done?

Judge Frank could have established that the "right of publicity" had a legal lineage. But if it had a legal lineage (which such scholars as Nimmer, Gordon, and, to some degree, Prosser, would later "discover" for it), then how could the "right of publicity" *enter* common law with the judgment in *Haelan*?[42] The wording of the opinion, in fact, does not imply that this new right had evolved from precedent following a logic inherent in the preexisting body of law. The majority opinion implied that it came into being because of the inadequacies of the right of privacy, but as Judge Frank stated, it was intended not to stand in lieu of privacy but instead to be an additional entitlement "independent" of the earlier right.[43] But if Judge Frank did not find the "right of publicity" by tracing its lineage, how did he find it? The answer, it seems, is that he found it in the entertainment marketplace, in the celebrity practice of entering into contractual agreements allowing the exclusive use of name and image for a specific purpose and a limited amount of time. Let me quote Judge Frank in full:

> This right might be called a "right of publicity." For it is common knowledge that many prominent persons (especially actors and ball-players), far from having their feelings bruised through public exposure of their likenesses, would feel sorely deprived if they no longer received money for authorizing advertisements, popularizing their countenances, displayed in newspapers, magazines, busses, trains and subways. This right of publicity would usually yield them no money unless it could be made the subject of an exclusive grant which barred any other advertiser from using their pictures.[44]

It would appear, then, that Frank has encoded an economic practice as a legal form—a right. And at the same time he says there is no economic value without the right. Which is it? Does the legal right create the economic value or does the economic practice create the right? I will return to this question.

Image appropriation cases following *Haelan* have also found the source of the right of publicity in the personhood of the plaintiff. Bela Lugosi's privacy right, the basis for his family's claim, inhered in his inviolate subjecthood. But if he had a *publicity* right in his likeness, as the dissent in *Lugosi* argued, does this distinctly different right inhere in the same way? Justice Rose Bird, in her dissenting opinion, discussed the origins of the right of publicity in terms of actors' creations of famous characters. She separated the actor from the role in arguing that a person could have rights to both a created character and a natural personhood. In addition to Lugosi, Charlie Chaplin (The Tramp), Carroll O'Connor (Archie Bunker), and Flip Wilson (Judge and Geraldine) could be considered actors who, she said, could have a right to a defining role as well as to a "natural" appearance. A "substantial publicity value," she went on, "exists" in the likeness of an actor playing such a role.[45] It is interesting to note that Bird did not consider how publicity value was produced by means of the creation of a role. Neither did this decision dwell on the issue of the ownership of the character Dracula, which technically belonged to Universal Pictures after it had purchased the motion picture rights to the Bram Stoker novel from the author's family.[46] It is quite possible that the Lugosi family could never establish a clear right to Lugosi as Dracula because Universal's motion picture character had so thoroughly taken over the Lugosi persona. But our concern here is with the natural likeness as a kind of text underlying the character. The question, in other words, is how publicity value can "exist" in a natural likeness *before* performance or before the exploitation that produces popular recognition. And these questions, in turn, telescope into one: Can an ordinary person have an inherent right of publicity?

Legal authorities such as Nimmer and McCarthy answer in the affirmative.[47] McCarthy says that the right of publicity is a recognition of the "potential *commercial* value of every person's identity."[48] Every one of us, according to this view, has a commercial value in an identity. Does entertainment law then anticipate Andy Warhol's prophecy of the fifteen minutes of fame we each have to look forward to in the media future? Justice Bird, in her dissent in *Lugosi*, went on to offer an answer to this riddle in relation to the actor or actress who had an as-yet-unused right of publicity. That right, she contended, might "remain dormant until a suitable medium and setting is found" in which to exploit it. Before exploitation, then, the ordinary person and the unknown actor can be said to have a right of publicity that, in its dormancy, is both there and not there. It is inherent *at the same time that it must be produced by exploitation.*

What I mean is that in current legal thought a person does not have publicity rights in himself or herself unless, at one time or another in the course of a career, he or she has transferred these rights to another party. Similarly, the standard counsel in the entertainment field is that right of publicity has its origin in the cast and creative personnel billing or in the advertising and promotion for a motion picture or television series.[49] These issues have been rehearsed most thoroughly in the question of exploitation as it relates to the post mortem uses of the celebrity image; and whether such an image could be merchandised if a star such as Bela Lugosi had not made commercial use of his likeness within his lifetime arose in *Lugosi* as it had in the earlier Laurel and Hardy case, *Price v. Hal Roach* (1975).[50]

It may seem that the celebrity's prior approval of commercial use is a rhetorical point that dismisses the concern with irreverence for the dead. But it is also the case that "exploitation" establishes a claim on the analogy with the use guaranteeing secondary meaning in a trademark. Moreover, the intellectual property convention recognizing entitlement to the "fruit of one's labors" acknowledges the work involved in building the wide popular recognition and sustaining the celebrity status of such luminaries as Elvis Presley. Not only does entertainment law credit the existence of the industries behind popular images; it also recognizes what might be called a "labor of promotion." Actually, in the version of contemporary mass-mediated culture given to us by entertainment law, there is no such thing as instant success, overnight fame, or spontaneous popularity. Samuel Spring makes a good summary statement of this point: "Why shouldn't publicity created by mental labor be viewed as property? Such publicity is not accidental. It is created by skill and labor. It goes and comes quickly. But it is the result of labor. . . . For though a human being is not property and can not be bought and sold, the personality of living persons is bought and sold in the market place."[51] We have seen that the right of publicity is justified by means of a legal lineage, by the rights-holding subject, by a legal agreement coupled with an economic practice, and by a labor of promotion. But before I show how the right of publicity becomes synonymous with publicity value, I want to digress briefly in order to locate these same issues in relation to current developments in cultural studies.

The Star as Microcosm of Capitalism

To a scholar who works within a cultural studies methodology, reading the literature of privacy and publicity is an uncanny experience. For in its recognition of the production of stardom and the labor of promotion, this literature invites a materialist consideration.[52] The important Marxist work in the analysis of the phenomenon of stardom probably begins with Peter Baechlin, who in his *Histoire économique du cinéma* remarked, "A star's way of life is in itself merchandise."[53] The industrial production, distribution, and consumption of stardom was first suggestively laid out in Edgar Morin's *The Stars*, but the job of reconciling the tempting economism of the production-consumption paradigm with post-Althusserian conceptions of ideology remained for Richard Dyer in his influential book *Stars*.[54] It was Dyer who introduced the notion of the star as constructed through publicity and promotion as well as by means of star vehicles, all of which adds up to a kind of Foucauldian "intertext," which the star produces as coherent.[55] Most important, Dyer has called our attention to the paradox of the real person/star construction, the one always reappearing to deny the other. This is part of the allure of stardom, he says, and the foregrounding of the artificial construction may be just as ideological as the return of the real person. It is, he says, "the insistent question of 'really' that draws us in, keeping us on the go from one aspect to another. Appearances are a kind of reality, just as manufacture and individual persons are. . . . Stars are obviously a case of appearance. . . . [Y]et the whole media construction of stars encourages us to think in terms of 'really.'"[56] The constructedness of stars, then, is quite available for ordinary persons to see and is undeniably *there* in the pronounced "artificiality" that commonsense wisdom falls back upon so repeatedly. But it could be the reality/falsehood dichotomy (which "keeps us going from one aspect to the other") that is the "real" ideological construction obfuscating that which is finally more difficult to see: What is more difficult to see is the way in which things are simultaneously true and false or, as Dyer says, the way "appearances are a kind of reality."[57]

Curiously, this same alternation, this back and forth between the "really" and the media construction also characterizes the right of publicity discourses. In my earlier discussion of the Jacqueline Onassis look-alike, I observed that commercial appropriation cases seemed to alternate between the real person and the construction, sometimes favoring the one and sometimes the other. *Lugosi*, as I said there, shows us that the real person is no legal match against the amalgamation of the character and the star image, which outlives the human Bela Lugosi. When Lugosi expired, and along with him his privacy right, Universal Pictures revitalized the construction, only to have Lugosi resurrected again, *not* as the real person half of the basis of privacy doctrine but (as I showed in the *Onassis* case) as the portion more real—the property right derived from the person.

Intellectual property gives itself to be read in a materialist way because it follows the lines of commodity production so closely. It tells us more straightforwardly what cultural forms like the novel can tell us only in roundabout ways. But the structure of intellectual property law, after laying everything out, still masks what it has told us. I come, then, to one of the places in U.S. law where Pashukanis's theory of the way in which the legal form replicates the commodity form holds up only too well. Recall that Judge Frank based his case for the existence of a right of publicity on the preexistence of enforceable contracts, reiterating that the right of publicity would not produce revenue for the celebrity unless it could be made subject of an exclusive contract that prohibited others from using his or her image. Entertainment law represents publicity value as something created by a labor of promotion or exploitation and realized in the transfer of the right of publicity. But at the same time, it contradicts itself by crediting itself with the creation of publicity value. Even as the law credits itself, however, it says that it does not create either property or value, but only recognizes existing value—value that is nevertheless value-less without legal protection.

In this space, I cannot hope to demonstrate fully the circularity of the reasoning with respect to the source of value, even in this small area of the law. Already I have suggested that the right of publicity has at least five different sources, all of which are used to argue for its preexistence. In the case of the argument for the existence of value, it is not even a matter of showing how a right becomes a value. It is not so much that this equivalence evolves or is reasoned by a logic with which we are already familiar, but that it is asserted: The right of publicity *is* publicity value.[58]

In his historically significant challenge to the structure of legal argument, Felix Cohen uses the treatment of the trade name in unfair competition law to illustrate the nonsensical nature of this reasoning. His example of the relationship between the word "Palmolive" and economic value is a parallel with the legal construction of publicity value. Cohen examines a pattern similar to the reasoning we find in the discourse around *Lugosi*. In his analysis, there is no single origin of right, property, or value in the law, because the reasoning by which each is brought into being is circular. Legal protection is purportedly based upon preexisting economic value, but then this same economic value depends upon the extent of protection. In reference to the value or valuelessness of the word "Palmolive," Cohen goes on:

> In other words, the fact that courts did not protect the word would make the word valueless, and the fact that it was valueless would then be regarded as a reason for protecting it. Ridiculous as this vicious circle seems, it is logically as conclusive or inconclusive as the op-

posite vicious circle, which accepts the fact that courts do protect private exploitation of a given word as a reason why private exploitation of that word should be protected.[59]

Let us apply this logic to Lugosi as Dracula, which, it would be argued after the 1979 decision, would be valueless if Lugosi's right of publicity were not upheld by the court. The same potential "worthlessness" of the image was then offered by the court as the reason for recognizing the right of publicity, that is, for giving the image protection. So this area of the law holds that without protection there is no valuable property. But then this discourse never exactly holds that *it* has created either value or property. As Cohen observes, rather than "creating" property, unfair competition authorities hold that they are "merely *recognizing* a pre-existent Something."[60] And whether this "Something" is the right of publicity inherent in every individual's identity or rather the publicity value produced in Lugosi-as-Dracula by the labor of publicity, we are left with the same question: How can a right preexist if it *depends* upon legal recognition?[61] How can the ordinary person have a right of publicity or publicity value in an identity to begin with if having that right is contingent upon the legal protection that it might or might not receive?

Whether legal discourse proceeds by the recognition of preexistent rights or by the protection of preexistent value, the consequences have been that many more entities have increasingly become legally designated as "property." Within the branch of privacy law we have been examining, every entity, it seems, can become a property—even one's right to be left alone.[62] But it is not just property per se that is at issue in the celebrity image cases. So far we have been concerned only with the Lockean, natural right foundations of Anglo-American law, in which property is derived from personhood and ownership is derived from the exertion of human labor over the natural object. This right to one's person also becomes the basis for its sale to others, the alienation of one's labor, and even the justification of unequal appropriation, which is the basis for bourgeois property.[63] In Locke we see the logic of private property based on a notion of inviolate personhood, but we do not necessarily see the implications of turning that property into more property—of using the original property to enlarge the domain of ownership. The difference, then, between a privacy right that does not survive the person and a publicity right that can be assigned and inherited is the difference between property in the legal subject and self-expanding property. What we see in the contradiction between right of privacy and right of publicity is the distance between Locke's origin of property in personhood and Marx's productive private property, which looks less and less like property in the self as it shows its propensity for accumulation.

Dracula—The Sucking Principle

To fill out the function of productive property, to illustrate it in its breadth and imagine its potentialities, there is no better lesson than *Dracula*. As Franco Moretti discusses Stoker's vampire, he is an entrepreneur who carefully plans an economic venture: to amass capital by taking his toll from the living population of London; in fact, to take over the city.[64] The count plans his domination by the principle of appropriation of the bodies of his victims who, once emptied of their own life forces, will work only in his interests. Dracula, more than the other classic vampires of Le Fanu or Polidori, fits Marx's description of capital as "dead labor, which, vampire-like, lives only by sucking living labor, and lives the more, the more labor it sucks."[65] Buying run-down real estate in different sections of the city, placing his fifty coffins at strategic points of operation, the vampire-entrepreneur calculates his expansion on what we might call the sucking principle. Dead labor (capital) gorges itself on the blood (labor) of others, expanding as they are depleted, and this unequal exchange between worker and capitalist is made to appear fair and equitable. As Marx explains it, "[W]hat really takes place is this—the capitalist again and again appropriates, without equivalent, a portion of the previously materialised labor of others, and exchanges it for a great quantity of living labor."[66] In Marxist theory, alienated labor—here, the blood sucked from the unknowing sleeping victim—and private property, stand in a reciprocal relationship; one can be substituted for the other. We can therefore speak of the connection between private property and the estrangement of workers separated from their labor in the same way that we can speak of the vampire, the creature who is totally estranged from its original self. The next step in this process, as Marx notes, is an almost magical reversal—as capitalist private property dehumanizes men, it humanizes capital.[67] But this process takes place by means of such a delicate siphoning from one to the other that no one seems to notice; and, indeed, since the monsters retain their human form, this draining, for all appearances, changes nothing. In fact, the principle of private property—at once the product and the producer of estranged labor, is naturalized.

Private property and alienated labor are only two of the interchangeable terms Marx uses to construct his theory of the interdependent workings of capital. More than that, each part contains the whole. Or, as Bertell Ollman describes Marx's analysis of capitalism, it is "a system contained relationally in each of its parts."[68] Thus, according to Marx, "just as we have found the concept of private property from the concept of estranged, alienated labor by analysis, in the same way every category of political economy can be evolved with the help of these two factors; and we shall find again in each category, e.g., trade, competition, capital, money, only a definite and developed expression of the first foundations."[69] This interchangeability also explains, in addition to the frustration of any attempt to find confirmation of bourgeois economic formulas, what has been noted as the peculiarity of Marx's writing style. As one of his translators has observed, words in Marx are like bats: Both birds and mice are recognizable in them.[70]

Dracula, too, is interchangeably bat, wolf, mist, or human form; he is both dead and alive. As capital, Dracula also takes on other forms— among them, significantly as Moretti notes, that of money. Like the gold that Harker finds hoarded in the castle, Dracula is the social form that has exchange value but no use value whatever.[71] Money, in Marx, is the universal equivalent to which all other commodities are equal; but that is so, he tells us, because "all other commodities make it the material embodiment of their uniform and universal form of value."[72] Money is something of a despot because it "imprints" other commodities with their equivalences; but, like the vampire, it is a despot whose powers are limited in strange ways.[73] This despotic equivalent, money, is itself only a glorified commodity because it is completely dependent on other commodities for its expression. Yet this interdependence is perceived in reverse: we think that commodities move because money is circulated, says Marx, whereas it is the commodities whose movement creates this universal value form. Both money and the vampire, then, have only an illusory freedom of mobility; they are really quite dependent on the circulatory system of satellite entities.

But the threat Dracula embodies is even a terror for the bourgeois capitalist who would welcome new injections of capital (foreign investment from Transylvania) into the modern city. The vampire-capitalist, although the product of the competitive market, is also the enemy of the market: monopoly. In Moretti's analysis, the Dracula figure represents the past and the future of monopoly, since to the nineteenth-century bourgeois, he appeared as the aristocratic grip of feudal monopoly, and at the same time, he is a vision of monopoly under capitalism.[74] Dracula shows us the powers of the monopolist unchecked—he thrives on accumulation without interference—and the helplessness of others against him once he has seduced his operatives and secured his properties. This is the monster produced by competition run rampant, and if Dracula doesn't stand out in metropolitan London, it is because his modes of operation, his transactions, are not significantly different from those of other entrepreneurs. Faced with such a plague, the entrepreneur, rather than denounce the free market system that produces the monster, denies that it is a threat to the whole.

Drawing on Marx, Moretti stresses the incredulity of the nineteenth-century bourgeois: "Monopoly is the *past* of competition, the middle ages. He cannot believe that competition itself can generate monopoly in new forms."[75] This disbelief is also a fitting characterization of contemporary attitudes toward monopoly: We blindly allow the burgeoning corporate entity to stretch to its fullest but then are horrified as competitive activity is wiped out, deadened. Marx, noting this contradiction (and in a sense explaining how the contemporary bourgeois could be fooled), describes postfeudal monopoly as a "true synthesis," says Moretti—"the negation of feudal monopoly insofar as it implies the system of competition, and the negation of competition insofar as it is monopoly."[76]

Regulating the Domain of Culture

Lugosi also speaks to another economy—the political economy of the availability of signs. I have wanted to offer in my analysis an alternative to the bleakest of the postmodern theories of culture giving us the thorough commodification of signs and the end of meaning.[77] However, my formal study of this area of intellectual property really does confirm the most negative portrait of the reification of social forms. I have not wanted to offer yet another disposition of the way the production of signs is the production of commodities.[78] And yet intellectual property law, in treating commercial "languages" interchangeably as products of intellectual labor and units of exchange-value, returns us to the classic description of the commodity, to the masking feature of commodity fetishism, whereby humans are unable to see that the product they have created is their own and that they are entitled to the value stored in it because it is their own congealed labor. This same substitution effect (the characteristic mechanism of commodity fetishism) also works in and through intellectual property law to transform works of culture into economic units and economic units back into works of culture. Consider, for instance, the way in which the First Amendment doubles as a trade regulation:[79] "Free dissemination of ideas" is often interchangeable with the "free marketplace of ideas" in intellectual property discourse, which, quite frankly, tells us that signs are commodities.

If there is a theoretical antidote to this (and I believe that there is), it is in the social uses of the sign. We understand, primarily from Volosinov, that although the sign may have an existence as a commodity, it may have another life and another meaning, and it may well have had a past life—a separate history not canceled out by its life as a commodity.[80] This is not to imply that the function of the sign as a commodity is merely one "use" among many, for a commodity always has an economic, structural function: The use-value of the commodity is a function of a different order than the social use of the sign. But the sign may be, as M. M. Bakhtin shows, accented in different ways by diverse social groups; and because the same sign may have significantly different meanings to such groups, it may become the center of conflict, an ideological "struggle over meaning."[81]

I want to suggest that intellectual property doctrine also lends itself to a reading in these terms. Various groups may attempt to influence the meaning of intellectual property, with less interest in building coherent law through adherence to precedent than in curtailing or encouraging various kinds of "speech." When the relatives of deceased celebrities opposed the outcome of *Lugosi*, they were motivated as much (or more) by desire to secure meaning as they were by an attempt to secure real property. While legislators in the state of California were concerned about a particular point of law—the extension of post mortem property rights to the dead—the families of deceased celebrities borrowed these legal mechanisms in an attempt to rearticulate the image of an ancestor. Since the families have explained their motivation as a response to images they find to be offensive—such as greeting cards featuring an image of John Wayne wearing lipstick and captioned, "It's a bitch being butch," or an image of Clark Gable carrying another man up the staircase of Tara—we might as well understand the politics here in the context of the reclamation of these stars for heterosexuality. And we might consider as well the significance of who controls the image capital produced by one member of a family in the name of that family. Strangely, the disputes over the inheritability of image capital echo Marx's analysis of primogeniture, also the basis for his critique of Hegel and one of his most profound examples of the operation of contradiction. The principle of entailed landed property, which for Hegel is the cement of ethical society, is for Marx a contradiction of Hegel's own ideal of the family bound together through love. In the passing of property to the eldest son—a passage that excludes the other children—the family is not unified in harmony but is brutally ruptured. This, says Marx, is the "barbarism of private property against family life," which appears as "the sovereign splendor of private property, of possession of land, about which so many sentimentalities have recently been uttered and on behalf of which so many multi-colored crocodile tears have been shed."[82]

The possible restriction of signs was an issue in *Lugosi* as it was in *Sinatra v. Goodyear Tire* and *Booth v. Colgate-Palmolive*, where the courts were concerned about monopolies on performance signs. Although the majority decision in *Lugosi* did not rest upon the issue of monopoly, Judge Mosk *did* offer a vision of the kind of proprietary claims on the U.S. cultural heritage that relatives of the now deceased forefathers might put forward if right of publicity were descendible without temporal limit:

> May the descendants of George Washington sue the Secretary of the Treasury for placing his likeness on the dollar bill? May the descendants of Abraham Lincoln obtain damages for the commercial exploitation of his name and likeness by the Lincoln National Life Insurance Company or the Lincoln division of the Ford Motor Company? May the descendants of James and Dolley Madison recover for the commercialization of Dolley Madison confections?[83]

The dissent, represented by Justice Bird, argued, as you will recall, *for* the descendible right of publicity. In contrast to the right of publicity based on privacy, which would put the image in the public domain upon the death of the celebrity, the right of publicity that passed to the estate heirs could have the effect of removing the image from circulation in the wider culture. It would put the celebrity image in the control of relatives or executors of the estate.

Critics of the dissent's position in *Lugosi* pointed out that in her opinion for the majority in *Guglielmi v. Spelling-Goldberg Productions*, heard one month after *Lugosi*, Justice Bird took an opposite position.[84] There, where the relatives of Rudolph Valentino brought action against television producers who used the star's image in a fictional work, Justice Bird argued that if the families of deceased celebrities were able to enjoin the fictional use of historical figures, "[a]n important avenue of self-expression would be blocked and the marketplace of ideas would be diminished."[85] But a closer look at Justice Bird's dissent reveals that she argued for a compromise—the relinquishment of the image of a popular figure to the control of relatives, but control under a temporal limit. After a certain time, she argued, the celebrity image would revert to its place in the public domain and in history: "Finally, with the passage of time, an individual's identity is woven into the fabric of history, as a heroic or obscure character of the past. In that sense, the events and measure of his life are in the public domain and are questionably placed in the control of a particular descendant."[86] The insurance against the removal of the celebrity image from history and the certainty that it would be returned to the public domain would be secured by the imposition of a limitation similar to that encoded in federal copyright law. As Justice Bird formulated this limitation on the right of publicity, it would work like the copyright limit, extending for the duration of life plus fifty years.[87]

As I said at the outset of this chapter, the dissent in *Lugosi* became the basis for section 990, the new section added to the California Civil Code in 1985, which nullified *Lugosi*. And in the hearings on Senate Bill 613, which introduced the changes in the code, we see the conflicts over the uses of celebrity images take recognizable shape; the political implications of the issues raised by *Lugosi* now become clearer.[88] First, I should explain that the amendments made to the code by the California legislature produced two different sections pertinent to commercial appropriation of the image—one applying to the living, the other to the dead. Section 3344, which had been added to the code in 1972, was amended to allow persons to recover profits from the unauthorized use of an image. Applicable to ordinary persons as well as celebrities, section 3344 was parallel to section 990 in the latter's reference to protection against uses of the voice, name, signature, photograph, and likeness.[89] Provisions also differed in that section 990 included a registration requirement, a time limitation corresponding with copyright law's life plus fifty years, and a retroactive clause pertaining to personalities who were already deceased.

Negative commentary in the aftermath of the passage of section 990 and its signature into law on 30 September 1984, focused on those categories of culture exempt from the provisions of the new amendments: areas traditionally considered what might be called free speech "zones." Within the provisions of the code, neither section 990 nor section 3344 can apply to public affairs, political campaigns, or news. Section 990 adds that books, plays, and magazines are privileged forms within which owners of celebrity images cannot assert the right of publicity of the deceased. However, the same provision does not extend to the living, since section 3344 (by omitting books, plays, and magazines from the list of exemptions) would make publishers and producers potentially liable if they used any aspect of the identity of a living person without his or her permission.[90]

It might seem from this list of exemptions that the California legislators were providing for First Amendment concerns—that they anticipated the possibility that the images of celebrities who had died in the state (and who had registered themselves in Sacramento as required) might become the subjects of news coverage, political commentary, historical fiction, or motion picture and television drama. But there are two ways in which we can see section 990 as consolidating signs in the interests of conservative ideologies in the contest over shared culture. First, section 990 exempts only works of art that, in its words, are "single and original."[91] And, not surprisingly, it does not exempt advertising or commercials. The legislators' position on advertising sends the message that the unauthorized appropriation of celebrity imagery is objectionable profiteering (in the words of Judge Greenfield, "hitching a free ride"). But it also means that certain celebrity images will be available only through licensing for payment of royalties or not available at all for either profit or not-for-profit promotions. The point here is that advertisements, like works that are not "single and original," may be the only means of access, for some groups, to these charged images. The most widely circulated forms of popular culture—posters, coffee cups, lunch pails, magazine ads, T-shirts, playing cards, ashtrays, statuettes, postcards, mementos—have the worst reputation in the eyes of judges and legal commentators. Such low forms—

which, in terms of "political speech," constitute a significant sphere of signification—are so saturated with the messages of commerce that they do not warrant exemption from the right of publicity monopoly grant on the grounds of "free speech." Justice Bird, for example, made it clear that some of the forms assumed by the image of Lugosi-as-Dracula were not legitimate cultural entities and therefore not worthy of defense as free expression:

> Finally, I am sensitive to the fact that enforcement of the right of publicity may conflict with freedom of expression in some cases. However, such a conflict is not presented in this case. Plaintiffs challenged Universal's licensing of Lugosi's likeness in his portrayal of Count Dracula in connection with the sale of such objects as plastic toy pencil sharpeners, soap products, target games, candy dispensers and beverage stirring rods. Such conduct hardly implicates the First Amendment.[92]

Legal commentators have tended to see this the other way around: Assuming that culture is produced for profit, only some forms of that culture—namely, those having "cultural or informative functions"—are "accorded a social value that transcends commercial enterprise."[93] The kind of "single and original" works sold in limited editions and exhibited in art galleries are not subject to liability. But where Justice Bird really *is* inconsistent is in her insistence that the same popular icons (the images of Lugosi's Dracula on plastic pencil sharpeners and soap products), as they are used in motion picture and television advertising, become constitutionally protectible utterances when they help to secure the economic viability of higher forms of popular culture—a motion picture or television program. The same pencil sharpeners, games, candy dispensers, and stirring rods, if sold as part of the advertising campaign tied to the original release, the re-release, or the videotape sale of *Dracula* starring Bela Lugosi, are, in this event, "protected speech."

This monopoly on signs, then, doesn't directly affect the circulation of star signs that promote the entertainment industry product. But it *does* limit the popular uses of those symbolic goods (T-shirts and posters) that are the cheapest to manufacture and the easiest for people's movements to use. In the same way, family control of the image is semiotically at odds with the meanings of star memorabilia and celebrity send-ups, which are the cultural sustenance of gay subcultures. My first concern, then, is that legal distinctions made between forms that are considered "culture" and those that are not translate into a right of publicity monopoly grant limit on the use of socially and sexually transgressive signs, a limitation on the very forms within which they have the most political volatility. And my first concern is only redoubled by my second objection: that the discussion of these uses and exclusions in terms of "freedom of speech" forgets that this right does not preexist. The right to speak, to manufacture in bulk, to represent in popular forms should be understood as a struggle between two rights-holding parties, each of which maintains that it has preeminent entitlement. If we cast this contest only in terms of the First Amendment we make the mistake of pitting historically flimsy speech rights against the solidity of property rights.

The political implications of section 990 thus sketched out, I want to return to the difference between the personal privacy right, which does not survive, and the publicity right, which is the basis of self-expanding capital. If the *Lugosi* case is a study in the fate of privacy, the Elvis Presley cases demonstrate the way privacy's personal monopoly becomes productive property. The debates around *Factors Etc., Inc. v. Pro Arts, Inc.* (1977) show us what is fully at stake in the survivability of the celebrity right of publicity, because the Presley image industry is threatened by the public domain as well as by the public, the fans themselves.[94] Here, the untimely and sensational death of the star illustrates how many interests are held together by the single thread of the celebrity's personal right. And finally, we see how the image industry justifies the continuance of its monopoly at the very point at which the celebrity seems most clearly to belong to us all.

In recent years, the deaths of John Lennon and Elvis Presley, in particular, provided a merchandising field day for newspapers and magazines as well as for the small industries that manufactured the first souvenirs. Only three days after Elvis Presley died, a poster titled "In Memory" (manufactured by Pro-Arts, an Ohio company) went on sale. Against what seemed an infringement of the right it held, Boxcar Enterprises—the corporation formed by Tennessee entrepreneur Colonel Tom Parker and Elvis to promote the diversification of the star into motion pictures in his later career—defended its interest in the Presley image against Pro Arts. In addition, Factors, the New York company to which Boxcar had transferred the exclusive right to exploit the name and likeness of the star, defended its licenses against Pro Arts and other companies that rushed into the souvenir market immediately after Presley's death.[95] Elvis's own right, then, served as a kind of funnel through which Boxcar Enterprises transferred exclusivity to a New York manufacturer, Factors—and through which, in turn, Factors transferred exclusivity to its licensees, the manufacturers of official Elvis souvenirs. The death of Elvis and the expiration of the right meant that the whole network of licensing entitlement broke down. Since 1977, the issue of the survivability of Elvis Presley's publicity right has been passed back and forth from New York to Tennessee courts as one has reversed the other. The most recent case held that Presley does have posthumous rights.[96]

In the Elvis Presley as well as the Bela Lugosi litigation, the debates around the cases focused on the "valuelessness" of an unprotected property and its relationship to "marketplace order." In the entertainment law commentary on *Factors Etc.*, the case made consistently against allowing the right of publicity to terminate with death was that chaos in the marketplace would ensue. As one commentator on *Lugosi* observed, "[I]f this right does have value as a commercial entity, placing the right of publicity in the public domain wrecks havoc in the marketplace."[97] But it is not as though there are no existing provisions in U.S. law for ensuring that such chaos will not break out in the marketplace. Trademark and patent law, for instance, organize manufacturers' claims for both the item produced and its distinctive mark, whether photographic image or abstract design. As an example of how such provisions work, imagine what the fate of the Lugosi image might have been if it had been indisputably in the public domain. If Lugosi's right of publicity, for example, had expired with his death and had not descended to his heirs, the fifty licensees who reproduced his image on paper products and games would merely have had to register the marked product with the U.S. Trademark Office in order to protect themselves from competitors. From this perspective, it is clear that the concern about marketplace disorder, which would recruit the monopoly right of publicity as a trade regulation, masks the fear that the image might fall into the public domain.

From the point of view of vampire capital, the public domain is like the stake through the heart; profits disseminated are like profits that have disintegrated. As our legal commentator on marketplace havoc puts it, "If survivability and descendability are denied, the right of publicity is placed in the public domain and no property interest in it is recognized. However, recognizing no property interest in an entity, i.e., no one owns it, is tantamount to recognizing an absolute property interest in the same thing, i.e., everyone owns it."[98] What the author of this article is finally not able to address is the disadvantage of "no property interest." Instead of a reasoned analysis of the social benefits, he offers a cliché—primitive as opposed to civilized property relations. No property, he says, is the "most primitive state of property law," one inappropriate to a more advanced civilization that has developed "increasingly sophisticated systems of ownership" for such "elusive property."[99]

In one of the Elvis Presley cases, however, we can consider the rationale behind the "primitive state of property law," in which "everyone owns it" means "no one owns it." The opinion in *Memphis Development Foundation v. Factors, Inc.* (1980) stands out from all of the recent right of publicity cases because it makes the argument against a surviving right to one's image in terms of common ownership of the mythic lives of the famous. In *Memphis Development*, the City of Memphis defended its right to produce statuettes of its favorite son in order to raise the funds to erect a memorial statue in his honor. Factors, Inc. (Boxcar's licensing agent) again defended the right that had been contractually transferred to it. The New York courts affirmed the claim of Factors, Inc., by recognizing the passage of the Presley legacy from Boxcar Enterprises to its licensee. But in the state of Tennessee this transfer was voided; there the *Memphis Development* case terminated Elvis's right of privacy with his death.[100] Thus, for several years the Presley image was available for merchandising in the state of Tennessee but not in the state of New York. The argument responsible for this temporary state of affairs in Tennessee centered on the idea that because the public "makes" the hero, the public is, in some senses, the "owner" of the image.[101] The court asked, "Who is the heir of fame?" and in answer it detailed the process of producing the famous. Notoriety, it held, was a "by-product" of a combination of "activities and personal attributes as well as luck and promotion." But even after all of that, the court concluded that fame finally "depends on the participation of the public."[102] Thus conceived, the *Memphis Development* court produced the likenesses and the memories of the famous as a kind of "common asset."[103] *Memphis Development*, like *Lugosi*, was subsequently overturned by state statute.[104]

The Legal Undead

"The law comes into constant conflict with its basic premise, private property," says Edelman.[105] This conflict is clear in the antithetical relation between the right of privacy and the right of publicity, which came to a head in the *Lugosi* case. In *Lugosi*, the question of privacy over publicity was the crucial legal issue. If it was found that Bela Lugosi's publicity right was dependent upon his right of privacy—a personal, nontransferrable right—then that right would cease after his death. But as we saw in that case, the central issue for capital was not that a person no longer existed to complain of an injury but that his personal right could no longer be enforced against commercial infringers using the Lugosi image. From the point of view of capital, the death that exhumed the star's natural right could turn a potentially valuable image property into a valueless sign, because the mechanism for protecting the face of Lugosi as Dracula no longer had a legal basis.

The value of the face lies in its guarantee of private property. The face is able to enter the commercial fray, to risk exposure and public possession, and still remain private. It is a natural No Trespassing sign and an index of the personal right that is the gold bullion behind all of the paper and plastic upon which the face is issued. But we must not think that the face stands out as the one sign of indivisibility, identity, singularity, or individuality. Deleuze and Guattari provocatively show us the face as only a functional part of the apparatus of the autonomous subject that operates as an "abstract machine of faciality."[106] Indeed, the phenomenon we are discussing is nothing more than the facialization of all the parts of the body, of ordinary objects, and of the entire surface, the "face" of the world. In these terms, as Deleuze and Guattari write, "[t]he face itself is a redundancy."[107]

Deleuze and Guattari capture something of the irony in the fact that although entertainment law represents privacy right as a threat to the growth of a right of publicity, the two rights have the same origin: the rights-holding subject who has property in himself. Whereas the one right finds its support in the human subject, the other finds its support in the self as property and in the property produced by expenditure of labor. The right of publicity is nothing more nor less than a personal monopoly reinforced, one that California Civil Code section 990 extended for an additional fifty years. The strategy behind section 990 is finally reminiscent of the strategy of the publishers who, faced with the expiration of their licenses after the Statute of Anne, borrowed the monopoly in perpetuity of authors' rights to extend and fortify their own rights to the literary works they published. The contemporary licensers of the images of the famous but now deceased, sometimes (but not always) in the name of the families, have similarly used the right of publicity, now fortified by statute in many states.[108] These new state laws create a fiction more marvelous than Bram Stoker's nightmare: a host of legal undead.

And yet, cultural image capital, although it is private property, resists such attempts to turn it into the wholly private speech that would "sever its social nerves."[109] On the one hand, the inheritable right of publicity may create a new nostalgia culture of the undead—Mae West, W. C. Fields, Marilyn Monroe, and James Dean with the subversive fluids drained out of them, featured in advertisements for Hershey's candy bars, Thom McAn shoes, and Maxell tapes. On the other, licensing may bring these images to life by pumping new capital into them. Or do these intangible undead unpropertylike properties still elude their owners, oscillating back and forth between decades, appearing to different groups in different forms?

CHAPTER SEVEN

Superman, Television, and the Protective Strength of the Trademark

The television text's characteristic segmentation, its capacity to ingest everything, to repeat infinitely, to stamp its imagery on every conceivable object of everyday life: These are the dimensions of television typically described as symptoms of postmodernism—that cultural phenomenon which, as Stuart Hall has so aptly put it, is really about "how the world dreams itself to be American."[1] In the U.S., then, where capitalism looms large and its symptomatic postmodern culture flows abundantly both within the country and across its borders, we would expect to find certain codes or rules governing this flow. And we do find them, not only in the formal conventions that govern works of cultural production in general but also in the codes of the entertainment law that seeks to regulate them. If intellectual property and unfair competition laws can be said to rule cultural texts, is this regulation in any way comparable to the governance of literary, cinematic, and televisual conventions? We may think that the laws of the state are significantly different from other kinds of codes because of the sharp edge of enforcement, but we might also consider how law silently shapes cultural forms even when it is not actually enforced. The law, in other words, has its implied *norms*, which legal commentators discuss in much the same way that theorists talk about cultural codes and conventions: Users put codes or rules into practice, and the cultural system functions because of loose agreement among culture members.

As I discussed in chapter 1, one way in which the study of the law has differed significantly from the study of culture has been in the availability of the concept of ideology. Theorists of culture have made extensive use of the concept since the late sixties, but it did not find its way into legal studies until the late seventies in Britain and the U.S.[2] This almost-ten-year lag presents an interesting problem for scholars. While it is crucial for legal theorists to begin work on the way law has functioned ideologically, those of us who study culture and society are currently looking for more elasticity in the concept of ideology. And whereas legal scholars are now refining their analysis of the structural function of ideology, scholars in cultural studies are looking more and more at the points of opposition to it.

For any critic who addresses the relationship between law and ideology, the recurring dilemma is whether the law asserts itself as material base or disengaged superstructure. I have already noted some of the ways in which the law *appears* to be a dimension of both in my discussion of star contracts. Commenting on the way in which rights to the land seemed inseparable from agricultural uses of it in seventeenth-century England, E. P. Thompson says that the law is "deeply imbricated" in the relations of production, so much so that it is often indistinguishable from the mode of production.[3] According to Hirst and Kingdom, this aspect of the law is its "mystery," but this elusiveness is also a condition of its efficacy: "[I]t stands to production in a mysterious form in that production is absent in it and yet by this 'absence' capitalism's conditions of operation are se-cured."[4] Do we have an inkling of the way the law silently "secures" capitalist "conditions of operation" when we see how the very design on the face of the object of culture can now be registered as a bona fide trademark? Thus, a scene from the television show "Star Trek" repro-duced on sheets and pillowcases can have an economic function at the same time that it has a decorative function. What the case of the bed linens tells us is that, more and more, the trademark on the consumer good (especially as label, shape, or design) represents economics as absent all the while that the mark "secures" the requisite conditions for economic production. After all, how is one to tell the purely decorative function of the scene from "Star Trek" from the entirely economic function of the same decoration?

The success of Paramount Pictures in registering the STAR TREK design as a trademark (which involved arguing to the U.S. Trademark Trial and Appeal Board that the design was not mere ornamentation) is part of a larger picture.[5] In fact, it is part of a marked historical shift in the use of particular legal theories in entertainment law from 1940 to the present. We might be tempted to locate the origins of this shift in the U.S. Trademark Act of 1946 (known as the Lanham Act), which took effect on 5 July 1947.[6] But the Lanham Act is, I think, a participant in, rather than an absolute determinant of, larger economic developments. From this perspective, the Lanham Act is itself just another symptom, and since we are looking at different levels of the social formation simultaneously, we therefore need to ask if the growing legal strategy of using trademark law to protect popular icons is related to another symptom: television's eclipse of the theatrical film.

A case in point is the transition of the character Superman from comic strip through radio and motion picture serials to television series and motion picture features—a transition that corresponds to the period in which trademark law overtakes copyright law as the governing principle of character protection in popular formats. Since 1940, DC Comics, the corporate proprietors of Superman, have aggressively defended their entitlement to the character in the U.S. courts. And the eight cases I have studied, spanning the years 1940 to 1983, are a remarkable record of realignment around the legal theories of character protection that would best strengthen the company's market position by reinforcing legal barriers around its image properties.[7] The DC Comics cases testify to the basic conflict between copyright and trademark as legal theories and practical remedies. But in another realm they speak as well of conflict over cultural values. In short, the Superman text is the cultural turf over which an important conflict between copyright and trademark has been waged.

On the side of copyright, we have authorship: the older, bourgeois, cultural value that has protected the comic strips since 1938 and that was invoked to defend the cartoon hero Superman against the infringing comic book hero Wonderman in 1940. Historically, the spirit of Anglo-American copyright law has been the protection of the author's expression. In the name of that expression, copyright law has traditionally justified the limited monopoly over a creative work by linking exclusive use with the protection of the livelihood of the author-originator. But, as I have been arguing, although Anglo-American law retains the Romantic notion of authorship in its emphasis on expression, uniqueness, and the self-contained work of art, in copyright law *originality* really denotes the work's point of origin rather than its novelty or creativity. We have already seen how the technical synonymity in copyright law between origin and author makes it possible for that law to recognize the owner of rights in a creative work over the claim of any real author. Thus it is that any legal entity can stand in as author, just as DC Comics has stood in for Superman's creators, Jerry Siegel and Joe Shuster, who tried for forty years to reclaim their work after having sold the rights to it in their youth.[8]

If Anglo-American copyright law has evolved from the need to protect an author against marketplace pirates, trademark law, a branch of unfair competition law, has evolved from a general philosophy of protection *for the public* against merchants who might deceive them about the true source of the goods or services they purchase. In principle, the merchant's mark has been protected traditionally because to the consumer it stood for *goodwill*—for the guarantee that the buyer could expect, from the source behind the goods, the same values and qualities received with the last purchase. Significant for us, however, is the inversion of this principle in American common law, where the trademark comes to ensure *not* that the public is protected from merchant fraud but that the merchant-owner of the mark is protected against infringers.[9] With the weight of unfair competition law behind them, merchants are able to defend their trademarks against others who would use them; and American (although not European) law has increasingly come to recognize the trademark as an asset or property. For while copyright law still upholds some remnant of the older cultural valuation of individual enterprise and creativity, the trademark unapologetically stands for market expansion and control. It is precisely this reversal in common law that makes it possible for DC Comics to defend the character Superman as its trademark, giving the company a significant market advantage not realizable under copyright theory.

As the preferred theory of legal defense for popular characters, copyright fell out of fashion in the entertainment industry with the often-cited 1954 Sam Spade case. The question in *Warner Brothers Pictures, Inc. v. Columbia Broadcasting Co.* turned on whether Warner Brothers' motion picture rights to the novel *The Maltese Falcon* included the right to enjoin author Dashiell Hammett from using the character in sequels. It would appear that the sympathy of the court was with Hammett, because the decision allowed him to continue to use his literary creation. But in the process of giving Spade back to the author, the court defined characters as mobile pieces in relation to the *work*, the wholeness and totality of which is crucial to copyright law. Characters—the "mere chessmen," devices, or

vehicles for telling the story—were now seen as less protectable as authorial creations than the work itself. Moreover, the court decided that the
character had to constitute the work as a whole in order for it to be protected by copyright.[10]

After the Sam Spade case, entertainment law literature associated copyright more and more with enigma and intellectual puzzle; in contrast to
trademark law, copyright was as tenuous as the works of authorship it
protected.[11] Sam Spade also demonstrated the consequences of copyright
law's preference for the single work as a whole upon which its component
parts (including its characters) depended for protection. Especially when
read in combination with the companion case, *Nichols v. Universal Pictures
Corp.* (1930), *Warner Brothers v. Columbia Broadcasting* seemed to say that
the literary character now had to take on the complex proportions of the
narrative undergirding in order to qualify for copyright protection.[12] As
if that weren't enough, the case reiterated the difference between the
ephemeral literary character—who is constructed with word portraits too
abstract and vague to be visualized (and hence protected)—and cartoon
characters, whose concrete existence as artistic renderings makes uniqueness (or imitative proclivities) easier to verify in court.[13]

The Sam Spade decision, a relic of the golden era of Hollywood cinema
when copyright law alone protected valuable literary properties, became a
textbook case, and the field of entertainment law gravitated toward trademark doctrine as a remedy for copyright law's failure to secure the profitability of either popular titles or characters. Copyright law was found to
be inadequate because it could not protect the title of a novel or motion
picture—those works understood by the doctrine of intellectual property
as descriptive of the work or like a proper name, but not part of the work
as a whole.[14] Trademark law, in contrast, with its emphasis on source,
origin, and sponsorship, not authorship, protected both title and character if one or the other "indicated" programs or stories emanating from the
same source.

It is interesting to note that the legal displacement of the author in the
shift from copyright to trademark is also roughly contemporaneous with
what postmodern theory has diagnosed as the eclipse of the author by his
or her own text. Bernard Edelman, commenting on the same feature in
French trademark law that I have identified in U.S. law, suggestively
argues that the character that breaks away from its author is a feature of
the very kind of writing that produced it: "With the character, the writing

circle closes—one could even claim that the author disappears. The author alienates himself within an infernal machine of his own making. The writing takes on a form beyond that of its own origin, a product that moves about freely on a stage, playing out its non-human role."[15]

Perhaps because of my American vantage point, I would stress the role of trademark law in facilitating the phenomenon described by Edelman—the tendency of popular characters to leave their textual origins and to disclaim their authors. In American law, where, as we have already seen, real authors may be contractually canceled out forever, it also seems that trademark law has encouraged the detachment of the character from the work.[16]

This situation seems especially true when we consider the importance of trademark law to the merchandising campaigns that grew out of early television programs. From the first days of television, series titles, as indicators of origin (as opposed to motion picture titles, which were considered to be detachable like proper names), attained legal status as trademarks. From the point of view of merchandising, then, "Maverick," "Howdy Doody," "Annie Oakley," and "Superman" were real ideal vehicles because both the name of the main character and the series title could be protected by trademark law. One of the early tests of trademark law in relation to television suggests the potency of this legal remedy and hence its attractiveness to television producers who were interested in turning popular characters and program titles into further capital. In *Wyatt Earp Enterprises, Inc. v. Sackman, Inc.* (1958), the court held that the owner of the program titled "The Life and Legend of Wyatt Earp" could enjoin a clothing manufacturer's use of the name "Wyatt Earp" on playsuits.[17] Without prior knowledge of trademark law, it must seem strange to us that any party could not lay claim to the name of a legendary figure; we would assume that history, of all the territories of shared culture, could not be monopolized. As we have seen, however, the doctrine of *secondary meaning* sorts commercial signs into a second (protected) order of meaning on the basis of their demonstrated popularity. And that was the case with the new meaning the popular television show gave to the name of the historical figure "Wyatt Earp."

Scholars have recently called attention to the way television programs exist to deliver viewers to advertisers, who calculate the matches between commercial airing and hypothetical viewing as "impressions" made on consumers. Here, the titles of the programs, as well as the names, physical appearances, and costumes of the characters are also impressed upon viewers, whose later recognition then substantiates the trademark status of such high-circulation signs.[18] The sheer fact of having been broadcast to millions of homes then made it possible for the producers of "The Life and Legend of Wyatt Earp" first to license Sackman, Inc., to use the trademark WYATT EARP on children's clothes—and, after Sackman's continued production beyond the expiration date of the license, to restrain the company from using the name of the legendary hero.

The *Wyatt Earp* case is but one example of the dynamics of product licensing, the parasitic industry that traces its parentage to the sound motion picture and radio industry. Licensing thrived in the early days of television, after the Lanham Act, enjoying a heyday it had not known since the thirties, when Herbert Kamen established the Walt Disney character licensing program and Shirley Temple and the Lone Ranger were licensed so successfully for dolls, games, and school supplies.[19] Decades later, the 1978 STAR WARS merchandise boom would reignite licensing after its lapse in popularity in the sixties and early seventies, and the success of that venture was followed almost immediately by Warner Brothers' duplication of the phenomenon with *Superman: The Movie* (1979). The past ten years, in turn, have seen further reduplication of the Superman phenomenon, with four motion picture sequels and at least forty half hours of syndicated television programming per week.[20]

All of these merchandise licensing ventures depend completely on the protectability of the trademark; it is the legal shield around the name, logo, shape, or character image, making it possible for the original proprietor to assign this sign to second and third parties for a limited period of time in exchange for royalties. But it is a shield made possible by the total reversal whereby in trademark law injury to the owner takes precedence over injury to the consumer. Moreover, the theories internal to trademark law seem to have reversed themselves as well: While unfair competition law is based on the prohibition against *palming off* one's goods as the goods of another, licensing itself is essentially a "passing off."[21] If, for instance, RJR Nabisco, through its merchandising agent, Columbia Pictures, licenses the image of Niagara Falls on the Nabisco Shredded Wheat cereal box cover to a manufacturer of beach towels, does Nabisco stand directly behind the towel in the same way it stands behind the box of breakfast cereal? Such unlimited transference, so basic to American merchandising, was anticipated and aptly described by a 1938 provision in British law against "trafficking in trademark." And it was invoked recently when American Greeting Cards tried to register its HOLLY HOBBY mark in the United Kingdom and was denied registration on grounds very close to the original spirit of U.S. trademark law. Rather than preserving the company's reputation, according to the British ruling, licensing would help American Greeting Cards to "dispose of [that] reputation as though it were a marketable commodity."[22]

Superman and Series Form

The point most often made about characters in television series is that the narrative returns them to the same situation and frame of mind we left them in the previous week. They learn nothing new; they neither grow nor change significantly.[23] Superman, the ideal series character, who was created to fit the frames of the comic book, fights the same battles every week; for all of his powers, he is unable to restore law and order or bring peace to the world. Each new story, says Umberto Eco in "The Myth of Superman," is a "virtual new beginning" because the character exhausts the narrative material he is given and requires that more be parceled out, week after week, year after year. For Eco, this "iterative scheme" is written into the very conditions of Superman's human/superhuman existence, as though Superman and series form were eternally one. His narrative is both driven by human problems and predicated upon superhuman strength and longevity.[24]

Recent developments in cultural studies, however, suggest two other important ways of explaining the relation between the Superman narrative and series form. First, following Tony Bennett and Janet Woollacott's paradigm for studying James Bond, Superman may be seen as one long intertext made up of all of the narratives, reviews, and biographies laid end to end. In their scheme, ancillary products (merchandising tie-ups) become "textual meteorites" shooting off from the intertextual chain.[25] In this configuration, each story does not necessarily start from a virtual beginning, but it instead is written onto as well as over the earlier story, creating a paradigmatic narrative buildup. The lethal powers of kryptonite, for instance, were introduced not in the comic strip but in the radio series, and they are now firmly embedded in the Superman story by the sheer accumulation of retellings. There is, however, a second and opposing explanation of the Superman phenomenon that would see the character as material that is significantly altered as is the cast in different media. From this vantage, Superman does not necessarily carry his narrative scheme within him like a genetic map. The character can always be rewritten for another medium. Although Superman would seem to epitomize the television series character who must always return to the beginning, in his earlier incarnations he is cast in different narrative schema and follows somewhat different rules. The history of the translation of the Superman narrative from comic book to television series bears this out.

Three years after Superman's famed launching of DC's *Action Comics* in June 1938, the stories took their first moving image form in the Max Fleischer/Paramount Pictures animated cartoons, seventeen of which were produced between 1941 and 1943. Columbia Pictures then produced two fifteen-part motion picture series starring Kirk Alyn in 1948 and 1950. But the failure of the second series relative to the first suggests that the logic of the connection between television and series form had occurred to audiences as well as producers. After 1950, it was inevitable that the next Superman series would be produced for television. A single transitional feature film, *Superman and the Moleman* (1951), almost a pilot for the television series, introduced George Reeves as Superman. Thereafter Reeves embodied the part in the 104 television episodes produced and aired between 1951 and 1957.[26]

Before television, the Superman character, in its comic book, animated cartoon, and motion picture serial incarnations, is ruled by the law of copyright. But in the fifties, in television, he comes more and more under the influence of the trademark. Under copyright law, the body of the text theoretically protects the character, but the character alone, outside the work, can be protected only by trademark law. So it is that the expansion of the story as a continuing serial is simultaneously the legal survival of the popular character. The first of two Columbia serials retells Superman's early life history from the disintegration of the planet Krypton, the arrival of the infant Superman on Earth and the death of his foster parents, to his arrival in Metropolis City. The feud with Lois Lane and the discovery of the powers of kryptonite are unfolded chronologically, with each episode ending in cliff-hanging anticipation of the consequence of a former action. Using the novelistic time frame, the continuing serial asserts its status as a work and reveals its ambition to be a motion picture feature— an inspiration it has historically had since the mid-teens, when it served as a compromise format in the transition from the short to the full-length feature.[27]

Significantly, in the pre-television period in which Superman is first represented by a mortal body (that of actor Kirk Alyn), the narrative takes the form of a continuing serial. One might also say that the 1948 motion picture serial tested the protectability of the character against the powers of the real, for in the serial's combination of animation and live action we are made aware of the continuity between DC Comics' thoroughly protected cartoon drawing and the new motion picture. Superman in cartoon form (the form with an already established record of toughness in court battles against pirates)[28] is imprinted on the film like the merchant's mark that ensures against infringement and defends against property claims made by the real-life actor playing the character.[29] In other words, the actor playing the part introduces a potential challenge to the total monopoly that DC Comics would have on Superman because the actor could conceivably argue that he had an ownership in a role with which he had become synonymous. The sign of the cartoon creator's authorial hand, which validates the iconic Superman as a protectable, artistic rendering, is invoked in the animated flying sequences in the series, which, in their unbounded defiance of physical laws, also reveal the limitations of the live action representation of flying "faster than a speeding bullet."

The use of live action to represent a character complicates an already complex issue. The difficulty that intellectual property had had with the literary character within the work tells us something about the antithetical relation between the novelistic character and narrative form. Taken together, *Warner Brothers v. Columbia Broadcasting* (Sam Spade) and *Nichols v. Universal Pictures* display a high-culture preference for the fully rounded character as opposed to the flat, one-dimensional type. These cases suggest that the ordinary character is subservient to the narrative work in which it appears and that in order for a character to be protected, it must rise to the condition of a uniquely created work of art in its own right. In other words, it must be the psychologically "deepened" novelistic character whose development and change is charted along the chronology of classical narrative form (although, of course, we know that novelistic time is only borrowed to help create the illusion of the birth-to-death sequence of human life). At the same time, however, the novelistic character has structural limitations unknown to narrative, which has a miraculous tapewormlike capacity to regenerate so as to ensure its own continuance.

While narrative can assure its self-perpetuation into infinity, the classic novelistic character, as he develops, will make life choices that only bring him closer to his own obliteration through aging and eventual death. As Eco has explained, the prohibition against action, change, and sexual encounter built into the Superman character is a stay against precisely such impermanence, that with every humanlike act he would, in approaching death, "consume" himself.[30]

If we compare the time frames of the novelistic character and the continuing narrative, we find an impending contradiction between the two. While the narrative can permutate *ad infinitum*, the character modeled after the human individual will be used up because of the very action-oriented growth and development that classical narrative requires of him as its agent. It is the necessary mortality of the character that explains why the continuing serial, the first model of the cultural-industrial form with the potential to carry on forever, requires multiple characters who reproduce over several generations if the form is to adhere to codes of realism and still follow its inclination to endure into infinity.[31] The genius of the mythic hero (Eco's "inconsumable" character), however, is that his actions will never extinguish him. Because he is mythic, he is doomed to repeat, but he is also most at home in the series form, which reconstructs the key components of his type each week. The immortal, semihuman character is ultimately incompatible with the novelistic form, which could expand infinitely to tell the history of the universe. For our purposes, however, this situation tells us less about the mythic hero and more about the inherent limitations of narrative realism and novelistic time. To get out of the bind, the Superman story resorts to fantasy time schemes and experimental temporalities. But finally, the profitability of the literary property requires this impossibility: a semihuman character who is immortal and a story that never really ends.

Capital and literary form appear as competing interests in Superman as in no other popular figure because of the peculiar conditions of his existence: He is both human and superhuman, and he obeys the temporal orders of both Earth and the universe. As Eco has put it, "Superman is a myth on condition of being a creature immersed in everyday life."[32] From the point of view of capital, Superman is under threat from two directions. First, his consumable aspect, the very human form that the character assumes in his live-action motion picture and television manifestations, is a potential danger to profit. But a still greater threat, whose effects are as dire and as certain as the effects of kryptonite on the body of this hero, is the possibility of copyright expiration. During the period of copyright protection (in the U.S., the life of the author or the date of first publication plus fifty years), the character may be somewhat shielded by the copyrighted story. But inevitably, if the story stands absolutely alone as a work, it will eventually fall into the public domain, taking the character with it. It will, that is, *unless it is part of a series.*

And here is precisely where television and trademark law come to the rescue of Superman. As I have already noted, the title of a television series is protected as a trademark because it indicates the source of the programs. And similarly, a character becomes a trademark when and if it comes to identify a series of narratives produced by the same creator. (One can faintly see the philosophy of producer "goodwill" and the ostensible concern for television viewers, who are protected by the promise that the trademarks MORK AND MINDY, THE DUKES OF HAZZARD, CHARLIE'S ANGELS, and STARSKY AND HUTCH mean that the audience can expect the same quality from the makers every time they choose one program over another.)[33]

But as though that were not enough protective strength for Superman, by virtue of his popularity, and because in legal theory "super" and "man" have achieved a *secondary meaning* in the minds of the public, the name, physical appearance, and costumes denoting SUPERMAN (but not the physical abilities or personal traits) are protected as trademarks.[34] And as a trademark, the name and the physical likeness of SUPERMAN are protected in perpetuity. So DC Comics, proprietor of the character, has a seemingly invincible monopoly on Superman that is guaranteed into infinity. It would seem, then, that the Superman character, as a free-floating entity, could outlast even the stories that launched him. Yet there is one final danger facing SUPERMAN as private property, the danger always lurking in non-use and its antithesis, overuse. I will explain these possibilities in my conclusion, but first I want to return to the pending crisis in entertainment law between copyright and trademark, a crisis bound up as well with motion picture and television form.

As if to reinforce his legal invincibility, SUPERMAN has found the ideal medium for ensuring his immortality. Because television is potentially never-ending, for THE MAN OF STEEL it could be the narrative form that corresponds perfectly with the conditions of his immortality. Theoretically, television would resolve the contradiction between narrative progression and mutable literary character by acknowledging that only the inconsumable, mythic character is temporally compatible with the never-ending proclivity of narrative. But for all of its apparent continuousness, television is also intermittent; its characteristic segmentation, as John Ellis argues, means that it "tend[s] never to coalesce into an overall totalising account," making it the perfect medium for the character who must never fulfill his complete mission in one episode.[35] And yet the weekly regularity of the 1950 series, now in syndication on American television, underscores the temporal and spatial impossibility of the Superman premise, one that defies the logic of narrative progression.[36] In each program the narrative continuity of the Superman story is undercut by the physical, spatial logic asserting that since Clark Kent and Superman are never in the same place together, they must be one and the same. Clark Kent's secret identity is a problem more insurmountable than the difficulty of finding for the character more action that would not slowly consume him. And it requires increasingly ingenious aesthetic solutions, pushing the series, at times, into an experimental and even self-reflexive mode (as in the episode where Lois and Jimmy watch Clark Kent interview Superman on television and he uses voiceover to speak to himself, eluding them once again).

And the insoluble time and space problems that place the stories in peril are only compounded in the television series by George Reeves's portrayal of Clark Kent. Reeves makes us interested in Kent as a morally committed journalist, which (in combination with the insistent tug of the black and white video image) takes "Superman" in the direction of the hard-hitting crime show and closer to social realism than at any time in the program's history.[37] Although, as Eco reminds us, it is Superman who is "real" and Clark Kent who is the fiction, it is in the Kent role that the split personality erupts as the full-blown troubled psyche of the novelistic character. In a strange foregrounding of the mortal time to which Superman is bound, signaled in the human fallibility of Clark Kent, Reeves would commit suicide in 1959, two years after the series ended.

In the Clark Kent–Superman dichotomy, we find something like an allegory for the tensions between copyright and trademark. George Reeves as Clark Kent dramatizes the artist locked into the role; as the actor develops a penetrating mind and a conflicted psychology for the character, he produces the very stuff of intellectual property—personal abilities and singular traits—which trademark law is not equipped to comprehend. Meanwhile, SUPERMAN the trademark, which subsumes and overrides the *Daily Planet* reporter, continues with each episode (every one of which constitutes another use) to stake out DC Comics' claim on the character in culture and in consciousness.

It is the super half of the character, the "immobility" and the historical shortsightedness of the mythic hero (which Eco and Thomas André diagnose as the political paralysis of the Superman format) that binds us to a "continuum" and a "repetition" rather than orienting us toward a future we can create. These recurrent terms in the political and aesthetic critique of Superman are, of course, the very same terms so often used to describe the conditions of American television as postmodern—its fragmentation, its infinitude, and its static quality.[38] But in describing the temporal immobility of television's episodic series (always a return to a position never outgrown), John Ellis asks that we consider another possibility—that this stasis is "more a basic contradiction or power relation than a zero degree."[39] Following Ellis, we could argue that the Clark Kent–Superman tension figures the immortal mythic character bound by conscience to the mortal, outdated values of humanism; locked as the two are into this antithesis, the episodes can only re-present a contradiction, at base one of the structural faults of bourgeois society.

Another structural fault, or in Macherey's terms, the "defect" at the core,[40] is more clearly written in the copyright-trademark dichotomy because it is here that capital announces its motives and clashes with bourgeois humanism. Recent trends in the interpretation of trademark law in the U.S., which have been such a boon to character merchandising, have also encouraged the growth of new industrial practices that challenge the humanist values of originality, creativity, and authenticity.[41] Corporations recoup their advertising expenses and further diversify their interests by licensing corporate logos, so that, for instance, R. J. Reynolds and Philip Morris can license their CAMEL and MARLBORO trademarks for leisure wear.[42] Moreover, with every successful defense against merchandise piracy and every license issued for these ancillary products (and even, in a sense, with every pair of MARLBORO jogging shorts produced and with every purchaser's wearing of them), Philip Morris shores up its monopoly on the word "Marlboro" and its ability to rent it again. Trademark law, as it has evolved in the entertainment industry over the last forty years, makes it possible for the owners of popular image properties to transfer them onto the surface of the culture, just as a decal is transferred onto a T-shirt.

To what extent, then, is SUPERMAN overlaid on the surface of contemporary culture? Imagine for a moment that you are growing up in the American suburbs in 1988. At home, you wear SUPERMAN house slippers, drink "Kryptonite-free" DIET COKE and eat pretzels in the shape of the SUPERMAN shield while you watch "Superman Week," an episode from the fifties television series rebroadcast on your local cable channel. During school, you mark your place in the SUPERMAN novelization with an American Library Association SUPERMAN bookmark, and you take a test on the official *SUPERGIRL Seatbelt Safety* book. After school, you go to your Girl Scout meeting at the YWCA, where you work on your WONDER WOMAN badge, which requires you to cook a meal from recipes in the *DC Super Heroes Super Healthy Cookbook*. On the way home from the meeting, you and your friends decide to get off the bus at the mall and play the SUPERMAN pinball machine (manufactured by ATARI, another subsidiary of Warner Communications), and after you run out of quarters, you snack on the free samples of SUPERMAN Trail Mix handed out by a man dressed up in the official, trademarked red and blue tights and cape.

My parody, I hope, will suggest that in urban culture under advanced capitalism, these commodities are linked with use-practices, so much so that the image colonization of daily life by the consumer product tie-up may be anything but a surface phenomenon. While Jean Baudrillard might describe this proliferation as the "collusion of Image and life, of the screen and daily life," which we experience at this time in history as "the most natural thing in the world," we need to counter his apocalyptic pessimism with a more comprehensive analysis: SUPERMAN tie-ups are inextricably intertwined with everyday life and deeply rooted in the culture.[43]

Imagine, then, that you are growing up in an American small town in 1948. The usher punches your SUPERMAN Club Card as you enter the local motion picture theater to see chapter 3, "The Reducer Ray," and as you go inside the dark house you carefully slip the card back into your SUPERMAN billfold, anticipating the fifteenth week, when a completely punched card entitles you to free admission. As you leave the theater, still chewing the free SUPERMAN bubble gum, compliments of the exhibitor (who paid fifty-two cents for a box of eighty sticks), you pass the dry goods store, where you see a SUPERMAN movie viewer exhibited in the window. You reach into the pocket of your SUPERMAN jacket to see if you have seventy-eight cents, almost two months' allowance, and since you don't, you decide to enter the SUPERMAN Contest advertised on the radio. With visions of SUPERMAN watches, school bags, and record albums in your hand, you walk home thinking (in twenty-five words or less), "If I Were Superman, I Would . . ."

DC Comics in Court

There is a temptation, understandable in materialist analyses of culture (and film theory has been particularly prone to this), to represent the production of meaning as the production of commodities. And while some recent critics rightfully object to the facile use of this homology, to say that the sign is the commodity is often an apt description of how the economy works under advanced capitalism.[44] Think of the "use" stipulation in U.S. trademark law, for example, which can be seen as encoding the transformation of sign-vehicles into commodities. American trademark law gives an emphasis to "use" that it doesn't have in other countries, where, for instance, it is not necessary to demonstrate "use" and secondary meaning *before* registering a mark. Whereas in other countries first registration guarantees the monopoly (which is why you may find Donald Duck ice cream in Hong Kong not licensed by Walt Disney), in the U.S. "use" stakes out the owner's claim.[45] In other words, to industrially produce an aluminum cake pan in the shape of Superman is to reassert (by a kind of high-finance squatter's rights) ownership and economic control over the most commonplace signs of culture in everyday circulation.

Unwittingly, the consumer too participates in this marking off of the territory of culture, which designates particular sign areas as legally out of bounds for users, some of whom are the very consumers whose use-practices helped to establish the claim in the first place. And, if secondary meaning exists "in the minds of the consuming public," then the owner of this cultural capital, even if a copyright or trademark has expired, can reestablish proprietorship.[46] Consider the case of *DC Comics, Inc. v. Powers* (1978). In this case, in which neither party held a registered trademark in the name "Daily Planet," the party that could demonstrate consumer awareness was able to assert prior claim to the name. DC Comics was better able to prove its entitlement to the name "Daily Planet" than Powers's underground newspaper, which had a limited circulation in Miami between 1969 and 1973 and which published an article titled "Superman Smokes Dope." To claim its monopoly on the name "Daily Planet," DC Comics needed only to show evidence that the newspaper title had figured in previous licensing contracts for SUPER-MAN, while the publishers of the underground *Daily Planet* (public awareness of which never reached beyond the audience of the 1969 Woodstock Music Festival) could not demonstrate the "duration and consistency" necessary to hold on to their expired trademark, which they had held from 1970 to 1976.[47] Copyright law, with its doctrine of fair use and its freedom of speech feature, might have allowed this kind of parodic use. But trademark law, the strong man for the expansion of capital, was more than ready, in this case, to stamp out oppositional culture.

And not only in this case. Coincident with the release of *Superman: The Movie* and its sequels between 1979 and 1982, DC Comics successfully enjoined at least three other uses of what the company calls the "family of SUPERMAN" properties. In 1979, it won a judgment for copyright and trademark infringement as well as unfair competition against Crazy Eddy, Inc., an electronic equipment company, by successfully arguing that the advertisement including the line "It's a bird, it's a plane, it's Crazy Eddy . . ." was not a parody but more of a "detailed copying" of the trailer for the fifties show, which was in syndication in New York City on the same channels.[48]

A year later, another New York court found in DC Comics' favor because the television cartoon characters Superstretch, as well as Manta and Moray, had the same abilities as DC's AQUAMAN and PLASTICMAN. Relying on copyright law—but also on section 43(a) of the Lanham Act, which refers to the dilution of trademark—the courts restrained Filmation Associates from producing its television series.[49] And in Chicago, an Illinois court concluded that the students of Richard J. Daley College could not name their school newspaper the *Daley Planet* (after one city's former mayor) because the students' use of the title violated the section of the Lanham Act pertaining to falsely designated source of origin. According to the state court, the students' use was *likely to cause confusion* and was *likely to dilute the distinctiveness* of the DAILY PLANET trademark.[50] David Lange, citing *DC Comics v. the Board of Trustees* (1981) along with the Marx Brothers and the John Philip Sousa cases from the same period, has identified a broad movement in copyright and trademark law indicating an "unconscionable overreaching" that significantly reduces the area of the public domain.[51] As he describes this realignment within case law, the "field of intellectual property can begin to resemble a game of conceptual Pac Man in which everything in sight is being gobbled up."[52]

So it is that a recent *Harvard Business Review* article recommends corporate logo licensing and trademark protection because of the limited number of brand names available. Some market researchers, the author says, are finding, in fact, that nearly all of the brand names they find desirable have already been registered.[53] While such a complaint may indicate the failure of corporate imagination as much as American multinational dreams of "gobbling up" the domain of culture, Lange's suspicion that the public domain is being devoured provides a metaphor for and an insight into the current relationship between popular culture and the state. Indeed, the cases we have just examined seem to confirm the thesis of an older Marxist instrumentalism, which would mean that the struggle over language in popular culture is a blatant example of ruling class manipulation of the law.[54]

But just when it appeared that DC Comics had gone too far in their overreaching and that U.S. law was clearly rigged in favor of concentrated power, the financial forces that protect SUPERMAN lost a landmark court case. In 1983, two years after the publication of Lange's article focusing on the Richard J. Daley College case, Warner Brothers (along with DC Comics, a subsidiary of Time Warner, Inc.), unsuccessfully tried to restrain ABC from producing its SUPERMAN takeoff, a television series titled "The Greatest American Hero."[55] The U.S. Second Circuit Court found, among other things, that the character Ralph Hinkley, who crash-landed in his flights and cowered at bullets, was "sufficiently dissimilar" and that he exhibited "Superman-like abilities in a decidedly unSuperman-like way." In its decision in favor of ABC and its unheroic Hinkley, the court, describing Hinkley as part of a "genre of superheros," concluded that "Superman has no monopoly among fictional heroes self-propelled in outer space."[56]

What made this decision possible is a provision in copyright and trademark law that comes to the rescue of the law in the nick of time, just when it is about to appear to be unfair. This stipulation is a loose translation of one of the basic dilemmas of capitalism, which characteristically fosters competition and at the same time remains deeply tied to a scale of economic expansion that wipes out all competition. In copyright law, this dilemma is reproduced in the doctrine that a limited monopoly rewards creativity but that a complete monopoly on the materials available for expression *doesn't* foster creativity because creative breakthrough depends upon the circulation of materials. And even the legal distinction between underlying *ideas* (which are not protectable) and their *expression* (which can be reserved) has, specialists admit, awkwardly dealt with the problems that arise from the need to free up the linguistic materials from which works are drawn.[57] The same general principle is at work in trademark law's prohibition against tying up language—hence the Lanham Act's distinctions between the *descriptive* meaning (defined as the literal or dictionary meaning) and the *secondary meaning*, which a word (or figure) acquires through use. Thus the primary meanings of the words "daily" and "planet" (or "mickey" and "mouse") are not removed from the language pool. This explains, as I have already said, why American trademark law exhibits a marked preference for *fanciful* or *arbitrary* marks such as the coined words "clorox," "sanka," and "kodak," which have no initial utility in the culture other than their use in reference to companies and products.[58]

Warner Brothers, Inc. v. American Broadcasting Co., Inc. marks a shift back toward the law's interest in defending an idea that is part of shared culture, the law's need to maintain a balance between "public interest in the free flow of ideas and the copyright holder's interest in exclusive use of his work."[59] In his argument that Superman is part of a genre of superheroes, circuit court judge Newman affirmed the theory developed in the case law on characters since *Nichols v. Universal* (1930): that the underlying "type" (much like an underlying "idea") must remain available to producers who need to use its basic features as building blocks.[60] The "superman" type must freely circulate in order for others to make use of the idea of a man with phenomenal powers who saves the human race, a concept made generic by the very success of the original SUPERMAN character. From this vantage, DC Comics' multiplication of the type into BATMAN, AQUAMAN, WONDER WOMAN, SUPERBOY, and SUPERGIRL (which, by their mere use, can deny existence to loose "imitations" such as Wonderman and Superstretch) is a corporate vision of the monopoly on culture that trademark and copyright law in practice encourage but in theory stand against.

So under the protection of trademark law, the only fear of extinction that SUPERMAN could conceivably have is not non-use or abandonment (hardly the concern of such a popular character), but rather the threat of emasculation brought on by popularity itself as a direct result of fifty years of merchandising and licensing. For built into the Lanham Act of 1946 is a seldom-invoked provision that gives the U.S. Federal Trade Commission the power to cancel a trademark in the name of competition if, through the success of its proprietors, it really does become the household term they set out to make it. Thus it was that Abercrombie and Fitch lost its monopoly on "safari" and Bayer lost its hold on "aspirin," which went the way of thermos, zipper, escalator, cellophane, ping-pong, yo-yo, brassiere, and shredded wheat: from protected trademark to generic *descriptive* term available to competitors. The final peril for the protectors of SUPERMAN may be read in the concern of the plastic laminate business; because the trademark may become generic through universal recognition, SUPERMAN might face the fate of "formica."[61]

CHAPTER EIGHT

Conclusion

OPPOSITIONAL CULTURE AND

CONTRABAND MERCHANDISE

So the courts say that DC Comics has no monopoly on heroes who fly through the air. And although in the heat of my argument I have characterized DC Comics as an overreacher that expands at the expense of counter-expression, I do not want to be misunderstood as having argued in any way that private claims could seriously reduce the pool of types and forms from which our common culture is produced. As I intimated in my discussion of the celebrity undead, the contrary may even be true. Capital may keep nostalgia culture in circulation in a way that facilitates and speeds up the production of a common culture, a culture that can be inflected oppositionally. The paradox here is that the owners of popular forms, which constitute our most widely shared culture (DC Comics, Walt Disney), are in the contradictory position of encouraging the widespread uses of BATMAN, SUPERMAN, and SNOW WHITE. But when these forms are used spontaneously—as in the recent cases of the SNOW WHITE parody on the Academy Awards show and the homegrown BATMAN stunt in Chicago—the owners want to take them back.

In most cases, unfair competition suits involving the uses of popular icons are undertaken as symbolic offensives against infringers. The initiation of such commercial infringement suits is in essence a statement of territoriality in which the owner of the property is backing up a proprietary right. This becomes especially important if the proprietor assigns the property through a license to other parties. DC Comics' crackdown on the lone Chicago Batman, for example, was an obligation to the hundreds 228 of small manufacturers who have licensed the BATMAN mark for novelties and clothes produced as tie-ups with the summer 1989 release of the Warner Brothers film. But in aggressively monitoring the uses of a popular form worldwide, does the entity that circulates the popular form also attempt to enforce *what* the popular form means? Can the corporate owners of popular properties own the meanings of these properties as well?

I have only begun to open up this most important question here. But it seems to me that further study of this problem will need to be prefaced by a consideration of the operative theory of *how things mean* underlying these intellectual property disputes. As I have indicated, U.S. courts approach such issues in terms of First Amendment speech rights, in which the rule seems to be that the more commercial the form, the less it is apt to be considered as protectable "speech." This leaves the T-shirt sporting an image of "Quaddafi" Duck at the mercy of the Licensing Corporation of America, a division of Warner Communications and owner of the Warner Brothers cartoon characters, including Daffy Duck. Not surprisingly, then, corporate owners may attempt to use intellectual property remedies as a form of censorship (as the cases against the pornographic versions of the Pillsbury Doughboy, Snoopy, and the Walt Disney characters show).[1] But finally, I am less concerned here with the confusion of speech and trade issues than I am with understanding the relationship operative in both the law and the wider culture, between the sign and its referent. Legal actions against appropriators and infringers almost always involve a common "mistake" in reading signs, one that treats the representational image as though it were the referent. As Stuart Hall has theorized it, this "mistake" is a function of a kind of naturalism that "tempts us to 'misread' the image for the thing it signifies."[2] And clearly, the products of mimetic technologics (look-alike and sound-alike signs) are by their very semiotic structure particularly susceptible to this kind of confusion.

Actions against appropriators may be motivated as well by the tacit assumption that combination and reinflection of popular signs does not produce creative expressions. This seemed to be the prevailing attitude where in a recent forum on the Phil Donahue television show the relatives of John Wayne, Clark Gable, Harpo Marx, and W. C. Fields spoke about their objections to the uses of the images of their ancestors. Objecting to a poster drawing portraying his grandfather in the nude, Everett Fields responded, "It doesn't mean anything." And using a term coined in the celebrity rights literature, he went on to say that this kind of expression should not be seen as creativity but as "re-creativity." This position is not significantly different from conventional wisdom. Creative meaning, it seems, must be uplifting. The possibility that the image of the comic iconoclast could be rearticulated to mean new, more outrageous things is stopped dead. Since the poster's message isn't uplifting, it doesn't mean anything at all. From this position, it is not even possible to enter into debates over "obscenity," since that would be to admit that these images have been provocatively recoded.

I suspect that if we investigated these matters further, we might find some relation between the structure of fundamentalist thought and the idea that things and their meanings are coincidental in time, or even that they are the same thing. Poststructuralism, in contrast, tells us that a sign and its meaning will never be in one place long enough for us to pin the two together for all time. My discussion of the legal protection of popular forms could be construed as a critique of the restriction of meaning. But, more important, I hope it reaffirms that the sign is disputed territory. After all, legal commentators themselves tell us that intellectual property law is an area of struggle over property and value, and the number of cases alone should indicate that there is significant conflict over the circulation of popular signs. But such conflict is not always motivated by the protection of valuable interests alone.

This is not to say that the private owners of popular forms don't succeed in their attempts to try to limit meaning as they stake out property claim. U.S. intellectual property law, in the last century, has generally yielded to such attempts. But we need to be more precise about the ways in which intellectual property can lend itself to such limitation. We need to examine the structure of the law in two different places: first, at the level of doctrine that *could* mandate the relation between signifier and signified; and second, at the broader level of doctrine that regulates the availability of signs through restriction and circulation.

The first of these two levels is the more difficult to address, and I have only touched on it in a limited way in my discussion of the likeness cases where two parties claim the same sign. What I have argued here is that in commercial cases the courts have tended to defer to a property right in returning signs to their proper referents. What makes the *Onassis* and *Lugosi* cases so interesting, however, is that they are examples of what courts try to do when the issue is not clearly one of property. In these cases, the courts have addressed questions of the real referent and the survival of a privacy right by turning privacy back into a property claim. Much more research needs to be done on this, and particularly on the "false light" and defamation cases in which real people object to the use of their names and "word portrait" likenesses in literary and cinematic fiction and nonfiction.[3]

Another way of looking at the structure of the sign in intellectual property law is to consider whether or not the doctrines of passing off and secondary meaning are modeled after the rules governing social discourses and languages. Or are they special rules of a different order? The legal rule would seem to follow custom and usage, so that, for instance, proof of secondary meaning (which entitles a trademark owner to defend a mark against other proprietors) is contingent upon recognition "in the minds of the consuming public." But because BETTY BOOP, BIG BIRD, and MR. T are heavily merchandised, are they "given" rather than socially "produced"? Are they popular signs by virtue of a kind of artificial semiotics? In his diagnosis of consumer society, Theodor Adorno argues that in the contemporary period *all* words have come to function automatically, like trademarks. Through reification, he says, words are conditioned so that "the more firmly linked to the things they denote, the less their linguistic sense is grasped."[4] From this perspective, we could argue that the secondary meaning encouraged by advertising and promotion works to eradicate other possible meanings.

More current theories describe mass culture as part of a space that originally functioned as a public sphere mediating between the family and society and that, as a space of public concerns, could operate as a check on the state. As Terry Eagleton describes it, mass culture has filled the public sphere by using the collective space to produce vehicles of meaning. But it has returned these new vehicles to the public as commodity forms that separate them from collectivity. For Eagleton, the culture industry in the contemporary period gives us a "gross caricature" of the public sphere by "drawing upon authentic personal experience, rearticulating it in its own idioms, and returning that message to its consumers in ways which lock them more deeply into a privatized world."[5] And yet we know so little about how these artificial idioms are changed in the process. Consider, for instance, how King Tut, the Statue of Liberty, the New York subway token, the pope, and images of Albert Einstein and Sigmund Freud have moved from public history to private licensed property and back again to public figure. These signs vacillate between elite and popular culture in such a way as to defy categorization. What they testify to, I think, is that in this continual "shuffling" of the "deck" of culture, as Tony Bennett has put it, it is difficult to predict where commercial signs will end up.[6] And although the majority of these popular signs will be used in quite harmlessly banal ways, there is nothing in their makeup to prevent them from being used to carry political messages. Commercial signs such as trademarks, television shows, and magazine covers may be different in structure from signs generated in noncommercial social discourse. But what difference does that make? Can intellectual property law tell us anything we don't already know even after the incredible number of semiotic analyses of consumer culture produced in the twenty years since the publication of Barthes's *Mythologies*?[7]

The doctrine of secondary meaning tells us that some signs take on new commercial connotations through their wide circulation, and that the new meaning becomes so common that it comes to seem the "natural" meaning of the sign. And the doctrine of passing off tells us in other terms, all over again, that the fundamental function of the sign is to stand to someone for something. So what is a passing off dispute about? Of what relevance is it to the structure of the sign that the *wrong* source is standing behind it (authorizing it) if the sign is successfully standing (to) the public? Do passing off disputes come into being *because* signification is essentially nothing more than successfully passing off one thing as another? Here is where trademark doctrine breaks down. The very success of public recognition—the goal of promotion, distribution, advertising— produces infringers as well as ordinary fans and potential buyers. What the proprietors of popular signs will always come up against is the predictable and desired result of their own popularity—imitation, appropriation, rearticulation.

Intellectual property can be used by the owners of popular signs to *attempt* to bind a sign to a single source that functions as if it were the only source of meaning. The corporate entity functions like an author in the way in which it resolves contradictory aspects of the image. But here we would have to say of the corporate source what we have said of the author as an enforcer of coherence: Once gone from the text he can never return to it. The popular property may be subject to quality control and design supervision up to the point at which it leaves its source. But once it has left the orbit of the owner, it can be reinterpreted and reinserted into the everyday lives of its users.

But what if we see the structures of ownership as facilitating the availability of some signs over others? In other words, do corporate owners control meanings by the sheer volume of the circulation of mass culture? In his important article on copyright and the record industry, Bob Christgau has argued that "the freedom to sell equals the freedom to disseminate."[8] Control of the copyright in sound recording, as Simon Frith adds, means "power over what the country sees and hears." This is especially true if what we hear is determined not necessarily by what we choose to purchase but rather by performing rights deals in which music is leased, in a sense, to motion picture, television, and theatrical producers.[9] We're back again to the issue of who controls the media, and although we can never ask this question often enough, it is not my aim to ask it again here, chiefly because arguments about media control so easily turn of their own accord into conspiracy theories. To offset this tendency, we need to do much more work on the politics of piracy.

The politics of piracy has two scales: the home and the world. I have not touched here upon the world scope of piratical reproduction of audio- and videotapes, or on the production of merchandise bearing counterfeit trademarks. Reading the law of merchandise in particular, however, one becomes aware of the way in which international differences in legal systems frustrate U.S. trademark proprietors. New developments in Japanese law are compatible with U.S. unfair competition law,[10] but developments in Latin American law range from hostility to ambivalence toward multinational commercial activity. As for the latter, Brazil is an interesting case study of how local enterprise expresses a kind of diffident opportunism by "occupying" French and U.S. trademarks when these marks show insufficient economic activity within the country. This practice then produces a kind of counterculture in which Brazilians manufacture a PEPSI and MARLBORO line of clothes as well as a PIAGET and a CARTIER, a VALENTINO drink, PHILLIPS dog food, and TIFFANY's construction material.[11] But reports suggest that in Southeast Asia, the magnitude of audiotape piracy is also a way of evening up the score against imperialist powers. Then how do we interpret piracy in Eastern bloc countries, where pirated music from the West also serves the purpose of cultural exchange? And what are the political concerns behind the U.S. Trademark Counterfeiting Act of 1984, which has produced international trademark "trafficking" as a criminal act?[12] What does the enforcement of this act—through the seizure of counterfeit goods without prior notice to infringers—tell us about the kind of threat that fly-by-night pirates pose to trademark proprietors?

We have no studies that address the broad scope of the international piracy of U.S. popular culture. But a good deal of data are now available because investors who want to expand their markets have started to look comparatively at the internal structure of intellectual property law in a variety of countries. Studies of the actual *uses* of contraband culture will be somewhat more difficult to undertake, however, since we are only now refining the tools we have for studying what people make of popular music, fiction, and television. Only in the last several years have scholars in cultural studies begun to consider cross-cultural interventions into popular forms. [13] And new studies of the "home use" of popular forms, which have become central to the field coincident with the increasing emphasis upon the reader, the viewer, and the listener, might examine how people get around buying audio- and videotapes by making them for each other. [14] Andy Lipman's suggestive remark that home tape reproduction in Britain might be calculated as lost revenue (substantial enough to put a small multinational corporation into bankruptcy) opens up one way of seeing home uses of popular culture as a kind of oppositional activity. [15] A less obvious approach to a study of home uses would be to consider the degree to which people consider taping as communal "sharing" rather than private "stealing." [16] One could then follow up L. Ray Patterson's argument that the current copyright laws tend to construct us as "infringers" as opposed to users. [17]

Categorically close to home use is educational use, to which I have referred only briefly in my discussion of "learning" as a rationale for extending the copyright monopoly grant. Here we would have to ask whether dedication to "learning" is hostage to a concern about "theft." One may be able to steal an original document, but one doesn't steal it if one copies it. Neither does one steal the rights to copy it by infringing upon them. To infringe may be to trespass and intrude on another's property, but it is a transgression that leaves the property intact. And here we need to ask how the prohibition against copying, reinforced by the deeply implanted original/copy dichotomy, works ideologically. That is, how does this prohibition encourage us to *not see* our relation to the private rights in the original, which allow it to be reproduced only with the consent of an owner? As Edelman reminds us, this owner has these rights by virtue of two structures. The first structure is a circular one in which rights given by the state are returned to it by rights-holding citizens. Second, the right to a work of authorship has its origins in the concept of the creative (human) subject whose labor is deposited in the object. Even though the work may later have a corporate, nonhuman owner (either by virtue of the employer-employee relation or by a transfer of rights), this corporate ownership is built upon the foundation of the natural rights-holding subject who created the object. And because that subject is endowed with natural rights, corporate rights-holders are vulnerable (as in privacy doctrine) to the return of the subject whose very person constituted the "work of authorship." This subject, in other words, may argue that the commercial use of a photograph or other likeness is a violation of either privacy or publicity rights.

The return of the photographic subject adds a significant new dimension to the study of the star image and accentuates the zone of exploitation as a problem area in which the star is divided and subdivided, crisscrossed and intersected with claims. For instance, can the Roger Richman Agency license for lamp bases the image of Marilyn Monroe wearing the famous white full-skirted dress from *The Seven Year Itch* if Twentieth-Century Fox claims that it owns the dress? What if a scholar wants to reproduce the same famous image of Monroe? If the shot was originally a publicity still (and not a frame enlargement from the motion picture itself), our scholarly reproduction could be considered a promotion for the film, which is now available on videotape. Under such circumstances, should we pay Fox Video for the rights to reproduce the photograph in an academic journal when we have in effect given them free promotion? These particular issues, of course, have arisen only in recent decades, after scholars in cultural studies began to engage in critical analysis of the very artifacts of culture that, because of their reproducibility, have the highest current commercial market value. It is an odd twist that the commercial availability of artifacts might make them unavailable to scholars. This is of course the reverse of the situation of the scholar who works on elite, one-of-a-kind culture that may be made accessible and easily reproducible with the help of expert archivists. If part of the original motivation of copyright law's "fair use" doctrine was to allow the kind of excerpting necessary for criticism, then we should consider critical discourse as a privileged zone, safe from proprietal incursions. Consider the disputed image of Jacqueline Kennedy Onassis, which is reproduced in this study. If the entitlement to an image reproduced in a commercial advertisement is in dispute, then the first place that the image should be reproduced without question is in the context of a critical commentary on that very controversy.

It is not as though contemporary critics of consumer culture haven't seriously analyzed the problem of the zones of possession, the domains of authorship, and the politics of appropriation. For a number of contemporary artists such as Barbara Kruger and Sherrie Levine, the problem of prohibited uses has become the subject and the object of their work. Kruger's tactic of "intercepting" visual and linguistic stereotypes and "reinscribing" them in her own counter-systems is a kind of model of semiotic disruption, one that requires us to think about sources and origins.[18] Kruger's mock-up collages work by refusing the myth of artistic originality, by refusing to start from scratch, showing us instead that we must use existing, available signs. As she pastes together advertising images and "found" graphics, Kruger creates objects that are received as "art" but that nevertheless gesture toward the impossibility of "creation."

Even more relevant to my previous discussion of authorship is the photographic work of Sherrie Levine. Generally critics have understood Levine's work, in which she rephotographs and remounts Walker Evans's and Edward Weston's photographic classics, as a reconsideration of authenticity and a direct challenge to existing copyrights in these works.[19] But Levine's work is also a testament to the inevitability of generic borrowing, to the possibility of the total exhaustion of signs and the consequent impossibility of producing anything entirely new.[20] Part of the power of Levine's work is in the way it works and keeps on working as conceptual art. (One never has to see her masterpieces of photography reframed in order to appreciate their concept.) As Hal Foster describes it, this work engages in a subversive "situational aesthetics" that both deploys and targets public space.[21] And yet it works its subversion primarily within the privileged space of the museum, where unauthorized borrowing can always be defended as parody or critical comment. To pose real trouble for the "author" in copyright doctrine, Sherrie Levine would have to reproduce her own copies of Edward Weston as postcards and then sell them—the stiffest test of "free commercial speech."

Both avant-garde practice and art criticism have concerned themselves with the process of recuperation; with the futility of producing the subversive sign, which inevitably will be appropriated for mainstream uses that void its oppositionality. In the face of this dilemma, culture critics have looked to the alternative space of the minority culture or subculture, theorized in terms of the trick code of an artificial mythology and the indeterminateness of symbolic ambivalence.[22] But while the theorist of the avant-garde finds no way out of the pattern of appropriation and reappropriation, the art worker must try to represent the "revolutionary" with what critics tell her is the increasingly limited number of signs at her disposal. Postmodern criticism, then, in its concern about the exhaustion of meaning, may begin to sound like those corporate analysts who are concerned that all of the laudatory words in the English language may have already been taken as trade names.

In my consideration of the structure of intellectual property that makes and breaks monopolies on cultural forms of expression, I have tried to stress the difference between the structure that makes such a monopoly possible and the actual implications of both for social discourse. But I have not been able to build a strong case for the social uses of popular forms that defy monopoly control. As yet, we have too few ethnographies of the use of popular icons in their travel from the avant-garde to the popular and back again; and we have too few cumulative histories. It would be a mistake, to paraphrase Hugh Collins, to look to the law instead of to custom and use as the primary indication of how ideological domains are configured.[23] What we can do, however, is to use the existence of legal conflicts arising around semiotic trouble areas to study popular meanings under duress, the advantage being that we also represent "the law" as in constant flux. To suggest how we might look at intellectual property law as it impinges on meaning at these two levels—the structure of the sign and the extent of its circulation—I want to use as a model the U.S. Supreme Court decision relative to the "Gay Olympic Games."

In *San Francisco Arts & Athletics, Inc. v. U.S. Olympic Committee* (1987), the U.S. Supreme Court was asked to decide if the OLYMPIC mark could be enforced by the U.S. Olympic Committee (USOC) without violating the First Amendment freedom of speech provisions. Affirming the decision of the court of appeals, the Supreme Court upheld the grant of exclusive rights to the name "Olympic" as well as to the signs and symbols of the Olympic Games, which had been given to the official U.S. committee, a private company, in a 1978 congressional act. At the level of the structure of the trademark, the Supreme Court decided that confusion of sponsorship was likely, and that "Olympic" was not generic, because the U.S. Olympic Committee had established secondary meaning in the word. And, the court went on, San Francisco Arts and Athletics could convey its meaning without using the word "olympic." So for the consequent circulation and distribution of the sign "olympic," the court agreed with the lower courts that the USOC could decide where and how its terms and symbols were used; and it held that this proprietary right to the terms and symbols was not in violation of the Fifth Amendment's guarantee of equal protection under the law.[24]

I would read this case as a dispute over the representation of sexuality in the symbolic terrain of the sports world. The attempt to "occupy" the trademark OLYMPIC was a strategic political maneuver on the part of gay men and lesbians, and it cut several ways at once. It subverted a symbol of traditional masculinity at the same time that it accommodated that symbol. Justice Brennan, the single dissenting vote on the court, seemed to recognize the latter, for in his opinion he argued that the image of the Olympics would help to mainstream homosexuals. But the USOC borrowed intellectual property doctrine in its attempt to settle the meaning of "Olympic" as a sign coterminous with a "healthy" heterosexual image of male and female sport. The USOC wanted, in short, to prohibit the connotative buildup that might be produced through the association of this sign with homosexuality.

But the question for us is how did the structure of intellectual property doctrine help to secure dominant meanings? I have stressed throughout that there is nothing necessarily *in* the law that guarantees outcomes for groups in dominance. Consider, for instance, how trademark law's provisions for "likelihood of confusion" and "secondary meaning" could have been used by the Supreme Court to secure the opposite linguistic and legal conditions. Trademark principles could have been used to argue that "olympic" was generic, that the USOC had not established the requisite secondary meaning, and that confusion between the Gay Games and the Olympic Games was unlikely. Does intellectual property law produce meaning as it ties up property rights? In this case, we would have to say yes. But we would need to qualify that answer by noting that this law is *made* to limit meanings under dispute by interested parties whose stated concern is the settlement of an unfair competition quarrel. *San Francisco Arts & Athletics* may serve as an example of how unfair competition may provide an alibi for the attempt to monopolize signs and legislate meaning.[25] Intellectual property, then, is an arena for the negotiation of meaning but is not necessarily the place where social meanings are made. The law is not simultaneous with either the industrial mode of production or the production of meaning. Although it may help to secure the conditions for both kinds of production, the ruling is always conditional. The legal rule may prevent some representational practices and may curtail some kinds of production, but social semiosis continues in spite of it.

One way that legal studies can supplement cultural studies, then, is in its identification of points of contention that we might want to interpret in terms of other ideological conflicts. Invariably, with every legal case, we enter a territory ruled by other codes; we find a system organized according to its own peculiar logic. Therefore, any study of the legal construction of cultural forms becomes a study of the law itself as constructed in Anglo-American history. Marxist studies of the relation between culture and other levels of the social formation often move between these levels without much ado, discussing the state, the family, and the mode of production in one sweep. But very few have taken legal strata into account in such cross-sectional accounts of society. Have they failed to do so because the strange rules constituting legal doctrine discourage straightforward, unspecialized reading? Others before me have warned that the law presents hazards for any study of the various levels of society. Marx's conclusion was that the law was "ambiguous," and E. P. Thompson has said that he found in his study of eighteenth-century Britain that the law "did not keep politely to a level but was at *every* bloody level."[26]

If there is an advantage to be gained from undertaking comparative studies of this kind, it is in the identification of marked shifts that may be more easily analyzed at one level than at another. The "distribution of causes and effects" to which I have referred is such that a phenomenon may be figured in a more readable way in the law than in the family, for instance. To take one example, the evolution of the right of publicity out of the right to privacy (and the problem of the disappearing author-subject in law) parallels the demise of humanism's subject. The first of these two developments is far easier to read than the second, since the publicity right has appeared as such a striking feature of American intellectual property in the current century. On the level of legal doctrine, we can trace the transformation of the bourgeois ideal of seclusion (private family life) into its antithesis, the publicity right, with a good deal of precision. And the history of this transformation tells us things about the ideological construction of the star image that we could not have known even after years of close textual analysis.

I have noted the eclipse of the author-subject in Anglo-American law at several points: at the turn of the century, in the ascendance of *Bleistein* over *Burrow-Giles*; at midcentury, in the trend that reversed *Warner Brothers v. Columbia Broadcasting*; and more recently, in *Time v. Geis*, where Abraham Zapruder was used to argue for authorial creativity in the Kennedy assassination film footage so that he could be displaced by Time-Life, Inc. In contrast, I have also stressed the fluidity of the law, in the arguments for the right of publicity based on a right of privacy offered in the *Lugosi* and Elvis Presley cases (and exemplified in the state and federal initiatives to insert a *droit moral* provision in copyright law). Nevertheless, as I emphasized in my discussion of the years following the 1709 Statute of Anne, Anglo-American intellectual property law has a long history of systematic displacement of the human subject. U.S. arts activists have discovered this fact at the same time in history as humanities scholars are discussing the demise of that same subject (man) as the focal point of Western culture. And that, perhaps, is the most intriguing and complex development of all.

For me, it is not a question of restoring that subject to a rightful place; rather, the issue is the contradiction inherent in any rhetoric of originality and authenticity that becomes evident when there is neither a singular person to produce an original work nor any possibility of the virginal uniqueness of that work. This is not to predict a future destitute of creativity; it is merely to challenge again the cult of the original. Intellectual property doctrine, as I have shown, has its own built-in contradiction in its minimal definition of the author-originator. And it faces challenges as well in its consideration of an increasing number of styles, types, genres, and forms—a consideration that it undertakes, I think, without grasping the social significance of its own mechanism.

James O'Connor, in his *Accumulation Crisis*, makes our connection between the features of the law that mirror commodity exchange and the crisis of individualism at this stage of advanced capitalism: "In short, the commodity form of need satisfaction together with the wage form of labor, means that to the degree that needs are satisfied in the 'individual' form, they are frustrated in the social form."[27] If we are to make a case against the current developments in American intellectual property doctrine that produce common culture as private property, it will have to be based upon this broader analysis—that as any aspect of culture is organized around the individual form, our needs will be "frustrated in the social form."

Notes

PREFACE

1. Marx, *Capital*, 1:163.
2. Farrell, "The Language of Hollywood," 205.
3. Denning, "'The Special American Conditions,'" 368.

CHAPTER 1. ON LIKENESS: THE LAW

1. Nimmer and Nimmer, *Nimmer on Copyright*; Nimmer, *Cases and Materials on Copyright and Other Aspects of Law Pertaining to Literary, Musical and Artistic Works*; Nimmer, *Cases and Materials on Copyright and Other Aspects of Entertainment Litigation*; Sobel, "A Memorial Tribute."
2. Poststructuralism, more a periodization than a consistent set of ideas, spreads out from the work of French theorists Louis Althusser, Roland Barthes, Jacques Lacan, Julia Kristeva, Michel Foucault, and Jacques Derrida.
3. Edelman, "The Character and His Double," 37.
4. Bleistein v. Donaldson Lithographic Co., 188 U.S. 239, 23 S. Ct. 298, 47 L. Ed. 460, as quoted in Nimmer, *Cases and Materials on Entertainment Litigation*, 4; For a concise overview of Holmes on this area of the law see S. Cohen, "Justice Holmes and Copyright Law."
5. To convey an idea of the way the legal community has responded to the poststructuralist suggestion that legal texts might be found to be incoherent, let me quote one judge (also a law professor) in response to the implications that the work of Jacques Derrida might have for legal theory:

> If (as I doubt) he thinks that no writing ever conveys a concept in approximately the form intended by the author, he is, if not barmy, then simply too remote from the legal culture to be heeded. *Literary* texts may or may not be self-referential and (if the former) therefore incoherent, but it would not follow that a legal text was self-referential and therefore incoherent too; the purposes and techniques of authors of literary texts are different from those of the authors of legal texts.
> (Posner, *Law and Literature*, 215)

Here is Terry Eagleton, almost in answer to Judge Posner:

> All language, as de Man rightly perceives, is ineradicably metaphorical, working by tropes and figures; it is a mistake to believe that any language is *literally* literal. Philosophy, law, political theory work by metaphor just as poems do, and so are just as fictional. . . . Literary works, however, are in a sense less deluded than other forms of discourse, because they implicitly acknowledge their own rhetorical status—the fact that what they say is different from what they do. Other forms of writing are just as figurative and ambiguous, but pass themselves off as unquestionable truth. (Eagleton, *Literary Theory*, 145).

6. Edelman, *Le droit saisi par le photographie*; Edelman, *Ownership of the Image*; Hirst and Kingdom, "On Edelman's 'Ownership of the Image'"; Porter, "Film Copyright and Edelman's Theory of Law." For an important use of Edelman, also see Saunders, "Copyright and the Legal Relations of Literature." Saunders also translates portions of one of Edelman's recent articles on new legislation, which removes the author's right in the protection of software in France (Edelman, "Commentaire").

7. Tagg, "Power and Photography."

8. Anderson and Greenberg, "From Substance to Form."

9. See, for instance, Burgin, "Looking at Photographs," in Burgin, ed., *Thinking Photography*.

10. I am thinking in particular of the classic "captains of industry" approach to the history of motion picture industry finance (Klingender and Legg, *Money Behind the Screen*). For a study that brings this approach up to date, see Wasko, *Movies and Money*; Allen and Gomery, *Film History*, 260, put this type of study in perspective in relation to other approaches to writing the history of the U.S. film industry. Unfortunately, there is no equivalent overview of the entertainment industry that pulls together studies of the publishing, recording, broadcasting, and motion picture industries.

11. Foucault, *History of Sexuality*, has been a model demonstration of the "interrelatedness" of state, church, law, and family. But especially see Foucault, *I, Pierre Riviere*, for a close parallel reading of the psychological, legal, medical, and criminological documents that converge in this strange case. The pathology of this family, as it turns out in Foucault's analysis, has to do with their emergence as a class of property owners. Foucault describes the crazed mother, whose son murders her (ostensibly for his father's sake), as undermining property relations and their signs, one symbol of which was the contract: "No doubt because as a woman and even more so as a wife married to thwart by rule a rule which itself was irregular, she felt that any contract remained a trick, an institutionalized assault—as if in a frozen, arrested, perpetual combat. She set herself up as the everlasting canceller of contracts, perpetually put them in doubt, and shifted their signs by setting them moving again—which is tantamount to repudiation and challenge" (181). In relation to medical discourse, I am thinking of all of the psychoanalytic

theory that also incorporates a critique of the medical profession. For instance, see Doane, *The Desire to Desire*, chap. 2, "Clinical Eyes: The Medical Discourse."

12. For all of the discussion of this rivalry, the difference in approach was fully laid out only in one debate within *Screen*. See Coward, "Class, 'Culture,' and the Social Formation"; Chambers et al., "Marxism and Culture"; Coward, "Response."

13. For an overview, see Hall, "Cultural Studies and the Centre." See also the *Journal of Communication Inquiry* 10, no. 2 (Summer 1986), special issue on the work of Stuart Hall.

14. Especially in its importation from Britain to the U.S. and in its incorporation into literary studies and American studies, cultural studies may be in the process of becoming diluted. In some circles it may be little more than an umbrella concept that covers the study of people's history, high and low literatures, new technologies, and material culture. If that trend continues, we can expect the part of cultural studies concerned with ideology, modes of production, and resistance culture to stay in Britain, while the part having to do with the dissolution of disciplinary boundaries and the amalgamation of feminism, poststructuralism, and semiotics finds a home in American studies. To some degree, this is a characterization of the new journal *Cultural Studies*, which is only tangentially related to the Marxist "cultural studies" that first came out of Britain. Two books that define the growth pattern of this enlarged "cultural studies" are Fiske, *Television Culture*, which popularizes the work of Stuart Hall, and Radway, *Reading the Romance*, a solidly American studies work written entirely without reference to an earlier Marxist cultural studies but nevertheless claimed for a new and broader cultural studies.

15. Hall, "Cultural Studies," 60.

16. Hall, "Notes on Deconstructing 'The Popular,'" 227.

17. Ibid., 228.

18. Ibid., 233.

19. Ibid. See Volosinov, *Marxism and the Philosophy of Language*.

20. As quoted in Hall, "Social Eye," 96.

21. Most of Walter Benjamin's theorization of the commodity "wish image" and "dream form" is found in his *Passagen-Werk*, the theory and commentary that grew out of his reflections on the Paris Arcades and is not yet translated completely into English. For a very rich explication of the utopian aspect of Benjamin's work, see Buck-Morss, "Benjamin's *Passagen-Werk*"; see also Buck-Morss, *The Dialectics of Seeing*. Also see Special Issue on Walter Benjamin, *New German Critique* 39 (Fall 1986); Bloch, *Natural Law and Human Dignity*.

22. Jameson, "Reification and Utopia," 144.

23. See Collins, *Marxism and Law*, 30–32, for more on this point.

24. Genovese, *Roll, Jordan, Roll*, 40.

25. E. P. Thompson, *Whigs and Hunters*, 263.

26. Ibid., 266. Morton Horwitz, "The Rule of Law," reviewing *Whigs and Hungers*, has followed Thompson up to this point and says this is going too far:

> It undoubtedly restrains power, but it also prevents power's benevolent exercise. It creates formal equality—a not inconsiderable virtue—but it *promotes* substantive inequality by creating a consciousness that radically separates law from politics, means from ends, processes from outcomes. By promoting procedural justice it enables the shrewd, the calculating, and the wealthy to manipulate its forms to their own advantage. And it ratifies an adversarial, competitive, and atomistic conception of human relations. (566)

Klare, "Law-Making as Praxis," also takes issue with Thompson's "unqualified human good" conclusion. This is how he would weigh the forces we are describing against one another:

> While acknowledging the difference between arbitrary and unbounded state power, on the one hand, and the checks and balances on domination imposed by the rule of law on the other, we need not be blind to the retrogressive character of the institutional and cultural practice embodied in the "rule of law ideal," i.e., liberal legalism. We must not confuse the concept of law with the historically specific forms that law assumed with the rise of capitalism. (134)

27. Tushnet, "A Marxist Analysis of American Law," 110.
28. Gabel and Feinman, "Contract Law as Ideology," 175; Forbath, "Taking Lefts Seriously," in a review of Kairys, ed., *The Politics of Law*, argues that the Knights of Labor vision of worker-owned industry was "built largely out of the utopian material of contract ideology" (1057).
29. Abrams, "The Historic Foundation of American Copyright Law," quotes Macaulay in an 1841 speech before the House of Commons on the extension of the term of the copyright: "The principle of copyright is this. It is a tax on readers for the purpose of giving a bounty to writers. The tax is an exceedingly bad one; it is a tax on one of the most innocent and salutary of human pleasures" (1120).
30. U.S. Constitution, art. 1, sec. 8, clause 8.
31. Sharpe, "The People and the Law," in a discussion of the use made of the law by the people during this period, says that there was a "two-way traffic" between the elite and the popular, and that the law was "one of the main routes through which this traffic passed" (248).
32. Porter, "Film Copyright and Edelman's Theory of Law," 146. One may wonder why I don't choose to deal with "fair use" here as part of the copyright provision for learning. I declined to do so because I have been convinced by L. Ray Patterson's argument that "fair use" is a compromised version of the "learning" provision, since it subjects the user to a potential infringement charge ("Free Speech, Copyright, and Fair Use").
33. Fitzpatrick and Hunt, "Critical Legal Studies," 11.

34. R. Williams, *The Sociology of Culture*, 102.

35. Ibid., 103.

36. Lovell, "The Social Relations of Cultural Production," 253.

37. Mensch, "The History of Mainstream Legal Thought," 20–21.

38. Gramsci, *Selections from "The Prison Notebooks,"* 328.

39. See Hall, Lumley, and McLennan, "Politics and Ideology: Gramsci," 49. A good overview of the relation between social class and the law is Collins, *Marxism and Law*, 45–61; Tushnet, "Corporations and Free Speech," 101–4, discusses social position in terms of Gramsci's concept of "organic" as opposed to "traditional" lawyers, with the former representing the interests of the new bourgeoisie and the latter defending the law against change.

40. O'Brien v. Pabst Sales Co., 124 F.2d 167 (5th Cir. 1941).

41. Tushnet, "A Marxist Analysis," 98.

42. Gabel and Feinman, "Contract Law as Ideology," 175.

43. Mensch, "The History of Mainstream Legal Thought," explains that the critique of legal reasoning as "artificial reasoning" depends upon contrasting it with "common sense," here meaning the opposite of mystification (21, n. 8). This is not the way in which I am using the term "commonsense knowledge."

44. See Lovell, "The Social Relations of Cultural Production," 246; Dyer, Introduction to *Coronation Street*, 2, describes common sense as "blinkered" in its inability to see beyond or above the immediate, but "wise" in its negotiation of the immediate business of living.

45. Hall, "The Rediscovery of 'Ideology,'" 75. It is a significant challenge to legal doctrine, a doctrine that promises science and gives us ideology instead. Here Hall emphasizes the importance of the ideology/science opposition in the Althusserian formulation that informs Edelman.

46. The one collection that brings both U.S. and British critical legal studies together is Beirne and Quinny, *Marxism and the Law*. The basic collection of work in the British variant is Fitzpatrick and Hunt, eds., *Critical Legal Studies*. A particularly accessible introduction to American critical legal studies with specially written chapters by some of the key participants in the movement is Kairys, ed., *The Politics of Law*. See also Kennedy and Klare, "A Bibliography of Critical Legal Studies."

47. Fitzpatrick and Hunt, eds., *Critical Legal Studies*, 1–3; Kelman, in *A Guide to Critical Legal Studies*, the most comprehensive overview to date, suggests that CLS *could* be placed within this larger scene and situated in terms of "the debates that rage in left academic circles on Neomarxism, structuralist Marxism, post-structuralism, the Frankfort School" (9). My sense is that although American critical legal studies is interested in these debates, they are *foregrounded* in British critical legal studies the way they aren't in the U.S.

48. See Mensch, "The History of Mainstream Legal Thought," 27–29. For examples of the work of the legal Realists, see M. Cohen, "Property and Sovereignty," and F. Cohen, "Transcendental Nonsense and the Functional Approach."

49. Burgin, Introduction to *Thinking Photography*, quotes MacCabe (8). On the problem as well as the importance of the "base" and the "superstructure," see Hall, "Re-thinking the 'Base-and-Superstructure' Metaphor," and R. Williams, *Problems in Materialism and Culture*, 31–49. For a cogent explication of the concept relative to legal theory, see Collins, *Marxism and Law*, 77–90.

50. Balibar, "On the Basic Concepts of Historical Materialism," says: "Such gaps are possible, or more precisely, since contradictions are induced within the law itself by its *non-correspondence* with the relations of production, law must be distinct and *second* in order of analysis to the relations of production" (pt. 3, 228).

51. See Collins, *Marxism and Law*, chap. 2.

52. Jameson, *The Political Unconscious*. In a footnote Jameson says: "The problem of mechanical causality imposes itself most vividly, perhaps, in film criticism, as a tension between the study of technological innovation and that of 'intrinsically' filmic languages; but it can be expected to be an issue in most other areas of mass culture as well" (26). I suppose Jameson is thinking here of the clear appeal to Marxists of the work of the *Cinéthique* and the *Cahiers du Cinéma* critics that emerged just before 1970. To see ideology, for instance, as "built into the lenses" was a performance of a brilliant synthesis of mode of production and cultural production (film language); see nn. 105–6. But that is not all. The study of technology is often a way of bringing the economic into the discussion automatically, and, somewhat like the law, technology (as industrial product, mass-producing machine, labor-saving instrument) is often difficult to *distinguish* from the mode of production. Jameson is generous when he sees the relation between studies of technological change and cinematic form as one of "tension." Mechanical causality is implicit, even in the extremely significant history of the "coming of sound" and its bearing on the motion picture aesthetic.

53. Benjamin, *Passagen-Werk*, as quoted in Buck-Morss, "Benjamin's *Passagen-Werk*," 229.

54. Balibar, *Reading "Capital,"* says: "It is difficult, firstly, to distinguish clearly between the relations of production and their 'legal expression'; this very concept of expression is difficult, too, once it no longer means duplication but rather the articulation of two heterogeneous instances; finally, so is the possible dislocation between the economic relations and the legal forms" (pt. 3, 229).

55. Marx and Engels, *The German Ideology*, say:

> That these general ideas and concepts are looked upon as mysterious forces is the necessary result of the fact that the real world, of which they are only the expression, has acquired an independent existence. Besides this meaning in everyday consciousness, these general ideas are further elaborated and given a social significance by politicians and lawyers who, as a result of the division of labor, are dependent on the culture of these concepts, and who see in them, and not in the relations of production, the true basis of all real property relations. (5:363)

56. See Cain and Hunt, *Marx and Engels on Law*, chap. 4.

57. Collins, *Marxism and Law*, 109, says that Pashukanis was correct to pose the individual over the group as the fundamental unit of contemporary law, especially as a contrast to the organization of prefeudal Europe. He goes on to describe Pashukanis as "crudely" reductionist in his characterization of the relation between the material base and the law. The consensus about the Soviet theorist is that he was wide of the mark in his prediction that the law would wither away with the commodity form that structured it and that his ideas about criminal law were unworkable. For detailed background on both Pashukanis and Soviet legal philosophy in the twenties, see Pashukanis, Introduction to *Selected Writings on Marxism and Law*.

58. Hirst, *Law, Socialism, and Democracy*, 18, says that the majority of the branches of the law cannot be explained on the model of commodity exchange.

59. Sumner, *Reading Ideologies*, 250.

60. Hirst, *Law, Socialism, and Democracy*, 56.

61. Pashukanis, *Law and Marxism*, 109.

62. Edelman, *Ownership of the Image*, 171.

63. Locke, *Two Treatises of Government*, 134; Edelman, *Ownership of the Image*, 52, echoes this when he says that the photographer had to "invest" the real world before the camera with his characteristics in order to make the photograph his property; Hirst and Kingdom, "On Edelman's 'Ownership of the Image,'" actually bring out the latent reference to Locke in Edelman's theory, explaining that "this image can only be property to the extent that it is mixed with the subject, that is re-presented and transformed through his creative labour" (136).

64. Hegel, *The Philosophy of Right*, 44.

65. Ibid., 37.

66. Pashukanis, *Law and Marxism*, 130.

67. The classic statement of Marx's theory of value, which sets persons against things, is this:

> There is an antithesis, immanent in the commodity, between use-value and value, between private labor and labor which must simultaneously manifest itself as directly social labor, and a particular concrete kind of labor which simultaneously counts as merely abstract universal labor, between the conversion of things into persons and the conversion of persons into things, the anti-thetical phases of the metamorphosis of the commodity are the developed forms of motion of this immanent contradiction. (Marx, *Capital*, 1:209)

68. Pashukanis, *Law and Marxism*, 125.

69. Ibid. This is another of the Soviet theorist's resounding echoes of Marx, who says that "both buyer and seller of a commodity, say of labor-power, are constrained only by their own free will. They contract as free agents, and the agreement they come to, is but the form in which they give legal expression to their common will" (*Capital*, 1:280).

70. For a modern version of this same concept, see Balbus, "Commodity Form and Legal Form."
71. Mensch, "Freedom of Contract as Ideology," 760.
72. Pashukanis, *Law and Marxism*, 121.
73. Edelman, *Ownership of the Image*, 33.
74. Although, for instance, literary criticism might speak of the contract between the reader and the author, this rule-governed relation is unlike the marriage contract between two persons. The rights and expectations are of a different order, certainly, but also marriage is one way that the *state* would organize and define us by means of contractual relations; Anderson and Greenberg, "From Substance to Form," 80, suggest marriage as an example here.
75. Edelman, *Ownership of the Image*, 194, fn. 8 and n. 61.
76. Heath, "The Turn of the Subject," 38.
77. Rosen, "Subject Formation and Social Formation," defines the subject as the "point of a fixed unity which guarantees knowledge and meaning" (169).
78. Foucault, "What Is an Author?" See also Foucault, *The Archaeology of Knowledge*, chap. 1.
79. See, for instance, the issue of *Texas Law Review* 60 (1982), reprinted as Mitchell, ed., *The Politics of Interpretation*.
80. Fish, "Don't Know Much About the Middle Ages," 306.
81. Althusser, *Lenin and Philosophy*, 170–71.
82. Ibid., 170.
83. See Forrester, "A Brief History of the Subject," for an overview that puts the contemporary concept in perspective.
84. Althusser, *Essays in Self-Criticism*, 129.
85. Eco, *Semiotics and the Philosophy of Language*, 45.
86. I refer here to the debates ensuing from the 1988 congressional decision to finally join the Berne Convention, the international agreement to respect creative rights, founded in 1886. Ostensibly, the U.S. had not signed the treaty with the now seventy-one member countries because the Berne provisions were to some degree incompatible with U.S. copyright law. Perhaps the most controversial question raised was whether the U.S. could comply with the Berne Convention standards without formally adopting a moral rights provision in the 1976 Copyright Act. In conclusion to the debate over the Berne Convention Implementation Act (BCIA), signed into law on 31 October 1988, both the House and the Senate decided that existing U.S. law, such as the Lanham Act and the doctrines of unfair competition, as well as libel, misrepresentation, and defamation, could provide the equivalent protection for authors from potential violation of their works. As requested by Congress, in March 1989, the U.S. Copyright Office reported on the implications of copyright law for future technologies (in particular the motion picture practices of altering the image by colorization, lexiconning, panning and scanning, and letterboxing). And in the context of this report, the Copyright Office, reviewing states' attempts to grant moral rights to authors of works of fine art, concluded that Congress should begin to

consider the adoption of a coherent federal system (see Heise, "Berne-ing Down the House [and Senate]).

87. Let me be clear that it is the death of the humanist subject that is not mourned. In its place, we would certainly want another version of subjectivity. See Heath, "The Turn of the Subject," 39, on this question; but also note that the implications are different for feminism. N. K. Miller, *Subject to Change*, says, "The postmodern notion that the Author is Dead and the subject along with him does not hold for women, and prematurely forecloses the question of agency for them" (106).

88. Edelman, *Ownership of the Image*, 51.

89. I also use the gendered pronoun "he" when I am analyzing those historically specific discourses (such as nineteenth-century law) that were spoken predominantly by and about men to the exclusion of women. My idea here is to reconstruct the heavy masculine flavor and the exclusivity of the legal discourse in earlier periods. In contrast, contemporary U.S. legal commentary, even when not dealing with issues specifically pertaining to women, will often use the personal pronoun "she" in place of the generic "he."

90. Althusser, *Lenin and Philosophy*, 171.

91. I am obliquely referring to Althusser's theory of the way individuals are "interpellated" as subjects. An accessible explanation of this theory of our "recruitment" into culture is Bennett, *Formalism and Marxism*, 119; Edelman, *Ownership of the Image*, adapts Althusser's theory to the law's signal to us: "Since you are a subject in law, you are capable of acquiring and selling (yourself)" (32). We participate in our own "interpellation," as we might automatically turn when called to, without thinking twice.

92. This is not a new critique, but MacDonell, *Theories of Discourse*, puts it well: "Meanwhile, it would seem that attempts to supply a theory of the subject (singular and general) for ideology or discourse will tend to idealism, speculating about what does not exist" (42).

93. Willemen, "Notes on Subjectivity," says on this point: "Real readers are subjects in history, living in given social formations, rather than mere subjects of a single text. The two types of subject are not commensurate. But for the purposes of formalism, real readers are supposed to coincide with the constructed readers" (48).

94. See E. P. Thompson, *The Poverty of Theory*. For a good account of the debates around Althusser, see Hall, "In Defence of Theory."

95. See P. Smith, *Discerning the Subject*, chap. 1, for a new account of this.

96. Hirst, "Althusser and the Theory of Ideology," 401.

97. Ibid.

98. Ibid.

99. Hirst, Introduction to Edelman, *Ownership of the Image*, 13.

100. R. Gordon, "Critical Legal Histories," 94–95, for instance, locates the work of Eugene Genovese and E. P. Thompson relative to class struggle and the law as number five in his spectrum; he gives the analysis of law as discourse a privilege by making it number six.

101. Anderson and Greenberg, "From Substance to Form," 82–83; Kennedy, "The Structure of Blackstone's Commentaries," in the introductory sections of one of the classic essays in American critical legal studies, explains that he will not try to explain "what brings legal consciousness into being, what causes it to change, and what effect it has on the actions of those who live it." He makes that decision because "we need to understand far more than we do now about the content and the internal structure of legal thought before we can hope to link it in any convincing way to other aspects of social, political or economic life" (220–21).

102. Edelman, *Ownership of the Image*, 23.

103. I refer to Edelman's adaptation of Althusser's concept of the "double speculary structure," or the double mirror of ideology, and it is, I think, extremely useful, as it suggests the reciprocity between the state and the legal subject. It is the law that awards the power to "right," which it then returns, giving the state its power (ibid., 32–33).

104. Edelman, *Ownership of the Image*, 65. He ties this development in film criticism into his own theory: "In other words, we are witnessing a *return of the camera/subject*. It is no longer the subject that is absorbed by the machine but the machine that is made subject. It has become creator in itself" (64).

105. The germ of this may be found in Pleynet and Thibaudeau, "Economique, Idéologique, Formel." The background on these developments is most completely given in Browne, ed., *Cahiers du Cinéma, 1969–1972*.

106. As quoted in Comolli, "Technique and Ideology."

107. Baudry, "The Apparatus," 108.

108. Baudry, "Ideological Effects," 44.

109. Edelman, *Ownership of the Image*, 32.

110. One of the more interesting avenues to pursue would be a feminist comparison of the way we are "gendered" in contract law and in cinema. As we know from feminist film theory, "looking" positions re-produce gender difference by organizing patterns of identification. Do contractual positions re-produce gender, but produce it as inequality because its blind categories insist that contracting parties are equal? That is, does contract law by *not seeing* subjects as male or female treat them unequally?

111. Edelman, *Ownership of the Image*, 57.

112. P. Smith, *Discerning the Subject*, 32.

113. Dyer, *The Stars*.

114. King, "The Hollywood Star System," 313, says that within the trade, the celebrity in actual life is referred to as the "private" person (chap. 5, n. 12).

115. Dyer, *Stars*.

116. Dyer, *Heavenly Bodies*; Dyer, "Four Films of Lana Turner."

117. King, "Articulating Stardom," 43. This is originally from Brady, "The Problem of Monopoly," who says that stardom works somewhat like the "ideal natural monopoly of talent in the voice of the opera singer . . . each star is to some extent a holder of a monopoly, and the owner of contracts for the

services of a star is the owner of a monopoly product. The majors dominate the employment of this individual monopoly talent" (131).

118. King, "Stardom and Symbolic Degeneracy."

119. Gledhill, "Signs of Melodrama."

120. Viera, "The Law of Star Images," 61; Dyer, *Stars*, 22–23.

121. Viera, "The Law of Star Images," 51.

122. Heath, "Film and System," 105–6.

123. Morin, *The Stars*, 105.

124. Clark, "Actors' Labor and the Politics of Subjectivity," 67–68.

125. Ibid., 154, 174.

126. Ibid; King, "The Hollywood Star System."

127. King, "The Hollywood Star System," 268.

128. Staiger, "Seeing Stars"; Janet Staiger in Bordwell, Staiger, and Thompson, *The Classical Hollywood Cinema*, on 1820s stars. To imagine the institution of cinema without stars, it is useful to think of how generic "moving" pictures were sold to early exhibitors by the foot (see Huettig, *Economic Control of the Motion Picture Industry*).

129. Tino Balio, "Part II: Struggles for Control," *The American Film Industry*, ed. Balio, 113–16.

130. Bordwell, Staiger, and Thompson, *The Classical Hollywood Cinema*, 96.

131. Ibid., 314.

132. DeCordova, "The Emergence of the Star System in America," 10–11.

133. See DeCordova, "The Emergence of the Star System and the Bourgeoisification of the American Cinema," 78–80, for a discussion of how studios handled scandal in the teens.

134. Morella and Epstein, *The "It" Girl*, 42.

135. Balio, ed., *The American Film Industry*, 114; Bordwell, Staiger, and Thompson, *The Classical Hollywood Cinema*, 101.

136. Klaprat, "The Star as Market Strategy," 35.

137. See my discussion in "From Elephants to Lux Soap," 37–38.

138. Staiger, "Announcing Wares," 7–8; Slide, *Aspects of American Film History*, 3.

139. Barry and Sargent, *Building Theatre Patronage*, 16, say that the first press book was for the Italian import *Quo Vadis* (1913); Reichenbach, "Press Books Then and Now," 318, says that he mimeographed the first press book for Jesse Lasky's feature *The Squaw Man* (1913).

140. Reichenbach, *Phantom Fame*. See Slide, *Aspects of American Film History*, 98–104, for an overview of early trade magazines and newspapers that did print news about motion pictures.

141. Teet Carle, Oral History, University of California at Los Angeles.

142. Staiger, "Announcing Wares," 9.

143. Griffith, *The Talkies*, xx.

144. Hilmes, "The 'Ban' That Never Was." See Hilmes, *Hollywood and Broadcasting*; Boddy, "The Stars Move into Prime Time"; Boddy, *Fifties Television*.

145. Hilmes, "The 'Ban' That Never Was," 43.

146. Gaines, "From Elephants to Lux Soap."

147. Hoff, "Publicity—What Is It?" 319; Staiger, "Announcing Wares," cites Cochrane, "Advertising Motion Pictures," 237–41, as making the following distinctions: "advertising: selling through the printed word; publicity—*'dissemination of interesting reading matter'* [italics in original], and exploitation—other techniques that help move the product"; Litwak, *Reel Power*, 236, explains studio marketing today as divided into *advertising* (television, radio, and newspaper advertising campaigns) and *publicity* (news coverage, press kit, interview arrangement, film screenings for critics).

148. Ramsaye, *A Million and One Nights*, 524.

149. Sargent, "The Development of Exploitation"; Sargent, "Exploitation."

150. Harry McWilliams, former publicist, Columbia Pictures, interview with author, 23 November 1986; McWilliams, "I Beat the Drum."

151. Lefebvre, *Everyday Life in the Modern World*, 97.

CHAPTER 2. PHOTOGRAPHY ''SURPRISES'' THE
LAW: THE PORTRAIT OF OSCAR WILDE

1. Ellmann, *Oscar Wilde*, 311.

2. Bazin, *What Is Cinema?*, 1:9.

3. Ibid., 1:13.

4. Wilde, *The Picture of Dorian Gray*.

5. Hirst, Introduction to Edelman, *Ownership of the Image*, 1.

6. See Fernand Laurent et Georges Daumas, *Dictionnaire Juridique anglais-français et français-anglais* (Paris: Rousseau and Co., 1927); Graham Oliver, *A French-English Dictionary of Legal and Commercial Terms* (1925; reprint, Littleton, Col.: Fred B. Rothman, 1988).

7. J. E. Mansion, ed., *Heath's Standard French and English Dictionary* (Boston: Heath, 1962).

8. Edelman, *Ownership of the Image*, 44.

9. For a good critique of the notion of "technological revolution," see Winston, *Misunderstanding Media*. I am not suggesting, however, anything like Winston's revolutionary curb, the "law of suppression of radical potential" accompanying technological innovation, which doesn't allow us either the glimpse of utopia or the hard edge of contradiction. Cubitt, "Time Shift," discusses videotaping as a technological threat. It is this kind of threat to existing intellectual property categories, to which legal institutions eventually have to respond, that I have in mind.

10. Edelman, *Ownership of the Image*, 44.

11. Alphonse Lamartine, *Cours familier de littérature. Entretiens sur Leopold Robert* (1848), as quoted in Edelman, *Ownership of the Image*, 45.

12. Ibid., 51.

13. Edelman, *Ownership of the Image*, 46; Edelman is vague about the actual time frame within which these changes took place. Some of this may have to do

with an assumption that his reader knows something about the evolution of French law. For instance, one needs to know that the recognition of photographers as able to claim *droits d'auteur* was developed entirely within common law; that is, it would evolve from case to case. Between the 1793 decree from the French Revolutionary period and the first proper French intellectual property law passed in 1957, the doctrine evolved in the courts. See Tournier, "The French Law of March 11, 1957." See especially the discussion of the protection of photographic works, which points out the inconsistency in the law that in article 2 extends protection of all works regardless of merit or the form the expression takes, and the stipulation that photographs must "be of an artistic or documentary character" (4).

14. Edelman, *Ownership of the Image*, 44.

15. Ibid., 43. In a nutshell, this is Edelman's theory of the "over-appropriation of the real," by which he means that the protection granted the art product by way of authorial creation is a double taking. The "reality" before the camera will always be property of some sort before the photographer "creates" it; it will be either public "communal" property or private property. What this emphasizes is the antithetical relation between reproduction and appropriation in Edelman's theory. Reproduction was not sufficient in French law; the photographer had to *produce* the "natural" world before the camera. One problem with the theory is that it seems to assume documentary or portrait photography and doesn't imagine the fully constructed "fictional" photograph to which the "reappropriation" of the real doesn't apply. Edelman does, however, make a distinction between photography as a "reflection of the real" and motion pictures as the "fiction of the real" (38).

16. Ibid., 51; Nesbitt, "What Was an Author?" 230–35, discusses the history of French reluctance to extend authorial status to the producers of technical drawings as well as photographs. It was not only that the operators of new machines aspired to be artists but that the cultural had to be distinguished from the industrial. The courts concluded that the technical drawing did not evidence the personality of the draftsman. She continues: "The bond between matter and spirit had been broken. In fact these sentiments were motivated by the basest instincts: industry did not want authors in its ranks; it wanted control over the property rights to every phase of production, from technical drawing to finished commodity" (234).

17. This important critique began as a debate between writers in *La Nouvelle Critique* and first *Cinéthique*, followed by *Cahiers du Cinéma*; The early seeds of it can be found in the discussion with Pleynet and Thibaudeau, "Economique, Idéologie, Formel." The representative articles in translation are Comolli, "Technique and Ideology"; Baudry, "Ideological Effects"; and Baudry, "The Apparatus."

18. See Neale, *Cinema and Technology*, 32–40, for a discussion of the way the scientific experiments of Eadweard Muybridge (human and animal motion) and M. J. Marey (the "gun" camera) originally posed challenges to human sight. In 1899 Marey wrote: "But in the end, what [the images] show could

have been perceived with the naked eye. They add nothing to the power of our sight, they in no way diminish our illusions. Whereas the true nature of scientific method is to remedy the insufficiency of our senses and to correct their errors. In order to achieve this, chronophotography must stop trying to reproduce the phenomena as we see them" (as quoted in Neale, 37).

19. This legislation was also enacted as a measure to curtail piracy. The effectivity of the statute in this regard can be seen in the contrast between the health of the British and the French publishing industries in these years. The French, who suffered far more than the British from the success of the Dutch book pirates, did not officially pass a protective decree until 1778. See Febvre and Martin, *The Coming of the Book*, 165, 196–97.

20. Burrow-Giles Lithographic Co. v. Sarony, 111 U.S. 53, 4 S. Ct. 279, 28 L. Ed. 349 (1884), in Nimmer, *Cases and Materials on Entertainment Litigation*, 10.

21. This is the account of U.S. copyright history recapitulated in a note in the Supreme Court case that reinforced the hard line on sound tape piracy. See Goldstein v. California, 412 U.S. 546, 93 S. Ct. 2303, 37 L. Ed. 2d 163 (1973), n. 17. Also see the 1976 U.S. copyright law revision, 17 U.S.C.A., sec. 5 (m) and (n). The relevant early references to copyright in photography are the Act of 3 Mar. 1865, ch. 126, 13 Stat. 540, and the Act of 8 July 1870, ch. 230, sec. 86, 16 Stat. 212.

22. Goldstein v. California, as quoted in Nimmer, *Cases and Materials on Entertainment Litigation*, 467.

23. House Report No. 756, 62d Congress, 2d Session (1912), 1. See Allen, "Copyright and Early Theatre, Vaudeville, and Film Competition," for the pioneering work on U.S. motion picture copyright from the point of view of film history.

24. Hirst, in Introduction to Edelman, *Ownership of the Image*, says, "In English law these contradictions and this problematic location of the subject appear not to exist. The relevant branch of English law is *copyright*, not *author's right*" (15). As I argue, even though in Anglo-American law the real author cannot claim a special relationship with the work as in French law, Anglo-American copyright law still invokes the author as a category. The difference between French and Anglo-American law becomes somewhat more clear if we think of French law as starting from the *moral right* of an author, which he could exercise even after the sale of his works—to intervene if his vision is compromised by altering his creation. For a good overview, see Whale and Phillips, *Whale on Copyright*, 16–18. The question may arise as to how, without a statutory *moral right* doctrine, the United Kingdom complies with the standards of the Berne Convention (see also chap. 1, n. 86). See Marvin, "Author's Status," for a close comparison of French and British law with a discussion of way the latter might be understood as containing equivalent protections for authors without recourse to *moral rights*.

25. For an early account of the British history with an American comparison, see Drone, *Treatise on the Law of Property*, 178–80.

26. Edelman, *Ownership of the Image*, 51.
27. Miller and Davis, *Intellectual Property*, 292. The reference here is to Bleistein v. Donaldson Lithographic Co., 23 S. Ct. 298 (1903), a Supreme Court decision involving circus posters produced by chromolithography. The significance of the case is that it answered the question of the amount of authorship required in the work, which Burrow-Giles had left undecided. It is therefore cited as authority more widely than Burrow-Giles on the issue of originality in works of authorship.
28. Time Incorporated v. Bernard Geis Associates, 293 F.Supp. 130 (1968), 141.
29. Miller and Davis, *Intellectual Property*, 292.
30. Sarony v. Burrow-Giles Lithographic Co., 17 F. 591 (S.D.N.Y. 1883).
31. Burrow-Giles v. Sarony, in Nimmer, *Cases and Materials on Entertainment Litigation*, 12.
32. Ibid., 10. The comparison with literary production, however, is *not* an uncomprehending anachronism. The requirement that the protected material be a "writing" is basic to U.S. intellectual property doctrine. But in the century and a half between the formulation of copyright doctrine on the literary model and the present, the increased variety of forms covered as "writings" has come to deform the original constitutional reference to literary works. In 1884 the list of copyrightable "writings" was already so expanded that the legal terminology had taken on a new, composite image no longer resembling the printed page, as the definition given here in Burrow-Giles attests in its reference to the language of the U.S. Constitution; see "Copyright," 1282–88, on how the definition of "writings" became liberally construed and the significance of Burrow-Giles v. Sarony in this development; Nimmer and Nimmer, *Nimmer on Copyright*, 1: sec. 1.08 [B].
33. I should be clear that although analogies were made between photographic printing and other printing processes, it was generally held that photography was *not* an art produced by printing. A good statement of this is Wood v. Abbott, 5 Blatchf. 325 (S.D.N.Y. 1866):

> The manufacture of these positives is called, in the language of this new art, "photographic printing." But names are not things. It is not printing in any sense known to the arts at the time this copyright was passed. . . . It is an entirely original and independent method of producing and multiplying pictures—an art, not of printing or engraving, but of securing the delineation of pictures by light operating on sensitive surfaces. (30 Fed. Cas. 425)

34. Burrow-Giles v. Sarony, in Nimmer, *Cases and Materials on Entertainment Litigation*, 11.
35. Ibid.
36. Jewelers' Circular Publishing Co. v. Keystone, 274 F. 932 (S.D.N.Y. 1921), as quoted in Nimmer, *Cases and Materials on Entertainment Litigation*, 13. I want to be clear that my interest in returning to Burrow-Giles is not to make an argument that it has been overlooked as precedent. If I suggest that its

definition of authorship could be construed as requiring no degree of personality at the same time that it requires a show of authorial personality, this is not to imply anything about the influence of either Bleistein or the Copyright Act of 1909 on Burrow-Giles. For my purposes, Burrow-Giles is a case microcosm for intellectual property doctrine within which two incompatibilities are set forth. Therefore, what I am saying about the structure of this doctrine applies to other parts of statutory and common law.

37. For instance, Mazer v. Stein, 347 U.S. 201 (1954) [lamp base statuettes]; Alfred Bell Co. v. Catalda Fine Arts, 191 F.2d 99 (1951) [mezzotint engravings], see especially 100, fn. 8.

38. Patterson, *Copyright in Historical Perspective*, 216–17.

39. Whale, "Copyright and Authors' Rights," says of the objective position of the author in the contemporary publishing industry: "Authors . . . as distinct from the other categories of copyright owners, have neither the corporate strength nor, except for the very few successful ones, the financial security to assert their legal rights on terms of equality with those to whom they entrust the exploitation of their works" (39).

40. Ibid., 15.

41. Ibid., 18.

42. Ibid., 219.

43. Notably, both the German Federal Republic and France now have a statutory "moral right," but it is particularly well developed in France. There the doctrine evolved after the Revolution to complement a new *droit d'auteur* (author's right), which was established as inherent in the artist as opposed to being conferred by the king. As set forth in the French copyright law of 11 March 1957, integral *droits moral* are distinguished from *droits patrimoniaux*, which can be sold or transferred. The *droit moral*, clearly in the spirit of Romanticism, belongs to the artist by virtue of his or her personhood and is both inalienable, unassignable, and perpetual. See DaSilva, "*Droit Moral* and the Amoral Copyright," 3–13. The movement to which I refer is part of the aftermath of the 1989 congressional hearings and consequent U.S. entry into the Berne Convention treaty. See Brown, "Adherence to the Berne Copyright Convention." Also see chap. 1, n. 86.

44. Alfred Bell v. Catalda Fine Arts, says the following:

> The defendants' contention apparently results from the ambiguity of the word "original." It may mean starting, novel or unusual, a marked departure from the past. Obviously this is not what is meant when one speaks of "the original package," or the "original bill," or . . . an "original" document; none of these things is highly unusual in creativeness. "Original" in reference to copyright work means that the particular work "owes its origin" to the "author." No large measure of novelty is necessary. (100)

45. Miller and Davis, *Intellectual Property*, 289.

46. R. Williams, *Keywords*, 73.

47. See, for instance, Crimp, "Appropriating Appropriation"; Owens, "The Discourse of Others," 57–82; Krauss, *The Originality of the Avant-Garde*.
48. Wolff, *The Social Production of Art*, 19.
49. R. Williams, *Culture and Society*, 36.
50. Becker, *Art Worlds*, says in one of the best basic critiques of the Romantic notion of the artist-genius, that "works and makers stand in reciprocal relation to one another. How do we know that artists have special gifts? By their works" (356).
51. Abrams, *The Mirror and the Lamp*, 226.
52. Ibid., 227.
53. Foucault, "What Is an Author?" 20, refers to this earlier state.
54. R. Williams, *Culture and Society*, 48.
55. Donaldson v. Becket, 4 Burr. 2408 (1774).
56. Rose, "The Author as Proprietor."
57. Francis Hargrave, *Argument in Defence of Literary Property* (London, 1774), as quoted in Rose, "The Author as Proprietor," 72.
58. Rose, "The Author as Proprietor," 73. In one of the very few objections to the assumptions behind hearings for the 1976 U.S. copyright law revision, which extended the term of coverage and increased the privileges of copyright, Stephen Breyer says that the property claim "rests on an intuitive, unanalyzed feeling that an author's book is his 'property.' But why do we have such a feeling? The intellectual creation differs radically from land and chattels. Since ideas are infinitely divisible, property rights are not needed to prevent congestion, interference, or strife. Nor does the fact that the book is the author's *creation* seem a sufficient reason for making it his *property*" ("The Uneasy Case for Copyright," 288–89).
59. Rose, "The Author as Proprietor," 74.
60. Frow, "Repetition and Limitation," 9.
61. Barthes, *Mythologies*, 152.
62. Rose, "The Author as Proprietor," 72. A comprehensive statement of the way contemporary literary theory views the text and its author is this, by Terry Eagleton:

> There is no such thing as literary "originality," no such thing as the "first" literary work: all literature is intertextual. A specific piece of writing thus has no clearly defined boundaries: it spills over constantly into the works clustered around it, generating a hundred different perspectives which dwindle to a vanishing point. The work cannot be sprung shut, rendered determinate, by an appeal to the author, for the "death of the author" is a slogan that modern criticism is now confidently able to proclaim. (*Literary Theory*, 138)

63. One might say, however, that moral rights does threaten to return the author to the work. Two of the four rights into which French law divides this doctrine would suggest that: *Droit de repentir ou de retrait* ("right to reconsider or to withdraw") allows the creator to reclaim a copyright that had

already been assigned, and *droit au respect de l'oeuvre* ("right of respect of the work," sometimes the "right of integrity") even allows the artist to oppose proposed modifications and distortions; see Reeves, Bauer, and Lieser, "Retained Rights," 7–12. To some degree, the provisions of the California and New York artists-rights acts may also be said to return the author to the work. These rights are extremely limited, however, and require a showing of what amounts to thorough alteration or defacement of the work or false attribution. See California Arts Preservation Act, California Civil Code, sec. 987; the New York Artists Authorship Rights Act, New York General Business Law, art. 12 J, secs. 228 m–q.

64. Hirst, Introduction to Edelman, *Ownership of the Image*, 17.
65. Esquire, Inc. v. Ringer, 591 F.2d 796 (1978) [light fixtures]; Kielselstein-Cord v. Accessories by Pearl, Inc., 632 F.2d 989 (1980) [belt buckles].
66. Krauss, *The Originality of the Avant Garde*, 162.
67. Bleistein v. Donaldson, in Nimmer, *Cases and Materials on Entertainment Litigation*, 4.
68. But copyright cases that need to make a case for copyright infringement in the more banal object would still use the "something irreducible" test to find the necessary authorial sign in the work. In F. W. Woolworth Co. v. Contemporary Arts, Inc. (193 F.2d 162 [1951]), the latter successfully enjoined the dry goods chain from selling sculptured plaster dogs. Again, the title to the statuettes had been assigned by the maker to Contemporary Arts, Inc., but using the name "Jan Allen" she had attained a copyright for each version of "Cocker Spaniel in Show Position." The court of appeals, in upholding the lower court's judgment for the plaintiff, citing Bleistein, went on to say:

> Here the "something irreducible" which was Jan Allen's alone was certainly not a matter of subject, nor was it a matter of size or material, nor even of color, for is it well known that cocker spaniels are typically of several colors. Her "something irreducible" was shape . . . proportion form, contour, configuration, and conformation, perhaps the latter in details too subtle for appreciation by anyone but a fancier, of the dog represented by the sculptured work of art.

69. See Nochlin, "Why Have There Been No Great Women Artists?" for a feminist analysis of the "golden nugget" of genius.
70. Edelman, *Ownership of the Image*, 51.
71. Ibid., 45. Edelman goes on to argue, "The photographer of 1860 is the *proletarian of creation*; he and his tool form one body." Here I think he betrays a concern for the real artist that is at odds with the main thrust of his argument, which I find complements the poststructuralist critique of authorship in important ways. And yet this is one of those points at which we have to admit that for real historical persons the immediate implications of poststructuralist insights are bleak.
72. William Alexandre Heydecker's translation of Eugène Pouillet's *Propriété Littéraire et Artistique* is included in the *Federal Reporter* report on *Sarony v.*

Burrow-Giles Lithographic Co., reprinted in *Decisions of the United States Courts Involving Copyright and Literary Properties*. The translation was probably taken from the first edition, *Traité théorique et pratique de la propriété littéraire et artistique et du droit de représentation* (Paris: Marchal et Billard, 1879).

73. Pouillet, *Propriété*, 2322.

74. Ibid.

75. Marx and Engels, *The German Ideology*.

76. Edelman, *Ownership of the Image*, 40.

77. Pouillet, *Propriété*, 2322.

78. Ibid., 2320.

79. As quoted in ibid., 2319.

80. Ibid.

81. As quoted in ibid., 2319.

82. Trib. Corr. Seine, 16 Mars, 1864, aff. Masson, Pataille, 64, 227, as quoted in ibid., 2319.

83. Newhall, *The History of Photography*, 12.

84. Ibid., 34.

85. Ibid., 16.

86. Ibid., 17.

87. Tagg, "A Democracy of the Image"; Newhall, *The Daguerreotype in America*, 18–19, says that Daguerre received six thousand francs per year for life from the French government in exchange for the process.

88. Newhall, *History of Photography*, 21.

89. Ibid., 57.

90. Tagg, "A Democracy of the Image," 26. See Krauss, "Tracing Nadar," for more on Nadar's early theory of the relationship between the photograph and its referent.

91. Newhall, *History of Photography*, 57, says of Sarony, "He posed his sitters and directed them, bringing out by flattery, threat, mimicry, their histrionic powers."

92. Ibid., 49; McCauley, *Disdéri*, 209.

93. Newhall, *History of Photography*, 14.

94. McCauley, *Disdéri*, 210.

95. See Staiger, "Seeing Stars," on the important, often overlooked connection between motion picture stars and their predecessors in the theater.

96. Bassham, *Theatrical Photographs*, 11–12.

97. Freund, *Photography and Society*, describes the *appui-tête* as "a chair with a metal brace which held the skull steady from behind and was hidden from the lens" (63); Bassham, *Theatrical Photographs*, 14, says that the "eye rest" gave subjects something upon which to "fix the gaze" so that eye movements would be kept to a minimum during the sitting.

98. Barthes, *Camera Lucida*, 14.

99. For example, see Gilbert and Gubar, *The Madwoman in the Attic*; Pollock, *Vision and Difference*.

100. For the original theorization of this, see Mulvey, "Visual Pleasure and Narrative Cinema."

101. Owens, "Posing," 15.

102. Here I quite literally mean that although feminists have thoroughly theorized conventional practice in the visual arts as phallocentrically authored, the eye and the head and more recently the voice have been the preferred centers of discussion. Although the *metteur en scène* has figured in motion picture and theater criticism, his function has not been fully elaborated as a mode of artistic positioning and control. I am wondering if a theory of the assertion of authorial rights flows more logically out of the hand. I am suggesting, though, that intellectual property law has found ways of dealing with claims to artistic property made via the ethereal "magic" of conception. Of course, this is foreign to the ways in which land was historically claimed as property—by foot.

103. Public sentiment was with this view. There was some prestige attached to the practice of sitting for the local commercial photographer if he was more than a mere mechanic. See W. Allen, "Legal Tests of Photography-as-Art," 221.

104. Falk v. Donaldson, 57 F. 32 (S.D.N.Y. 1893), in *Decisions of the United States Courts Involving Copyright and Literary Properties*, 944.

105. Ibid.

106. Ibid., 945.

107. This invisibility has been theorized in relation to film. Heath, "Film and System," 104, describes this disappearance as the way the signifiers put on by the actor work by "absorbing face and body into character significance." Also see King, "Articulating Stardom," 46, on the vogue in acting technique that produces the effacement of artistry.

108. Bassham, *Theatrical Photographs*, 14.

109. Ibid., 10, 14. Lily Langtry's photographs could command a price of $5 apiece. At the time she received the $5,000 fee, Sarony had an order for five hundred of her photographs from France. Oscar Wilde was in the category of the celebrity who early saw the value of the mass-produced photograph, and his agent, D'Oyly Carte, who scheduled this photographic session at the beginning of Wilde's lecture tour of the U.S., did not demand such an outrageous fee for his client (74).

110. Foucault, "What Is an Author?" 20.

111. Staiger, "The Eyes Are Really the Focus," describes the Kemble "Teapot" School of Acting in this way.

112. Naremore, *Acting in the Cinema*, 52, says that Francois Delsarte (1811–71) was interested in a kind of semiotics of gesture, which he understood from Locke, long before either Charles Sanders Peirce or Ferdinand Saussure. He refers readers to two typical works from the period that describe this general method: Henry Siddon, *Practical Illustrations of Rhetorical Gesture & Action* (1882), and Gustave Garcia, *Actor's Art* (1882); Wilden, *The Rules Are No Game*, 142, refers to John Locke as the first to use "semiotics" as a term in its modern sense.

113. Bassham, *Theatrical Photographs*, 8, says that Sarony was the "original pioneer of the theatrical poster."

114. Ibid., 22. The comparison with Rembrandt is especially interesting in light of Svetlana Alpers's recent discussion of Rembrandt's self-portraiture as a new aesthetic of "self-possession," which proclaimed property in the self and claimed its advantages in the emerging seventeenth-century Dutch market economy (*Rembrandt's Enterprise*). Thanks to Mark Rose for this reference.

115. Newhall, *The History of Photography*, 60–61.

116. Bassham, *Theatrical Photographs*, 19.

117. Ibid., 20.

118. *Wilson's Photographic Magazine*, 11 January 1893, as quoted in Newhall, *The History of Photography*, 57.

119. Benjamin, "Art in the Age of Mechanical Reproduction," 228.

120. Benjamin, "A Small History of Photography," 241.

121. Nimmer, *Cases and Materials on Entertainment Litigation*, 9.

122. Baily, *The Gilbert and Sullivan Book*, 212. I am indebted to my colleague George W. Williams for this reference.

123. Lewis and Justin, *Oscar Wilde Discovers America*, 7.

124. Ellmann, *Oscar Wilde*, 191.

125. Ibid., 167.

126. For an interesting comparison, see Solomon-Godeau's discussion in "The Legs of the Countess" of the way the Second Empire beauty the Countess de Castiglione "authored" her own image through commercial photographic portraiture.

127. Hirst and Kingdom, "On Edelman's 'Ownership of the Image,'" 138.

128. Gross v. Seligman, 212 F. 930 (1914).

129. Ibid., 203, 205. To understand the contemporary significance of Gross v. Seligman, one might consider Nimmer's discussion of the two situations in which a photograph could be denied copyright protection for want of originality. First, he gives the example of "slavish copying," which would be nothing more than printing a negative, photographing a print, or making a microfilm, thermofax or xerox copy. (A photograph of a painting, because it is a conversion to a different medium, however, might be another case.) The second example would be a situation in which a photographer, as in Gross v. Seligman, "attempts to duplicate" all of the elements in another photographic work, even though he may be dealing with a "live subject." See Nimmer and Nimmer, *Nimmer on Copyright*, sec. 2.08 [E].

130. Gross v. Seligman, 203. It is this fixed legal subject position, says Edelman, which is the foot in the door for capital. In motion pictures, the next state of technological development, capital becomes the creative subject (*Ownership of the Image*, 58).

131. For the consideration of the transgressive possibilities of Wilde's commitment to "striking a pose" throughout life, I am indebted to Dollimore, "Different Desires." The other ramification that haunts this chapter, of course, is the double "death" of both the author and the humanist subject,

developments that have implications for any notion of "origin." In Barthes, *The Rustle of Language*, the modern "scriptor" who has replaced the author can do nothing more than "trace": "[F]or him, on the contrary, his hand, detached from any voice, born by a pure gesture of inscription (and not of expression), traces a field without origin—or at least with no origin but language itself, i.e., the very thing which ceaselessly calls any origin into question" (52).

CHAPTER 3. DEAD RINGER: JACQUELINE ONASSIS AND THE LOOK-ALIKE

1. Edelman, *Ownership of the Image*, 42–43.
2. See Hegel, *The Philosophy of Right*.
3. Edelman, *Ownership of the Image*, 39.
4. Bleistein v. Donaldson Lithographic Co., 188 U.S. 239 (1903).
5. Edelman, *Ownership of the Image*, 51.
6. This is a reference to André Bazin, "The Ontology of the Photographic Image," *What Is Cinema?*, 1:12; Burgin, "Photographic Practice and Art Theory," 61, discusses the degree to which the photograph is "caused" by the referent. For an account of the correspondence between Bazin's theory of photography and Charles Sanders Peirce's notion of the indexical sign, see Rosen, "History of Image, Image of History," 11–13.
7. Holmes, "The Stereoscope and the Stereograph," 81.
8. See McCarthy, *The Rights of Publicity and Privacy*, chap. 1; Nimmer, *Cases and Materials on Entertainment Litigation*, chap. 16.
9. Lugosi v. Universal Pictures, 25 Cal.3d 813 (1979).
10. Onassis v. Christian Dior–New York, Inc., 122 Misc.2d 603 (1984), 605.
11. Ibid., 603. Technically, Onassis brought suit against Christian Dior, Lansdowne Advertising, Inc., Ron Smith Celebrity Look-Alikes, and Barbara Reynolds.
12. Ibid., 605. If the socialite had been agreeable to the commercialization of her name and likeness, we would have had "Jackie Onassis" instead of "Gloria Vanderbilt" jeans. Hong Kong jeans manufacturer Murjani was turned down by Onassis before he settled on the Vanderbilt image for his line of designer clothes (Sudjic, *Cult Heroes*, 83).
13. Onassis v. Dior, 603.
14. Hirst and Kingdom, "On Edelman's 'Ownership of the Image,'" 139.
15. Onassis v. Dior, 611. The Woody Allen cases following Onassis seem to have avoided the problem of having to conclude that the look-alike was legally the "picture or portrait" of the celebrity. In the first, Allen sued National Video, Inc., Phil Boroff, the look-alike, and Ron Smith of Celebrity Look-Alikes for violation of his right to privacy and his right of publicity as well as unfair competition. The actor objected to the use of the "Woody Allen" look-alike in an advertisement (in which he is portrayed standing in line in a video

store) captioned "Become a V.I.P. at National Video. We'll Make You Feel Like a Star." Judge Motley dealt with the issue of the photographic likeness more squarely than Judge Greenfield had the year before (Allen v. National Video, Inc., 610 F.Supp. 612 [S.D.N.Y. 1985]). For a comparison between Onassis and Allen v. National Video in this regard, see Rufflo, "Unfair Competition."

16. Eco, "Articulations of the Cinematic Code," 595.

17. I refer to Barthes, "The Photographic Message," and "Rhetoric of the Image," *Image/Music/Text*, 15–51.

18. Eco goes on to say, "[I]t may be enough for the moment to have recognized processes of codification concealed in the mechanisms of perception themselves" ("Articulations of the Cinematic Code," 595). It is generally accepted that Eco's argument here for seeing the image as coded at the level of perception successfully unseated the notion of photography as uncoded. I am drawing attention to the tentativeness he has expressed about his own conclusions. For further background, see Burgin, *Thinking Photography*, 60–63.

19. Baudrillard, "Beyond Right and Wrong," 8.

20. Onassis v. Dior, 605.

21. Thanks to William Price for this idea about readership, as well as invaluable legal research assistance and advice.

22. I allude to the "impasse" in feminist film criticism, effected by the theorization of "woman" as absence. For an overview, see Doane, Mellencamp, and Williams, eds., "Feminist Film Criticism," 1–17.

23. Doane, "Film and the Masquerade."

24. See Kaplan, *Women and Film*, chap. 10, for a good overview of this position.

25. For a succinct discussion of Roberson v. Rochester Folding Box Co. and its relationship to the 1903 New York statute enacted as the result of its outcome, see McCarthy, *The Rights of Publicity and Privacy*, 1.14–1.16, 6.56–6.65.

26. Onassis v. Dior, 612.

27. The irony of my introduction of "publicity" into a discussion of *Onassis* will not escape the attention of legal commentators who will know that New York has notoriously resisted the evolution of a concept of "right of publicity" within state courts and consistently backed off from enacting the kind of legislation that exists in other states. That does not, however, mean that common law "right of publicity" remedies would be totally unavailable or that celebrities would not be able to find relief under other doctrines in the state. For a full discussion of the issues within an argument *for* a New York statute, see Lind, "The Right of Publicity in New York." In 1988, Senator Gold sponsored a bill in the New York legislature to amend the state civil rights law to grant a property right in the image to the heirs of deceased personalities. Named "the 'Mommie Dearest' bill" in reference to the biography of Joan Crawford written by her daughter, the bill met substantial opposition on First Amendment grounds (see Zeldis, "Public Hearing Focuses on Bill on Use of Deceased's Likeness").

28. Sennett, *The Fall of Public Man*, chap. 8; Susman, *Culture as History*, chap. 14.

29. See Sekula, "The Traffic in Photographs," 133, for a discussion of the "scientific" portraiture of August Sandler.

30. Balázs, *Theory of the Film*, 51–52, 60–61.

31. Deleuze, *Cinema 1*, 87–88.

32. Barthes, *Mythologies*, 56.

33. Deleuze, *Cinema 1*, 100.

34. Onassis v. Dior, 610.

35. Ibid., 611.

36. Ibid.

37. Mitchell, *Iconology*, 29. Part of the difficulty of this case has to do with the tendency to confuse iconicity (similarity) with indexicality (the contiguity between photograph and photographed). For a useful discussion of the photograph as both indexical and iconic, see Metz, "Photography and Fetish," 82.

38. See Miller and Davis, *Intellectual Property*, 255–68, for a discussion of similarity as it applies to both copyright and trademark.

39. Onassis v. Dior, 613.

40. Ibid.

41. Lee, "Celebrity Look-Alikes," argues that one of the issues that the Onassis court overlooked pertained to Barbara Reynolds's right to labor, since under the Fourteenth Amendment this right would be constitutionally guaranteed property. For Lee, who especially objected to the tendency to make individual look-alikes liable, "[t]he constitutionally protected right to labor should take precedence over the publicity right" (217).

42. McCarthy, in a different vein, says, "One is not the 'author' of one's face, no matter how much cosmetic surgery has been performed. Either God, fate, or our parents' genes 'authored' this 'work'" (*The Rights of Publicity and Privacy*, 5.44).

43. Morin, *Stars*, 140, first referred to the actor's physiognomy as "raw material," but later Dyer, *The Stars*, 17, would integrate the concept into his theory of the industrial production of the star image; McCarthy, *Trademarks*, 1:656–717.

44. Edelman, *Ownership of the Image*, 38.

45. Ibid., 101.

46. Onassis v. Dior, 614.

47. McCarthy, *Trademarks*, 1:54–55, 666–68. The issue of "likelihood of confusion" is more submerged in Onassis because the issue at hand was invasion of privacy. In other cases in which celebrities have tried to enjoin look-alikes under the Lanham Act, the test has clearly been a "likelihood of confusion" (between celebrity and look-alike), which implied endorsement or involvement. Woody Allen, for instance, successfully enjoined both National Video, Inc., and Men's World Outlet on this theory (Allen v. National Video, Inc.,

610 F.Supp. 612 [S.D.N.Y. 1985]; Allen v. Men's World Outlet, Inc., 679 F.Supp. 360 [S.D.N.Y. 1988]).

48. Indeed, the Duke University counsel's office was not willing to let the *South Atlantic Quarterly* take this risk, and, based on that advice, the Duke Press decided not to reproduce the Dior advertisement along with this chapter (in the form of an article) in vol. 88, no. 2 (Winter 1989). At the eleventh hour, Duke law school professor David Lange persuaded the counsel's office to change its position, and the ad finally was reproduced in the issue. However, Duke University Special Collections, which houses the J. Walter Thompson Advertising Archives, was unable to release the original tear sheets for reproduction, since Christian Dior's letter to me stated that the company could not authorize the use of the image. The image that appeared in the journal was reproduced directly from a page in the 10 October 1983 issue of *The New Yorker*.

49. McCarthy, *Trademarks*, 1:663.

50. Gauthier, "The Semiology of the Image," 9. For more on the methodology, see Alvarado, "Photographs and Narrativity."

51. Berger, *Ways of Seeing*, chap. 7.

52. Deleuze, *Cinema 1*, 99; Grant v. Esquire, Inc., 367 F.Supp. 876 (1973); Cher v. Forum, International, 692 F.2d 634 (9th Cir. 1982); Eastwood v. Superior Court, 149 Cal.App. 3d 409 (1983).

53. See Pat Paulsen v. Personality Posters, Inc., 59 Misc.2d 444 (1969).

54. See International News Service v. Associated Press, 248 U.S. 215 (1918); National Tel. News Co. v. Western Union, 119 Fed. 294 (1902); Pamela Samuelson, "Information as Property," argues that two recent Supreme Court decisions could be interpreted as unproblematically acknowledging property rights in information. Within this article she rereads International News Service, the case remembered for Justice Brandeis's dissent in which he provided the basis for a strong resistance to expanding the category of property in his remark that the "noblest of human productions—knowledge, truths ascertained, conceptions, and ideas—become, after voluntary communication to others, free as the air to common use" (as quoted in Samuelson, 395).

55. See Hoehling v. Universal City Studios, 618 F.2d 972 (1980), for a discussion of the proprietal claims on the historical facts related to the *Hindenberg* explosion. The courts have also generally held that public interest can outweigh a privacy right. One example is actress Ann-Margret's failure in a privacy action against *High Society* magazine for the reproduction of an image from the film *Magic* (1978) that showed her naked from the waist up. The New York court concluded that that reproduction of a performance by a public figure in which there was public interest was protected by the First Amendment (Ann-Margret v. High Society, 498 F.Supp. 401 [S.D.N.Y. 1980]).

56. Onassis v. Galella, 487 F.2d 986 (2d Cir. 1973), 43–44. In his essay

"Papparazzo Notes," Alan Sekula provocatively analyzes this case as a replay of an old "antagonism between the literal and popular press and the sequestered economic elite" (31). The piece also contains a discussion of the social inequality of Galella and Onassis, photographer and subject, as well as the relationship of celebrity journalists to their publishers (*Photography Against the Grain*).

57. Time Incorporated v. Bernard Geis Associates, 293 F.Supp. 130 (1968).

58. Ibid., 138.

59. Ibid., 143.

60. See, for instance, Barthes, *The Rustle of Language*, 131–32, for a critique of the "chastity of History," untouched by historians and their forms.

61. See Michel DeCerteau, *The Writing of History*, 21, for a discussion of the peculiarity of the discipline that uses the same term ("history") to refer to both the object of study and the discourse on it. In my argument I am taking advantage of the ambiguity.

62. Onassis v. Dior, 143.

63. Edelman, *Ownership of the Image*, 67–66, reading Time Inc. v. Geis with fresh eyes from the point of view of French law, is astounded to find that Judge Wyatt had stated that the "form" of history was copyrightable but not the "foundation," or underlying ideas. Porter, "Film Copyright and Edelman's Theory of Law," 144–45, quite rightly points out that Edelman had not read enough U.S. law to know that the distinction was basic to intellectual property doctrine.

64. Frow, "Repetition and Limitation," 8.

65. Onassis v. Dior, 613.

66. See Warner Brothers, Inc. v. American Broadcasting Co., Inc., 720 F.2d 231 (2d Cir. 1983), 242–43, for a discussion of Superman as a generic type that cannot be reserved.

67. Onassis v. Dior, 613.

CHAPTER 4. "THESE BOOTS ARE MADE FOR WALKIN'": NANCY SINATRA AND THE GOODYEAR TIRE SOUND-ALIKE

1. R. Williams, *The Sociology of Culture*, 50.

2. Hirst and Kingdom, "On Edelman's 'Ownership of the Image,'" 140.

3. McCarthy, *The Rights of Publicity and Privacy*, 4.90.

4. Sinatra v. Goodyear Tire & Rubber Co., 435 F.2d 711 (1970), 712.

5. Ibid., 713.

6. Thus if one merchant adopts a familiar product trade name for his completely dissimilar product, the merchant who has been imitated has no cause for complaint. For example, it was held that a chocolate company could adopt the name "Vassar" since it was not in competition with the women's college by the same name. In the case of the girdle manufacturer that adopted the

name "Seventeen," however, the magazine *Seventeen* successfully claimed unfair competition because of the market overlap between the lingerie company and the young women's magazine (Triangle Publications v. Rohrlich, 167 F.2d 969 [1948]).

7. Miller and Davis, *Intellectual Property*, 250, say that "palming off" is the paradigm of federal unfair competition law, codified in sec. 43(a) of the 1946 Lanham Act.

8. Prosser, *Law of Torts*, 982–83, as quoted in Sinatra, 715.

9. Lahr v. Adell Chemical Co., 300 F.2d 256 (1962), 259.

10. Ibid.

11. *Sinatra*, 716.

12. McCarthy, *Trademarks*, 1:665.

13. Newhall, *The History of Photography*, 89; Eder, *History of Photography*, 489.

14. Lipman, *The Electronic Pirates*, 9, says that Standard Oil tried to establish copyright protection for the distinctive mark EXXON, arguing that "research, skill and imagination" were used in the creation of the word. From Lipman's account, it apparently did not meet the copyright requirement as an "original work of authorship."

15. Derenberg and Morofsky, *European Trademark Law and Practice*, 27.

16. Hereafter I will use the graphic convention employed in legal publications of representing trademarked terms in capital letters.

17. Miller and Davis, *Intellectual Property*, 162. To suggest the economic significance of the difference between a descriptive and a distinctive word, consider the dispute over UNCOLA heard on appeal before the Trademark Trial and Appeal Board. While Coca-Cola argued that "uncola" was a common "descriptive" and "generic" term, Seven-Up argued that it was "distinctive." The board found for Seven-Up, that UNCOLA was "distinctive," but held that it had not acquired a secondary meaning, or marketplace meaning, as yet (Coca-Cola Co. v. Seven-Up Co., 497 F.2d 1351 [1974]).

18. Eco, *A Theory of Semiotics*, 54–57.

19. An example of how one commercial entity "hitches a free ride" on another is the case of the "Jaws One" and "Jaws Two" trash compactors manufactured by Montgomery Ward and first advertised around the time of the first broadcast of *Jaws* on television in 1979. In support of the argument that they had created a secondary meaning in the word "Jaws," Universal City Studios cited the $15 million in advertising expenses for *Jaws* (1975) and *Jaws 2* (1978); the $200 million in revenues from exhibition, the mechanical attraction *Jaws* in the Universal Studios tour; three books (including a novelization), merchandising (including stockings, costume jewelry, plastic cups, neckties) earning $35 million retail and $2.5 million in royalties; the *Jaws* game (a best-seller from 1976 to 1979), the sound-track album, with sales around $295,000; a tie-up with Datsun coordinated with the fall 1979 broadcast of the film (Universal City Studios, Inc. v. Montgomery Ward & Co., Inc., 207 U.S.P.Q. 852 [1980]).

20. As quoted in McCarthy, *Trademarks*, 1:659.

21. Miller and Davis, *Intellectual Property*, 164.

22. Barthes, *Mythologies*.

23. In 1938 secondary meaning existed only in the vague concept of "special significance." Since the 1946 Lanham Act it has evolved out of the stipulation mentioned there that a symbol "has become distinctive" (McCarthy, *Trademarks*, 1:665).

24. This interesting "about-face" was one of the developments that struck me first when I began to read the history of trademark law. Since then I have encountered legal commentators who have confirmed this outsider's first impression. Lange, "Recognizing the Public Domain," says: "Unfair competition theory no longer is confined to its legitimate original purpose, which was to prevent deception or confusion in the context of actual competition. Nor is it confined to its later, more doubtful task of preventing competitive misappropriation" (168); F. Cohen, "Transcendental Nonsense and the Functional Approach," 814, makes a similar point from the point of view of Legal Realism.

25. Miller and Davis, *Intellectual Property*, 164.

26. See Saussure, *Course in General Linguistics*, 113–14. For a good introduction, see Hawkes, *Structuralism and Semiotics*.

27. Vandevelde, "The New Property," 329.

28. Ibid., 344.

29. Acheson, *Trade-Mark Advertising as an Investment*, 11.

30. Vandevelde, "The New Property," 347.

31. Ibid., 329.

32. Ibid., 330.

33. Booth v. Colgate-Palmolive, 362 F.Supp. 343 (S.D.N.Y. 1973), 345; There is also another important doctrinal issue at stake in both Sinatra and Booth relative to the concern about the monopoly on performance signs. What has become known as the Sears-Compco doctrine holds that the states cannot grant copyright protection in areas that federal copyright law has left unprotected (Sears, Roebuck & Co. v. Stiffel Co., 376 U.S. 225 [1964]; Compco Corp. v. Day-Brite Lighting, Inc., 376 U.S. 234 [1964]). While the difference between federal and state courts is significant for legal scholars, I will draw it into the picture only when it seems pertinent to my argument. Here I would say that in the light of my model of the double movement of restriction-circulation, the Sears-Compco doctrine is a swing to the more generous side, which leaves more cultural area in circulation.

34. Sinatra, 713.

35. Musicians call this disappearance of the performance the "sandcastle syndrome." It produces the need to "re-create" sound patterns in every performance. Thanks to Nancy Monsman for this insight and other help with this section.

36. Durand, "The Disposition of the Voice," 100.

37. Barthes, *Image/Music/Text*, 179–89.

38. Kristeva, "On the Melancholic Imaginary," asks the question we all ask:

"Presuming that affect is the most archaic inscription of internal and external events, how does one get from there to signs?" (8). In answering her own question, she takes us back to where we were when we started: "Affect is not conveyed by language; or, more precisely, when referred to in language, the affect is not bound to it as is the idea" (13).

39. Gorbman, *Unheard Melodies*.

40. Ibid., 60.

41. Psychoacoustics relies upon voice "printouts," or "pictures" of wave-forms. I think the question of the comparison between the "voiceprint" and the photograph's light trace on celluloid is still an open one. See Hodges, ed., *Handbook of Music Psychology*.

42. Ibid., 71.

43. Doane, "Ideology and the Practice of Sound Editing and Mixing," 48–49.

44. Durand, "The Disposition of the Voice," 103.

45. A. Williams, "Godard's Use of Sound," 322, derives this by analogy with Paul Willemen's "profilmic event," the event before the camera. For an ideological analysis of the technology of the microphone, see Altman, "The Technology of the Voice."

46. Crissel, *Understanding Radio*, 3. The notion of the "blindness" of radio (and its virtues) is originally from Arnheim, *Radio*.

47. Act of 3 Feb. 1831, ch. 16, 4 Stat. 436.

48. Act of 18 Aug. 1856, ch. 169, 11 Stat. 138.

49. Act of 4 Mar. 1909, which came to be known as the "Copyright Act." This act and the amendments to it were codified as Title 17 of the U.S. Code in 1947 under "Copyrights."

50. Sound Recording Act of 1971.

51. 17 U.S.C.A., sec. 114(b) (1976). For further discussion of the contemporary situation regarding "performance" for profit, which gives it some historical perspective, see Morgan, "Sound Recording Copyright Law."

52. Lardner, *Fast Forward*, 214; Sony Corporation of America v. Universal City Studios, Inc., 464 U.S. 417, 104 S. Ct. 744, 78 L. Ed. 2d 574 (1984).

53. Armes, "Entendre, C'est Comprendre," 11, says that we should begin our analysis of contemporary mass-produced entertainment with the videocassette recording as "the crucial device." In this article he also argues that we would make the transition from film theory to video more easily if we were to look at the history of sound tape, which not only gives us a paternity for videotape but transformed motion picture technology in ways we have yet to consider.

54. Lipman, *The Electronic Pirates*, 36–37.

55. Ibid., 37.

56. 17 U.S.C.A., sec. 101(a), defines fixation:

> A work is "fixed" in a tangible medium of expression when the embodiment in a copy of phonorecord, by or under the authority of the author, is sufficiently permanent or stable to permit it to be perceived, re-

produced, or otherwise communicated for a period of more than transitory duration. A work consisting of sounds, images, or both, that are being transmitted, is "fixed" for purposes of this title if a fixation of the work is being made simultaneously with its transmission.

57. See Lukács, *History and Class Consciousness*, for this concept.
58. Abrams, "The Historic Foundations of American Copyright Law," says that the "common law copyright" is a "misnomer since all ability to control the copying of a work—the essence of copyright—is lost upon publication. Without statutory protection, the author loses his or her exclusive rights to the work" (1133).
59. See, for example, California Civil Code, sec. 990 (n).
60. Booth v. Colgate-Palmolive, 345.
61. Gelatt, *The Fabulous Phonograph*, 137, 143; Gelatt reports that Caruso's royalties from the Victor recordings were $2 million.
62. Adorno, "A Social Critique of Radio Music," 211.
63. Adorno, *Aesthetic Theory*, 83.
64. Gardella v. Log Cabin Products, Inc., 89 F.2d 871 (2d Cir. 1937).
65. Silverman, *The Acoustic Mirror*, 44.
66. Lawrence, "The Pleasures of Echo," 8.
67. Eisler, *Composing for the Films*, 20.
68. Ibid., 21.
69. Ellis, *Visible Fictions*.
70. Altman, "Television/Sound," 50.
71. Ellis, *Visible Fictions*, 158.
72. Altman, "MOVING LIPS," 74.
73. Altman, "Television/Sound," 50.
74. Barthes, *The Responsibility of Forms*, 259.
75. Grossberg, "'I'd Rather Feel Bad Than Not Feel Anything at All,'" 102.
76. Guattari, *Molecular Revolution*, as quoted in ibid.
77. Goldstein and Kessler, "The Twilight Zone," 822, say that allowing "imitation" has been an attempt to deal with the problem of potential monopolies.
78. White-Smith Music Co. v. Apollo Co., 209 U.S. 1, 28 S. Ct. 319, 52 L. Ed. 655 (1908). For an important discussion of the ambiguity of the legal definition of "copying" as seen in White-Smith and Harper Bros. v. Kalem, a parallel case relevant to the issue of motion picture "copying," see Porter, "Copyright: The New Protectionism." J. T. Allen, "The Industrialization of Culture," situates the player piano in relation to changes in American leisure activity and daily life produced by industrialization.
79. White-Smith v. Apollo, as quoted in Nimmer, *Cases and Materials on Entertainment Litigation*, 200.
80. Ferris v. Frohman, 223 U.S. 424 (1912), describes the phonorecord as a "captured performance."
81. Levin, "The Acoustic Dimension," 55–58, is the best overview and analysis

of the errors of theorists of the image as they have (tardily) turned their attention to sound.

82. Baudry, "The Apparatus," 110.

83. Williams, "Is Sound Recording Like a Language?" in one of the most succinct and useful critiques of the notion of "sound reproduction" says:

> Microphones being more like ears than they are like rooms (they function as points and not as volume), it is never the literal, original "sound" that is reproduced in recording, but one perspective on it, a *sample*, a *reading* of it. . . . The notion of sound recording as *reproduction* and not *representation* would have us believe that sound, a three-dimensional event . . . is turned into a three-dimensional event in another medium (electricity or impressions on wax, versus air), then recreated as still another three-dimensional event in the original medium (but not necessarily the original acoustic environment) and all this without loss of essence or "aura." (53–54)

84. More work needs to be done to consider the correspondence between copyright's fixed/unfixed dichotomy and the hierarchy within the art world seemingly based upon the relative substantiality of the "work." Choreography, for instance, because it is regarded as "unfixed," is protected under theories of state common law copyright, but federal law does not include dances in its list of copyrightable "works." Choreographic works recorded on videotape, however, can be registered.

85. Goodwin, "Sample and Hold," 257. Goodwin's discussion implies that new technologies that could challenge Romantic notions of authorship and originality may get reinflected as "authentic," as happened to the analogue synthesizer, which was once understood as an alienating music production technology (269).

86. Welsh, "Writing and Copying in the Age of Steam," 37, finds this insight in Charles Babbage, *On the Economy of Machinery and Manufactures* (1835), in the chapter "Of Copying."

87. R. Williams, *The Sociology of Culture*, 184; Frow, "Repetition and Limitation," 6, says that the difference between the work and the copy is positional.

88. Tushnet, "Critical Legal Studies and Constitutional Law," remarks in his analysis of the politics of U.S. Supreme Court opinions: "Saying that the Court lied about the facts is an irrelevant observation, for the facts don't matter much, except insofar as one must bow in their direction to satisfy certain retrograde cultural perceptions about what courts do. The courts must await a case with real facts before they can act, but once a case is in hand they are free to use it, and to construct its facts, for the policy goals they wish to advance" (634).

89. Cain and Hunt, *Marx and Engels on Law*, 65.

90. There is another way of understanding the court's decision in White-Smith, but it is not central to my argument. One reason for leaving the status of

sound software unclear, that is, defining piano rolls as neither works them-selves nor copies of works, becomes more clear when we consider the phonorecord, heir to the legal construction of the piano roll. The question for composers whose works were embodied in phonorecords became this: Did storing the work in this new form constitute a publication of the underlying music composition or did the work remain in an unpublished state still protected by a common law copyright? Leaving the work un-published gave the composer two advantages: He still held the composition in perpetuity, and he could authorize a sound recording. Making a sound recording, then, was analogous to having a band, an orchestra, or a singer perform the work. Tape recording a jam session produced an unfixed (un-published) performance, meaning that composers retained performance rights and that they weren't legally bound to let others reproduce their music for compulsory royalty fees. Let me bring this up to date. The 1976 Copy-right Act took away the monopoly in perpetuity, which a composer had enjoyed under common law, producing the change by shifting the terms of the unfixed-fixed dichotomy. Now both the sound recording and the musical composition stored in it are fixed (published) works.

91. White-Smith v. Apollo, as quoted in Nimmer, *Cases and Materials on Enter-tainment Litigation*, 201.

92. Whale and Phillips, *Whale on Copyright*, 35.

93. For discussion of "style" as a kind of secret code apprehended by gay and lesbian subcultures, see Feuer, "Reading *Dynasty*," and my "The QUEEN CHRISTINA Tie-ups."

94. Homburg, *Legal Rights of Performing Artists*, 14.

95. Ibid., 78.

96. The 1976 Copyright Act (17 U.S.C.A., sec. 114 [d]) makes provision for a report on the pros and cons of performance rights solicited from representa-tives of both labor and management in the entertainment industry. How-ever, legal commentators who follow these developments report that broad-casters (who are concerned that multiple royalty payments to performers would make broadcasting costs prohibitive for them) have blocked legisla-tion that might institute such protection in the U.S. See D'Onofrio, "In Support of Performance Rights in Sound Recordings," 169. See chap. 1, n. 86, and chap. 2, n. 43, for an update on the U.S. position regarding the artists' rights in light of the 1988 Berne Convention hearings.

97. Midler v. Ford Motor Co., 849 F.2d 460 (1988).

98. Hodgson, "Intellectual Property," 569.

99. Nimmer and Nimmer, *Nimmer on Copyright*, 1:sec. 3.01.

100. Levine, "The Right of Publicity as a Means of Protecting Performers' Style," 142.

101. Davis v. Trans World Airlines, 297 F.Supp. 1145 (1969).

102. Sinatra, 913.

103. Homburg, *Legal Rights of Performing Artists*, 39, explains that in German law the artist who performs a work is treated as its "reviser" or adapter.

104. Bennett, "Texts, Readers, and Reading Formations," 3. See also Bennett and Woollacott, *Bond and Beyond*, 55.

105. Barthes, *The Responsibility of Forms*, 283.

106. Ibid., 255.

107. Barthes, *Image/Music/Text*, says, "The 'grain' is the body in the voice as it sings, the hand as it writes, the limb as it performs" (188).

108. Marofloti, *Caruso's Method of Vocal Production*.

109. Barthes, *The Responsibility of Forms*, 307.

110. Ibid., 259, 308.

111. Two of the most interesting and controversial musical plagiarism cases are Selle v. Gibb, 741 F.2d 896 (1984) ("How Deep Is Your Love"), and Bright Tunes Music Corp. v. Harrisongs Music, Ltd., 420 F.Supp. 177 (1976) ("My Sweet Lord").

112. Metzger, "Name That Tune," 151.

113. Semiotically, it would seem that the opposite would be true. In cases of literary plagiarism, for instance, the issues often revolve around the similarity of "ideas" versus the dissimilarity of "expression." This situation can become quite complicated if, for instance, one considers two similar narrative "ideas," which find form in a theatrical as opposed to a novelistic "expression." One could think of it as the semiotic problem of separating the contents from the expression plane. Then one could argue that if a comparison of two similar musical compositions did not deal with "ideas" and thus was restricted to the expression plane only—to musicological elements—a court could make a relatively scientific determination about similarity. Here I am thinking of the semiotic model devised by Scandinavian Louis Hjelmslev in the forties (Eco, *A Theory of Semiotics*, 55–56). The case that could become the model for the use of the ideas/expression dichotomy in musical plagiarism cases, however, dealt with the similarity of iconic signs. The question was whether the mise-en-scène of the "McDonaldland" commercials infringed the copyright of the "H. R. Pufnstuf" television cartoon program (Sid & Marty Krofft Television Productions, Inc. v. McDonald's Corp., 562 F.2d 1157 [1977]). See Hughes, "The Philosophy of Intellectual Property," 310–14, for a good analysis of the ideas/expression distinction.

114. It is not really enough here to consider "style" without making a distinction between a style of musical playing and a style of singing or acting. The issue of the protectability of instrumentation style and musical arrangement has arisen in the Glenn Miller and Artie Shaw cases, where orchestras not conducted by either Miller or Shaw performed renditions of the popular band leaders' musical work and recorded these performances. In Miller v. Universal Pictures (214 N.Y.S.2d 645 [1960]), the studio sold record albums of *The Glenn Miller Story* sound track with the studio orchestra playing Miller's hit songs in the manner he popularized. The case was dismissed for other reasons, but the fact that the dissent argued that Miller's widow had no "property right" in the "Glenn Miller sound" is frequently cited in entertainment law commentary. Shaw v. Time-Life (38 N.Y.2d 210 [1975]) is slightly

different from *Miller* in that *Reader's Digest* had an orchestra play Shaw's arrangements instead of re-recording the original recordings, and consequently Shaw sued for unfair competition and palming off. The judge decided in favor of Time-Life, again on the basis that there was no "property interest" in sound arrangements (see McCarthy, *Rights of Publicity and Privacy*, 4.85, and Nimmer and Nimmer, *Nimmer on Copyright*, 1:sec. 2.05, for criticism of *Shaw*, which Nimmer considers incorrect).

115. Levine, "The Right of Publicity as a Means of Protecting Performers' Style," 114, asks why Sinatra's or Booth's voices couldn't have been understood as distinctive characterizations, and thus why they wouldn't follow Chaplin v. Amador (93 Cal.App. 358 [1928]), in which actor Charles Chaplin successfully asserted the right to his character and won a judgment against an imitator. In Chaplin, all of the signs of performance—from use of costume, facial expression, mannerisms, and body movement—were credited to the originator, and the look-alike Amador was said to have been "counterfeiting" the Charlie role. Significantly, it was not found that Chaplin had a property in the character, only that the imitator, in passing himself off, was "likely to deceive." Levine also suggests that in sound-alike and look-alike cases the "ordinary observer" test could be applied (148). Duggan, "A Cause of Action for Simulation of Sound Recordings? Yes!" 157, argues that audience "recognition" of a sound-alike is a solid basis for arguing "secondary meaning" and "passing off."

116. David Laing, *Buddy Holly* (London: Studio Vista, 1971), as quoted in Frith, *Music for Pleasure*, 122.

117. Frith, *Music for Pleasure*, 120.

118. Boggs, "The Blues Tradition from Poetic Revolt to Cultural Impasse," 281. The best analysis of rock music in its historical context is Gilroy, *There Ain't No Black in the Union Jack*, chap. 5.

119. One might say that the description of Sinatra's new sound on the originally released album is a translation of her singing style into a kind of poetry: "A young fragile living thing, on its own in a wondrous-wicked-woundup-wasted-wild-worried-wised-up-warmbodied world. On her own. Earning her daily crepes and Cokes by singing the facts of love. Her voice tells as much as her songs. No faked up grandure, her voice is like it is: a little tired, little put down, a lot loving" (cover copy compliments of Larry Grossberg).

120. This is a good example of how the law will analogize and borrow freely. Although sec. 990(b) of the California Civil Code *does* pertain only to the deceased, the point is that the court in Midler is willing to consider rights to voice and likeness as "property rights" because the concept is recognized as of 1985 under state law.

121. Midler, 143.

122. Legal commentary often cites Motschenbacher v. R. J. Reynolds Tobacco Company, 498 F.2d 821 (1974), as the case that marks the common law recognition of a right of publicity. It is interesting to us as a contrast with Onassis and Midler. Although famous race car driver Motschenbacher was

the actual referent in the television commercial for Winston cigarettes, he was not recognizable in the videotape clip. However, the court ruled that he was identifiable by the distinctive insignia on his car. His privacy was not invaded, but his signs were appropriated.

123. Generally, rights in the work produced are assigned to other entities by means of a contract within which the terms of ownership are worked out. If the second party is an employer, that entity may become legal author of the performer's work, unless the contract states otherwise.

CHAPTER 5. READING STAR CONTRACTS

1. "Opinion and Award of Arbitrator: Arbitration between Screen Actors Guild and Producers," 28 June 1986 (unpublished arbitration proceeding), 16 (hereafter SAG Arbitration).

2. 1960 Screen Actors Guild Television Agreement, sec. 10(a), as quoted in SAG Arbitration, 12.

3. Ibid., 15.

4. Ibid., 5.

5. Ibid., 16.

6. SAG Agreement, sec. 22(a), as quoted in SAG Arbitration, 18.

7. Ibid., 8.

8. Ibid., 9.

9. Ibid., 21.

10. Youngman, "Negotiation of Personal Service Contracts," 8, explains how sec. 3005 of the U.S. Labor Code holds that any kind of employee can be discharged for "misconduct"; an interesting example of the use of the force majeure clause in a star contract was the case in which Warner Brothers argued that the 1960 Writers Guild strike was such a casualty, which relieved the studio of the obligation to continue to keep actor James Garner on the payroll during a layoff on the television show "Maverick." Garner's suit is the story of one actor's battle with the studio over his attempt to get out of a studio term contract (Warner Bros. Pictures, Inc. v. James Bumgarner, 17 Cal. Rptr. 171 [1961]). For background on this case and some of the insight it gives us into the economics of the transition from motion pictures to television in relation to labor issues, see Strait, *James Garner*, 140–65.

11. Griffith, *The Talkies*, xvii.

12. See chap. 1, n. 112, on the "private" person; Dyer, "*A Star Is Born*," says something about the star inside and outside of the text and the elusiveness of the star/person relation:

> To say that stars exist outside of the media texts in real life would be misleading, but stars are carried in the person of people who do go on living away from their appearances in the media, and the point is that we know this. When he got home John Wayne may have become Marion Morrison again, but there was a real human being with a continuous

existence, that is, who existed in between all the times he was "being" John Wayne. But there is no way in which Elizabeth Bennett can leave the pages of *Pride and Prejudice*. (16)

13. Chaneles, *Collecting Movie Memorabilia*, 117. In March 1990, a restaurateur in Toronto reported that an original film contract signed by Marilyn Monroe from around the time of *Some Like It Hot* (1959) had been stolen from the wall of his establishment. Although he had paid $8,000 for the signature two years earlier, he estimated that it was now worth two times as much and was offering a $2,000 reward.

14. Wilkinson, "Crazy Contracts," 30–31, 60–62.

15. Ellis, "Star/Industry/Image," 3, refers to the "ordinary and extraordinary paradox." The concept was really formulated by Dyer, in *Stars*, 49, when he refers to the "star-as-ordinary" and the "star-as-special" as an "ambiguity," "paradox," and "contradiction." For a more current statement of this, see Dyer on Judy Garland's "special relation to ordinariness," *Heavenly Bodies*, 156–59; Morin, *The Stars*, 141.

16. See Dyer, *Stars*, 30, on the way stars "effect a 'magic' reconciliation of incompatible terms."

17. Wilkinson, "Crazy Contracts," 30.

18. Ibid.

19. Ibid., 61.

20. Ibid. See King, "The Hollywood Star System," 281, for further on the way the preservation of assets was written into star contracts.

21. Wilkinson, "Crazy Contracts," 61.

22. Clark, "Actors' Labor and the Politics of Subjectivity," 159.

23. Kindem, "Hollywood's Movie Star System," 14; Paul A. Samuelson, *Economics*, and Sidney R. Finkle and Vincent J. Tarascio, *Wage Employment Theory* (New York: Ronald Press, 1971), as quoted in Kindem, "Hollywood's Movie Star System."

24. Kindem, "Hollywood's Movie Star System," 15; Clark, "Actors' Labor and the Politics of Subjectivity," asks these important questions about the issue of class: "Would one address class divisions between actors and studio executives, between actors and spectators, or among the actors themselves? Assuming that class fractions could be identified, is the problematic position of actors within the film industry best characterized as a conflict of class?" (79).

25. King, "The Star and the Commodity," 152.

26. Balio, "Stars in Business," 157–62, discusses Mary Pickford's 1916 contract within which Adoph Zukor allowed her 50 percent of the profits on her films and in addition set up a separate unit, the Pickford Film Corporation. He compares the details of her contract, which made her the first star to produce her own films, with those of Jimmy Cagney's best contract with Warner Brothers, which gave him only 10 percent of the box office gross in 1938.

27. Clark, "Actors' Labor and the Politics of Subjectivity," 146.

28. Ibid., 154; Prindle, *The Politics of Glamour*, 22.

29. Prindle, *The Politics of Glamour*, 28.

30. Until the publication of Prindle's history, the only book-length history was Ross, *Stars and Strikes*. On the stratification of the union, see Kindem, "Hollywood's Movie Star System," 19.

31. Clark, "Actors' Labor and the Politics of Subjectivity," 219.

32. The decrees to which the five major studios (Paramount, RKO, Warner Brothers, Twentieth-Century Fox, and MGM) finally agreed after losing the important antitrust suit to the government (United States v. Paramount Pictures, Inc., 344 U.S. 131 [1948]), provided for the prohibition of unfair trade practices in the area of distribution, as well as a reorganization of company holdings. While the decrees *did* significantly restructure the entire industry, other factors were also involved in the transformation, among them, certainly, the end of World War II and the evolution of television. For a concise account of these changes, see Conant, "The Paramount Decrees Reconsidered." This article is essentially an update of his earlier work, *Antitrust in the Motion Picture Industry*.

33. Prindle, *The Politics of Glamour*, 72; Mann, "The Spectacularization of Everyday Life," says that in this period, "star names were reconstituted as 'property' to be administered primarily by the celebrity rather than by the studio or network" (52).

34. Kindem, "Hollywood's Movie Star System," 15.

35. SAG Arbitration, 9.

36. Boddy, "The Studios Move into Prime Time," 27.

37. Ibid.

38. Ibid., 32; Sinclair, "Should Hollywood Get It for Free?" 31, criticizes this kind of programming for being nothing more than "straight commercials."

39. Barnouw, *Tube of Plenty*, 195.

40. Boddy, "The Studios Move into Prime Time," 30.

41. Braverman, *Labor and Monopoly Capital*, chap. 4; see Kindem, "Hollywood's Movie Star System," 15.

42. See Schatz, *The Genius of the System*, 62–63, for background on the Warner Brothers structure during this period.

43. Yeck, "De Havilland vs. Warner Brothers."

44. De Havilland v. Warner Bros. Pictures, 67 C.A.2d 225 (1944).

45. See R. C. Allen, "'The Guiding Light,'" 322, for reference to how contemporary television serials get around this problem by distributing the dramatic emphasis in such a way that the program cannot be affected by the fate of a single character.

46. Zimmerman, "Exclusivity of Personal Services," 73.

47. Warner Brothers Pictures, Inc. v. Nelson, 1 K.B. 209 (1936).

48. Behlmer, ed., *Inside Warner Brothers*, 16, 28; Schatz, *The Genius of the System*, 218–20. It is clear that control as much as studio finance was an issue here, since to some degree star vehicles produced by different studios on loan-outs were always in competition with each other. In the case of legal loan-outs, however, the studio was always compensated by the producer who bor-

rowed the talent. Although it was common practice for studios to loan out actors, Warner Brothers loaned out Davis only once—to Samuel Goldwyn for *The Little Foxes* (1941) in exchange for Gary Cooper, who was to star in *Sergeant York*.

49. See chap. 1, n. 70.

50. Gabel and Feinman, "Contract Law as Ideology," 177, explain that fairness was originally a concern of Anglo-American courts in the eighteenth century; Bloch, *Natural Law and Human Dignity*, 190, says that the bourgeois contract has historically been based on the Roman *pactum*, law of the creditor. The *pactum*, however, was predated by the concept of *pax*, the agreement to abandon grievances.

51. Warner Brothers v. Nelson, 211.

52. Bloch, *Natural Law and Human Dignity*, in reference to the magical nature of the contract, suggests that it is condensed in the fairy tale within which the bargain is either richly rewarding or fatal, especially if it is a "pact made with the devil," as in the Rumpelstiltskin story. See also Mensch, "Freedom of Contract as Ideology," 760, for a discussion of the contradiction between coercion and freedom in the contemporary contract. The classical contract masked this internal inconsistency with the image of the contract agreement as a magical moment when free wills appeared to create a new right (which then had to be enforced in order to protect free will).

53. Pashukanis, *Law and Marxism*, 127.

54. The classic definition of commodity fetishism is this: "The mysterious character of the commodity-form consists therefore simply in the fact that the commodity reflects the social characteristics of men's own labor as objective characteristics of the products of labor themselves, as the socio-natural properties of these things." In reference to religion, Marx goes on: "There the products of the human brain appear as autonomous figures endowed with a life of their own, which enter into relations both with each other and with the human race. I call this the *fetishism* which attaches itself to the products of labour as soon as they are produced as commodities . . . this fetishism arises from the peculiar social character of the labor which produces them" (Marx, *Capital*, 1:164–65). For one of the best applications of Marx's concept of fetishism (in addition to a comparison with Freud's concept), see L. Williams, *Hard Core*, chap. 4.

55. Lugosi v. Universal Pictures, 25 Cal.3d 813 (1979), 331, took up this issue in regard to the proprietorship of Bela Lugosi's image of the character Dracula. The judge cited the U.S. Labor Code, sec. 2860, to the effect that everything that an employee "acquires" within the terms of his employment belongs to the employer. In support of the argument that Lugosi's creative product belonged to Universal Studios, the judge cited Famous Players-Lasky Corp. v. Ewing, 49 Cal.App. 676 (1920), in which an earlier court ruled that the electrical lighting device invented by an electrician employed by the motion picture studio belonged to the employer.

56. See Youngman, "Negotiation of Personal Service Contracts," 7–8, for a basic description of the "grant of rights."

57. On the historic and economic importance of sound to Warner Brothers in particular, see Gomery, "Writing the History of the American Film Industry," and "The 'Warner-Vitaphone Peril.'"

58. Warner Brothers–Gretchen Young ("Loretta Young") Agreement, 11 April 1927, 2 (Loretta Young personnel file, Warner Brothers Collection, University of Southern California Archive of the Performing Arts, hereafter WB/USC).

59. Warner Brothers–Gretchen Young Agreement, 23 May 1930, 3 (Young file, WB/USC). Also important here is the stipulation regarding both body doubles and voice doubles. One of the most productive discussions of the phenomenon of dubbing and standing in from a materialist point of view, which theorizes this *bricolage* in relation to the actor's craft, is King, "The Hollywood Star System," 268–73.

60. King, "The Hollywood Star System," 3. Around this time, the studios had begun to buy music publishing and recording businesses. MGM bought Robbins Music Corp., Fox acquired DeSylva, Paramount began the Famous Music Corporation, and Warner Bros. bought Witmarks, Inc. (Neale, *Cinema and Technology*, 80).

61. See Anson, "A Licensing Retrospective and Glimpse into the Future," 4.

62. The program for "Licensing 89," the Ninth Annual Licensing and Merchandising Conference and Exposition held 13–15 June 1989 at the Jacob Javits Center in New York, states that the industry now does a yearly $55 million in sales; Battersby and Grimes, "The Year in Merchandising Law," 4–7, say that 1985 was a significant year for the merchandising and licensing industry. As the authors of *The Law of Merchandise and Character Licensing*, Battersby and Grimes attribute the new viability of licensing and the health of the industry to the enactment of the Trademark and Counterfeiting Act of 1984. Here, the U.S. Congress gave owners of registered trademarks more power against counterfeiters than they had previously had under the 1946 Lanham Act. Others point to the success of the E.T. and STAR WARS licensing programs ("Maggie Young—the 'Force' at Lucasfilm"; "Les Borden—Columbia's Dealmaker"). See also Gustafson, "'What's Happening to Our Pix Biz?'" on the conglomerate of which the Licensing Corporation of America is a part. Today, Warner's Licensing Corporation of America handles the licensing for Superman, Bugs Bunny, and "Dynasty," as well as some of the old MGM properties such as the Wizard of Oz characters.

63. "Pete Smith—Mickey's Mentor." See Schickel, *The Disney Version*, 135–39, for an account of Disney merchandising worldwide as well as one of the earliest criticisms of the Disney philosophy.

64. Lester and Lester, *The Shirley Temple Story*, 62–63.

65. In Agreement between Loew's and Godette Products, Newark, New Jersey (13 February 1941), the licensee (Godette) agrees to pay the licensor

(Loew's/MGM) a two-and-one-half-cent royalty on every hair bow sold "up to and including 25 cents retail" on bows that sold for five and ten cents apiece. Other arrangements for *Ziegfeld Girl* included those with Ostby & Barton Co., makers of "premium jewelry," Uniform Guild, Inc., manufacturers of "uniforms for beauticians, manicurists, salesladies, waitresses, factory workers, fountain attendants, nurses, maids, clerks, etc.," and Louis Herman & Co., makers of women's and ladies' rayon and silk slips. Correspondence to MGM from R. Gross, Flatto Ribbon Co. (25 April 1941), notes that the manufacturer has seen the images of Judy Garland, Hedy Lamarr, and Lana Turner on counters in S. S. Kresge promoting the Godette bows, and he asks if the studio would be interested in a similar arrangement with Flatto Ribbon; telegram from Prinzmetal to Irwin (5 February 1941) asks if they have the right to use the name and likeness of the stars in addition to feature players and twelve models on tie-ups for *Ziegfeld Girl*, either on a royalty arrangement or for regular advertising (Metro-Goldwyn-Mayer Collection, Academy of Motion Pictures Arts and Sciences). Thanks to Sam Gill for rescuing this material.

66. Stallings and Mandelbaum, "Moonlighting with the Stars."
67. Martin, "Those Ad Endorsements," 86.
68. Marchand, *Advertising the American Dream*, 96.
69. Resor, "Personalities and the Public," 2–3.
70. Marchand, *Advertising the American Dream*, 97.
71. Jones, "Celebrity Endorsements," 525–26.
72. Ibid., 529, 533.
73. Freedland, *Fred Astaire*, 110.
74. *Photoplay*, May 1933, 81; R. J. Obringer (WB Head Office, Burbank) to Morris Ebenstein (WB Publicity, New York), 20 April 1933; George H. Thomas (WB New York) to Obringer, 26 April 1933; Obringer to Frank Joyce (Francis's attorney), 27 April 1933; Obringer to Ebenstein, 27 April 1933; Obringer to Ralph Lewis (Freston and Files, WB attorneys), 27 April 1933 (Kay Francis personnel file, WB/USC).
75. R. J. Obringer to Ralph Lewis, 18 March 1935; Lewis to Obringer, 20 March 1935; Obringer to Irving Nathanson (WB Legal Dept., New York), 21 March 1935; Obringer to Lewis, 19 April 1935; Lewis to Lucking, Van Auken, and Sprague (Detroit lawyers retained), 24 April 1935; Lewis to Obringer, 24 April 1935; Laurence Sprague to Lewis, 20 May 1935; Lewis to Obringer, 10 August 1935 (Francis file, WB/USC).
76. Warner Brothers–Bette Davis Agreement, 27 January 1949, 8, par. 8 (Bette Davis personnel file, WB/USC).
77. Ibid., 7 June 1943, 11, par. 14.
78. King, "The Hollywood Star System," 33, 363.
79. Ibid., 358.
80. Warner Brothers–Bette Davis Agreement, 27 January 1949, 8, par. 8 (Davis file, WB/USC).

81. Warner Brothers–Betty Bogart Agreement, 26 July 1945, 8, rider to par. 11 (Lauren Bacall personnel file, WB/USC).

82. Undated typescript (Bacall file, WB/USC).

83. Warner Brothers–Betty Bogart Agreement, 8 (Bacall file, WB/USC).

84. J. Walter Thompson–Betty Bogart signed release, 2 August 1946 (Bacall file, WB/USC).

85. Ibid., 3 February 1947 (Bacall file, WB/USC).

86. See chap. 1, n. 117.

87. Warner Brothers–Bette Davis Agreement, 7 June 1943, 9b, par. 11 (Davis file, WB/USC).

88. Ibid., 27 January 1929, 9, par. 8 (Davis file, WB/USC).

89. Memo to J. L. Warner from Alex Evelove (Warner Brothers Legal Dept.), 26 April 1944; Warner Brothers–Joan Crawford Agreement, 20 May 1947, 9, rider to par. 8 (Joan Crawford personnel file, WB/USC).

90. King, "The Hollywood Star System," 338–41.

91. Memo to R. J. Obringer from Sam Clark, 3 March 1950; Warner Brothers–Joan Crawford Agreement, 11 December 1950, 11, par. 8 (Crawford file, WB/USC).

92. Rogers v. Republic Pictures, 104 F.Supp. 328 (1952).

93. Ibid., 333. Fifty years later, the commercialization had grown into the Roy Rogers fast food franchise owned by the Marriott Corporation along with Hot Shoppes and Big Boy. But this may be the end of the line for the "Roy Rogers" name as a commodity. Early in 1990, Marriott announced plans to sell the chain to Hardee's, which will in turn take up a name change with owners of the franchises (*Washington Post*, 31 January 1990, sec. A, 1, col. 3).

94. Rogers v. Republic, 335.

95. Ibid., 331.

96. Ibid., 334.

97. Ibid.

98. Ibid., 341.

99. Ibid., 342.

100. Ibid., 354.

101. Ibid., 355–56.

102. Ibid., 356.

103. Ibid., 357.

104. Bennett and Woollacott, *Bond and Beyond*, 232.

105. Rogers v. Republic, 332.

106. Ibid., 356.

107. Ibid., 354.

108. Ibid., 353.

109. Ibid., 355.

110. Ibid.

111. Ibid., 337.

112. Elber et al., "An Agreement with a Performer," 21–22.

113. Republic Pictures Corp. v. Rogers, 213 F.2d 662 (9th Cir. 1954) pet. for recall mandate denied, 222 F.2d 950 (9th Cir. 1955), 666.

114. Autry v. Republic Productions, Inc. 104 F.Supp. 918 (1952), 921.

115. Ibid., 922.

116. Ibid., 924.

117. Autry v. Republic Productions, Inc., 213 F.2d 662 (1954), 670.

118. Ibid., 669.

119. Viera, "The Law of Star Images," 160.

120. P. D. Knecht (WB Burbank) to Harold Berkowitz (WB New York), 15 August 1958 (Publicity Files, Warner Brothers Archive, Princeton University Theatre Collection), hereafter WB/Pr.

121. Boddy, "The Studios Move into Prime Time," 30.

122. Ibid. See chap. 4, n. 19, for statistics on Universal's profits from merchandising on *Jaws* and *Jaws* 2. While I would argue that profits from merchandising have never compared favorably with box office receipts or advertising revenue in motion picture and television entertainment history, in the late seventies one finds a new argument for seeing "spin-offs" as a source of income. See Blum, "Merchandising a Theatrical Motion Picture."

123. In 1934, MGM's animal supplier, Goebel's Lion Farm, wanted to use the phrase "Home of M-G-M's Leo the Lion" on ashtrays sold at the farm. The MGM lawyer advised signing a nonexclusive license that could be revoked at any time (F. L. Henderson to Asher, 13 November 1934; F. L. Henderson to Asher, 19 November 1934; David Shattuck to Henderson, 27 November 1934); (Goebel's Lion Farm file, MGM/AMPAS). See M. C. Miller, "Hollywood," for a discussion of the way product placement works today through middlemen who look for chances to place clients' products as props; Litwak, *Reel Power*, 243, also discusses product placement; see also *The Hollywood Reporter*, 2 June 1987, for an entire issue devoted to product placement and merchandising.

124. Memo to H. E. Holman from Bryan S. Moore, 14 January 1958, 3 (Publicity files, WB/Pr). With television, the studio also began to divide merchandising rights three ways, so that on the original "Maverick" merchandising contract, for instance, the revenue from sales of comic books, puzzles, hats, and playsuits was split among ABC, Kaiser, and Warner Brothers, with ABC functioning as licensing agent (American Broadcasting Company Merchandising, Inc.–Warner Brothers Pictures, Inc., Licensing Agreement, 29 January 1958 [Publicity files, WB/Pr]).

125. Knecht to Berkowitz, 15 August 1958 (Publicity files, WB/Pr).

126. Rand Marlis, president, Creative Licensing Corp., interview with author, Los Angeles, California, 4 April 1987.

127. L. A. Thompson, "The Prime Time Crime."

128. Davidson, "Crackup in Hazzard County!"

129. L. A. Thompson, "The Prime Time Crime."

130. See n. 6.

CHAPTER 6. *DRACULA* AND THE RIGHT
OF PUBLICITY

1. Lugosi v. Universal Pictures, Inc., 172 U.S.P.Q. 541, 551 (1972), rev'd, 70 Cal.App. 3d 552, 139 Cal. Rptr. 35 (1977), aff'd, 25 Cal.3d 813, 603 P.2d 425, 160 Cal. Rptr. 323 (1979), 329.
2. Ibid., 333.
3. Lenning, *The Count*, 317.
4. Lugosi v. Universal Pictures, 333.
5. Ibid., 334.
6. Prosser, *Law of Torts*, chap. 20.
7. Roberson v. Rochester Folding Box (1902), O'Brien v. Pabst (1941), Gautier v. Pro-Football (1952), Haelan Laboratories v. Topps Chewing Gum (1954).
8. On French law, see Wagner, "The Right to One's Own Likeness in French Law," which explains that the personal right one has in one's likeness has the same philosophical origins as the authorial right in the work. On English law, see McCarthy, *The Rights of Publicity and Privacy*, 6.21–22.
9. Ibid., sec. 1.4.
10. Warren, "The Right to Privacy." Although the legal commentary on the right of privacy refers to this article as authored by both Warren and Louis D. Brandeis, only Warren is listed as author in the original.
11. McCarthy, *The Rights of Publicity and Privacy*, 1.11–12.
12. Barron, "Warren and Brandeis," 921, concludes that the best explanation is that this article is a reflection of elitist Republican Mugwumpery and the view that that tight group held of the press in the late nineteenth century.
13. Dworkin, *Taking Rights Seriously*, 119.
14. Warren, "The Right to Privacy," 197.
15. Kalven, "Privacy in Tort Law," 329.
16. R. Williams, *Keywords*, 204.
17. Ibid. For another view of the relation between the history of a twentieth-century notion of personhood and privacy doctrine, see Hixon, *Privacy in a Public Society*, chap. 7.
18. Prosser, "Privacy."
19. Friedman, *A History of American Law*, 18.
20. Nimmer, *Cases and Materials on Entertainment Litigation*, 832.
21. Fish, "Working on the Chain Gang," 558.
22. Nimmer, "The Right of Publicity." Nimmer wrote this article while he was employed as a lawyer for Paramount Pictures, where he had gone to work after his 1950 graduation from Harvard Law School. After six years in the studio's legal department, he went into private practice, where he had a chance to try out his theory of the right of publicity by defending client Kenneth Strickler. In *Strickler v. National Broadcasting Co.*, 167 F.Supp. 68 (S.D. Cal. 1958), Nimmer argued that NBC had appropriated his client's

right of publicity by casting him as a character in a television drama based on an airplane crash and subsequent South Seas rescue. The California court did not recognize the right of publicity in 1958, but by the seventies it was clearly recognized in the state common law. Nimmer went on to join the UCLA Law School faculty in 1962, write the four-volume treatise *Nimmer on Copyright*, first published in 1963, and become, by the time of his death, one of the one hundred most powerful lawyers in the U.S. (Sobel, "A Memorial Tribute to Melville B. Nimmer").

23. Nimmer, "The Right of Publicity," 217; Nimmer, *Cases and Materials on Entertainment Litigation*, 852.

24. McCarthy, *The Rights of Publicity and Privacy*, 1–4.

25. Tushnet, "A Marxist Analysis," 103–4.

26. Macherey, *A Theory of Literary Production*, 99.

27. Adorno, *Aesthetic Theory*.

28. Hirst, *Law, Socialism, and Democracy*, 25, says that laws "*always* have an 'outside'" since they are subject to the transformation by the Supreme Court or the legislature; Dworkin, *Taking Rights Seriously*, says that although "'rules' may be changed overnight, 'principles' alter gradually" (40).

29. Kairys, "Legal Reasoning," 15–16.

30. Jackson, *Semiotics and Legal Theory*, says that one of the characteristics of judicial discourses is the way they will "purport to provide an account of their own production" (305).

31. Macherey, *A Theory of Literary Production*, 194.

32. Roberson v. Rochester Folding Box Co., 171 N.Y. 538, 64 N.E. 442 (1902); New York Civil Rights Law, secs. 50–51.

33. Barthes, *Image/Music/Text*, 32–51, introduced this concept into discussions of photographic form as a way of theorizing tense in the photograph; further embellishment of the concept in regard to the photograph can be found in Metz, "Photography and Fetish."

34. Maxine Martin v. F.I.Y. Theatre Co., Inc., 10 *Ohio Opinions* 340 (1938). Also in Paramount Pictures, Inc. v. Leader Press, Inc., 24 F.Supp. 338 (W.D. Okla. 1938), it was held that since Paramount stars had waived their right of privacy, Leader Press could produce advertising accessories bearing their names and likenesses.

35. O'Brien v. Pabst Sales Co., 124 F.2d 167 (5th Cir. 1941).

36. Dworkin, *Taking Rights Seriously*, 4.

37. King, "Articulating Stardom," 23.

38. Haelan Laboratories, Inc. v. Topps Chewing Gum, Inc., 202 F.2d 866 (2d Cir. 1953).

39. Ibid., 868.

40. Gordon, "Right of Property," 556.

41. Kennedy, "Legal Education as Training for Hierarchy," says that this discourse is "internally inconsistent, vacuous, or circular" (48); Hirst, *Law, Socialism, and Democracy*, says that "attempting to solve questions of divided interests in terms of rights can only lead to impossible contradictions" (15).

42. Nimmer, "The Right of Publicity"; Prosser, "Privacy"; Gordon, "Right of Property."
43. Haelan Labs, 868.
44. Ibid.
45. Lugosi v. Universal, 342.
46. Ibid., 325, explains that the novel *Dracula* (1897) has always been in the U.S. public domain because the author did not deposit a copy in compliance with copyright regulations here. Universal purchased motion picture rights from Florence Stoker as well as Hamilton Deane and John Balderston, authors of the play *Dracula* (1927). Although Universal Pictures has copyright in the motion picture *Dracula*, Count Dracula the character is in the public domain in the U.S.
47. McCarthy, *The Rights of Publicity and Privacy*, 1–6; Nimmer, "The Right of Publicity," quoting the dissent in O'Brien v. Pabst, has the following to say on this point:

> It is impractical to attempt to draw a line as to which persons have achieved the status of celebrity and which have not; it should rather be held that every person has the property right of publicity, but that the damages which a person may claim for infringement of the right will depend upon the value of the publicity appropriated which in turn will depend in great measure upon the degree of fame attained by the plaintiff. Thus, the right of publicity accorded to each individual "may have as much or little, or only a nominal value," but the right should be available to everyone. (217)

48. McCarthy, *The Rights of Publicity and Privacy*, 1–46.
49. Selz and Simensky, *Entertainment Law*, 1:9-24.
50. Price v. Hal Roach, 400 F.Supp. 836 (S.D.N.Y. 1975). The issue for entertainment law has to do with the viability of the analogy between "exploitation" and trademark law's "use" as opposed to abandonment (non-use). But in the popular press this issue gets rearticulated as a question of whether the deceased would have approved of the continued use of his or her image after death if the image had not been merchandised in the celebrity's lifetime. The "exploitation within the lifetime" issue as raised in the Laurel and Hardy as well as the Lugosi case, however, does not distinguish between studio-arranged promotion and the star's own self-merchandising. Examples of the difference between self-merchandising and studio-arranged promotion might be the difference between Roy Rogers (as discussed in chap. 5) and Marilyn Monroe, whose situation as a studio contract player is continually misunderstood. For instance, Grove, "Death Be Not Proud," 28, gives these examples of Monroe's having "actively merchandised" herself in her lifetime: House of Westmore Cosmetics, Lustre-Creme Shampoo, City Club Shoes, and Idaho potatoes. But to say that Monroe "actively merchandised" herself doesn't take account of the actress's position under the studio system. The Lustre-Creme and Westmore endorsements were standard endorsements the

star would be contractually obligated to do in conjunction with advertising for a forthcoming motion picture. The Idaho potatoes merchandising is probably a reference to the 1950 photograph of Monroe taken by Earl Theisen. At that time Monroe was a starlet under contract to Twentieth-Century Fox studios and posing for pinup photos was a condition of her employment. According to Dyer, *Star Dossier One*, 35, the "Miss Idaho Potato" photograph, featuring Monroe wearing nothing but a bag of Idaho potatoes, was taken as a publicity stunt, purportedly the studio's answer to a newspaper columnist's comment that she would even look good in a sack. Technically, then, it was the studio and not Monroe who "actively merchandised" the star, and although she may have participated in the exploitation as an enthusiastic model, she did not set up any kind of merchandising enterprise as Roy Rogers had done.

51. Spring, *Risks and Rights*, 244–45.

52. Frow, "Repetition and Limitation," 11, suggests that copyright law lends itself to rethinking in these terms, starting, for instance, with the way "originality" requires an expenditure of labor.

53. Baechlin, *Histoire économique du cinéma*, 64.

54. Morin, *The Stars*; Dyer, *Stars*.

55. Dyer, *Stars*, 68–69. While Dyer is responsible for suggesting that the star is constructed over a variety of texts, King, "Articulating Stardom," 29, discusses the actor's relation to the text in terms of Foucault, but in somewhat different terms, since King asks here how the star as auteur, like the myth of the literary author, works ideologically to deny intertextuality (see Foucault, "What Is an Author?").

56. Dyer, *Heavenly Bodies*, 2.

57. Ibid.

58. Nimmer, "The Right of Publicity," was really the first to articulate this right as a valuable property; Haelan v. Topps had stopped short of making publicity a right. However, in the enthusiasm over the development of a new property right, entertainment law commentators have often forgotten that a number of celebrities use publicity "value" to prevent the use of their image by anyone, including themselves. Judge Whitman Knapp for the majority in Cary Grant v. Esquire, Inc., admittedly stated the dilemma this way: "There is obvious difficulty in defining a 'right of privacy' for public personages. Moreover, plaintiff Grant has complicated the difficulty by asserting that he does not want anyone—himself included to profit by the publicity value of his name and reputation" (880) (367 F.Supp. 876 [S.D.N.Y. 1973]).

59. F. Cohen, "Transcendental Nonsense and the Functional Approach," 815; Elizabeth Mensch refers to this article as one of the best examples of the project of the legal Realists (1920–39), whose work has been carried on by contemporary critical legal studies scholars ("The History of Mainstream Legal Thought," 26–29).

60. F. Cohen, "Transcendental Nonsense and the Functional Approach," 815.

61. Dworkin, *Taking Rights Seriously*, 80, says that although the way in which

legal opinions are written would lead one to believe that either the defendant or the plaintiff had a preexisting right, that is "only a fiction." The judge has actually "legislated new rights and applied them retrospectively."

62. Macpherson, "The Meaning of Property," 2, says that there are two misuses of the concept of property that appear in the period coincident with the development of a capitalist market economy: one, the use of property to mean *things* when it has to do with "rights in or to things"; two, the treatment of property as synonymous with *private* property.

63. Macpherson, *The Political Theory of Possessive Individualism*, says that, contrary to the arguments that Locke provides the foundation for an alternative to the capitalist mode of production, he actually laid the groundwork and provided the moral justification:

> Starting from the traditional assumption that the earth and its fruits had originally been given to mankind for their common use, he has turned the tables on all who derived from this assumption theories which were restrictive of capitalist appropriation. He has erased the moral disability with which unlimited capitalist appropriation had hitherto been handicapped. . . . He also justifies, as natural, a class differential in rights and in rationality, and by doing so provides a positive moral basis for capitalist society. (221)

64. Moretti, *Signs Taken for Wonders*, 83.
65. Marx, *Capital*, 1:342.
66. Ibid., 730.
67. Ibid., 798–99.
68. Ollman, *Alienation*, 19.
69. Karl Marx, 1844 *Manuscripts*, as quoted in Ollman, *Alienation*, 164.
70. Ollman, *Alienation*, 3.
71. Moretti, *Signs Taken for Wonders*, 90.
72. Marx, *Capital*, 1:160.
73. Ibid.
74. Moretti, *Signs Taken for Wonders*, 93.
75. Ibid.
76. Ibid.
77. See, for instance, Baudrillard, *For a Critique of the Political Economy of the Sign*, and Baudrillard, *Simulations*. One of the best critiques of Baudrillard is Morris, *The Pirate's Fiancée*, 187–211.
78. One model of this approach is Rossi-Landi, *Linguistics and Economics*.
79. This possibility is suggested by Treece, "Commercial Exploitation of Names, Likenesses, and Personal Histories."
80. See Volosinov, *Marxism and the Philosophy of Language*, chap. 1.
81. Bakhtin, *The Dialogic Imagination*, says:

> Thus at any given moment of its historical existence, language is heteroglot from top to bottom: it represents the co-existence of socio-ideolog-

ical contradictions between the present and the past, between differing epochs of the past, between different socio-ideological groups in the present, between tendencies, schools, circles and so forth, all given bodily form. These "languages" of heteroglossia intersect each other in a variety of ways, forming new socially typifying "languages." (291)

There is disagreement among scholars in Slavic studies about the authorship of several works of literary criticism attributed to Bakhtin. Editor Holquist says that over 90 percent of *Marxism and the Philosophy of Language*, published under the name of V. N. Volosinov, was written by Bakhtin (xxvi).

82. Marx, *Critique of Hegel's Philosophy of Right*, 99. Significantly, the critique of Hegel is also Marx's first attempt to understand private property as the organizing principle of the bourgeois state, the examination he took further in *Capital*, vol. 1, and *1844 Manuscripts*.

83. Lugosi v. Universal Pictures, 827.

84. Rohde, "Dracula: Still Undead," 53.

85. Lugosi v. Universal Pictures, 827.

86. Ibid., 847.

87. Ibid.

88. Groups lobbying *against* sec. 990 included the ACLU, the Alliance of Motion Picture and Television Producers, the Motion Picture Association of America, NBC, CBS, and Ron Smith's Celebrity Look-Alikes. Working hard *for* the bill were Screen Actors Guild president Ed Asner and relatives of such "deceased personalities" as Groucho Marx and John Wayne. Elizabeth Taylor and Burt Lancaster appeared in Sacramento to testify in support of the amendment, and President Ronald Reagan and his wife, Nancy, exerted influence (Rohde, "Dracula: Still Undead," 53. Roger Richman, president, Roger Richman Agency, interview with author, Los Angeles, California, 16 April 1987); John Wayne's son Michael continues to work actively for post mortem publicity rights legislation in other states. Michael Wayne and Everett Fields (grandson of W. C. Fields) testified in 1988 in the hearings on the New York State Celebrity Rights Act and in that context exhibited a poster of W. C. Fields reclining in the nude, an advertisement for a Pope John Paul II look-alike, an Albert Einstein noisemaker, and a videotape of a Marilyn Monroe impersonator, in addition to the cards portraying Clark Gable and John Wayne "in sexual situations" (Hevesi, "Heirs Warn of 'Poachers' in Afterlife of the Famous"). Thanks to Rod and Karen Gibbs for this information on the New York hearings. Before Andy Warhol's death, Michael Wayne sued the artist and Gaultney-Klineman Art Publishers for selling the image of John Wayne as part of the Warhol silk-screen portfolio. (Zeldis, "Public Hearing Focuses on Bill on Use of Deceased's Likeness"). For more on the New York hearings see, chap. 3, n. 27.

89. McCarthy, *The Rights of Publicity and Privacy*, 6.24–25.

90. See Rohde, "Dracula: Still Undead," 53–55; Brassel and Kulzick, "Life After Death for the California Celebrity." (This article is the germ of the

discussion of the look-alike I take up in chap. 3.) See also Gross, "The Right of Publicity Revisited."

91. *California Civil Code*, sec. 990 (n), 3.

92. Lugosi v. Universal Pictures, 851.

93. Fletcher and Rubin, "Privacy, Publicity, and the Portrayal of Real People by the Media," 1599.

94. Factors Etc., Inc. v. Pro Arts, Inc., 444 F.Supp. 288 (S.D.N.Y. 1977), aff'd 579 F.2d 215, 205 U.S.P.Q. 751 (2d Cir. 1978) cert. denied. 440 U.S. 908. This is only the first of several Presley estate court cases. See McCarthy, *The Rights of Publicity and Privacy*, 9.35–37, for a full account.

95. Goettsch, "The Right of Publicity," 1009; Viera, "Elvis Presley," 34, quoting *Factors, Inc. v. Creative Card*, says that Presley's death would produce an industry worth an estimated $1 billion.

96. Elvis Presley Enterprises v. Elvisly Yours, 817 F.2d 104 (6th Cir. 1987).

97. Goettsch, "The Right of Publicity," 994.

98. Ibid., 993.

99. Ibid., 993–94.

100. Memphis Development Foundation v. Factors, Inc., 616 F.2d 956, 205 U.S.P.Q. 784 (6th Cir. 1980).

101. Ibid., 959.

102. Ibid., 957–59; Viera, "The Law of Star Images," chap. 4, takes an opposite point of view on Memphis Development. He says that the case doesn't make a distinction between famous persons and commercially produced images such as "Elvis Presley." Viera makes a distinction between "Elvis-the-person," who would have privacy rights, and "Elvis-the-'image,'" who should be seen as an artificial corporate entity with few privacy rights. In conclusion, Viera proposes a Federal Personhood Statute, which would deal with "intertextual media images" such as Presley and Lugosi (chap. 6). Also see Viera, "Images as Property."

103. Memphis Development, 960.

104. Tennessee Statute, secs. 47-25-1101 and 47-25-1108 (1984); Brassel and Kulzick, "Life After Death for the California Celebrity," 16, say that the provisions of this statute are such that if the entitlement were periodically renewed and not allowed to lapse, the celebrity right of publicity could be kept alive for eternity in the state of Tennessee.

105. Edelman, *Ownership of the Image*, 25.

106. Deleuze and Guattari, *A Thousand Plateaus*, 181.

107. Ibid., 168.

108. Curtis Licensing, a Division of Curtis Publishing, longtime publisher of *The Saturday Evening Post*, now handles licensing for Elvis Presley Enterprises, the Charlie Chaplin Estate, the Babe Ruth Estate, the Abbott and Costello Estate, and the Buddy Holly Estate, among others. Before the tenth anniversary of Elvis Presley's death, in 1988, James Dean was Curtis's most popular licensing property. The James Dean Foundation licensee summary dated 1 November 1987 lists sixty-three different manufacturing companies produc-

ing James Dean novelty products in the U.S., Sweden, Italy, France, the Netherlands, Australia, Hong Kong, England, and Switzerland. In Hollywood, California, the Roger Richman Agency has handled licensing for such deceased celebrities as W. C. Fields, Mae West, Clark Gable, Albert Einstein, and Sigmund Freud, as well as living stars, among whom have been Dorothy Lamour, Sophia Loren, and Marlene Dietrich. Richman's agency does the most licensing for the Estate of Marilyn Monroe. Since Monroe died without heirs, leaving her estate to Lee Strasberg and her psychiatrist, Marianne Kris, both now deceased, the royalties from the licensing of her image go to the Hampstead Child Therapy Clinic in London, run by Anna Freud (Grove, "Death Be Not Proud," 29). McCarthy, *The Rights of Publicity and Privacy*, chap. 6, says that some kind of right of privacy is recognized at the level of common law or statutory law in nearly all states; nearly half of these have recognized a right of publicity at one or the other of these levels. Technically, twelve states give statutory recognition to privacy or publicity or both. Only California, Tennessee, and Kentucky have passed statutes recognizing the right of publicity as a descendible property right. New York has historically resisted the codification of a right of publicity, but that does not mean that New York doesn't recognize the right; it means only that in this state that right is governed by common law (see Ross, "Thirty-one Years after *Haelan Laboratories*").

109. Marx, *Critique of Hegel's Philosophy of Right*, lvi.

CHAPTER 7. SUPERMAN, TELEVISION, AND THE PROTECTIVE STRENGTH OF THE TRADEMARK

1. Hall, "On Postmodernism and Articulation," 46.
2. For an overview of these developments, see Collins, *Marxism and Law*; Kairys, ed., *The Politics of Law*; Fitzpatrick and Hunt, eds., *Critical Legal Studies*.
3. E. P. Thompson, *Whigs and Hunters*, 261.
4. Hirst and Kingdom, "On Edelman's 'Ownership of the Image,'" 139.
5. Paramount Pictures Corp., 217 U.S.P.Q. 292 (T.T.A.B. 1983).
6. Trade-Mark Act of 5 July 1946, ch. 540, secs. 1–45, 60 Stat. 427–43, *as amended*, 15 U.S.C., secs. 1051–1127 (1970); Germain, "Unfair Trade Practices," 84, says that although it was noted in 1965 that few cases had been brought to trial under the section, since that time there has been a remarkable increase in "passing off" litigation under 43(a).
7. Detective Comics, Inc. v. Bruns Pub., Inc., 111 F.2d 432 (2d Cir. 1940); Detective Comics, Inc. v. Fox Pub., Inc., 46 F.Supp. 872 (S.D.N.Y. 1942); Detective Comics, Inc. v. Powers 465 F.Supp. 843, 201 U.S.P.Q. 99 (1978); Detective Comics, Inc. v. Crazy Eddie, Inc., 205 U.S.P.Q. 1177 (S.D.N.Y. 1979); Detective Comics, Inc., v. Filmation Assoc., 486 F.Supp.

1273 (S.D.N.Y. 1980); Detective Comics, Inc., v. Board of Trustees, No. 81 C, 2402 (N.D. Ill., filed 17 June 1981); Detective Comics v. Reel Fantasy, Inc., 696 F.2d 24 (2d Cir. 1982); Warner Brothers, Inc. v. American Broadcasting Co., Inc., 720 F.2d 231 (2d Cir. 1983).

8. Friedrich, "Up, Up, and Away!!!" 69, says that Warner Communications, now the owners of DC Comics, finally paid each author $20,000 per year for life at the time that Warner produced *Superman: The Movie* (1979).

9. Schechter, *The Historical Foundations of Law Relating to Trademarks*, 5; Moore, *The Legal Protection of Goodwill*, 40; Lange, "Recognizing the Public Domain," 168.

10. Warner Brothers Pictures, Inc. v. Columbia Broadcasting Co., 216 F.2d 945 (9th Cir. 1954) cert. denied. 348 U.S. 971, 75 S. Ct. 532 (1955); for Melville Nimmer's fuller discussion of this case, see "Copyright 1955."

11. Adams, "Superman, Mickey Mouse, and Gerontology," 191.

12. Nichols v. Universal Pictures Corp., 45 F.2d 119, 7 U.S.P.Q. 84 (CA 2 1930); Harrison, "The Protection of Titles and Characters."

13. Brylawski, "Protection of Characters," 83–84.

14. Battersby and Grimes, *The Law of Merchandise and Character Licensing*, sec. 8.10.

15. Edelman, "The Character and His Double," 36.

16. See Waldheim, "Characters—May They Be Kidnapped?" 1030, on this.

17. Wyatt Earp Enterprises, Inc. v. Sackman, Inc., 157 F.Supp. 621 (S.D.N.Y. 1958).

18. Ibid., 622, uses as evidence for the establishment of *secondary meaning* the fact that between 1955 and 1957, 107 programs were produced and aired for fifty-two weeks each year, "viewed weekly on millions of television receivers by additional millions of persons." All U.S. registered trademarks discussed will be designated by all caps in the text, following the graphic convention used in the legal literature on unfair competition.

19. Anson, "A Licensing Retrospective and Glimpse into the Future," 4–5, cites Theodore Roosevelt's 1913 royalties earned from the sale of "Teddy" bears (which supported the National Parks system) as the earliest American use of licensing, followed by the radio, television, and film licensing campaigns for Buck Rogers (1929), the Lone Ranger and Shirley Temple (thirties), Hopalong Cassidy and Tom Mix (forties), and Zorro and Davy Crockett (fifties); Battersby and Grimes, *The Law of Merchandise and Character Licensing*, sec. 1.6, say that in the fifties more than seventeen ANNIE OAKLEY trademark registrations were approved for more than seventy different products. See also chap. 5, nn. 62 and 63, for an overview of licensing.

20. Turan, "Superman! Supersell!," 49–52; "Maggie Young—The 'Force' at Lucasfilm."

21. Nimmer, *Cases and Materials on Entertainment Litigation*, says that "the essence of unfair competition consists in the palming off of the goods or business of one person as that of another" (837).

22. Battersby and Grimes, "English Legal Decision Jars Licensing Commission"; see Derenberg and Morofsky, eds., *European Trademark Law and Practice*, 452, on this aspect of British law.

23. Ellis, *Visible Fictions*, 125. See Feuer, "Narrative Form in American Network Television," 108, 112, for a challenge to the notion that series characters do not develop, which takes into account the political significance of the concept of character development.

24. Eco, *The Role of the Reader*, 117, 120.

25. Bennett and Woollacott, *Bond and Beyond*, 44.

26. Grossman, *Superman*, 318–20.

27. Stedman, *The Serial*, 10.

28. Warner Brothers, Inc. v. American Broadcasting Co., Inc., 720 F.2d 231 (2d Cir. 1983), 240, cites King Features Syndicate v. Fleischer (1924) [Barney Google's horse Spark Plug], Hill v. Whalen & Martell, Inc. (1914) [Mutt and Jeff], and Empire City Amusement Co. v. Wilton (1903) [Alphonse and Gaston].

29. Although legal commentators have concurred that cartoon characters cannot lose their identities to actors, the Lone Ranger and Lugosi cases (in which the actors' rights to the roles they had played were asserted) are often cited in cautionary footnotes (The Lone Ranger, Inc. v. Cox, 39 F.Supp. 487 [W.D.S. Car. 1941]; The Lone Ranger, Inc. v. Currey, 79 F.Supp. 190 [M.D. Pa. 1948]; Lugosi v. Universal Pictures, 160 Cal. Rptr. 323 [1979]).

30. Eco, *The Role of the Reader*, 111.

31. R. C. Allen, "'The Guiding Light,'" 311, describes the character Bert Bauer, who was played by the same actress for thirty years on this soap opera, which, if we count its origin in radio in 1937, had been broadcast for more than forty years. My point is merely polemical. Broadcast television *could* produce a narrative that continued into infinity, but even the serial that runs for several years is the exception.

32. Eco, *The Role of the Reader,* 111.

33. Paramount Pictures Corp., 213 U.S.P.Q. 1111 (T.T.A.B. 1983) (MORK AND MINDY decals); Warner Brothers v. Gay Tops, Inc., 724 F.2d 327 (2d Cir. 1981) (DUKES OF HAZZARD—the General Lee car); Spelling-Goldberg v. Levi (1978) (STARSKY & HUTCH, CHARLIE'S ANGELS iron-on heat transfers).

34. McCarthy, *Trademarks*, 1:chap. 7.

35. Ellis, *Visible Fictions*, 120.

36. Eco, *The Role of the Reader*, 115, says the "confused notion of time is the only condition which makes the story credible."

37. In the fifties, on black and white television, "Superman" has its resemblances with "Dragnet" and "Eliot Ness and the Untouchables," but today—seen in the color in which it was originally shot—instead of hard edge we see soft nostalgia.

38. André, "From Menace to Messiah," 124–38; Eco, "Innovation and Repetition," 179–80.

39. Ellis, *Visible Fictions*, 125.

40. Macherey, *A Theory of Literary Production*, 197.

41. Kuzui, "Japanese Licensing," 30–31, describes how in 1962, *shohinka-ken*, a new word meaning "product-making rights," had to be added to the Japanese language as the number of animated television series with licensing programs increased.

42. Quelch, "How to Build a Product Licensing Program," 187.

43. Baudrillard, "Beyond Right and Wrong," 10. I am indebted to McRobbie, "Postmodernism and Popular Culture," for this way of reading Baudrillard, as well as for an idea of how we might see realities and fictions as intermingling at this time in history.

44. See Jameson, *The Political Unconscious*, 45, on this point.

45. Battersby and Grimes, *The Law of Merchandise and Character Licensing*, sec. 5.35.

46. Ibid., sec. 4.18.

47. DC Comics, Inc. v. Powers (1978), 847.

48. DC Comics, Inc. v. Crazy Eddie, Inc. (1979). Other characters in the "family of SUPERMAN" are WONDERWOMAN, SUPERBOY, AQUAMAN, PLASTICMAN, and BATMAN.

49. DC Comics, Inc. v. Filmation Associates (1980).

50. DC Comics, Inc. v. Board of Trustees, as quoted in Lange, "Recognizing the Public Domain," 166.

51. In Groucho Marx Productions, Inc. v. Day and Night Co., Inc., 523 F.Supp. 485 (S.D.N.Y. 1981), the heirs of the Marx Brothers successfully enjoined the off-Broadway comic spoof *A Day in Hollywood, a Night in the Ukraine*, which, they argued, used Groucho, Chico, and Harpo in violation of their right of publicity. In Instrumentalist Co. v. Marine Corps League, 509 F.Supp. 323 (N.D. Ill. 1981), an Illinois court awarded the exclusive use of the name and likeness of John Philip Sousa to a relatively unknown magazine, in effect prohibiting its use by the Marine Corps League. Lange, "Recognizing the Public Domain," 170, argues that trademark and unfair competition law in this case could not take account of the cultural or historical significance of Sousa's relationship to the Marine Corps Band, which he directed at the time he wrote the march "Semper Fidelis" (which took its name from the Marine Corps motto); Lange, "Intellectual Property under the Constitution," defines the public domain as "that seedbed of impulses and ideas, that common ground of human experience from which all creativity ultimately must come" (16). Professor Lange's work stands out in this field, since he is one of a very few legal commentators with an interest in defending a public domain of culture.

52. Lange, "Recognizing the Public Domain," 156.

53. Quelch, "How to Build a Product Licensing Program," 186.

54. See Collins, *Marxism and Law*, 41, for further on the instrumentalist theory that saw the law as carrying out the interests of the ruling class.

55. *Institutional Investor* 24 (January 1990), 139, called Time Inc.'s $14.9 billion

acquisition of Warner Communications one of the most "noteworthy deals" of 1989.

56. Warner Brothers, Inc. v. ABC, 233.

57. See Nimmer, *Cases and Materials on Entertainment Litigation*, 89, on the expression/ideas dichotomy. See Frow, "Repetition and Limitation," 7, for an analysis of the problems posed by this distinction from the point of view of linguistics.

58. See McCarthy, *Trademarks*, 1:656–79. British trademark law often cites Lord Justice Farwell on the need for vigilance in registering only those marks that genuinely "distinguish," lest "the large and wealthy firms with whom the smaller folk are unwilling to litigate, could by a system of log-rolling, divide amongst themselves all the ordinary words of description and laudation in the English language" (as quoted in Derenberg and Morofsky, eds., *European Trademark Law*, 81–82).

59. Warner Brothers v. ABC, 242.

60. "Protection for Literary and Cartoon Characters," 359. An alternative reading of the cultural significance of this line of Superman cases can be found in Harris, "Who Owns Our Myths?" Harris decries the ownership of contemporary mythic heroes such as Superman and finds it paradoxical that because of the structure of intellectual property the only way one can intervene is to create legitimate parody. Although the outcome of Warner Brothers v. ABC did not hinge on the argument for seeing Ralph Hinkley as a parody of Superman, this is a broad way of understanding why the character wouldn't be considered infringing.

61. Margulies, "FTC vs. Formica, Inc."

CHAPTER 8. CONCLUSION: OPPOSITIONAL CULTURE
AND CONTRABAND MERCHANDISE

1. The Pillsbury Co. v. Milky Way Productions, Inc., 215 U.S.P.Q. 124 (N.D. Ga. 1981); Walt Disney Productions v. The Air Pirates, 581 F.2d 751 (9th Cir. 1978); Edelman, "The Character and His Double," 38.

2. Hall, "Encoding/Decoding," 132.

3. The issue of "false light" portrayals arises in an entirely different branch of privacy doctrine with its own special issues. For more, see McCarthy, *The Rights of Publicity and Privacy*.

4. Horkheimer and Adorno, *Dialectic of Enlightenment*, 166.

5. Eagleton, *The Function of Criticism*, 122.

6. Bennett, "Popular Culture as a 'Teaching Object,'" 23.

7. Barthes, *Mythologies*.

8. As quoted in Frith, "Copyright and the Music Business," 72.

9. Ibid.

10. Kuzui, "Japanese Licensing."

11. Daniel, "Trademark Piracy," 12.

12. Krieger, "The Trademark Counterfeiting Act of 1984."

13. See, for instance, Ang, *Watching DALLAS*, for an analysis of the Dutch reception of "Dallas."

14. One example is Morley, *Family Television*.

15. Lipman, *The Electronic Pirates*, 19.

16. Ibid., 44.

17. Patterson, "Free Speech, Copyright, and Fair Use."

18. Foster, *Recodings*, 111, 170.

19. Krauss, *The Originality of the Avant-Garde*, 168, 170.

20. Owens, "Sherrie Levine at A&M Artworks," 148; Owens, "The Discourse of Others," 73.

21. Foster, *Recodings*, 100.

22. Ibid., 171.

23. Collins, *Marxism and Law*.

24. San Francisco Arts & Athletics, Inc. v. U.S. Olympic Committee, 107 S. Ct. 2971 (1987).

25. Kravitz, "Trademarks, Speech, and the *Gay Olympics* Case," makes a similar point regarding the way trademark rights take priority over free expression in this case.

26. E. P. Thompson, *The Poverty of Theory*, 288.

27. O'Connor, *Accumulation Crisis*, 20.

Bibliography

MANUSCRIPT COLLECTIONS

Durham, North Carolina
  Duke University
    Perkins Library
      Special Collections, J. Walter Thompson Archives
Los Angeles, California
  Academy of Motion Picture Arts and Sciences
  University of Southern California
    Doheny Library
      Special Collections, Warner Brothers Archive
New York, New York
  New York Public Library at Lincoln Center
  Library and Museum of the Performing Arts
Princeton, New Jersey
  Princeton University
    Princeton University Library
      Theatre Collection, Warner Brothers Archive

WORKS IN CULTURAL STUDIES

Abrams, M. H. *The Mirror and the Lamp: Romantic Theory and the Critical Tradition.* 1953. Reprint. London: Oxford University Press, 1971.

Adorno, Theodor. *Aesthetic Theory.* Translated by C. Lenhardt. 1970. Reprint. London and New York: Routledge and Kegan Paul, 1984.

———. *Prisms.* Translated by Samuel Weber and Shierry Weber. 1967. Reprint. Cambridge: MIT Press, 1981.

———. "A Social Critique of Radio Music." *Kenyon Review* 7, no. 2 (1945): 208–17.

Allen, Jeanne Thomas. "Copyright and Early Theater, Vaudeville, and Film Competition." In *Film Before Griffith*, edited by John Fell. Berkeley and London: University of California Press, 1983.

———. "Film and Photography as Legal Evidence." In *The Social Relations of American Communications Technology* (forthcoming).

————. "The Industrialization of Culture: The Case of the Player Piano." In *Popular Culture and Media Events*, edited by Vincent Mosco and Janet Wasko. Norwood, N.J.: Ablex Publishing Co., 1985.

Allen, Robert C. "'The Guiding Light': Soap Opera as Economic and Cultural Document." In *American History/American Television*, edited by John E. O'Connor. New York: Frederick Ungar, 1983.

Allen, Robert C., and Douglas Gomery. *Film History: Theory and Practice*. New York: Knopf, 1985.

Alpers, Svetlana. *Rembrandt's Enterprise: The Studio and the Market*. Chicago: University of Chicago Press, 1988.

Althusser, Louis. *Essays in Self-Criticism*. Translated by Grahame Lock. London: New Left Books, 1976.

————. *Lenin and Philosophy and Other Essays*. Translated by Ben Brewster. New York and London: Monthly Review Press, 1971.

Althusser, Louis, and Etienne Balibar. *Reading Capital*. Translated by Ben Brewster. London: New Left Books, 1970.

Altman, Rick. "MOVING LIPS: Cinema as Ventriloquism." *Yale French Studies* 60 (1980): 67–79.

————. "The Technology of the Voice." *Iris* 3, no. 1 (1985): 3–20.

————. "Television/Sound." In *Studies in Entertainment: Critical Approaches to Mass Culture*, edited by Tania Modleski. Bloomington and Indianapolis: Indiana University Press, 1986.

Alvarado, Manuel. "Photographs and Narrativity." *Screen Education*, nos. 32–33 (Autumn–Winter 1979–80): 5–17.

André, Thomas. "From Menace to Messiah: The History and Historicity of Superman." In *American Media and Mass Culture: Left Perspectives*, edited by Donald Lazere. Berkeley: University of California Press, 1987.

Ang, Ien. *Watching DALLAS: Soap Opera and the Melodramatic Imagination*. Translated by Della Couling. London and New York: Methuen, 1985.

Armes, Roy. "Entendre, C'est Comprendre—In Defence of Sound Reproduction." *Screen* 29, no. 2 (Spring 1988): 8–23.

Arnheim, Rudolph. *Radio*. Translated by Margaret Ludwig and Herbert Read. 1936. Reprint. New York: Arno Press, 1971.

Baechlin, Peter. *Histoire économique du cinéma*. Paris: Nouvelle Edition, 1947.

Baily, Leslie. *The Gilbert and Sullivan Book*. New York: Coward-McCann, 1957.

Bakhtin, M. M. *The Dialogic Imagination*. Translated by Caryl Emerson and Michael Holquist. Edited by Michael Holquist. Austin and London: University of Texas Press, 1981.

Balázs, Béla. *Theory of the Film*. Translated by Edith Bone. 1952. Reprint. New York: Arno Press, 1970.

Balio, Tino. "Stars in Business: The Founding of United Artists." In *The American Film Industry*, edited by Tino Balio. 2d. ed. Madison: University of Wisconsin Press, 1985.

————, ed. *The American Film Industry*. 2d ed. Madison: University of Wisconsin Press, 1985.

Baran, Paul A., and Paul M. Sweezy. *Monopoly Capital: An Essay on the American Economic and Social Order*. New York: Monthly Review Press, 1966.

Barnouw, Erik. *Tube of Plenty: The Evolution of American Television*. Oxford and New York: Oxford University Press, 1982.

Barry, John F., and Epes W. Sargent. *Building Theatre Patronage*. New York: Chalmers Publishing Co., 1927.

Barthes, Roland. *Camera Lucida: Reflections on Photography*. Translated by Richard Howard. New York: Farrar, Straus and Giroux, 1981.

————. *Image/Music/Text*. Translated by Stephen Heath. New York: Hill and Wang, 1977.

————. *Mythologies*. Translated by Annette Lavers. New York: Hill and Wang, 1972. Reprint. In *Film Theory and Criticism*, edited by Gerald Mast and Marshall Cohen. 3d ed. New York: Oxford University Press, 1985.

————. *The Responsibility of Forms: Critical Essays on Music, Art, and Representation*. Translated by Richard Howard. New York: Hill and Wang, 1985.

————. *The Rustle of Language*. Translated by Richard Howard. New York: Hill and Wang, 1986.

Bassham, Ben L. *The Theatrical Photographs of Napoleon Sarony*. Kent, Ohio: Kent State University Press, 1978.

Baudrillard, Jean. "Beyond Right and Wrong or the Mischievous Genius of Image." In *Resolution: A Critique of Video Art*, translated by Laurent Charreyron and Amy Gerstler, edited by Patti Podesta. Los Angeles: Los Angeles Contemporary Exhibitions, 1986.

————. *For a Critique of the Political Economy of the Sign*. Translated by Charles Levin. St. Louis: Telos Press, 1981.

————. *Simulations*. Translated by Paul Foss, Paul Patton, and Philip Beitchman. New York: Semiotext(e), 1983.

Baudry, Jean-Louis. "The Apparatus." Translated by Jean Andrews and Bertrand Augst. *Camera Obscura* 1 (Fall 1976): 104–28. Reprint. In *Narrative, Apparatus, Ideology: A Film Theory Reader*, edited by Philip Rosen. New York: Columbia University Press, 1986.

————. "The Ideological Effects of the Basic Cinematographic Apparatus." Translated by Alan Williams. *Film Quarterly* 28, no. 2 (Winter 1974–75): 39–47.

Bazin, André. *What Is Cinema?* Vol. 1. Translated by Hugh Gray. Berkeley: University of California Press, 1967.

Becker, Howard. *Art Worlds*. Berkeley: University of California Press, 1982.

Behlmer, Rudy, ed. *Inside Warner Brothers (1935–1951)*. New York: Viking, 1985.

Belton, John, and Elizabeth Weis, eds. *Film Sound: Theory and Practice*. New York: Columbia University Press, 1985.

Benamou, Michel, and Charles Caramello, eds. *Performance in Postmodern Culture*. Madison: Coda Press, 1977.

Benjamin, Walter. *Charles Baudelaire: Lyric Poet in the Era of High Capitalism*. Translated by Harry Zohn. London and New York: Verso, 1983.

————. "A Small History of Photography." In *One-Way Street and Other Writings*, translated by Edmund Jephcott and Kingsley Shorter. London: Verso, 1985.

————. "The Work of Art in the Age of Mechanical Reproduction." In *Illuminations*, translated by Harry Zohn, edited by Hannah Arendt. Glasgow: Fontana/Collins, 1973.

Bennett, Tony. *Formalism and Marxism*. London and New York: Methuen, 1979.

————. "Popular Culture as a 'Teaching Object.'" *Screen Education*, no. 34 (Spring 1980): 17–29.

————. "Text and History." In *Re-reading English*, edited by Peter Widdowson. London and New York: Methuen, 1982.

————. "Texts, Readers, and Reading Formations." *Bulletin of the Midwest Modern Language Association* 16 (Spring 1983): 3–17.

Bennett, Tony, and Janet Woollacott. *Bond and Beyond: The Political Career of a Popular Hero*. New York: Methuen, 1987.

Bennett, Tony, Susan Boyd-Bowman, Colin Mercer, and Janet Woollacott, eds. *Popular Television and Film*. London: Open University Press, 1981.

Bennett, Tony, Graham Martin, Colin Mercer, and Janet Woollacott, eds. *Culture, Ideology, and Social Process*. London: Open University Press, 1981.

Bennett, Tony, Colin Mercer, and Janet Woollacott, eds. *Popular Culture and Social Relations*. Milton Keynes, England, and Philadelphia: Open University Press, 1986.

Benton, Ted. *The Rise and Fall of Structural Marxism: Althusser and His Influence*. London: Macmillan, 1984.

Benveniste, Emile. *Problems in General Linguistics*. Translated by Mary Elizabeth Meek. Coral Gables: University of Miami Press, 1971.

Berger, John. *And Our Faces, My Heart, Brief as Photos*. New York: Pantheon, 1984.

————. *Selected Essays and Articles*. Harmondsworth, Middlesex: Penguin, 1972.

————. *The Sense of Sight*. New York: Pantheon, 1985.

————. *Ways of Seeing*. New York: Penguin, 1977.

Berger, John, and Jean Mohr. *Another Way of Telling*. New York: Pantheon, 1982.

Bill, George. "What's Wrinkled, Bug-eyed, and Worth Billions?" *Cinefantastique* 13, nos. 2–3 (November–December 1982): 17–18.

Bloch, Ernst. "Dialectics and Hope." Translated by Mark Ritter. *New German Critique* 9 (Fall 1976): 3–10.

————. *The Utopian Function of Art and Literature: Selected Essays*. Translated by Jack Zipes and Frank Mecklenburg. Cambridge and London: MIT Press, 1988.

Blum, Stanford. "Merchandising a Theatrical Motion Picture." In *U.C.L.A. Entertainment Symposium: Sources of Revenue and Presale Financing for Theatrical Motion Pictures*, edited by Peter J. Dekom, Lawrence P. Mortorff, and Michael Sherman. Los Angeles: University of California Press, 1977.

Boddy, William. *Fifties Television: The Industry and Its Critics*. Urbana and
  Chicago: University of Illinois Press, 1990.
———. "The Rhetoric and the Economic Roots of the American Broadcast
  Industry." *Ciné-tracts* 2 (Spring 1979): 37–54.
———. "The Studios Move into Prime Time: Hollywood and the Television
  Industry in the 1950s." *Cinema Journal* 24, no. 4 (Summer 1985): 23–37.
Boggs, Carl. "The Blues Tradition from Poetic Revolt to Cultural Impasse." In
  American Media and Mass Culture: Left Perspectives, edited by Donald Lazere.
  Berkeley and London: University of California Press, 1987.
Bordwell, David, Janet Staiger, and Kristin Thompson. *The Classical Hollywood
  Cinema: Film Style and Mode of Production to 1960*. New York: Columbia
  University Press, 1985.
Brady, Robert A. "The Problem of Monopoly." *Annals of the American Academy
  of Political and Social Sciences* 254 (November 1947): 125–36.
Braudel, Fernand. *Afterthoughts on Material Civilization and Capitalism*.
  Translated by Patricia M. Ranum. Baltimore: Johns Hopkins University
  Press, 1977.
Braverman, Harry. *Labor and Monopoly Capital: The Degradation of Work in the
  Twentieth Century*. New York: Monthly Review Press, 1974.
Brenkman, John. "Mass Media from Collective Experience to the Culture of
  Privatization." *Social Text* 1 (Winter 1979): 94–109.
Brittan, Arthur. *The Privatized World*. London and Boston: Routledge and
  Kegan Paul, 1977.
Browne, Nick, ed. *Cahiers du Cinéma, 1969–1972: The Politics of
  Representation*. Cambridge: Harvard University Press, 1990.
Buchloh, Benjamin H. D., Serge Guilbaut, and David Solkin, eds. *Modernism
  and Modernity*. Halifax, Nova Scotia: Nova Scotia College of Art and Design,
  1983.
Buck-Morss, Susan. "Benjamin's *Passagen-Werk*: Redeeming Mass Culture for
  the Revolution." *New German Critique* 29 (1983): 211–40.
———. *The Dialectics of Seeing: Walter Benjamin and the Arcades Project*.
  Cambridge and London: MIT Press, 1989.
———. "The Flaneur, the Sandwichman, and the Whore: The Politics of
  Loitering." *New German Critique* 39 (1986): 99–140.
Burgin, Victor. "Photographic Practice and Art Theory." In *Thinking
  Photography*, edited by Victor Burgin. London: Macmillan, 1982.
———, ed. *Thinking Photography*. London: Macmillan Press, 1982.
Chambers, Ian, John Clarke, Ian Connell, Lidia Curti, Stuart Hall, and Tony
  Jefferson. "Marxism and Culture." *Screen* 18, no. 4 (Winter 1977–78): 109–
  19.
Chaneles, Sol. *Collecting Movie Memorabilia*. New York: Arno Press, 1977.
Clark, Danae. "Actors' Labor and the Politics of Subjectivity: Hollywood in the
  1930s." Ph.D. diss., University of Iowa, 1989.
Clayton, Sue, and Jonathon Curling. "On Authorship." *Screen* 20, no. 1 (Spring
  1979): 35–61.

Cochrane, Robert. "Advertising Motion Pictures." In *The Story of Films*, edited by Joseph P. Kennedy. Chicago: A. W. Shaw Co., 1927.

Comolli, Jean-Louis. "Machines of the Visible." In *The Cinematic Apparatus*, edited by Teresa DeLauretis and Stephen Heath. New York: St. Martin's Press, 1980.

———. "Technique and Ideology: Camera, Perspective, Depth of Field." Translated by Diana Matias. *Film Reader* 2 (January 1977): 128–40. Reprint. In *Movies and Methods*, edited by Bill Nichols. Vol. 2. Berkeley and Los Angeles: University of California Press.

Conant, Michael. *Antitrust in the Motion Picture Industry*. Berkeley and Los Angeles: University of California Press, 1960.

———. "The Paramount Decrees Reconsidered." In *The American Film Industry*, edited by Tino Balio. 2d ed. Madison: University of Wisconsin Press, 1985.

Corrigan, Paul, and Derek Sayer. "Hindess and Hirst: A Critical Review." *Socialist Register* (1978): 194–214.

Coward, Rosalind. "Class, 'Culture,' and the Social Formation." *Screen* 18, no. 1 (Spring 1977): 75–105.

———. "Response." *Screen* 18, no. 4 (Winter 1977–78): 120–22.

Crimp, Douglas. "Appropriating Appropriation." In *Image Scavengers: Photography*, edited by Paula Marincola. Philadelphia: Institute of Contemporary Art, 1982.

Crissel, Andrew. *Understanding Radio*. London and New York: Methuen, 1986.

Cubitt, Sean. "Time Shift: Reflections on Video Viewing." *Screen* 29, no. 2 (Spring 1988): 74–81.

DeCerteau, Michel. *The Practice of Everyday Life*. Translated by Steven Tendall. Berkeley and Los Angeles: University of California Press, 1984.

———. *The Writing of History*. Translated by Tom Conley. New York: Columbia University Press, 1988.

DeCordova, Richard. "The Emergence of the Star System and the Bourgeoisification of Society." In *Star Signs*, edited by Christine Gledhill. London: British Film Institute, 1982.

———. "The Emergence of the Star System in America." *Wide Angle* 6, no. 4 (1985): 4–13.

DeLauretis, Teresa, and Stephen Heath, eds. *The Cinematic Apparatus*. New York: St. Martin's Press, 1980.

Deleuze, Gilles. *Cinema 1: The Movement-Image*. Translated by Hugh Tomlinson and Barbara Habberjam. Minneapolis: University of Minnesota Press, 1986.

Deleuze, Gilles, and Félix Guattari. *A Thousand Plateaus: Capitalism and Schizophrenia*. Translated by Brian Massumi. Minneapolis: University of Minnesota Press, 1988.

Denning, Michael. "The 'Special American Conditions': Marxism and American Studies." *American Quarterly* 38, no. 3 (1986): 357–80.

Doane, Mary Ann. *The Desire to Desire: The Woman's Film of the 1940's*. Bloomington: Indiana University Press, 1987.

———. "Film and the Masquerade—Theorising the Female Spectator." *Screen* 23, nos. 3–4 (September–October 1982): 74–87.

———. "Ideology and the Practice of Sound Editing and Mixing." In *The Cinematic Apparatus*, edited by Teresa DeLauretis and Stephen Heath. New York: St. Martin's Press, 1980.

———. "The Voice in Cinema: The Articulation of Body and Space." *Yale French Studies* 60 (1980): 33–50.

Doane, Mary Ann, Patricia Mellencamp, and Linda Williams. "Feminist Film Criticism: An Introduction." In *Re-vision*, edited by Mary Ann Doane, Patricia Mellencamp, and Linda Williams. Frederick, Md.: University Publications of America, 1984.

Dollimore, Jonathan. "Different Desires: Subjectivity and Transgression in Wilde and Gide." *Genders* 2 (Summer 1988): 24–41.

Durand, Régis. "The Disposition of the Voice." In *Performance in Postmodern Culture*, edited by Michel Benamou and Charles Caramello. Madison: Coda Press, 1977.

Dutton, Denis, ed. *The Forger's Art: Forging and the Philosophy of Art*. Berkeley: University of California Press, 1983.

Dyer, Richard. "Four Films of Lana Turner." *Movie*, no. 25 (Winter 1977–78): 30–52.

———. *Heavenly Bodies: Film Stars and Society*. London: Macmillan, 1987.

———. *Star Dossier One*. London: British Film Institute, 1980.

———. "*A Star Is Born* and the Construction of Authenticity." In *Star Signs*, edited by Christine Gledhill. London: British Film Institute, 1982.

———. *Stars*. London: British Film Institute, 1979.

———. *The Stars: Teachers' Study Guide 1*. London: British Film Institute, 1979.

Dyer, Richard, Christine Geraghty, Marion Jordan, Terry Lovell, Richard Patterson, and John Stewart, eds. *Coronation Street*. London: British Film Institute, 1981.

Eagleton, Terry. *Against the Grain: Selected Essays*. London: Verso, 1986.

———. *The Function of Criticism: From "The Spectator" to Post-Structuralism*. London: Verso, 1984.

———. *Literary Theory: An Introduction*. Minneapolis: University of Minnesota Press, 1983.

———. *The Rape of Clarissa*. Oxford: Basil Blackwell, 1982.

Eco, Umberto. "Articulations of the Cinematic Code." In *Movies and Methods*, edited by Bill Nichols. Berkeley: University of California Press, 1976.

———. "Innovation and Repetition: Between Modern and Post-Modern Aesthetics." *Daedalus* 114 (Fall 1985): 161–84.

———. *The Role of the Reader*. Bloomington: Indiana University Press, 1979.

———. *Semiotics and the Philosophy of Language*. Bloomington: Indiana University Press, 1986.

————. *A Theory of Semiotics*. Bloomington: Indiana University Press, 1976.

Eder, J. M. *History of Photography*. Translated by E. Epstean. New York: Columbia University Press, 1945.

Eisler, Hanns (with Theodor Adorno). *Composing for the Films*. New York: Oxford University Press, 1947.

Ellis, John. "Star/Industry/Image." In *Star Signs*, edited by Christine Gledhill. London: British Film Institute, 1982.

————. *Visible Fictions: Cinema, Television, Video*. London: Routledge and Kegan Paul, 1982.

Ellmann, Richard. *Oscar Wilde*. New York: Alfred A. Knopf, 1988.

Farrell, James T. "The Language of Hollywood." In *The Mint: A Miscellany of Literature, Art, and Criticism*, edited by Geoffrey Grigson. London: Routledge and Sons, 1946.

Febvre, Lucien, and Henri-Jean Martin. *The Coming of the Book: The Impact of Printing, 1450–1800*. Translated by David Gerard. Edited by Geoffrey Nowell-Smith and David Wootton. 1958. Reprint. London: Verso, 1986.

Feuer, Jane. "Narrative Form in American Network Television." In *High Theory/Low Culture: Analysing Popular Television and Film*, edited by Colin MacCabe. New York: St. Martin's Press, 1986.

————. "Reading *Dynasty*: Television and Reception Theory." *South Atlantic Quarterly* 88, no. 2 (Spring 1989): 443–60.

Fish, Stanley. *Doing What Comes Naturally*. Durham, N.C.: Duke University Press, 1989.

Fiske, John. *Television Culture*. New York: Methuen, 1987.

Forrester, John. "A Brief History of the Subject." In *The Real Me: Post-Modernism and the Question of Identity*. ICA Documents 6, edited by Lisa Appignanesi. London: Institute of Contemporary Arts, 1987.

Forty, Adrian. *Objects of Desire: Design and Society from Wedgewood to IBM*. New York: Pantheon, 1986.

Foster, Hal. *Recodings: Art, Spectacle, Cultural Politics*. Port Townsend, Wash.: Bay Press, 1985.

————, ed. *The Anti-Aesthetic: Essays on Postmodern Culture*. Port Townsend, Wash.: Bay Press, 1983.

Foucault, Michel. *The Archaeology of Knowledge and the Discourse on Language*. Translated by A. M. Sheridan Smith. New York: Pantheon, 1972.

————. *The History of Sexuality*. 3 vols. Translated by Robert Hurley. New York: Pantheon, 1978.

————. *I, Pierre Riviere, Having Slaughtered My Mother, My Sister, and My Brother . . .: A Case of Parricide in the 19th Century*. Translated by Frank Jellinek. Lincoln and London: University of Nebraska Press, 1975.

————. *Language, Counter-Memory, and Practice. Selected Essays and Interviews*. Translated by D. F. Bouchard and Sherry Simon. Edited by D. F. Bouchard. Ithaca: Cornell University Press, 1977.

————. *The Order of Things: An Archeology of the Human Sciences*. New York: Pantheon, 1971.

———. "What Is an Author?" *Screen* 20, no. 1 (Spring 1979): 13–33.

Freedland, Michael. *Fred Astaire*. London: W. H. Allen, 1976.

Freund, Gisèlle. *Photography and Society*. Boston: David R. Godine, 1980.

Friedrich, Otto. "Up, Up, and Away!!!" *Time* 131, no. 11 (14 March 1988): 68–69.

Frisby, David. *Fragments of Modernity: Georg Simmel, Siegfried Kracauer, and Walter Benjamin*. Cambridge: MIT Press, 1986.

Frith, Simon. "Copyright and the Music Business." *Popular Music* 7, no. 1 (1987): 57–75.

———. *Music for Pleasure: Essays in the Sociology of Pop*. New York: Routledge, Chapman, and Hall, 1988.

Frith, Simon, and Andrew Goodwin, eds. *On Record: Rock, Pop, and the Written Word*. New York: Pantheon, 1990.

Frow, John. "Film, Commodity Production, and the Law." *Australian Journal of Cultural Studies* 2, no. 1 (May 1984): 3–22.

———. "Repetition and Limitation—Computer Software and Copyright Law." *Screen* 29, no. 1 (Winter 1988): 4–20.

———. "Spectacle Binding: On Character." *Poetics Today* 7, no. 2 (1986): 227–50.

Gaines, Jane. "From Elephants to Lux Soap: The Programming and Flow of Early Motion Picture Exploitation." *The Velvet Light Trap*, no. 25 (Spring 1990): 29–43.

———. "The QUEEN CHRISTINA Tie-ups: Convergence of Show Window and Screen." *Quarterly Review of Film and Television Studies* 11, no. 1 (1989): 35–60.

Garnham, Nicholas. "Subjectivity, Ideology, Class, and Historical Materialism." *Screen* 20, no. 1 (Spring 1979): 121–33.

Gauthier, Guy. *The Semiology of the Image*. London: British Film Institute, 1976.

Gelatt, Roland. *The Fabulous Phonograph: From Tin Foil to High Fidelity*. Philadelphia: Lippincott, 1955.

Genovese, Eugene. *Roll, Jordan, Roll: The World the Slaves Made*. New York: Random House, 1972.

Gilbert, Sandra M., and Susan Gubar. *The Madwoman in the Attic: The Woman Writer and the Nineteenth-Century Imagination*. New Haven: Yale University Press, 1979.

Gilroy, Paul. *There Ain't No Black in the Union Jack: The Cultural Politics of Race and Nation*. London: Hutchinson, 1987.

Gledhill, Christine "Signs of Melodrama." In *Stardom: Industry of Desire*, edited by Christine Gledhill. London: British Film Institute, 1991.

———, ed. *Star Signs*. London: British Film Institute, 1982.

———, ed. *Stardom: Industries of Desire*. London: British Film Institute, forthcoming, 1991.

Gomery, Douglas. "Corporate Ownership and Control in the Contemporary U.S. Film Industry." *Screen* 25, nos. 4–5 (July–October 1984): 60–69.

———. "Failed Opportunities: The Integration of the U.S. Motion Picture and Television Industries." *Quarterly Review of Film Studies* 9, no. 3 (Summer 1984): 219–28.

———. "The 'Warner-Vitaphone Peril': The American Film Industry Reacts to the Innovation of Sound." *Journal of the University Film Association* 27, no. 1 (Winter 1976): 11–19.

———. "Writing the History of the American Film Industry—Warner Bros. and Sound." *Screen* 17, no. 1 (Spring 1976): 40–53.

Goodman, Nelson. *The Languages of Art*. Indianapolis: Bobbs-Merrill, 1968.

Goodwin, Andrew. "Sample and Hold: Popular Music of the Digital Age of Reproduction." In *On Record: Rock, Pop, and the Written Word*, edited by Simon Frith and Andrew Goodwin. New York: Pantheon, 1990.

Gorbman, Claudia. *Unheard Melodies: Narrative Film Music*. Bloomington and Indianapolis: Indiana University Press, 1987.

Gramsci, Antonio. *Selections from "The Prison Notebooks" of Antonio Gramsci*. Edited by Quintin Hoare and Geoffrey Nowell-Smith. London: Lawrence and Wishart, 1971.

Griffith, Richard. *The Talkies: Articles and Illustrations from a Great Fan Magazine, 1928–40*. New York: Dover, 1971.

Griffith, Richard, Arthur Mayer, and Eileen Bowser. *The Movies*. Rev. ed. New York: Simon and Schuster, 1981.

Gross, Larry, John Katz, and Jay Ruby, eds. *Image Ethics: The Moral Rights of Subjects in Photographs, Film, and Television*. New York and Oxford: Oxford University Press, 1988.

Grossberg, Lawrence. "'I'd Rather Feel Bad Than Not Feel Anything at All': Rock and Roll, Music and Pleasure." *Enclitic* 8, nos. 1–2 (1984): 94–111.

Grossman, Gary. *Superman: Serial to Cereal*. New York: Popular Library, 1976.

Grove, Martin A. "Death Be Not Proud: Deceased Stars Can Still Endorse." *Adweek* 32, no. 38 (20 September 1982): 28.

Guattari, Felix. *Molecular Revolution: Psychiatry and Politics*. New York: Penguin, 1984.

Gurevitch, Michael, Tony Bennett, James Curran, and Janet Woollacott, eds. *Culture, Society, and the Media*. London and New York: Methuen, 1982.

Gustafson, Robert. "'What's Happening to Our Pix Biz?' From Warner Bros. to Warner Communications to Warner Communications Inc." In *The American Film Industry*, edited by Tino Balio. 2d ed. Madison: University of Wisconsin Press, 1985.

Hall, Stuart. "Cultural Studies and the Centre: Some Problematics and Problems." In *Culture, Media, Language*, edited by Stuart Hall, Dorothy Hobson, Andrew Lowe, and Paul Willis. London: Hutchinson, 1980.

———. "Cultural Studies: Two Paradigms." *Media, Culture, and Society* 2 (1980): 57–72.

———. "Encoding/Decoding." In *Culture, Media, Language*, edited by Stuart Hall, Dorothy Hobson, Andrew Lowe, and Paul Willis. London: Hutchinson, 1980.

————. "The Hinterland of Science: Ideology and the 'Sociology of Knowledge.'" *Working Papers in Cultural Studies* 9 (1977): 9–32.

————. "In Defence of Theory." In *People's History and Socialist Theory*, edited by Raphael Samuel. Boston: Routledge and Kegan Paul, 1981.

————. "Notes on Deconstructing 'The Popular.'" In *People's History and Socialist Theory*, edited by Raphael Samuel. Boston: Routledge and Kegan Paul, 1981.

————. "On Postmodernism and Articulation: An Interview." *Journal of Communication Inquiry* 10, no. 2 (Summer 1986): 45–60.

————. "Popular Culture and the State." In *Popular Culture and Social Relations*, edited by Tony Bennett, Colin Mercer, and Jane Woollacott. Milton Keynes, England, and Philadelphia: Open University Press, 1986.

————. "The Problem of Ideology—Marxism Without Guarantees." *Journal of Communication Inquiry* 10, no. 2 (Summer 1986): 28–43.

————. "A Reading of Marx's 1857 'Introduction to the Grundrisse.'" *Working Papers in Cultural Studies* 6 (1974): 132–70.

————. "The Rediscovery of 'Ideology': Return of the Repressed in Media Studies." In *Culture, Society, and the Media*, edited by Michael Gurevitch, Tony Bennett, James Curran, and Janet Woollacott. London and New York: Methuen, 1982.

————. "Re-thinking the 'Base-and-Superstructure' Metaphor." In *Class, Hegemony and Party*, edited by J. Bloomfield. London: Lawrence and Wishart, 1977.

————. "Signification, Representation, Ideology: Althusser and the Post-Structuralist Debates." *Critical Studies in Mass Communication* 2, no. 2 (June 1985): 91–114.

————. "The Social Eye of Picture Post." *Working Papers in Cultural Studies* 2 (1972): 71–120.

Hall, Stuart, Bob Lumley, and Gregor McLennan. "Politics, and Ideology: Gramsci." *Working Papers in Cultural Studies* 10 (1977): 45–76.

Harris, Neil. *Cultural Excursions: Marketing Appetites and Cultural Tastes in Modern America*. Chicago and London: University of Chicago Press, 1990.

————. "Who Owns Our Myths? Heroism and Copyright in an Age of Mass Culture." *Social Research* 52, no. 2 (Summer 1985): 241–67.

Hawkes, Terence. *Structuralism and Semiotics*. London: Methuen, 1977.

Heath, Stephen. "Film and System: Terms of Analysis, Pt. I." *Screen* 16, no. 2 (1975): 105–6.

————. "The Turn of the Subject." *Ciné-Tracts* 2, no. 2 (1979): 32–48.

Heath, Stephen, and Gillian Skirrow. "An Interview with Raymond Williams." In *Studies in Entertainment*, edited by Tania Modleski. Bloomington: Indiana University Press, 1986.

Hegel, Georg Wilhelm Friedrich. *The Philosophy of Right*. Translated by T. M. Knox. 1821. Reprint. London: Oxford University Press, 1965.

Hilmes, Michele. "The 'Ban' That Never Was: Hollywood and the Broadcasting Industry in 1932." *The Velvet Light Trap*, no. 23 (Spring 1989): 39–48.

———. *Hollywood and Broadcasting: From Radio to Cable*. Urbana and Chicago: University of Illinois Press, 1990.

Hindess, Barry, and Paul Q. Hirst. *Pre-Capitalist Modes of Production*. London: Routledge and Kegan Paul, 1975.

Hirst, Paul Q. "Althusser and the Theory of Ideology." *Economy and Society* 5, no. 4 (November 1976): 385–412.

Hodges, Donald A., ed. *Handbook of Music Psychology*. Dubuque, Iowa: Kandall/Hunt, 1980.

Hoff, James L. "Publicity—What Is It?" *Moving Picture World* 37 (20 July 1918): 319–21.

Holmes, Oliver Wendell. "The Stereoscope and the Stereograph." In *Classic Essays on Photography*, edited by Alan Trachtenberg. New Haven: Leete's Island Books, 1980.

Horkheimer, Max, and Theodor W. Adorno. *Dialectic of Enlightenment*. Translated by John Cumming. 1944. Reprint. New York: Continuum, 1987.

Huettig, Mae D. *Economic Control of the Motion Picture Industry: A Study in Industrial Organization*. Philadelphia: University of Pennsylvania Press, 1944.

Jameson, Fredric. *The Political Unconscious: Narrative as a Socially Symbolic Act*. Ithaca: Cornell University Press, 1981.

———. "Postmodernism, or the Cultural Logic of Late Capitalism." *New Left Review*, no. 146 (July–August 1984): 53–92.

———. "Reification and Utopia in Mass Culture." *Social Text* 1, no. 1 (1979): 129–48.

Jenkins, Reese. *Images and Enterprise: Technology and the American Photographic Industry*. London and Baltimore: Johns Hopkins University Press, 1975.

Johnston, Richard. "What Is Cultural Studies Anyway?" *Social Text* 6, no. 1 (1986–87): 38–80.

Kaplan, E. Ann. *Women and Film: Both Sides of the Camera*. New York: Methuen, 1983.

Kellner, Ulrich F. "The Myth of the Art Photograph: A Sociological Analysis." *History of Photography* 8 (October 1984): 249–75.

Kindem, Gorham. "Hollywood's Movie Star System: A Historical Overview." In *The American Movie Industry: The Business of Motion Pictures*, edited by Gorham Kindem. Carbondale and Edwardsville, Ill.: Southern Illinois University Press, 1982.

———. "Hollywood's Movie Star System During the Studio Era." *Film Reader* 6 (1985): 13–26.

King, Barry. "Articulating Stardom." *Screen* 26, no. 5 (September–October 1985): 27–50.

———. "The Hollywood Star System." Ph.D. diss., University of London, 1984.

———. "Screen Acting: Reflections on the Day." *Screen* 27, nos. 2–4 (August 1986): 134–39.

———. "The Star and the Commodity: Notes Towards a Performance Theory of Stardom." *Cultural Studies* 1, no. 2 (May 1987): 145–61.

————. "Stardom and Symbolic Degeneracy: Television and the Transformation of Stars as Public Symbols." Paper presented at the annual meeting of the Society for Cinema Studies, Washington, D.C., May 1990, forthcoming in *Semiotica*, 1992.

Klaprat, Cathy. "The Star as Market Strategy: Bette Davis in Another Light." In *The American Film Industry*, edited by Tino Balio. 2d ed. Madison: University of Wisconsin Press, 1985.

Klingender, F. D., and Stuart Legg. *Money Behind the Screen*. London: Lawrence and Wishart, 1937.

Krauss, Rosalind. *The Originality of the Avant-Garde and Other Modernist Myths*. Cambridge: MIT Press, 1985.

————. "Tracing Nadar." In *Reading into Photography*, edited by Thomas F. Barrow, Shelley Armitage, and William E. Tydeman. Albuquerque: University of New Mexico Press, 1982.

Krieger, Murray, ed. *The Aims of Representation: Subject/Text/History*. New York: Columbia University Press, 1988.

Kristeva, Julia. "On the Melancholic Imaginary." *New Formations* 3 (Winter 1987): 5–18.

Lahue, Kalton. *Continued Next Week: A History of the Moving Picture Serial*. Norman: University of Oklahoma Press, 1964.

Lardner, James. *Fast Forward: Hollywood, the Japanese, and the VCR Wars*. New York and London: W. W. Norton, 1987.

Lawrence, Amy. "The Pleasures of Echo: The Listener and the Voice." *Journal of Film and Video* 40, no. 4 (Fall 1988): 3–14.

Lazere, Donald, ed. *American Media and Mass Culture: Left Perspectives*. Berkeley and London: University of California Press, 1987.

Lefebvre, Henri. *Everyday Life in the Modern World*. Translated by Sacha Rabinovitch. 1967. Reprint. London: Penguin, 1971.

Lenning, Arthur. *The Count: The Life and Films of Bela "Dracula" Lugosi*. New York: G. P. Putnam, 1974.

Lester, David, and Irene Lester. *The Shirley Temple Story*. New York: G. P. Putnam, 1983.

Levin, Tom. "The Acoustic Dimension: Notes on Cinema Sound." *Screen* 25, no. 3 (1984): 55–68.

Lewin, George. "Dubbing and Its Relation to Sound Picture Production." *Journal of the Society of Motion Picture Engineers* 16, no. 1 (January 1931): 38–48.

Lewis, Lloyd, and Henry Justin. *Oscar Wilde Discovers America*. New York: Harcourt Brace, 1936.

Lipman, Andy. *The Electronic Pirates*. London: Comedia/Marion Boyars, 1986.

Litwak, Mark. *Reel Power: The Struggle for Influence and Success in the New Hollywood*. New York: William Morrow, 1986.

Locke, John. *Two Treatises of Government*. Edited by Thomas I. Cook. 1690. Reprint. London: MacMillan, 1947.

Lovell, Terry. "The Social Relations of Cultural Production: Absent Centre of a

New Discourse." In *One-Dimensional Marxism: Althusser and the Politics of Culture*, edited by Simon Clarke, Victor Jeleniewski Siedler, Kevin McDonnel, Kevin Robbins, and Terry Lovell. London: Allison and Busby, 1980.

Lukács, Georg. *History and Class Consciousness*. Translated by Rodney Livingstone. Cambridge: MIT Press, 1971.

MacCabe, Colin, ed. *High Theory/Low Culture*. New York: St. Martin's Press, 1986.

McCanell, Dean. *The Time of the Sign: A Semiotic Interpretation of Modern Culture*. Bloomington: Indiana University Press, 1982.

———. *The Tourist: A New Theory of the Leisure Class*. New York: Schocken, 1985.

McCauley, Elizabeth Anne. *A. A. E. Disdéri and the Carte de Visite Portrait Photograph*. New Haven: Yale University Press, 1985.

MacDonell, Diane. *Theories of Discourse: An Introduction*. Oxford: Basil Blackwell, 1986.

Macherey, Pierre. *A Theory of Literary Production*. Translated by Geoffrey Wall. London: Routledge and Kegan Paul, 1978.

Macpherson, C. B. *The Political Theory of Possessive Individualism: Hobbes to Locke*. Oxford: Oxford University Press, 1962.

McRobbie, Angela. "Postmodernism and Popular Culture." *Journal of Communication Inquiry* 10, no. 2 (Summer 1986): 108–16.

McWilliams, Harry. "I Beat the Drum: 1907–1946." Unpublished manuscript.

Maltby, Richard. "The Political Economy of Hollywood: The Studio System." In *Cinema, Politics, and Society in America*, edited by Philip Davies and Brian Neve. Manchester: University of Manchester Press, 1982.

Mandell, Ernest. *Late Capitalism*. Translated by Joris DeBres. London: New Left Books, 1975.

Mann, Denise. "The Spectacularization of Everyday Life: Recycling Hollywood Stars and Fans in Early TV Variety Shows." *Camera Obscura* 16 (January 1988): 49–77.

Marchand, Roland. *Advertising the American Dream: Making Way for Modernity, 1920–1940*. Berkeley and Los Angeles: University of California Press, 1985.

Marcus, Greil. *Lipstick Traces: A Secret History of the Twentieth Century*. Cambridge: Harvard University Press, 1989.

Marofloti, Pasqual Mario. *Caruso's Method of Vocal Production: The Scientific Culture of the Voice*. Austin: Cadica Enterprises, 1958.

Martin, Martin. "Those Ad Endorsements." *Screenland*, March 1928.

Marx, Karl. *Capital*. Vol. 1. Translated by Ben Fowkes. 1867. Reprint. New York: Vintage Books, 1977.

———. *Critique of Hegel's Philosophy of Right*. Translated by Annette Jolin and Joseph O'Malley. Edited by Joseph O'Malley. 1843. Reprint. Cambridge: Cambridge University Press, 1970.

Marx, Karl, and Friedrich Engels. *The German Ideology, Collected Works*. Vol. 5. London: Lawrence and Wishart, 1976.

Mauss, Marcel. *Sociology and Psychology: Essays*. Translated by Ben Brewster. London: Routledge, 1979.

Mayer, Michael F. *The Film Industries*. New York: Hastings House, 1973.

Metz, Christian. "Photography and Fetish." *October* 34 (1985): 81–90.

Miller, Mark Crispin. "Hollywood: The Ad." *Atlantic Monthly* 265, no. 4 (April 1990): 41–68.

Miller, Nancy K. *Subject to Change: Reading Feminist Writing*. New York: Columbia University Press, 1988.

Mitchell, W. J. T. *Iconology: Image, Text, Ideology*. Chicago and London: University of Chicago Press, 1986.

———, ed. *The Politics of Interpretation*. Chicago and London: University of Chicago Press, 1982.

Modleski, Tania, ed. *Studies in Entertainment*. Bloomington: Indiana University Press, 1986.

Monaco, James. *Celebrity: The Media as Image Makers*. New York: Dell, 1978.

Morella, Joe, and Edward Epstein. *The "It" Girl: The Incredible Story of Clara Bow*. New York: Delacorte Press, 1976.

Moretti, Franco. *Signs Taken for Wonders*. Translated by Susan Fischer, David Forgacs, and David Miller. London and New York: Verso, 1983.

Morin, Edgar. *The Stars*. Translated by Richard Howard. London and New York: Grove Press, 1961.

Morley, David. *Family Television: Cultural Power and Domestic Leisure*. London: Comedia, 1986.

Morris, Meaghan. *The Pirate's Fiancée: Feminism, Reading, Postmodernism*. London: Verso, 1988.

Mosco, Vincent, and Janet Wasko, eds. *Popular Culture and Mass Media*. Norwood, N.J.: Ablex, 1983.

Mulvey, Laura. "Visual Pleasure and Narrative Cinema." *Screen* 16, no. 3 (Autumn 1975): 6–18.

Naremore, James. *Acting in the Cinema*. Berkeley: University of California Press, 1988.

Neale, Steve. *Cinema and Technology: Image, Sound, Colour*. Bloomington: Indiana University Press, 1985.

Nesbitt, Molly. "What Was an Author?" *Yale French Studies* 73 (1987): 229–57.

Newhall, Beaumont. *The Daguerreotype in America*. 3d ed., rev. New York: Dover Publications, 1976.

———. *The History of Photography*. New York: Museum of Modern Art, 1978.

Nichols, Bill. "The Work of Culture in the Age of Cybernetic Systems." *Screen* 29, no. 1 (Winter 1988): 22–46.

———, ed. *Movies and Methods*. Berkeley and Los Angeles: University of California Press, 1976.

———, ed. *Movies and Methods*. Vol. 2. Berkeley and Los Angeles: University of California Press, 1985.

Nochlin, Linda. "Why Have There Been No Great Women Artists?" In *Art and*

Sexual Politics, edited by Elizabeth Baker and Thomas B. Hess. London: Collier Macmillan, 1973.

O'Connor, James. *Accumulation Crisis*. London: Basil Blackwell, 1984.

Ollman, Bertell. *Alienation*. 2d ed. Cambridge and London: Cambridge University Press, 1978.

Owens, Craig. "The Discourse of Others: Feminists and Postmodernism." In *The Anti-Aesthetic: Essays on Postmodern Culture*, edited by Hal Foster. Port Townsend, Wash.: Bay Press, 1983.

———. "Posing." In *Difference: On Representation and Sexuality*, edited by Kate Linker. New York: New Museum of Contemporary Art, 1985.

———. "Sherrie Levine at A&M Artworks." *Art in America* 70, no. 6 (Summer 1982): 148.

Pleynet, Marcelin, and Jean Thibaudeau. "Economique, Idéologie, Formel." *Cinéthique*, no. 3 (1971).

Podesta, Patti, ed. *Resolution: A Critique of Video Art*. Los Angeles: Los Angeles Contemporary Exhibitions, 1986.

Pollock, Griselda. "Artists, Mythologies, and Media—Genius, Madness, and Art History." *Screen* 21, no. 3 (1980): 57–96.

———. *Vision and Difference: Femininity, Feminism, and Histories of Art*. New York: Routledge, 1988.

Prindle, David F. *The Politics of Glamour: Ideology and Democracy in the Screen Actors' Guild*. Madison: University of Wisconsin Press, 1988.

Radway, Janice. *Reading the Romance: Women, Patriarchy, and Popular Literature*. Chapel Hill: University of North Carolina Press, 1984.

Ramsaye, Terry. *A Million and One Nights*. 1926. Reprint. New York: Simon and Schuster, 1964.

Reichenbach, Harry. *Phantom Fame: The Anatomy of Ballyhoo*. London: Noel Douglas, 1932.

———. "Press Books Then and Now." *Moving Picture World* 85, no. 4 (March 1927): 318.

Resor, Stanley. "Personalities and the Public: Some Aspects of Testimonial Advertising." *J. Walter Thompson News Bulletin*, no. 138 (April 1929).

Rosen, Philip. "History of Image, Image of History: Subject and Ontology in Bazin." *Wide Angle* 9, no. 4 (1987): 7–34.

———. "Subject Formation and Social Formation: Issues and Hypotheses." In *Cinema and Language*, edited by Stephen Heath and Patricia Mellencamp. Frederick, Md.: University Publications of America, 1983.

———, ed. *Narrative, Apparatus, Ideology: A Film Theory Reader*. New York: Columbia University Press, 1986.

Ross, Murray. *Stars and Strikes*. New York: Columbia University Press, 1941.

Rossi-Landi, Ferruccio. *Linguistics and Economics*. The Hague and Paris: Mouton and Co., 1975.

Ryan, Allan. *Property*. Minneapolis: University of Minnesota Press, 1987.

———. *Property and Political Theory*. Oxford: Basil Blackwell, 1984.

Samuel, Raphael, ed. *People's History and Socialist Theory*. Boston: Routledge and Kegan Paul, 1981.

Samuelson, Paul A. *Economics*. New York: McGraw Hill, 1976.

Sargent, Epes W. "The Development of Exploitation." *Variety*, 29 December 1931, 12.

———. "Exploitation: Its Beginning and Its Advance." *Moving Picture World* 85, no. 4 (March 1927): 286–87.

Saunders, David. "Copyright and the Legal Relations of Literature." *New Formations*, no. 4 (Spring 1988): 125–43.

Saussure, Ferdinand de. *Course in General Linguistics*. Translated by Wade Baskin. 1959. Reprint. New York: McGraw Hill, 1974.

Schatz, Thomas. *The Genius of the System*. New York: Pantheon, 1988.

Schickel, Richard. *The Disney Version: The Life, Times, Art, and Commerce of Walt Disney*. New York: Avon, 1968.

Sekula, Alan. "The Body and the Archive." *October* 39 (Winter 1986): 3–64.

———. *Photography Against the Grain: Essays and Photoworks, 1973–1983*. Halifax, Nova Scotia: Press of the Nova Scotia College of Art and Design, 1984.

———. "The Traffic in Photographs." In *Modernism and Modernity: The Vancouver Conference Papers*, edited by Benjamin H. D. Buchloh, Serge Guilbaut, and David Solkin. Halifax, Nova Scotia: Press of the Nova Scotia College of Art and Design, 1983.

Sennett, Richard. *The Fall of Public Man*. New York: Vintage Books, 1974.

Shell, Marc. *Money, Language, and Thought: Literary and Philosophical Economies From the Medieval to the Modern Era*. Berkeley: University of California Press, 1982.

Siedler, Victor Jeleniewski, Kevin McDonnel, Kevin Robbins, and Terry Lovell, eds. *One-Dimensional Marxism: Althusser and the Politics of Culture*. London: Allison and Busby, 1980.

Silverman, Kaja. *The Acoustic Mirror: The Female Voice in Psychoanalysis and Cinema*. Bloomington and Indianapolis: Indiana University Press, 1988.

Simmel, Georg. *Philosophy of Money*. Translated by Tom Bottmore and David Frisby. London: Routledge and Kegan Paul, 1978.

Sinclair, Charles. "Should Hollywood Get It for Free?" *Sponsor*, 8 August 1955.

Slide, Anthony. *Aspects of American Film History Before 1920*. Metuchen, N.J.: Scarecrow Press, 1978.

———. "The Evolution of the Film Star." *Films in Review* 25 (December 1974): 591–94.

Smith, Gary. *Thinking Through Benjamin*. Chicago: University of Chicago Press, 1984.

Smith, Paul. *Discerning the Subject*. Minneapolis: University of Minnesota Press, 1988.

Solomon-Godeau, Abigail. "The Legs of the Countess." *October* 39 (Winter 1986): 65–108.

Sparks, Colin. "The Evolution of Cultural Studies." *Screen Education* 22 (Spring 1977): 16–30.

Staiger, Janet. "Announcing Wares, Winning Patrons, Voicing Ideals: Thinking About the History and Theory of Film Advertising." *Cinema Journal* 29, no. 3 (Spring 1990): 3–31.

———. "The Eyes Are Really the Focus: Photoplay Acting and Film Form and Style." *Wide Angle* 6, no. 4 (1985): 14–23.

———. "Seeing Stars." *The Velvet Light Trap*, no. 20 (Summer 1983): 10–15.

Stallings, Penny, and Howard Mandelbaum. "Moonlighting with the Stars." *American Film* 9, no. 2 (November 1983): 40–46.

Stedman, Raymond. *The Serial: Suspense and Drama by Installment*. 2d ed. Norman, Okla.: University of Oklahoma Press, 1977.

Stewart, Susan. *On Longing: Narratives of the Miniature, the Gigantic, the Souvenir, the Collection*. Baltimore: Johns Hopkins University Press, 1984.

Strait, Raymond. *James Garner*. New York: St. Martin's Press, 1985.

Sudjic, Deyan. *Cult Heroes: How to Be Famous for More than Fifteen Minutes*. London: André Deutsch, 1989.

Susman, Warren. *Culture as History: The Transformation of American Society in the Twentieth Century*. New York: Pantheon, 1984.

———. " 'Personality' and the Making of Twentieth-Century Culture." In *New Directions in American Intellectual History*, edited by John Higham and Paul K. Conklin. Baltimore: Johns Hopkins University Press, 1979.

Tagg, John. *The Burden of Representation: Essays on Photographies and Histories*. Amherst: University of Massachusetts Press, 1988.

Tagg, John. "A Democracy of the Image: Photographic Portraiture and Commodity Production." *Ten-8*, no. 13 (1984): 18, 23. Reprint. In *The Burden of Representation: Essays on Photographies and Histories*, by John Tagg. Amherst: University of Massachusetts Press.

———. "Power and Photography—Part II, A Legal Reality: The Photograph as Property in Law." *Screen Education* 37 (Winter 1981): 17–27. Reprint. In *The Burden of Representation: Essays on Photographies and Histories*, by John Tagg. Amherst: University of Massachusetts Press, 1988.

Thompson, E. P. "The Grid of Inheritance." In *Family and Inheritance: Rural Society in Western Europe, 1200–1800*, edited by Jack Goody, Joan Thirsk, and E. P. Thompson. Cambridge: Cambridge University Press, 1976.

———. *The Poverty of Theory and Other Essays*. London: Merlin Press, 1978.

———. *Whigs and Hunters: The Origins of the Black Act*. New York: Pantheon, 1975.

Trachtenberg, Alan. *The Incorporation of America: Culture and Society in the Gilded Age*. New York: Hill and Wang, 1982.

———. *Reading American Photographs: Images as History, Mathew Brady to Walker Evans*. New York: Hill and Wang, 1989.

———, ed. *Classic Essays on Photography*. New Haven: Leete's Island Books, 1980.

Turan, Kenneth. "Superman! Supersell!" *American Film* 4, no. 3 (December–January 1979): 49–52.

Viera, John David. "Images as Property." In *Image Ethics: The Moral Rights of Subjects in Photographs, Film, and Television*, edited by Larry Gross, John Katz, and Jay Ruby. New York and Oxford: Oxford University Press, 1988.

———. "The Law of Star Images, Media Images, and Personal Images: Personality as Property." Ph.D. diss., University of Southern California, 1985.

Volosinov, V. N. *Marxism and the Philosophy of Language*. Translated by Ladislav Matejk and I. R. Titunik. 1929. Reprint. New York: Seminar Press, 1973.

Waites, Bernard, Tony Bennett, and Graham Martin, eds. *Popular Culture: Past and Present*. London: Croom Helm, 1982.

Wallis, Brian, ed. *Art after Modernism: Rethinking Representation*. New York: New Museum of Contemporary Art, 1984.

Wasko, Janet. *Movies and Money: Financing the American Film Industry*. Norwood, N.J.: Ablex Publishing, 1982.

Weis, Elisabeth, and John Belton, eds. *Film Sound: Theory and Practice*. New York: Columbia University Press, 1985.

Weiss, Ken, and Ed Goodgold. *To Be Continued*. New York: Crown Publishing, 1972.

Welsh, Alexander. "Writing and Copying in the Age of Steam." In *Victorian Literature and Society: Essays Presented to Richard D. Altick*, edited by J. R. Kincaid and A. J. Kuhn. Columbus: Ohio State University Press, 1984.

Wilde, Oscar. *The Picture of Dorian Gray*. New York: Book League of America, 1931.

Wilden, Anthony. *The Rules Are No Game: The Strategy of Communication*. London and New York: Routledge, 1987.

Wilkinson, Lupton A. "Crazy Contracts of the Stars." *Motion Picture-Hollywood Magazine*, April 1943.

Willemen, Paul. "Notes on Subjectivity—On Reading Ed Branigan's 'Subjectivity Under Siege.'" *Screen* 19, no. 1 (Spring 1978): 41–69.

Williams, Alan. "Godard's Use of Sound." In *Film Sound: Theory and Practice*, edited by Elisabeth Weis and John Belton. New York: Columbia University Press, 1985.

———. "Is Sound Recording Like a Language?" *Yale French Studies* 60 (1980): 51–66.

Williams, Linda. *Hard Core: Power, Pleasure, and the "Frenzy of the Visible."* Berkeley and Los Angeles: University of California Press, 1989.

Williams, Raymond. *Communications*. Harmondsworth, Middlesex: Penguin, 1967.

———. *Culture and Society: 1780–1950*. New York: Columbia University Press, 1983.

———. *Keywords*. New York and Oxford: Oxford University Press, 1976.

———. "The Magic System." *New Left Review*, no. 41 (July–August 1960): 27–32.

————. *Problems in Materialism and Culture*. London: Verso, 1980.

————. "Problems of Materialism." *New Left Review*, no. 109 (May–June 1978).

————. *The Sociology of Culture*. New York: Schocken Books, 1982.

Winston, Brian. *Misunderstanding Media*. Cambridge: Harvard University Press, 1986.

Wolff, Janet. *The Social Production of Art*. New York: New York University Press, 1984.

Wolin, Richard. *Walter Benjamin: An Aesthetic of Redemption*. New York: Columbia University Press, 1982.

Woodmansee, Martha. "The Genius and the Copyright: Economics and Legal Conditions for the Emergence of the 'Author.'" *Eighteenth-Century Studies* 17, no. 4 (1984): 425–48.

Yeck, Joanne L. "De Havilland vs. Warner Bros.: A Trial Decision That Marked a Turning Point." *American Classic Screen* 6, no. 3 (1983): 7–11.

WORKS IN LEGAL STUDIES

Abraham, K. "Statutory Interpretation and Literary Theory." *Rutgers Law Review* 32 (1979): 676–94.

Abrams, Howard B. "The Historic Foundations of American Copyright Law: Exploding the Myth of Common Law Copyright." *Wayne Law Review* 29, no. 3 (Spring 1983): 1119–85.

Acheson, Arthur. *Trade-Mark Advertising as an Investment*. New York: The New Evening Post, 1917.

Adams, Paul E. "Superman, Mickey Mouse, and Gerontology." *Trademark Reporter* 64 (1974): 183–91.

Allen, William. "Legal Tests of Photography-as-Art: Sarony and Others." *History of Photography* 10, no. 3 (July–September 1986): 221–28.

American Bar Association. *Two Hundred Years of English and American Patent, Trademark, and Copyright Law. Papers Delivered at the Bicentennial Symposium of the Section of Patent, Trademark, and Copyright Law Meeting, Atlanta, Georgia, August 9, 1976, American Bar Association*. Chicago: American Bar Center, 1977.

Anderson, Nancy E., and David Greenberg. "From Substance to Form: The Legal Theories of Pashukanis and Edelman." *Social Text* 7 (Spring–Summer 1983): 69–84.

Anson, Weston. "A Licensing Retrospective and Glimpse into the Future." *Merchandising Reporter* 3, no. 5 (June–July 1984): 4–5.

Apfelbaum, Marc J. "Copyright and Right of Publicity: One Pea in Two Pods?" *Georgetown Law Review* 71 (1983): 1567–94.

Arthur, C. J. "Towards a Materialist Theory of Law." *Critique* 7 (1976): 31–46.

Balbus, Isaac D. "Commodity Form and Legal Form: An Essay on the 'Relative

Autonomy' of the Law." *Law and Society Review* 11, no. 3 (Winter 1977): 571–88.

Balibar, Etienne. "On the Basic Concepts of Historical Materialism." In *Reading "Capital,"* by Louis Althusser and Etienne Balibar. Translated by Ben Brewster. London: New Left Books, 1970.

Banks, John C. "Photographer's Common Law Rights in the Product of His Art." *Rocky Mountain Law Review* 7 (1934–35): 238–46.

Barron, James. "Warren and Brandeis, The Right to Privacy: Demystifying a Landmark Citation." *Suffolk University Law Review* 13 (1979): 875–922.

Battersby, Gregory J., and Charles W. Grimes. "English Legal Decision Jars Licensing Commission." *The Licensing Book* 1, no. 5 (April 1984): 10–12.

———. *The Law of Merchandise and Character Licensing.* New York: Clark Boardman, 1985.

———. "The Year in Merchandising Law." *Merchandising Reporter* 4, no. 10 (November–December 1985): 4–7.

Beirne, Piers, and Richard Quinny, eds. *Marxism and the Law.* New York: John Wiley and Sons, 1982.

Bloch, Ernst. *Natural Law and Human Dignity.* Translated by Dennis J. Schmidt. 1961. Reprint. Cambridge: MIT Press, 1986.

Boorstin, Daniel J. *The Mysterious Science of Law: An Essay on Blackstone's Commentaries.* Cambridge: Harvard University Press, 1941.

Brassel, Roz, and Ken Kulzick. "Life After Death for the California Celebrity." *Los Angeles Lawyer* (January 1985): 12–15.

Brenner, Daniel. "A Two-Phase Application to Copyrighting the Fine Arts." *Bulletin of the Copyright Society of the U.S.A.* 24 (1976): 85–117.

Breyer, Stephen. "The Uneasy Case for Copyright in Books, Photocopies, and Computer Programs." *Harvard Law Review* 84 (December 1970): 281–351.

Brown, Ralph S. "Adherence to the Berne Copyright Convention: The Moral Rights Issue." *Journal of the Copyright Society of America* 35 (April 1988): 196–209.

Brylawski, E. Fulton. "Protection of Characters—Sam Spade Revisited." *Bulletin of the Copyright Society of America* 22 (1974): 77–103.

Cain, Maureen. "The Main Themes of Marx's and Engels's Sociology of Law." *British Journal of Law and Society* 1, no. 2 (1974): 136–68.

Cain, Maureen, and Alan Hunt. *Marx and Engels on Law.* London: Academic Press, 1979.

Chernoff, George, and Hershel Sarbin. *Photography and the Law.* 5th ed. New York: AMPHOTO, 1977.

Cohen, Felix. "Transcendental Nonsense and the Functional Approach." *Columbia Law Review* 35, no. 6 (1935): 809–49.

Cohen, Morris. "Property and Sovereignty." *Cornell Law Quarterly* 13 (1927): 8–30.

Cohen, Saul. "Justice Holmes and Copyright Law." *Southern California Law Review* 32 (1959): 263–79.

Collins, Hugh. "Contract and Legal Theory." In *Legal Theory and Common Law*, edited by W. Twining. Oxford: Basil Blackwell, 1986.

———. *The Law of Contract*. London: Weidenfeld and Nicholson, 1986.

———. *Marxism and Law*. New York: Oxford University Press, 1984.

Copinger, Walter Arthur. *Copinger and Skone James on Copyright*. London: Sweet and Maxwell, 1980.

"Copyright—Study of the Term 'Writings' in the Copyright Clause of the Constitution." *New York University Law Review* 31 (1956): 1263–1312.

Daniel, Denis Allan. "Trademark Piracy: The Brazilian Way." *Merchandising Reporter* 4, no. 3 (March 1985): 11–14.

DaSilva, Russell J. "*Droit Moral* and the Amoral Copyright: A Comparison of Rights in France and the United States." *Bulletin of the Copyright Society of America* 28 (1980): 3–58.

Davidson, Bill. "Crackup in Hazzard County! Here's the Casualty Report." *TV Guide* 30, no. 52 (25 December 1982): 13–15.

Decisions of the United States Courts Involving Copyright and Literary Properties, 1789–1909. Bulletin no. 13. Washington, D.C.: Copyright Office, Library of Congress.

Dekom, Peter J., Lawrence P. Mortorff, and Michael Sherman, eds. *U.C.L.A. Entertainment Symposium: Sources of Revenue and Presale Financing for Theatrical Motion Pictures*. Los Angeles: U.C.L.A., 1977.

Derenberg, Walter J., and Paul B. Morofsky, eds. *European Trademark Law and Practice*. New York: Practicing Law Institute, 1971.

D'Onofrio, Steven J. "Performance Rights in Sound Recordings—To Pay or Not to Pay, That Is the Question." *Beverly Hills Bar Association Journal* (Winter 1980): 347–71.

———. "In Support of Performance Rights in Sound Recordings." *U.C.L.A. Law Review* 29 (October 1981): 168–98.

Drone, Eaton S. *A Treatise on the Law of Property in Intellectual Productions in Great Britain and the United States*. Boston: Little, Brown and Co., 1879.

Duggan, James. "A Cause of Action for Simulation of Sound Recordings? Yes!: Reflections on the 1976 Copyright Act." *Rutgers Law Review* 38 (Fall 1985): 139–63.

Dworkin, Ronald. "Law as Interpretation." *Texas Law Review* 60, no. 3 (1982): 527–50.

———. *Taking Rights Seriously*. Cambridge: Harvard University Press, 1977.

Edelman, Bernard. "The Character and His Double." In *The Real Me: Postmodernism and the Question of Identity*. ICA Documents 6, edited by Lisa Appignanesi. London: Institute of Contemporary Arts, 1987.

———. "Commentaire de la loi n. 85–660 (du 3 juillet 1985), relative au droits d'auteur et aux droits voisins." *Actualité Législative Dalloz*, Numéro spécial (1987).

———. *Le droit saisi par le photographie: éléments pour une théorie marxiste du droit*. Paris: Maspéro, 1973.

———. *La légalisation de la classe ouvrière*. Paris: C. Bourgois, 1978.

———. *L'Homme des foules*. Paris: Payot, 1981.

———. *Ownership of the Image: Elements for a Marxist Theory of Law*. Translated by Elizabeth Kingdom. London: Routledge and Kegan Paul, 1979.

———. "The Transition in Kant's 'Doctrine of Right.'" Translated by Keith Tribe. *Economy and Society* 6, no. 2 (May 1977): 145–65.

Edelman, Bernard, and Marie-Angèle Hermite, eds. *L'Homme, la nature et le droit*. Paris: C. Bourgois, 1988.

Elber, George A., et al. "An Agreement with a Performer for His Services on a Television Program." In *Television Agreements*, edited by David Morris Solinger. New York: Practicing Law Institute, 1956.

Fallon, Perlie P. "Some Influences of Justice Holmes' Thought on Current Law—Conflict of Laws, Contempt, Contracts, Copyright, and Corporations." *Tennessee Law Review* 19 (1946): 118–27.

Feinman, Jay M. "Critical Approaches to Contract Law: *U.C.L.A. Law Review* 30 (1983): 829–60.

Fish, Stanley. "Don't Know Much About the Middle Ages: Posner on Law and Literature." In *Doing What Comes Naturally*, by Stanley Fish. Durham, N.C.: Duke University Press.

———. "Interpretation and the Pluralist Vision." *Texas Law Review* 60 (1982): 495–505.

———. "Working on the Chain Gang: Interpretation in Law and Literature." *Texas Law Review* 60 (1982): 527–61. Reprint. In *The Politics of Interpretation*, edited by W. J. T. Mitchell. Chicago and London: University of Chicago Press, 1982.

Fitzpatrick, Peter, and Alan Hunt, eds. *Critical Legal Studies*. London: Basil Blackwell, 1987.

Fletcher, Peter L., and Edward L. Rubin. "The Descendibility of the Right of Publicity: Is There Commercial Life After Death?" *Yale Law Journal* 89 (1980): 1125–32.

———. "Privacy, Publicity, and the Portrayal of Real People by the Media." *Yale Law Journal* 88, no. 8 (July 1979): 1577–1622.

Forbath, William E. "Taking Lefts Seriously." *Yale Law Journal* 92, no. 6 (1983): 1041–64.

Fox-Genovese, Elizabeth. "Property and Patriarchy in Classical Bourgeois Political Theory." *Radical History Review* 4 (Spring–Summer 1977): 36–59.

Fraser, Andrew. "The Corporation as Body Politic." *Telos* 57 (1983): 5–40.

———. "The Legal Theory We Need Now." *Socialist Review* 40–41 (1978): 147–87.

Friedman, Lawrence M. *A History of American Law*. 2d ed. New York: Simon and Schuster, 1985.

Gabel, Peter. "A Critical Anatomy of the Legal Opinion." *ALSA* (Fall 1980): 5–11.

———. Review of *Taking Rights Seriously*, by Ronald Dworkin. *Harvard Law Review* 91 (1977): 302–15.

Gabel, Peter, and Jay M. Feinman. "Contract Law as Ideology." In *The Politics of*

Law: A Progressive Critique, edited by David Kairys. New York: Pantheon, 1982.

Germain, Kenneth B. "Unfair Trade Practices Under Section 43(a) of the Latham Act: You've Come a Long Way, Baby—Too Far, Maybe?" *Indiana Law Journal* 49 (1973): 84–116.

Ginsburg, Jane, and John M. Kernpochan. "One Hundred and Two Years Later: The U.S. Joins the Berne Convention." *Columbia Law Review* 13 (1988): 1–38.

Goettsch, Raymond H. "The Right of Publicity: Premature Burial for California Property Rights in the Wake of *Lugosi*." *Pacific Law Journal* 12 (1981): 987–1011.

Goldstein, Richard, and Arthur Kessler. "The Twilight Zone: Meandering in the Area of Performers' Rights." *U.C.L.A. Law Review* 9 (1962): 819–61.

Goodrich, Peter. *Reading the Law: A Critical Introduction to Legal Method Techniques*. London: Basil Blackwell, 1986.

Gordon, Harold. "Right of Property in Name, Likeness, Personality, and History." *Northwestern University Law Review* 55 (1960): 553–613.

Gordon, Robert. "Critical Legal Histories." *Stanford Law Review* 36 (1984): 57–125.

———. "Historicism in Legal Scholarship." *Yale Law Journal* 90 (1981): 1017, 1028–45.

Gross, Joan. "The Right of Publicity Revisited: Reconciling Fame, Fortune, and Constitutional Rights." *Boston Law Review* 62, no. 4 (July 1982): 986–95.

Harrison, Thomas E. "The Protection of Titles and Characters." *Merchandising Reporter* 4, no. 7 (August 1985): 9–10.

Heise, Cathryn A. "Berne-ing Down the House [and Senate]. The Berne Convention Implementation Act of 1988." *Florida Bar Journal* 63 (July–August 1989): 62–65.

Hevesi, Dennis. "Heirs Warn of 'Poachers' in Afterlife of the Famous." *New York Times*, 26 February 1988, B1, col. 2.

Hirst, Paul Q. *Law, Socialism, and Democracy*. London and Boston: Allen and Unwin, 1986.

———. *On Law and Ideology*. London: Macmillan, 1979.

Hirst, Paul, and Elizabeth Kingdom. "On Edelman's 'Ownership of the Image.'" *Screen* 20, nos. 3–4 (Winter 1979–80): 135–40.

Hixon, Richard. *Privacy in a Public Society*. New York: Oxford University Press, 1987.

Hodgson, Cheryl. "Intellectual Property—Performer's Style—A Quest for Ascertainment, Recognition, and Protection." *Denver Law Journal* 52 (1975): 561–94.

Homburg, Robert. *Legal Rights of Performing Artists*. Translated by Maurice J. Speiser. New York: Baker and Voorhis, 1934.

Horwitz, Morton. "The Rule of Law: An Unqualified Human Good?" *Yale Law Journal* 86 (1977): 561–66.

———. *The Transformation of American Law, 1780–1860.* Cambridge: Harvard University Press, 1977.

———. "The Transformation of the Idea of Property in American Law, 1780–1860." *University of Chicago Law Review* 40 (1973): 248–90.

Hughes, Justin. "The Philosophy of Intellectual Property." *Georgetown Law Journal* 77 (1988): 288–366.

"Human Cannonballs and the First Amendment: Zacchini v. Scripps-Howard Broadcasting." *Stanford Law Review* 30 (1978): 1185–86.

Humphreys, Sally, ed. *The Discourse of Law.* London: Harwood Press, 1985.

Hutchinson, Allan C., and Patrick J. Monahan. "Law, Politics, and the Critical Legal Scholars: The Unfolding Drama of American Legal Thought." *Stanford Law Review* 36 (1984): 199–244.

Jackson, Bernard S. *Semiotics and Legal Theory.* London: Routledge and Kegan Paul, 1988.

Jaszi, Peter. "Towards a Theory of Copyright: The Metamorphoses of 'Authorship.'" *Duke Law Review* (forthcoming).

———. "When Works Collide: Derivative Motion Pictures, Underlying Rights, and the Public Interest." *U.C.L.A. Law Review* 28, no. 3 (1981): 715–30.

Jones, Michael E. "Celebrity Endorsements: A Case for Alarm and Concern for the Future." *New England Law Review* 15, no. 3 (1979–80): 521–44.

Kairys, David. "Legal Reasoning." In *The Politics of Law: A Progressive Critique*, edited by David Kairys. New York: Pantheon, 1982.

———, ed. *The Politics of Law: A Progressive Critique.* New York: Pantheon, 1982.

Kalven, Harry. "Privacy in Tort Law—Were Warren and Brandeis Wrong?" *Law and Contemporary Problems* 31, no. 2 (1966): 326–41.

Kaplan, Benjamin. "Encounters with O. W. Holmes, Jr." *Holmes and the Common Law: A Century Later.* Cambridge: Harvard Law School, 1983.

———. "Performer's Right and Copyright: The Capitol Records Case." *Harvard Law Review* 69 (1956): 409–39.

———. "Publication in Copyright Law: The Question of Phonograph Records." *University of Pennsylvania Law Review* 103 (1955): 469–90.

Kase, Francis J. *Copyright Thought in Continental Europe.* South Hackensack, N.J.: Fred B. Rothman, 1969.

Kelman, Mark. *A Guide to Critical Legal Studies.* Cambridge and London: Harvard University Press, 1987.

———. "Trashing." *Stanford Law Review* 36 (1984): 293–348.

Kennedy, Duncan. "Legal Education as Training for Hierarchy." In *The Politics of Law: A Progressive Critique*, edited by David Kairys. New York: Pantheon, 1982.

———. "The Structure of Blackstone's Commentaries." *Buffalo Law Review* 28 (1979): 209–382.

Kennedy, Duncan, and Karl E. Klare. "A Bibliography of Critical Legal Studies." *Yale Law Review* 94, no. 2 (December 1984): 461–89.

Klare, Karl E. "Law-Making as Praxis." *Telos* 40 (Summer 1979): 123–35.

Kravitz, Robert N. "Trademarks, Speech, and the *Gay Olympics* Case." *Boston University Law Review* 69, no. 1 (January 1989): 131–84.

Krieger, Paul E. "The Trademark Counterfeiting Act of 1984." *Merchandising Reporter* 4, no. 7 (August 1985): 4–6.

Kulzick, Ken. "Celebrity Jeopardy." *Entertainment Law Reporter* 5, no. 11 (1984): 3.

Kurnit, Richard. "'Dior' Case Leaves Constitutional Questions Unanswered." *New York Law Journal* (27 January 1984): 5.

Kuzui, Kaz. "Japanese Licensing: An Ever-Changing Market." *Merchandising Reporter* 3, no. 5 (June–July 1984): 30–31.

Lange, David. "Intellectual Property under the Constitution." *Duke Law Magazine* 7, no. 2 (Summer 1989): 15–18.

———. "Recognizing the Public Domain." *Law and Contemporary Problems* 44, no. 4 (Autumn 1981): 147–78.

Lee, Elizabeth C. "Celebrity Look-Alikes: Rethinking the Right to Privacy and Right to Publicity." *Entertainment and Sports Law Journal* 2 (Fall 1985): 193–217.

"Les Borden—Columbia's Dealmaker." *Merchandising Reporter* (November–December 1982): 14–19.

Levine, Marla. "The Right of Publicity as a Means of Protecting Performers' Style." *Loyola Law Review* 14 (1980): 129–63.

Licensing Law Handbook. New York: Clark Boardman, 1985.

Liebig, Anthony. "Style and Performance." *Bulletin of the Copyright Society of America* 17 (1969): 40–47.

Lind, Joel S. "The Right of Publicity in New York: A Practical Analysis." *Columbia Journal of Art and the Law* 7 (1982): 355–72.

Lindey, Alexander. *Entertainment Publishing and the Arts.* Vol. 1. New York: Clark Boardman, 1977.

McCarthy, J. Thomas. "Melville B. Nimmer and the Right of Publicity: A Tribute." *U.C.L.A. Law Review* 34 (June–August 1987): 1703–12.

———. *The Rights of Publicity and Privacy.* New York: Clark Boardman, 1988.

———. *Trademarks and Unfair Competition.* 2d ed. 2 vols. Rochester, N.Y.: Lawyers Co-operative Publishing Co., 1984.

Macpherson, C. B. "The Meaning of Property." In *Property: Mainstream and Critical Positions*, edited by C. B. Macpherson. Toronto and Buffalo: University of Toronto Press, 1978.

———, ed. *Property: Mainstream and Critical Positions.* Toronto and Buffalo: University of Toronto Press, 1978.

"Maggie Young—The 'Force' at Lucasfilm." *Merchandising Reporter* 3, no. 5 (June–July 1984): 15–16.

Margulies, Walter P. "FTC vs. Formica, Inc.: Trademarks Face Challenge of Their Lives." *Advertising Age*, 13 August 1979, 52–54.

Marvin, Charles A. "Author's Status in the United Kingdom and France: Common Law and the Moral Right Doctrine." *International and Comparative Law Quarterly* 20 (October 1971): 675–705.

Mensch, Betty [Elizabeth]. "Freedom of Contract as Ideology." Review of *The Rise and Fall of Freedom of Contract*, by P. S. Atiyah. *Stanford Law Review* 33, no. 75 (April 1981): 753–72.

———. "The History of Mainstream Legal Thought." In *The Politics of Law: A Progressive Critique*, edited by David Kairys. New York: Pantheon, 1982.

Metzger, Raphael. "Name That Tune: A Proposal for an Intrinsic Test of Musical Plagiarism." *Copyright Law Symposium* 34 (Summer 1987): 139–201.

Meyer, Michael, and Susan Oman. "Production Company Remedies for 'Star' Breaches." *Entertainment Law Journal* 1, no. 1 (April 1981): 25–30.

Miller, Arthur R., and Michael H. Davis. *Intellectual Property: Patents, Trademarks, and Copyright*. St. Paul: West Publishing Co., 1983.

Moore, Frank S. *The Legal Protection of Goodwill*. New York: Ronald Press, 1936.

Morgan, Bryan. "Sound Recording Copyright Law—Its Application to the Performance of Records and Tapes." *Cumberland Law Review* 11 (Fall 1980): 447–63.

Nimmer, Melville B. *Cases and Materials on Copyright and Other Aspects of Entertainment Litigation—Including Unfair Competition, Defamation, and Privacy*. 3d ed. St. Paul: West Publishing, 1985.

———. *Cases and Materials on Copyright and Other Aspects of Law Pertaining to Literary, Musical and Artistic Works*. St. Paul: West Publishing, 1971.

———. "Copyright and Quasi-Copyright Protection for Characters, Titles, and Phonograph Records." *Trademark Reporter* 59 (1969): 63–75.

———. "Copyright 1955." *California Law Review* 43 (1955): 791-808.

———. "The Law of Ideas." *Southern California Law Review* 27, no. 2 (1954): 120–48.

———. "The Right of Publicity." *Law and Contemporary Problems* 19 (1954): 203–23.

Nimmer, Melville B., and David Nimmer. *Nimmer on Copyright: A Treatise on the Law of Literary, Musical, and Artistic Property and the Protection of Ideas*. 8th ed. 4 vols. Albany, N.Y.: Matthew Bender, 1989.

Pashukanis, Evgeny B. *Law and Marxism: A General Theory*. Translated by Barbara Einhorn. Edited by Chris Arthur. 1924. Reprint. London: Ink Links, 1978.

———. *Selected Writings on Marxism and Law*. Translated by Peter B. Maggs. Edited by Piers Beirne and Robert Sharlett. New York: Academic Press, 1980.

Patterson, Lyman Ray. *Copyright in Historical Perspective*. Nashville: Vanderbilt University Press, 1968.

———. "Free Speech, Copyright, and Fair Use." *Vanderbilt Law Review* 40, no. 1 (January 1987): 1–66.

Pattishall, Beverly N. "Trademarks and the Monopoly Phobia." *Michigan Law Review* 50 (May 1952): 967–88.

"Pete Smith—Mickey's Mentor." *Merchandising Reporter* (June–July 1984): 12–14.

Philbin, Stephen H. "Judge Learned Hand and the Law of Patents and Copyright." *Harvard Law Review* 60 (1947): 394–404.

Pilpel, Harriet. "The Right of Publicity." *Bulletin of the Copyright Society of America* 27 (1980): 249–63.

Porter, Vincent. "Copyright: The New Protectionism." *Intermedia* 17, no. 1 (January 1989): 10–17.

———. "Film Copyright and Edelman's Theory of Law." *Screen* 20, nos. 3–4 (Winter 1979–80): 141–47.

———. "Film Copyright: Film Culture." *Screen* 19, no. 1 (Spring 1978): 90–107.

———. "On Authorship: A Reply." *Screen* 20, no. 2 (Summer 1979): 113–17.

Posner, Richard. *Law and Literature: A Misunderstood Relation*. Cambridge: Harvard University Press, 1988.

Prosser, William. *Law of Torts*. 3d ed. St. Paul: West Publishing, 1964.

———. "Privacy." *California Law Review* 48 (1960): 383–423.

"Protection for Literary and Cartoon Characters." *Harvard Law Review* 68 (1954): 349–63.

Quelch, John A. "How to Build a Product Licensing Program." *Harvard Business Review* 65, no. 3 (May–June 1985): 186, 188.

Reeves, Van Kirk, Ronald G. Bauer, and Stéphanie Lieser. "Retained Rights of Authors, Artists, and Composers under French Law on Literary and Artistic Property." *Journal of Arts Management and Law* 14, no. 4 (Winter 1985): 7–30.

Rohde, Stephen. "Dracula: Still Undead." *California Lawyer* (April 1985): 51–55.

Rose, Mark. "The Author as Proprietor: *Donaldson v. Becket* and the Genealogy of Modern Authorship." *Representations* 23 (Summer 1988): 51–85.

Ross, Seth. "Thirty-one Years after *Haelan Laboratories*: The Descendibility of Rights of Publicity." *Probate Law Journal* 5 (Winter 1985): 227–42.

Rudell, M. I. *Behind the Scenes: Practical Entertainment Law*. New York: Harcourt, 1984.

Rufflo, Suzanne. "Unfair Competition: Copycats Can No Longer 'Take the Money and Run.'" *Loyola Entertainment Law Journal* 7, no. 1 (1987): 191–99.

Samuelson, Pamela. "Information as Property: Do *Ruckleshaus* and *Carpenter* Signal a Changing Direction in Intellectual Property Law?" *Catholic University Law Review* 38 (1989): 365–400.

Schechter, Frank Isaac. *The Historical Foundations of Law Relating to Trademarks*. New York: Columbia University Press, 1925.

Selz, Thomas D., and Melvin Simensky. *Entertainment Law: Legal Concepts and Business Practices*. 3 vols. Colorado Springs: Shepard's McGraw-Hill, 1986.

Sharpe, James. "The People and the Law." In *Popular Culture in Seventeenth-Century England*, edited by Barry Reay. New York: St. Martin's Press, 1985.

Shears, Peter. "Character Merchandising: Holly Hobby and the Dukes of Hazzard." *Patent and Trademark Review* 82 (1984): 307–13.

Shipley, David E. "Publicity Never Dies; It Just Fades Away: The Right to Publicity and Federal Preemption." *Cornell Law Review* 66 (1981): 672–737.

Sobel, Lionel. "A Memorial Tribute to Melville B. Nimmer (1923–1985)." *Loyola Entertainment Law Journal* 6 (1985): 1–6.

Spring, Samuel. *Risks and Rights in Publishing, Television, Radio, Motion Pictures, Advertising, and Theater.* 2d ed. New York: W. W. Norton, 1952.

Strait, Raymond. *James Garner.* New York: St. Martin's Press, 1985.

Sugarman, D., ed. *Legality, Ideology, and the State.* New York: Academic Press, 1983.

Sumner, Colin. *Reading Ideologies: An Investigation into the Marxist Theory of Ideology and Law.* London: Academic Press, 1979.

Tannenbaum, David. "Enforcement of Personal Service Contracts in the Entertainment Industry." *California Law Review* 42, no. 1 (1954): 18–27.

Thompson, Larry A. "The Prime Time Crime." *Entertainment Law Journal* 1, no. 3 (July 1982): 1–11.

Toner, Michael E. "Celebrity Endorsements: A Case for Alarm and Concern for the Future." *New England Law Review* 15 (1980): 521–44.

Tournier, Jean-Loup. "The French Law of March 11, 1957, on Literary and Artistic Property." *Bulletin of the Copyright Society* 6, no. 1 (October 1958): 1–26.

"Transfer of the Right of Publicity: Dracula's Progeny and Privacy's Stepchild." *U.C.L.A. Law Review* 32 (1975): 1103–28.

Treece, James M. "Commercial Exploitation of Names, Likenesses, and Personal Histories." *Texas Law Review* 51 (1973): 637–72.

Tushnet, Mark. "Corporations and Free Speech." In *The Politics of Law: A Progressive Critique,* edited by David Kairys. New York: Pantheon, 1982.

———. "Critical Legal Studies and Constitutional Law: An Essay in Deconstruction." *Stanford Law Review* 36 (January 1984): 623–47.

———. "An Essay on Rights." *Texas Law Review* 62, no. 8 (1984): 1363–1403.

———. "A Marxist Analysis of American Law." *Marxist Perspectives* 1, no. 1 (1978): 96–116.

———. "The United States Constitution and the Intent of the Framers." *Buffalo Law Review* 36 (1987): 217–26.

Unger, Roberto. *The Critical Legal Studies Movement.* Cambridge: Harvard University Press, 1983.

———. *Knowledge and Politics.* New York: Macmillan, 1975.

Vandevelde, Kenneth. "The New Property of the Nineteenth Century: The Development of the Modern Concept of Property." *Buffalo Law Review* 29 (1980): 325–67.

Viera, David. "Elvis Presley: The New Twists." *Entertainment Law Journal* (April 1981): 31–39.

Wagner, Wenceslas J. "The Right to One's Own Likeness in French Law." *Indiana Law Journal* 46 (1970): 1–36.

Waldheim, Franklin. "Characters—May They Be Kidnapped?" *Trademark Reporter* 55 (1965): 1022–31.

Warren, Samuel D. "The Right to Privacy." *Harvard Law Review* 4, no. 5 (1890): 193–216.

Whale, R. F. "Copyright and Authors' Rights." *European Intellectual Property Law Review* 1 (1979): 38–39.

Whale, R. F., and Jeremy J. Phillips. *Whale on Copyright*. 1971. Reprint. Oxford: ESC Publishing, 1983.

Youngman, Gordon. "Negotiation of Personal Service Contracts." *California Law Review* 42, no. 1 (Spring 1954): 2–17.

Zeldis, Nancy. "Public Hearing Focuses on Bill on Use of Deceased's Likeness." *New York Law Journal* 4 (26 February 1988): 1, 7–8.

Zimmerman, Jory Bard. "Exclusivity of Personal Services: The Viability and Enforceability of Contractual Rights." *Beverly Hills Law Journal* (Spring 1985): 73–100.

Index

DENAVIBVS · E